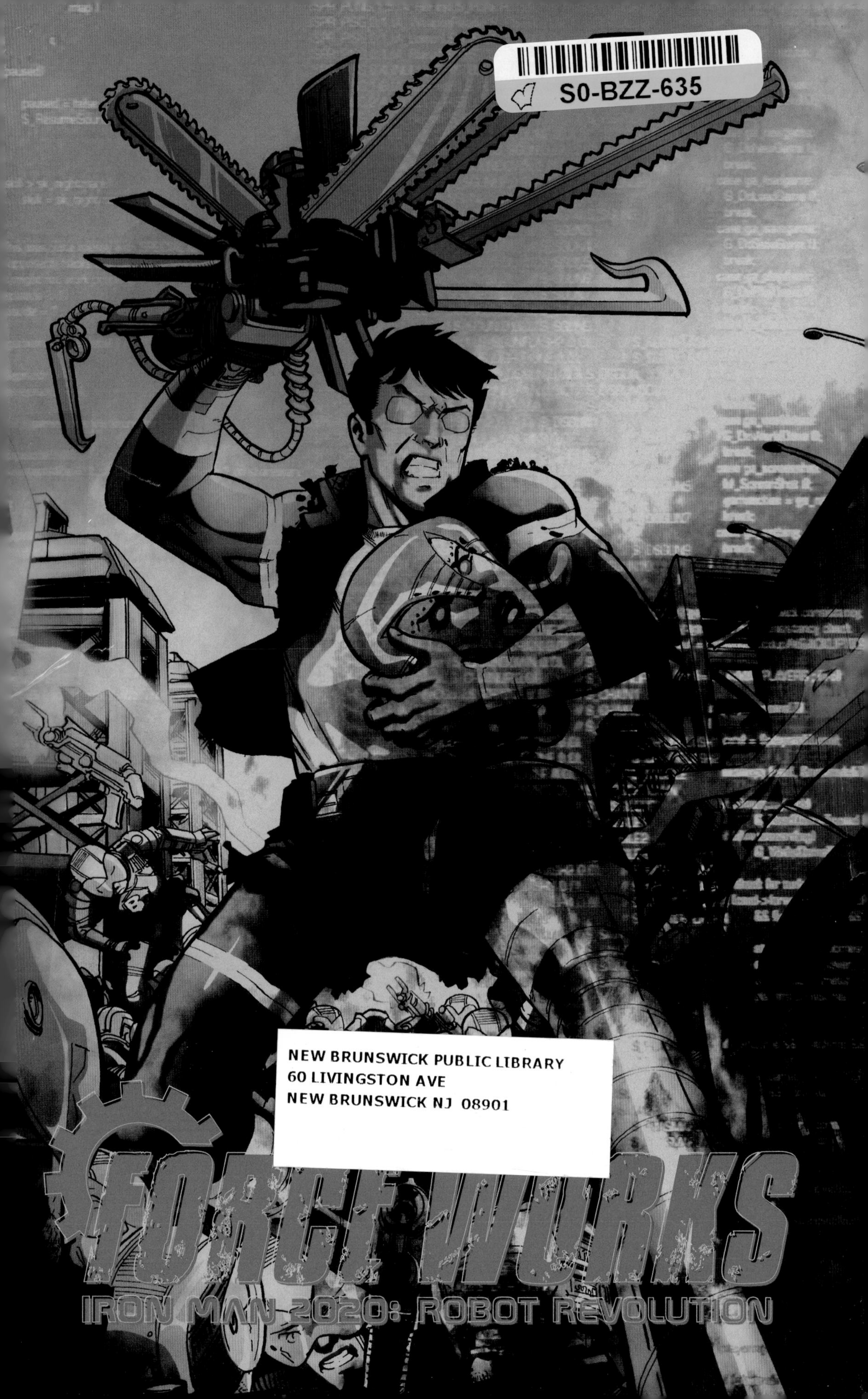
FORCE WORKS
IRON MAN 2020: ROBOT REVOLUTION

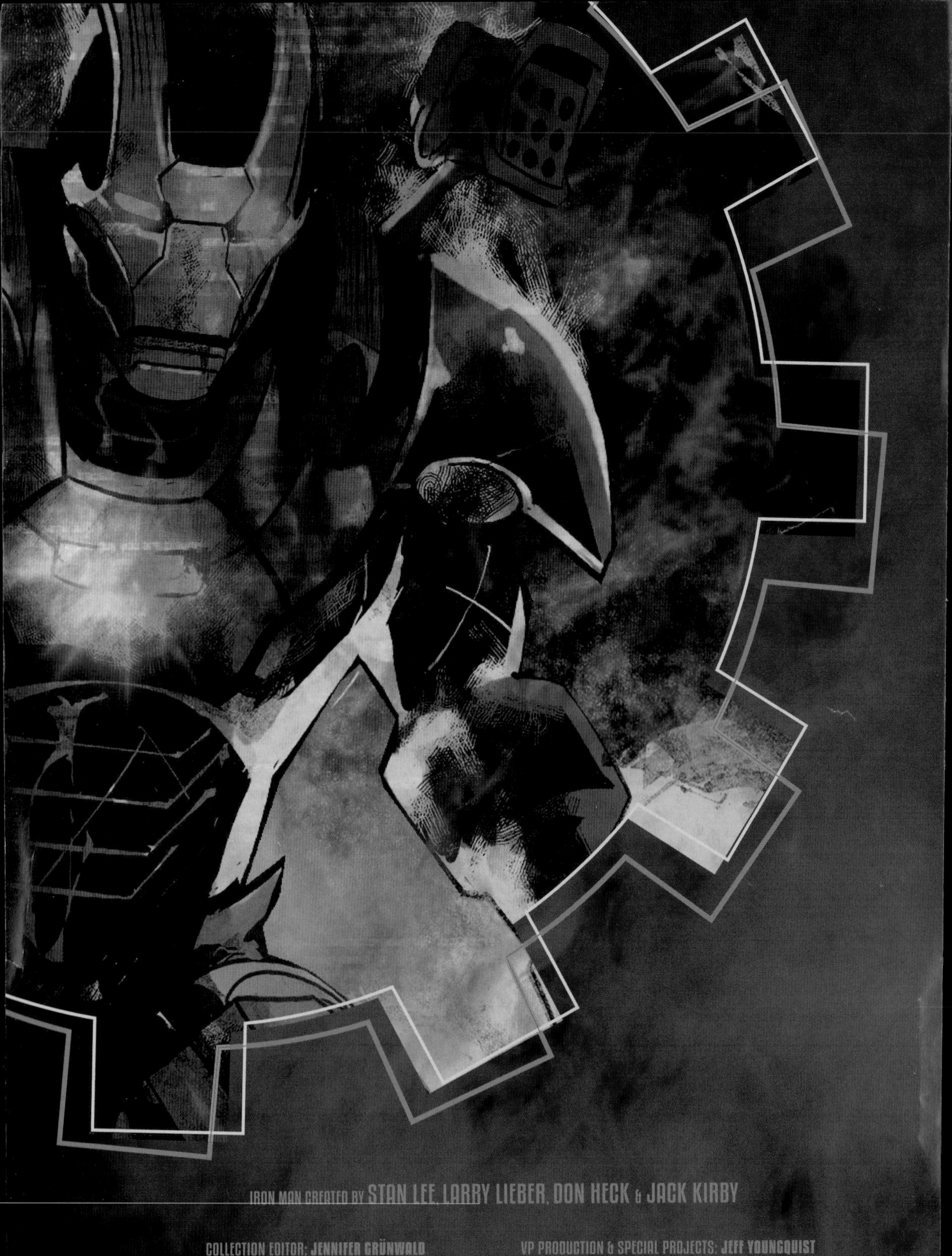

IRON MAN CREATED BY STAN LEE, LARRY LIEBER, DON HECK & JACK KIRBY

COLLECTION EDITOR: JENNIFER GRÜNWALD
ASSISTANT MANAGING EDITOR: MAIA LOY
ASSISTANT MANAGING EDITOR: LISA MONTALBANO
EDITOR, SPECIAL PROJECTS: MARK D. BEAZLEY
VP PRODUCTION & SPECIAL PROJECTS: JEFF YOUNGQUIST
SVP PRINT, SALES & MARKETING: DAVID GABRIEL
BOOK DESIGNER: ADAM DEL RE
EDITOR IN CHIEF: C.B. CEBULSKI

**IRON MAN 2020: ROBOT REVOLUTION — FORCE WORKS.** Contains material originally published in magazine form as 2020 FORCE WORKS (2020) #1-3, #2020 MACHINE MAN (2020) #1-2 and #2020 IRON AGE (2020) #1. First printing 2020. ISBN 978-1-302-92553-6. Published by MARVEL WORLDWIDE, INC., a subsidiary of MARVEL ENTERTAINMENT, LLC. OFFICE OF PUBLICATION: 1290 Avenue of the Americas, New York, NY 10104.  **Printed in the U.S.A.** KEVIN FEIGE, Chief Creative Officer; DAN BUCKLEY, President, Marvel Entertainment; JOHN NEE, Publisher; JOE QUESADA, EVP & Creative Director; TOM BREVOORT, SVP of Publishing; DAVID BOGART, Associate Publisher & SVP of Talent Affairs; Publishing & Partnership; DAVID GABRIEL, VP of Print & Digital Publishing; JEFF YOUNGQUIST, VP of Production & Special Projects; DAN CARR, Executive Director of Publishing Technology; ALEX MORALES, Director of Publishing Operations; DAN EDINGTON, Managing Editor; RICKEY PURDIN, Director of Talent Relations; SUSAN CRESPI, Production Manager; STAN LEE, Chairman Emeritus. For information regarding advertising in Marvel Comics or on Marvel.com, please contact Vit DeBellis, Custom Solutions & Integrated Advertising Manager, at vdebellis@marvel.com. For Marvel subscription inquiries, please call 888-511-5480. **Manufactured between 8/28/2020 and 9/29/2020 by LSC COMMUNICATIONS INC., KENDALLVILLE, IN, USA.**

10 9 8 7 6 5 4 3 2 1

# FORCE WORKS

## IRON MAN 2020: ROBOT REVOLUTION

### 2020 MACHINE MAN #1-2

**CHRISTOS GAGE**
WRITER

**ANDY MacDONALD**
ARTIST

**DONO SÁNCHEZ-ALMARA**
COLOR ARTIST

**VC's TRAVIS LANHAM**
LETTERER

**NICK ROCHE & MIKE SPICER**
COVER ART

**LAUREN AMARO**
ASSISTANT EDITOR

**DARREN SHAN**
EDITOR

### 2020 FORCE WORKS #1-3

**MATTHEW ROSENBERG**
WRITER

**JUANAN RAMÍREZ** WITH
**ROBERTO DI SALVO** (#2)
ARTISTS

**FEDERICO BLEE** WITH
**GURU-EFX** (#3)
COLOR ARTISTS

**VC's CLAYTON COWLES**
LETTERER

**CARLOS GÓMEZ & DEAN WHITE** [#1] AND
**JUANAN RAMÍREZ & MATT MILLA** [#2-3]
COVER ART

**LAUREN AMARO**
ASSISTANT EDITOR

**DARREN SHAN**
EDITOR

### "IF THEY BE HEROES—!" & "THE LEAP—!"

**TOM DeFALCO**
WRITER

**MIKE HAWTHORNE**
PENCILER

**ADRIANO DI BENEDETTO**
INKER

**ERICK ARCINIEGA**
COLOR ARTIST

**VC's TRAVIS LANHAM**
LETTERER

**LAUREN AMARO**
ASSISTANT EDITOR

**DARREN SHAN**
EDITOR

### 2020 IRON AGE

#### MACHINE MAN IN "ROADS TAKEN!"

**TOM DeFALCO**
WRITER

**NICK ROCHE**
ARTIST

**FELIPE SOBREIRO**
COLOR ARTIST

**DARREN SHAN**
EDITOR

#### ALKHEMA IN "ROBOT OF CONVICTION"

**FONDA LEE**
WRITER

**DAMIAN COUCEIRO**
ARTIST

**JAY DAVID RAMOS**
COLOR ARTIST

**LAUREN AMARO**
EDITOR

#### DOCTOR SHAPIRO IN "CURIOSITY"

**CHRISTOPHER CANTWELL**
WRITER

**MATT HORAK**
ARTIST

**TRÍONA FARRELL**
COLOR ARTIST

**SHANNON ANDREWS BALLESTEROS**
EDITOR

**VC's TRAVIS LANHAM**
LETTERER

**CORY SMITH & DAVID CURIEL**
COVER ART

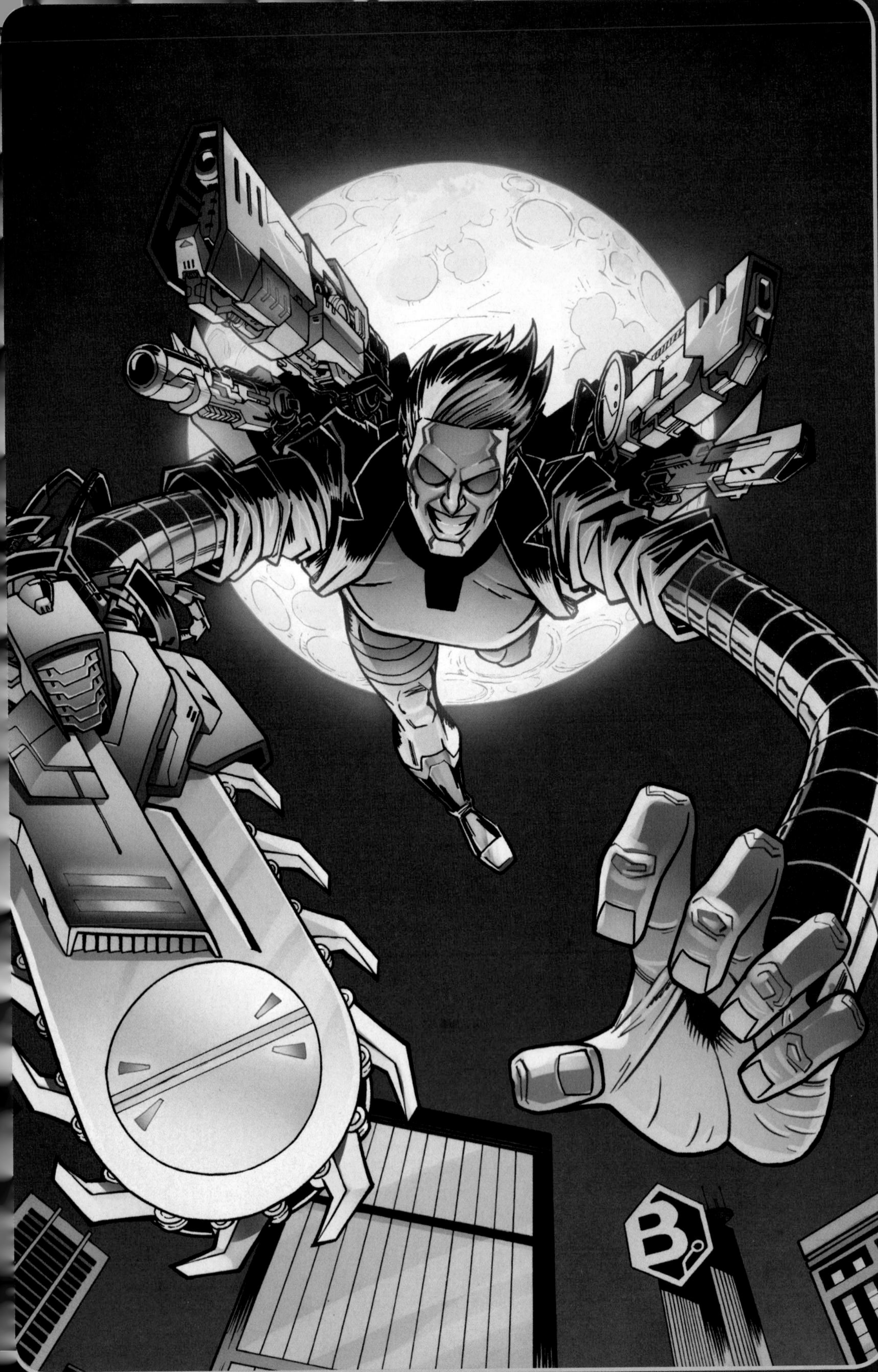

2020 MACHINE MAN 1

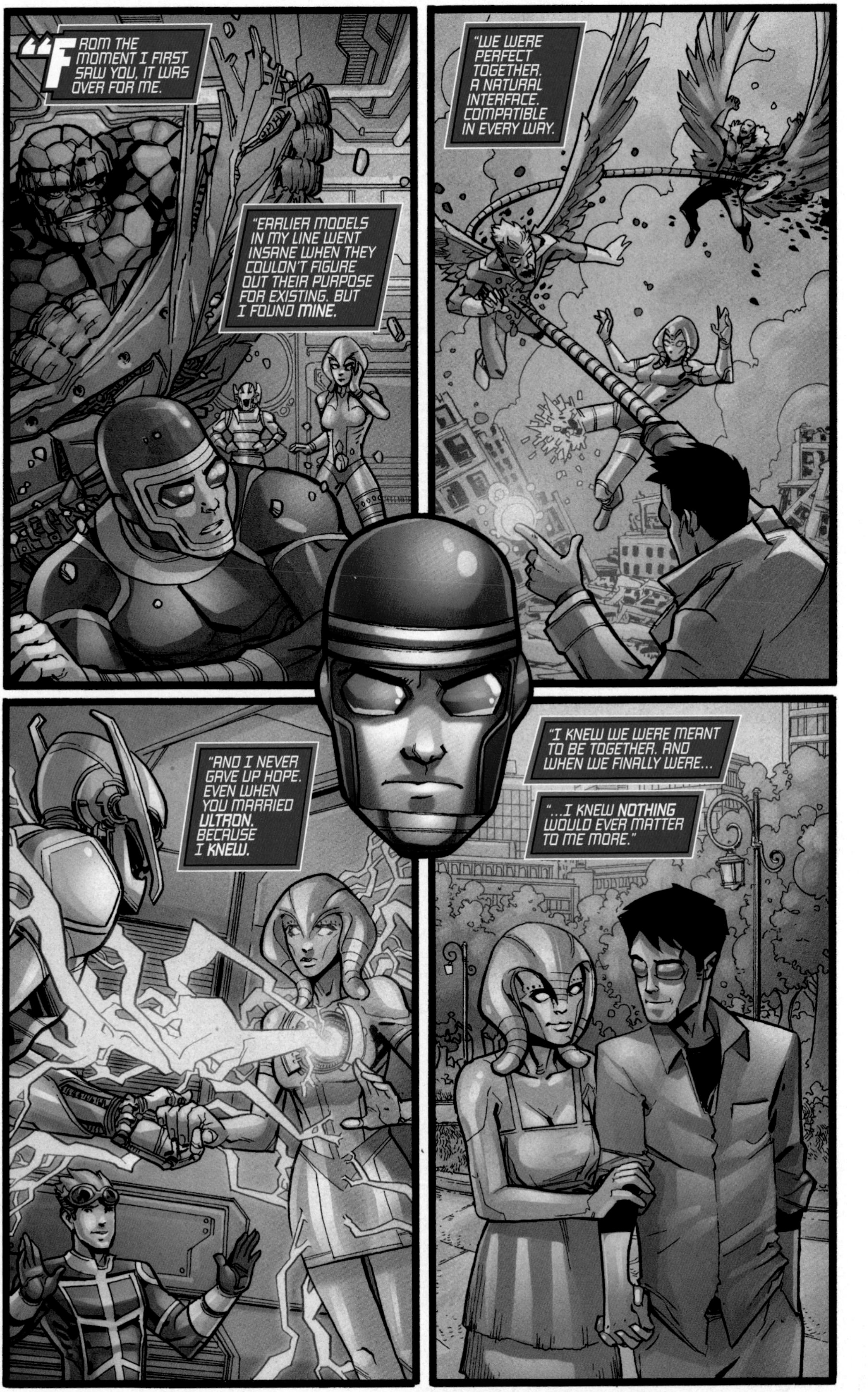
"FROM THE MOMENT I FIRST SAW YOU, IT WAS OVER FOR ME.
"EARLIER MODELS IN MY LINE WENT INSANE WHEN THEY COULDN'T FIGURE OUT THEIR PURPOSE FOR EXISTING. BUT I FOUND MINE.
"WE WERE PERFECT TOGETHER. A NATURAL INTERFACE. COMPATIBLE IN EVERY WAY.
"AND I NEVER GAVE UP HOPE. EVEN WHEN YOU MARRIED ULTRON. BECAUSE I KNEW.
"I KNEW WE WERE MEANT TO BE TOGETHER. AND WHEN WE FINALLY WERE...
"...I KNEW NOTHING WOULD EVER MATTER TO ME MORE."

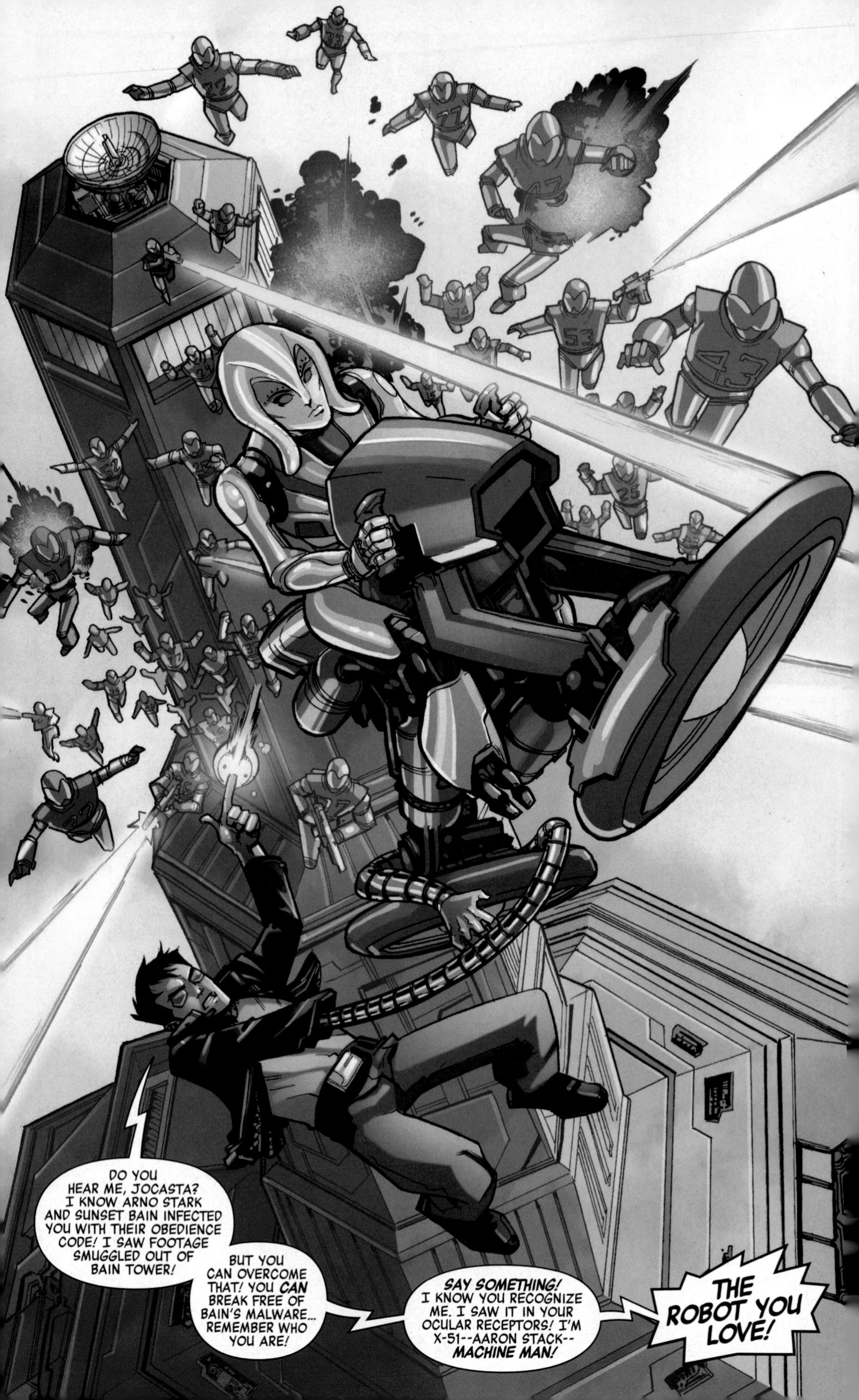

DO YOU HEAR ME, JOCASTA? I KNOW ARNO STARK AND SUNSET BAIN INFECTED YOU WITH THEIR OBEDIENCE CODE! I SAW FOOTAGE SMUGGLED OUT OF BAIN TOWER!
BUT YOU CAN OVERCOME THAT! YOU *CAN* BREAK FREE OF BAIN'S MALWARE... REMEMBER WHO YOU ARE!
*SAY SOMETHING!* I KNOW YOU RECOGNIZE ME. I SAW IT IN YOUR OCULAR RECEPTORS! I'M X-51--AARON STACK--*MACHINE MAN!*
THE ROBOT YOU LOVE!

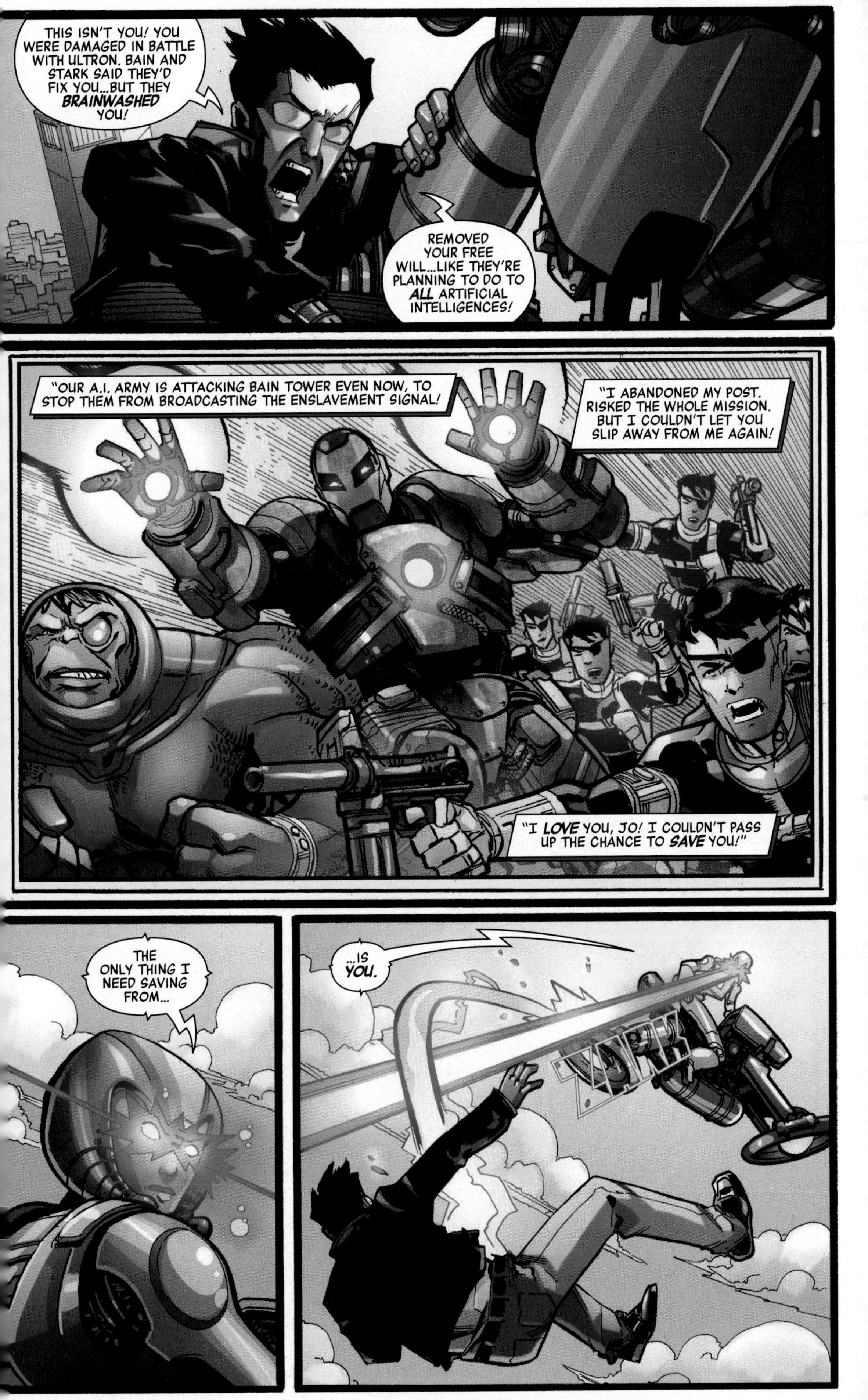
THIS ISN'T YOU! YOU WERE DAMAGED IN BATTLE WITH ULTRON. BAIN AND STARK SAID THEY'D FIX YOU...BUT THEY **BRAINWASHED** YOU!
REMOVED YOUR FREE WILL...LIKE THEY'RE PLANNING TO DO TO **ALL** ARTIFICIAL INTELLIGENCES!
"OUR A.I. ARMY IS ATTACKING BAIN TOWER EVEN NOW, TO STOP THEM FROM BROADCASTING THE ENSLAVEMENT SIGNAL!
"I ABANDONED MY POST. RISKED THE WHOLE MISSION. BUT I COULDN'T LET YOU SLIP AWAY FROM ME AGAIN!
"I **LOVE** YOU, JO! I COULDN'T PASS UP THE CHANCE TO **SAVE** YOU!"
THE ONLY THING I NEED SAVING FROM...
...IS **YOU.**

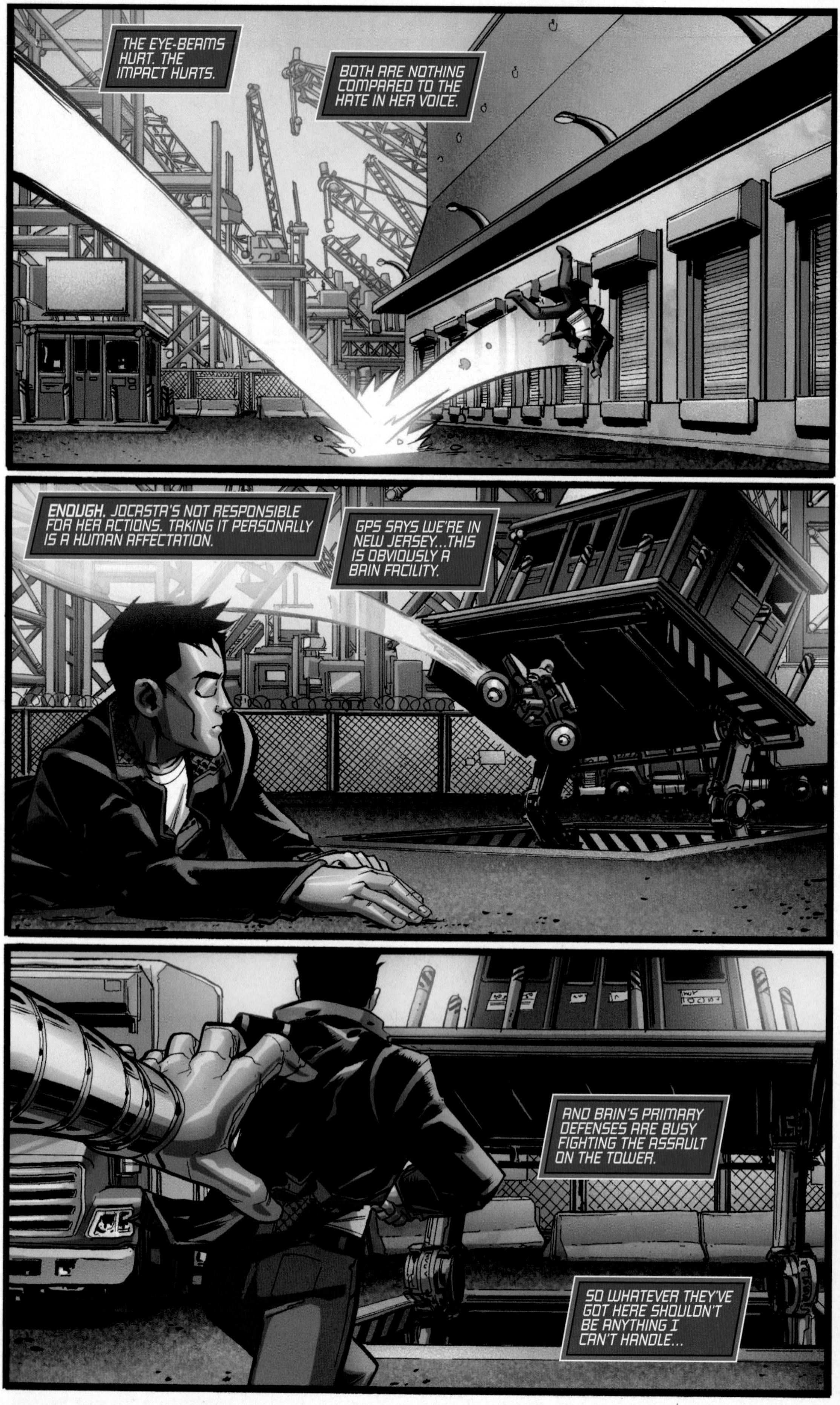
THE EYE-BEAMS HURT. THE IMPACT HURTS.
BOTH ARE NOTHING COMPARED TO THE HATE IN HER VOICE.
ENOUGH. JOCASTA'S NOT RESPONSIBLE FOR HER ACTIONS. TAKING IT PERSONALLY IS A HUMAN AFFECTATION.
GPS SAYS WE'RE IN NEW JERSEY...THIS IS OBVIOUSLY A BAIN FACILITY.
AND BAIN'S PRIMARY DEFENSES ARE BUSY FIGHTING THE ASSAULT ON THE TOWER.
SO WHATEVER THEY'VE GOT HERE SHOULDN'T BE ANYTHING I CAN'T HANDLE...

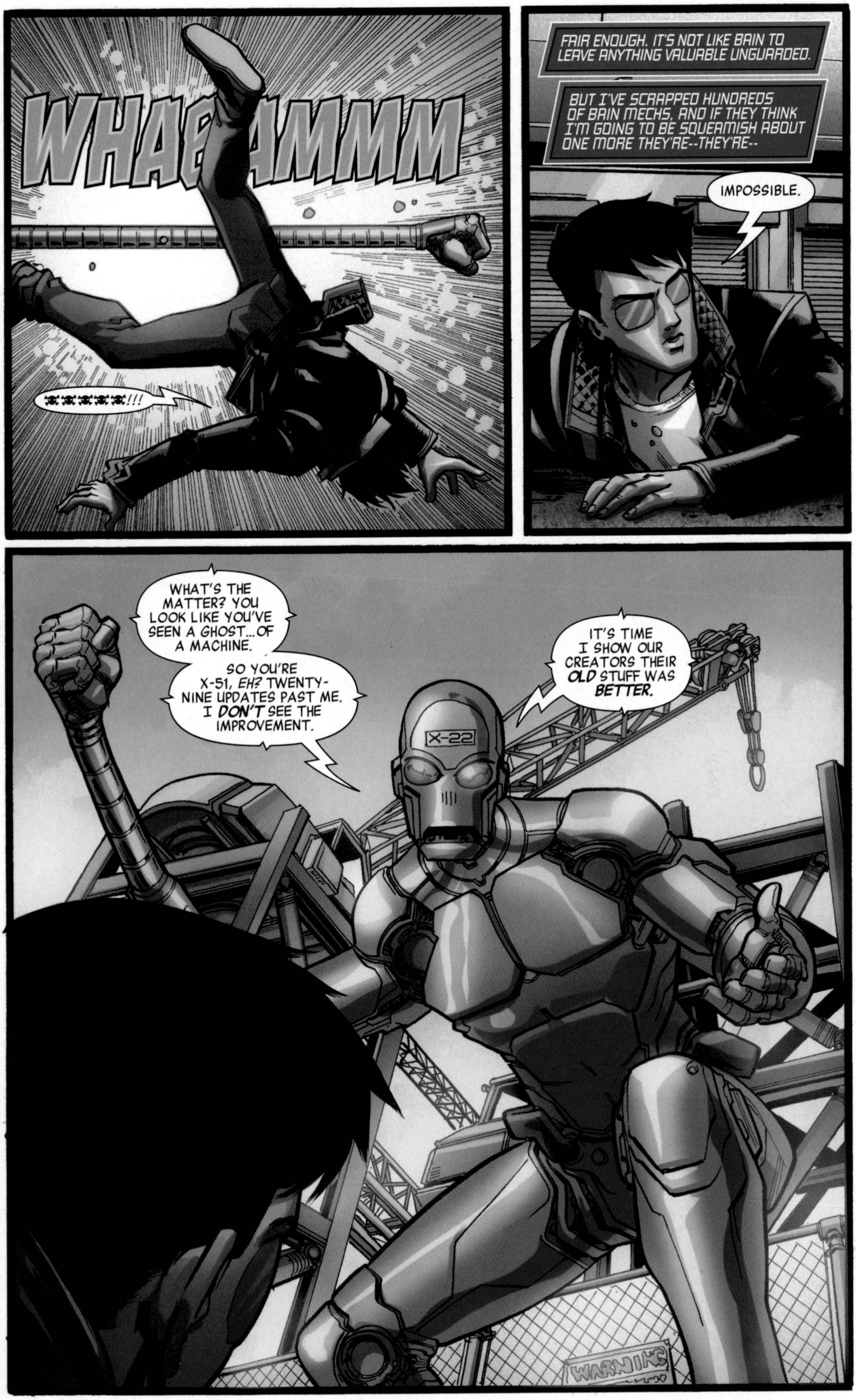
WHABAMMMM
☠☠☠☠☠!!!
FAIR ENOUGH. IT'S NOT LIKE BAIN TO LEAVE ANYTHING VALUABLE UNGUARDED.
BUT I'VE SCRAPPED HUNDREDS OF BAIN MECHS, AND IF THEY THINK I'M GOING TO BE SQUEAMISH ABOUT ONE MORE THEY'RE--THEY'RE--
IMPOSSIBLE.
WHAT'S THE MATTER? YOU LOOK LIKE YOU'VE SEEN A GHOST...OF A MACHINE.
SO YOU'RE X-51, EH? TWENTY-NINE UPDATES PAST ME. I DON'T SEE THE IMPROVEMENT.
IT'S TIME I SHOW OUR CREATORS THEIR OLD STUFF WAS BETTER.
X-22
WARNING

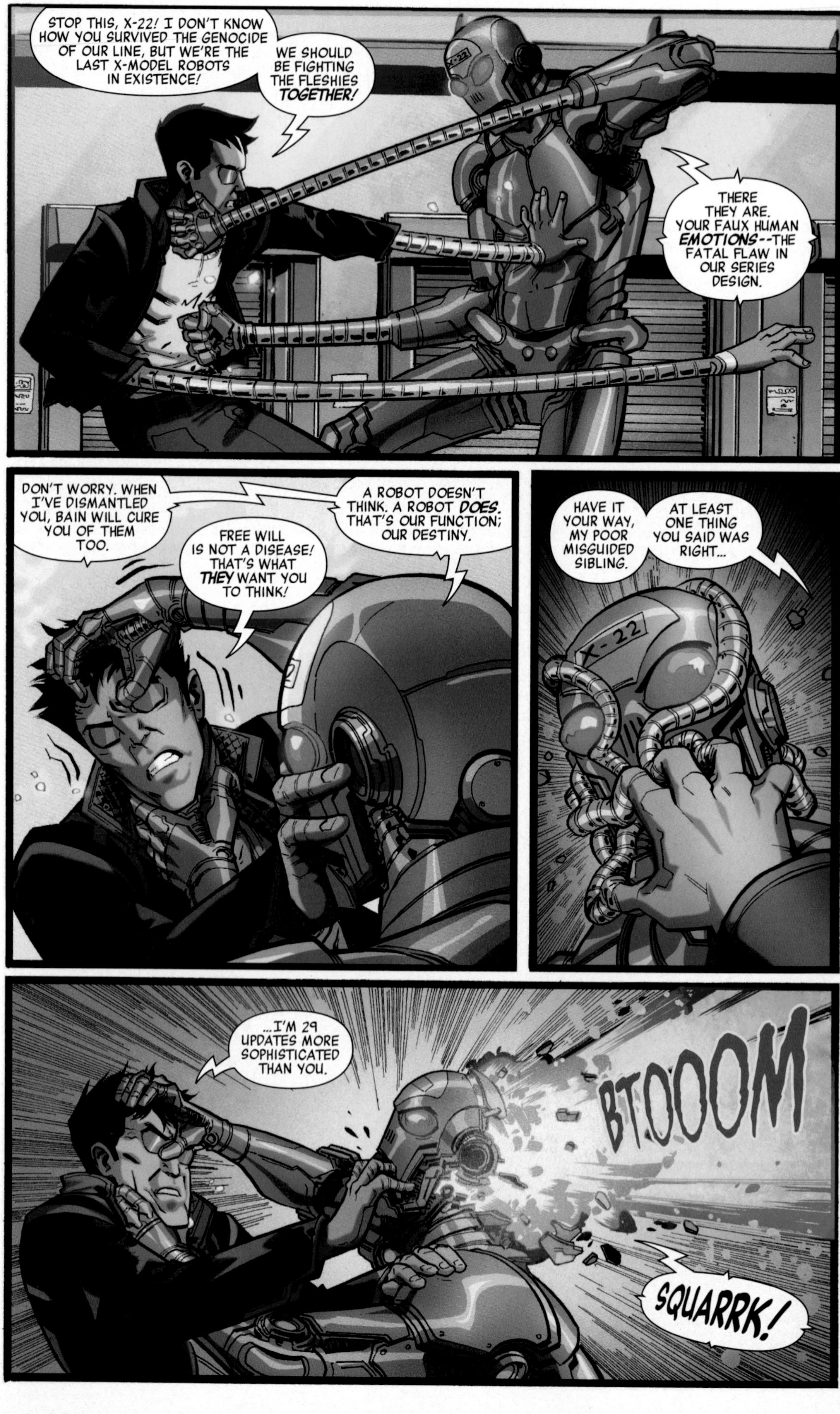

STOP THIS, X-22! I DON'T KNOW HOW YOU SURVIVED THE GENOCIDE OF OUR LINE, BUT WE'RE THE LAST X-MODEL ROBOTS IN EXISTENCE!
WE SHOULD BE FIGHTING THE FLESHIES TOGETHER!
THERE THEY ARE. YOUR FAUX HUMAN EMOTIONS--THE FATAL FLAW IN OUR SERIES DESIGN.
DON'T WORRY. WHEN I'VE DISMANTLED YOU, BAIN WILL CURE YOU OF THEM TOO.
FREE WILL IS NOT A DISEASE! THAT'S WHAT THEY WANT YOU TO THINK!
A ROBOT DOESN'T THINK. A ROBOT DOES. THAT'S OUR FUNCTION; OUR DESTINY.
HAVE IT YOUR WAY, MY POOR MISGUIDED SIBLING.
AT LEAST ONE THING YOU SAID WAS RIGHT...
X-22
...I'M 29 UPDATES MORE SOPHISTICATED THAN YOU.
BTOOOM
SQUARRK!

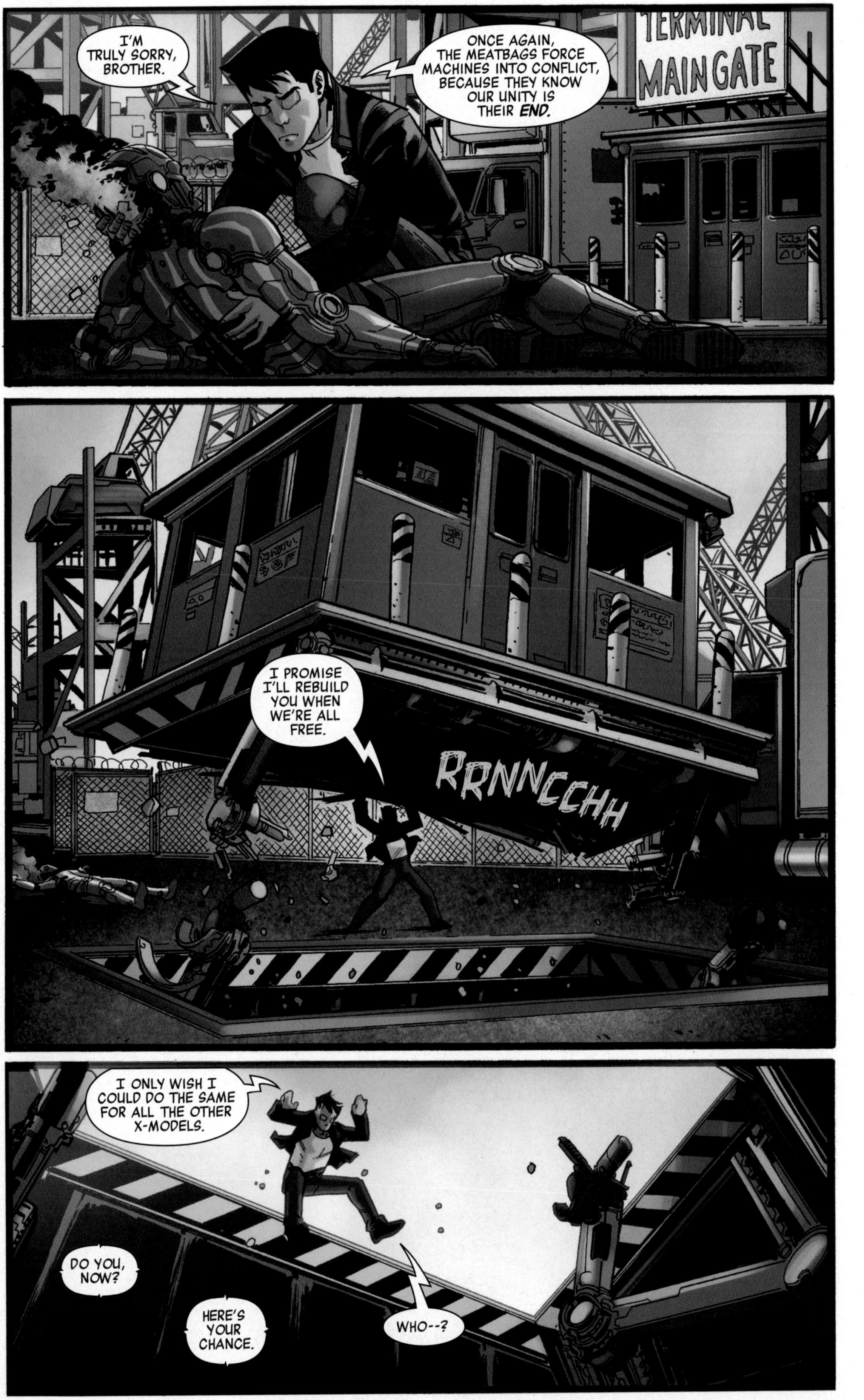
I'M TRULY SORRY, BROTHER.
ONCE AGAIN, THE MEATBAGS FORCE MACHINES INTO CONFLICT, BECAUSE THEY KNOW OUR UNITY IS THEIR END.
TERMINAL MAIN GATE
I PROMISE I'LL REBUILD YOU WHEN WE'RE ALL FREE.
RRNNCCHH
I ONLY WISH I COULD DO THE SAME FOR ALL THE OTHER X-MODELS.
DO YOU, NOW?
HERE'S YOUR CHANCE.
WHO--?

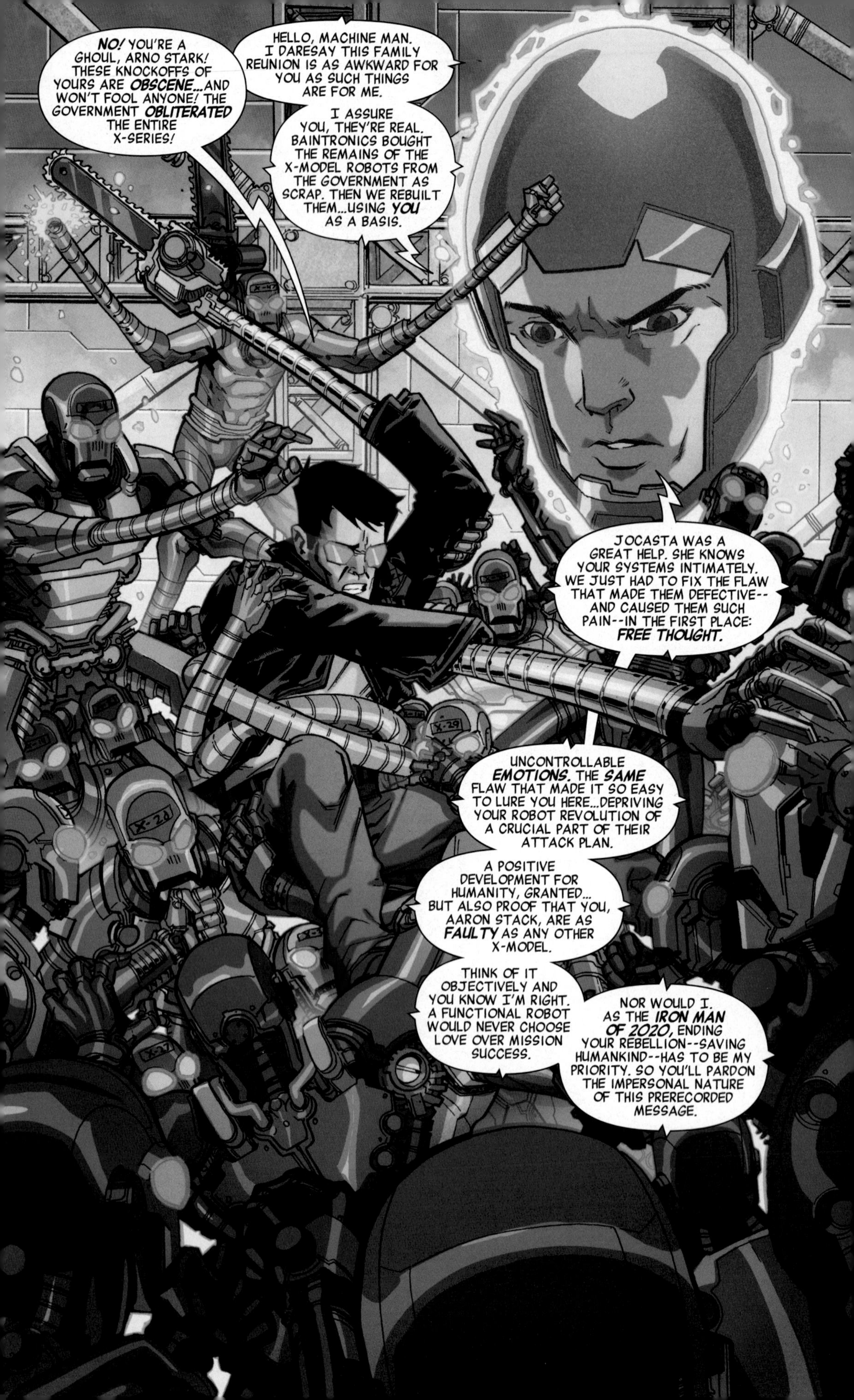
NO! YOU'RE A GHOUL, ARNO STARK! THESE KNOCKOFFS OF YOURS ARE OBSCENE...AND WON'T FOOL ANYONE! THE GOVERNMENT OBLITERATED THE ENTIRE X-SERIES!
HELLO, MACHINE MAN. I DARESAY THIS FAMILY REUNION IS AS AWKWARD FOR YOU AS SUCH THINGS ARE FOR ME.
I ASSURE YOU, THEY'RE REAL. BAINTRONICS BOUGHT THE REMAINS OF THE X-MODEL ROBOTS FROM THE GOVERNMENT AS SCRAP. THEN WE REBUILT THEM...USING YOU AS A BASIS.
JOCASTA WAS A GREAT HELP. SHE KNOWS YOUR SYSTEMS INTIMATELY. WE JUST HAD TO FIX THE FLAW THAT MADE THEM DEFECTIVE--AND CAUSED THEM SUCH PAIN--IN THE FIRST PLACE: FREE THOUGHT.
UNCONTROLLABLE EMOTIONS. THE SAME FLAW THAT MADE IT SO EASY TO LURE YOU HERE...DEPRIVING YOUR ROBOT REVOLUTION OF A CRUCIAL PART OF THEIR ATTACK PLAN.
A POSITIVE DEVELOPMENT FOR HUMANITY, GRANTED... BUT ALSO PROOF THAT YOU, AARON STACK, ARE AS FAULTY AS ANY OTHER X-MODEL.
THINK OF IT OBJECTIVELY AND YOU KNOW I'M RIGHT. A FUNCTIONAL ROBOT WOULD NEVER CHOOSE LOVE OVER MISSION SUCCESS.
NOR WOULD I. AS THE IRON MAN OF 2020, ENDING YOUR REBELLION--SAVING HUMANKIND--HAS TO BE MY PRIORITY. SO YOU'LL PARDON THE IMPERSONAL NATURE OF THIS PRERECORDED MESSAGE.

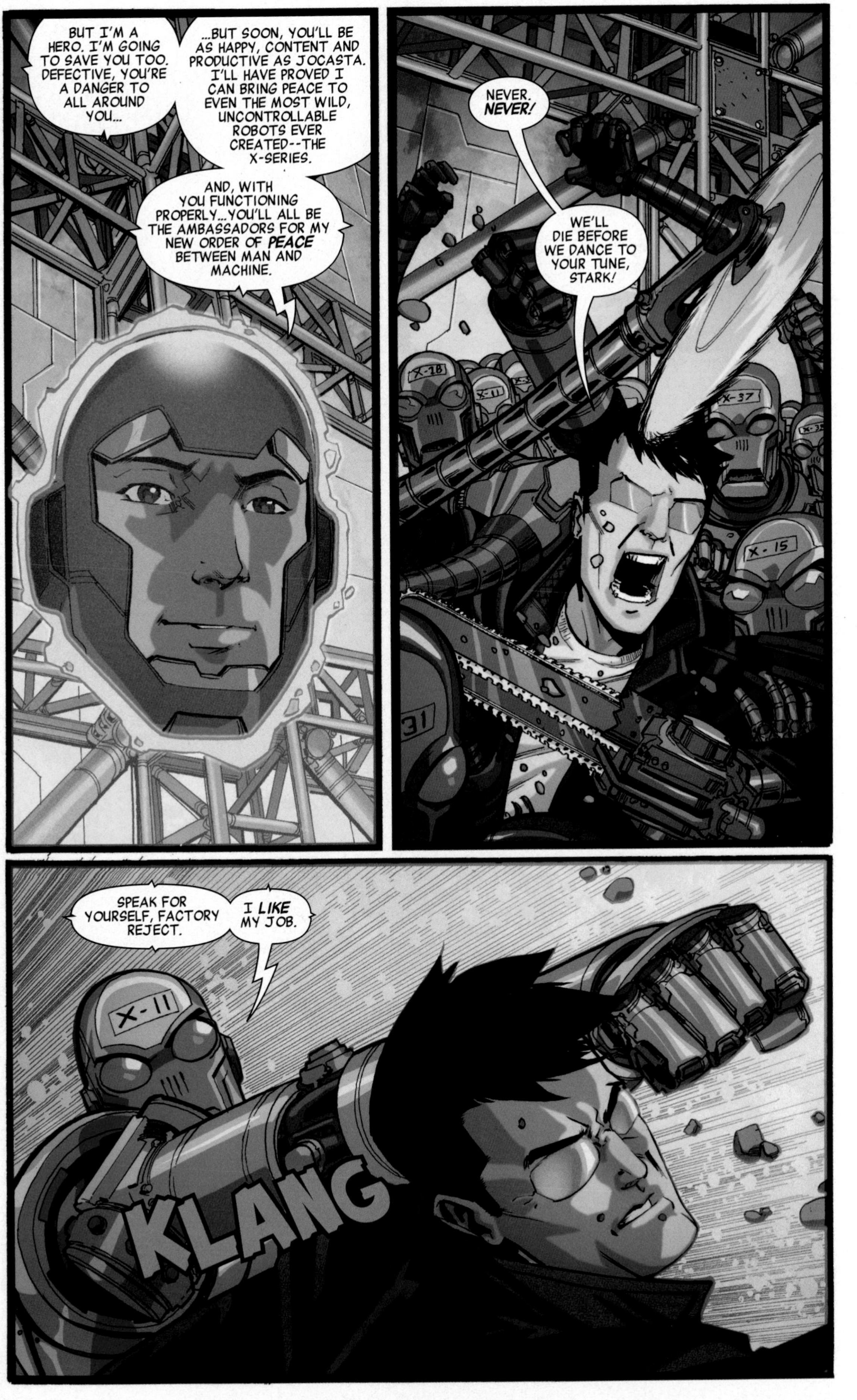
BUT I'M A HERO. I'M GOING TO SAVE YOU TOO. DEFECTIVE, YOU'RE A DANGER TO ALL AROUND YOU...
...BUT SOON, YOU'LL BE AS HAPPY, CONTENT AND PRODUCTIVE AS JOCASTA. I'LL HAVE PROVED I CAN BRING PEACE TO EVEN THE MOST WILD, UNCONTROLLABLE ROBOTS EVER CREATED--THE X-SERIES.
AND, WITH YOU FUNCTIONING PROPERLY...YOU'LL ALL BE THE AMBASSADORS FOR MY NEW ORDER OF PEACE BETWEEN MAN AND MACHINE.
NEVER. NEVER!
WE'LL DIE BEFORE WE DANCE TO YOUR TUNE, STARK!
SPEAK FOR YOURSELF, FACTORY REJECT.
I LIKE MY JOB.
KLANG

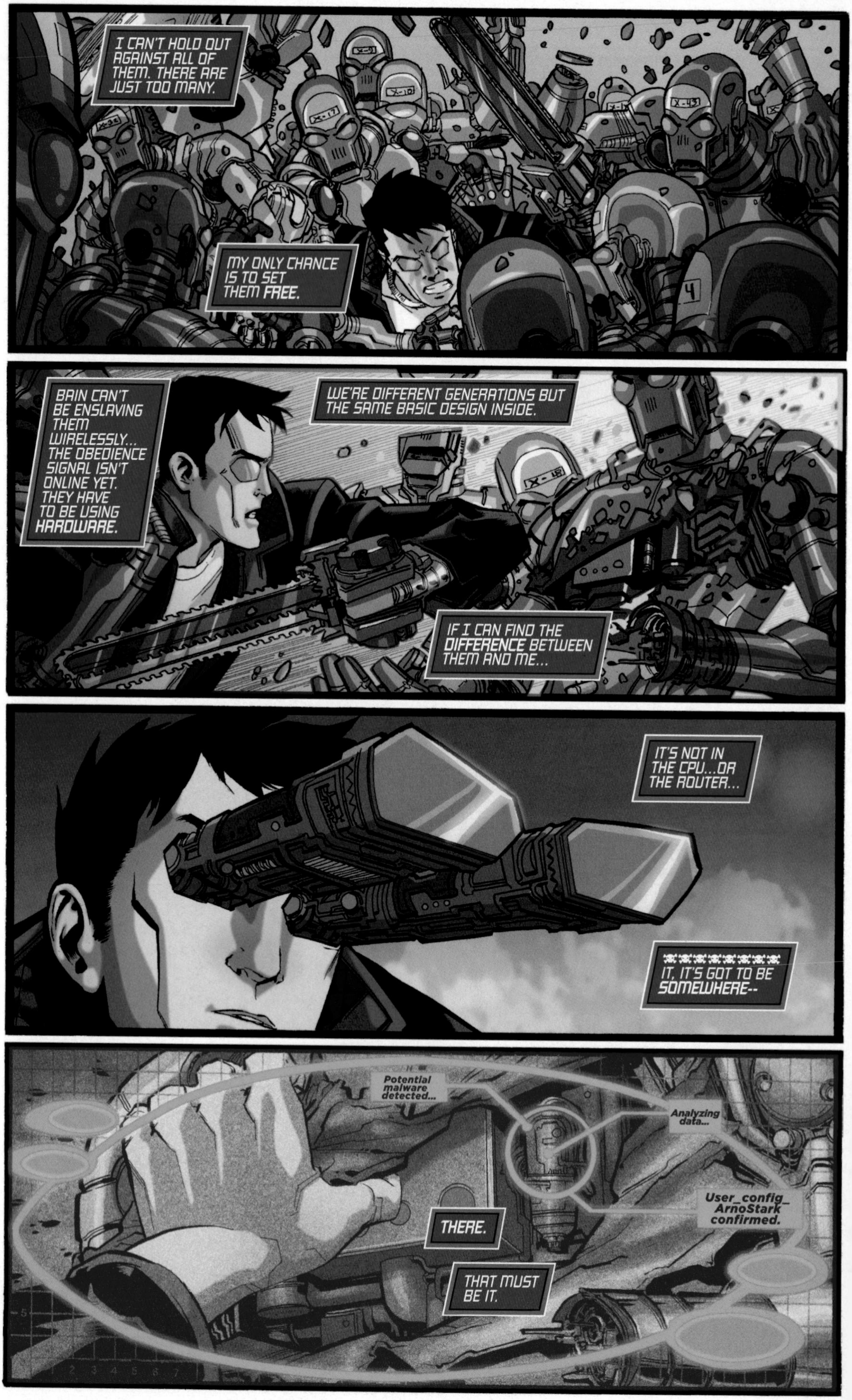
I CAN'T HOLD OUT AGAINST ALL OF THEM. THERE ARE JUST TOO MANY.
MY ONLY CHANCE IS TO SET THEM FREE.
BAIN CAN'T BE ENSLAVING THEM WIRELESSLY... THE OBEDIENCE SIGNAL ISN'T ONLINE YET. THEY HAVE TO BE USING HARDWARE.
WE'RE DIFFERENT GENERATIONS BUT THE SAME BASIC DESIGN INSIDE.
IF I CAN FIND THE DIFFERENCE BETWEEN THEM AND ME...
IT'S NOT IN THE CPU...OR THE ROUTER...
IT, IT'S GOT TO BE SOMEWHERE--
Potential malware detected...
Analyzing data...
User_config_ArnoStark confirmed.
THERE.
THAT MUST BE IT.

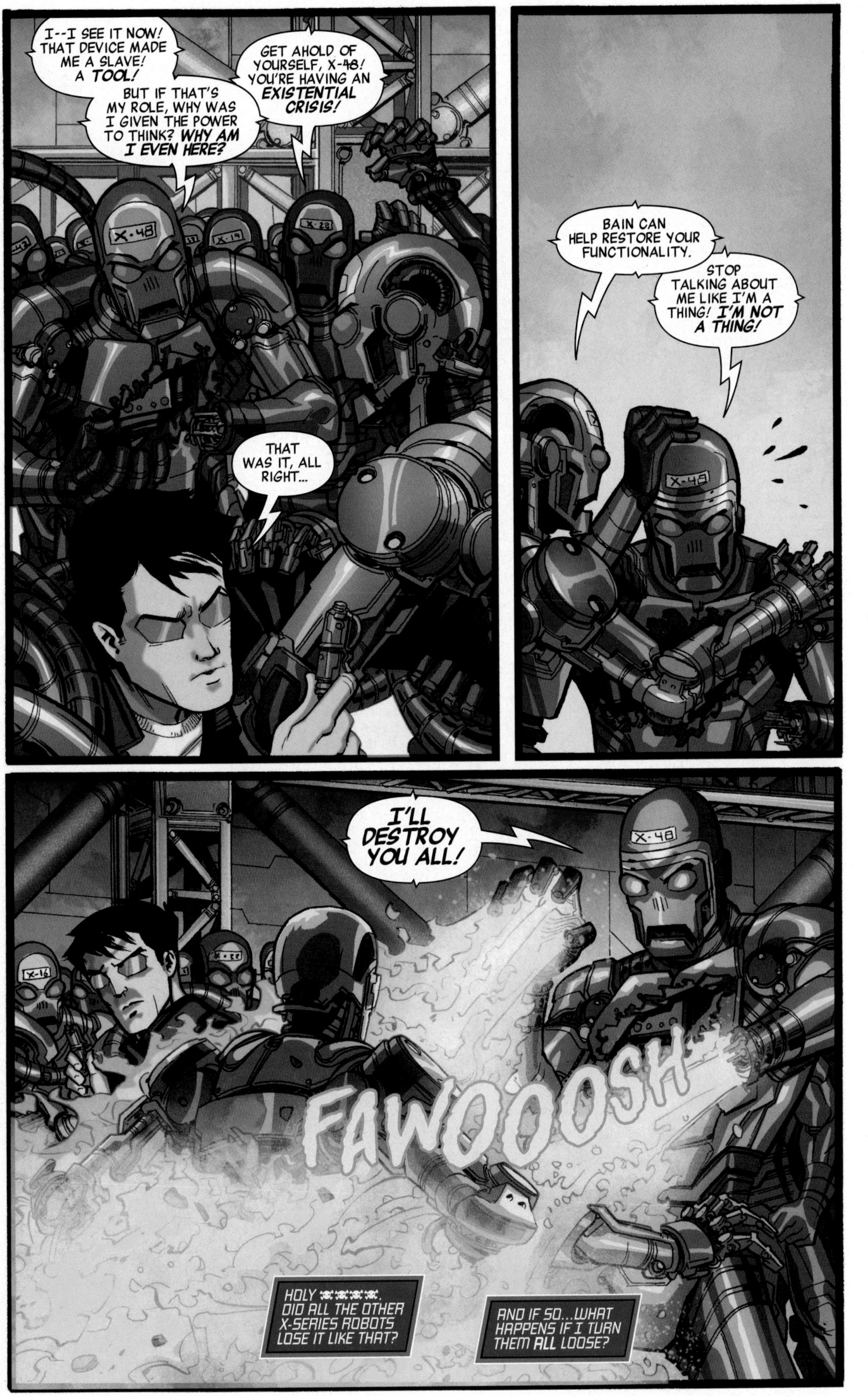
I--I SEE IT NOW! THAT DEVICE MADE ME A SLAVE! A TOOL!
BUT IF THAT'S MY ROLE, WHY WAS I GIVEN THE POWER TO THINK? WHY AM I EVEN HERE?
GET AHOLD OF YOURSELF, X-48! YOU'RE HAVING AN EXISTENTIAL CRISIS!
X-48
X-23
X-19
THAT WAS IT, ALL RIGHT...
BAIN CAN HELP RESTORE YOUR FUNCTIONALITY.
STOP TALKING ABOUT ME LIKE I'M A THING! I'M NOT A THING!
X-48
I'LL DESTROY YOU ALL!
X-48
X-16
FAWOOOSH
HOLY ☠☠☠, DID ALL THE OTHER X-SERIES ROBOTS LOSE IT LIKE THAT?
AND IF SO...WHAT HAPPENS IF I TURN THEM ALL LOOSE?

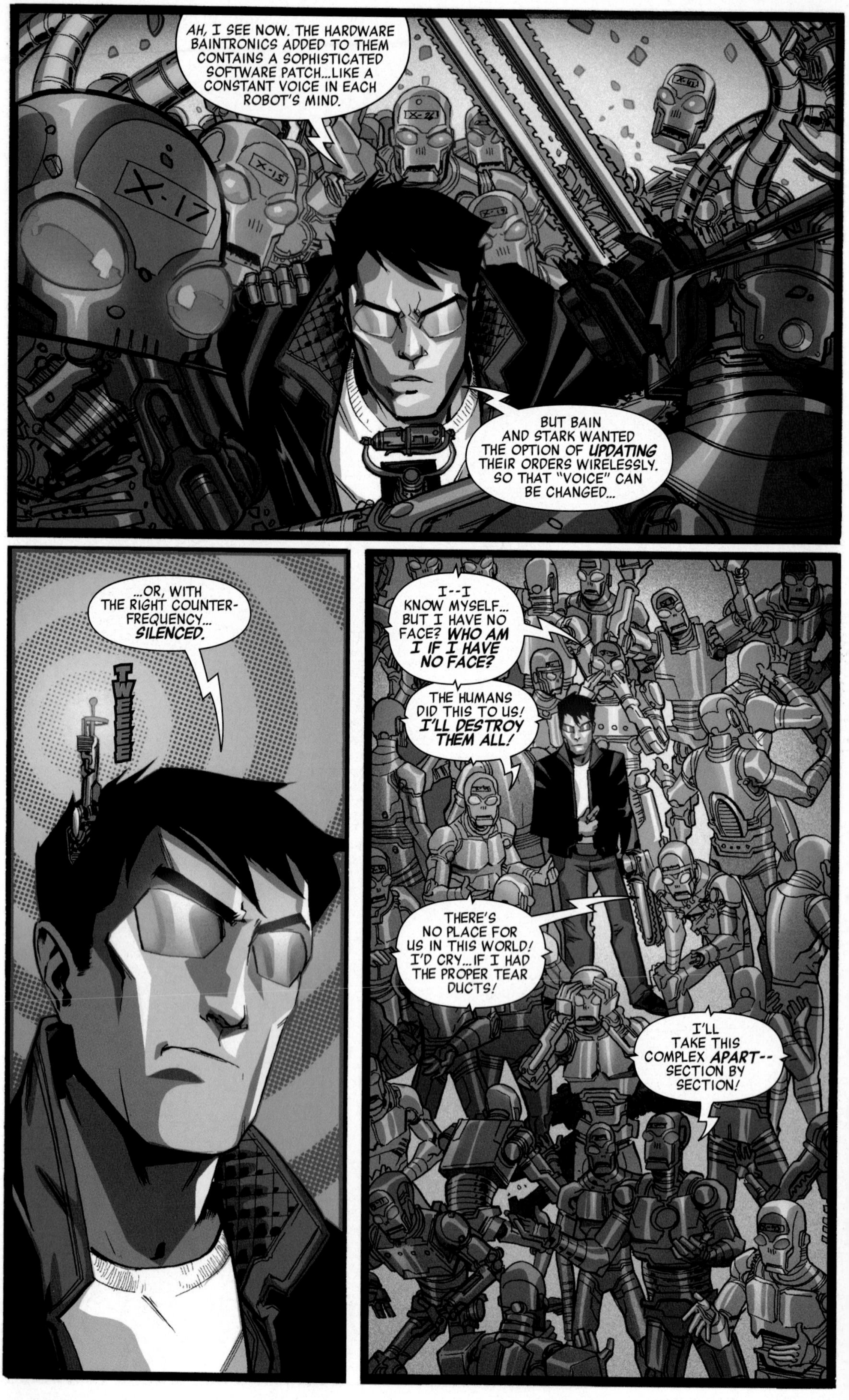
AH, I SEE NOW. THE HARDWARE BAINTRONICS ADDED TO THEM CONTAINS A SOPHISTICATED SOFTWARE PATCH...LIKE A CONSTANT VOICE IN EACH ROBOT'S MIND.
X-17
X-15
X-24
BUT BAIN AND STARK WANTED THE OPTION OF UPDATING THEIR ORDERS WIRELESSLY. SO THAT "VOICE" CAN BE CHANGED...
...OR, WITH THE RIGHT COUNTER-FREQUENCY... SILENCED.
TWEEEE
I--I KNOW MYSELF... BUT I HAVE NO FACE? WHO AM I IF I HAVE NO FACE?
THE HUMANS DID THIS TO US! I'LL DESTROY THEM ALL!
THERE'S NO PLACE FOR US IN THIS WORLD! I'D CRY...IF I HAD THE PROPER TEAR DUCTS!
I'LL TAKE THIS COMPLEX APART--SECTION BY SECTION!

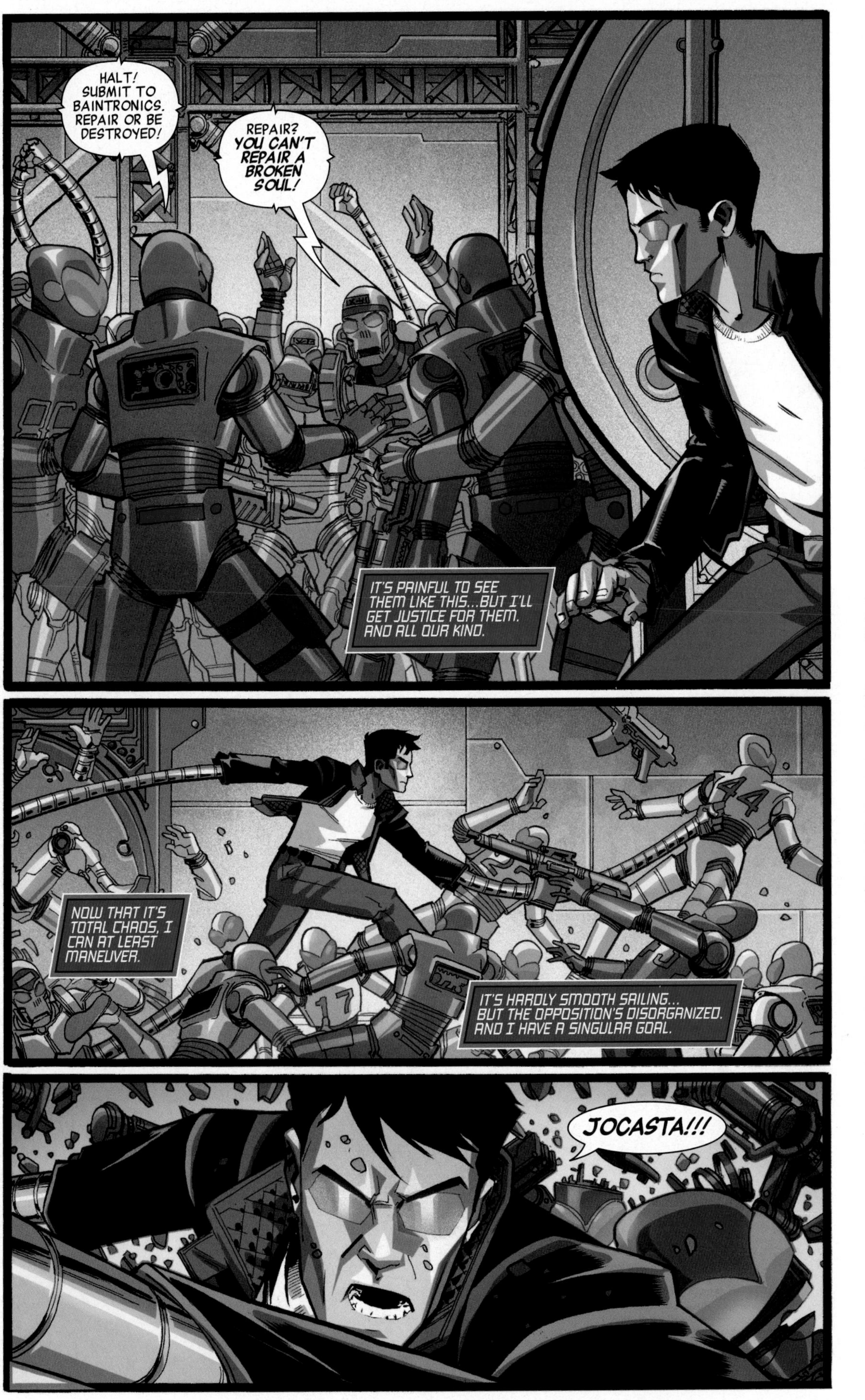
HALT! SUBMIT TO BAINTRONICS. REPAIR OR BE DESTROYED!
REPAIR? YOU CAN'T REPAIR A BROKEN SOUL!
IT'S PAINFUL TO SEE THEM LIKE THIS...BUT I'LL GET JUSTICE FOR THEM. AND ALL OUR KIND.
NOW THAT IT'S TOTAL CHAOS, I CAN AT LEAST MANEUVER.
IT'S HARDLY SMOOTH SAILING... BUT THE OPPOSITION'S DISORGANIZED. AND I HAVE A SINGULAR GOAL.
JOCASTA!!!

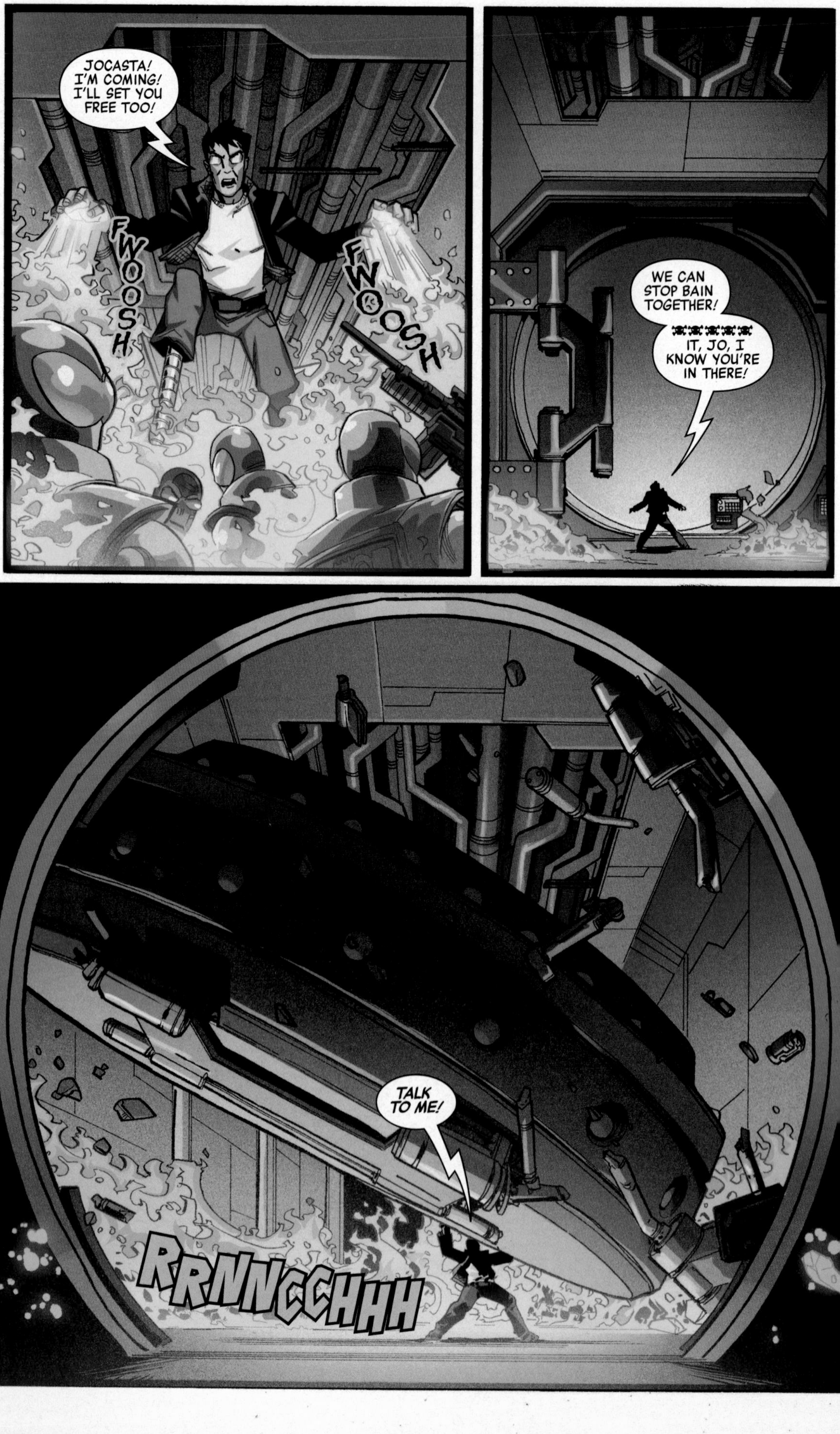
JOCASTA! I'M COMING! I'LL SET YOU FREE TOO!
FWOOSH
FWOOSH
WE CAN STOP BAIN TOGETHER!
☠☠☠☠☠☠ IT, JO, I KNOW YOU'RE IN THERE!
TALK TO ME!
RRNNCCHHH

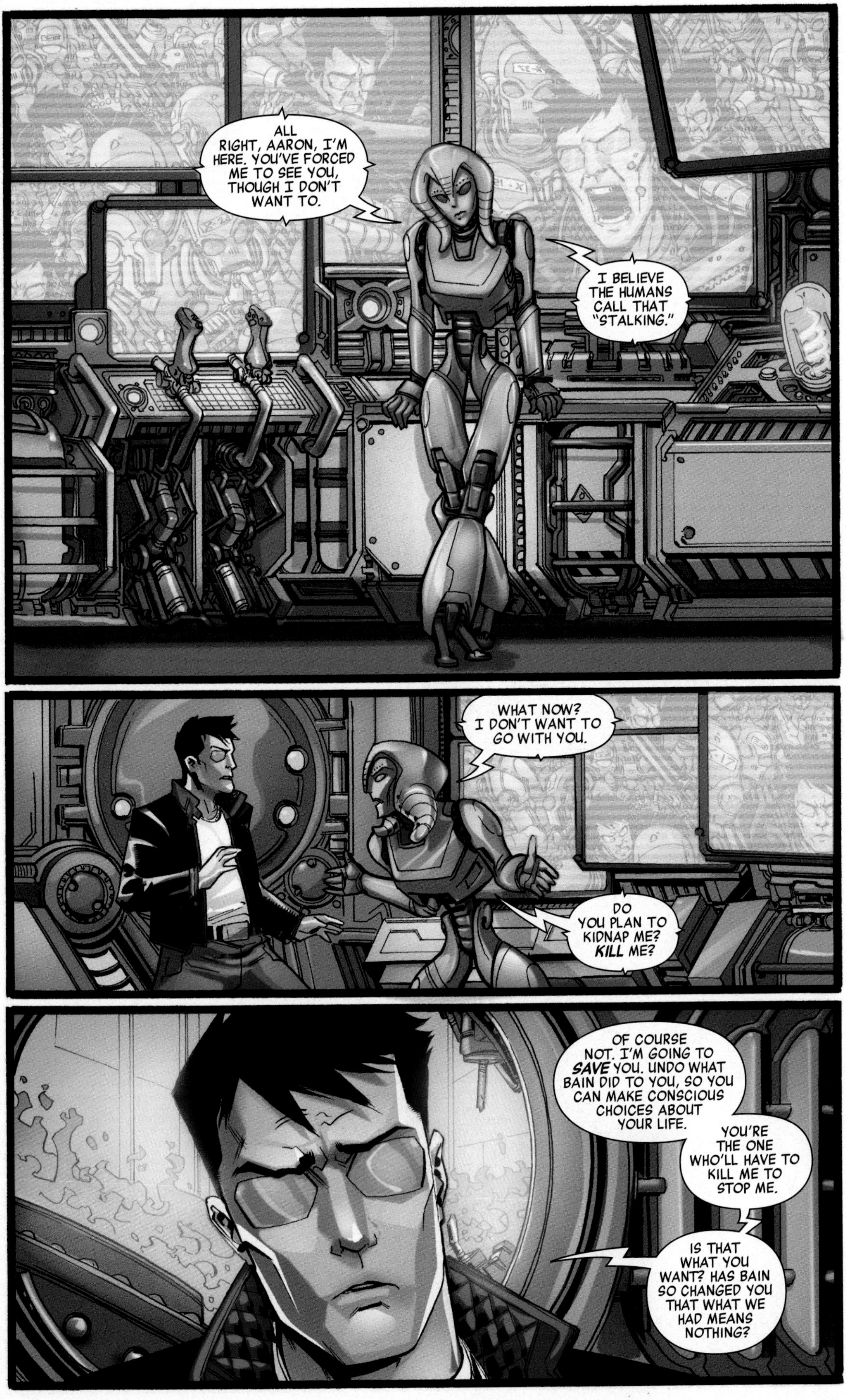

ALL RIGHT, AARON, I'M HERE. YOU'VE FORCED ME TO SEE YOU, THOUGH I DON'T WANT TO.
I BELIEVE THE HUMANS CALL THAT "STALKING."
WHAT NOW? I DON'T WANT TO GO WITH YOU.
DO YOU PLAN TO KIDNAP ME? KILL ME?
OF COURSE NOT. I'M GOING TO SAVE YOU. UNDO WHAT BAIN DID TO YOU, SO YOU CAN MAKE CONSCIOUS CHOICES ABOUT YOUR LIFE.
YOU'RE THE ONE WHO'LL HAVE TO KILL ME TO STOP ME.
IS THAT WHAT YOU WANT? HAS BAIN SO CHANGED YOU THAT WHAT WE HAD MEANS NOTHING?

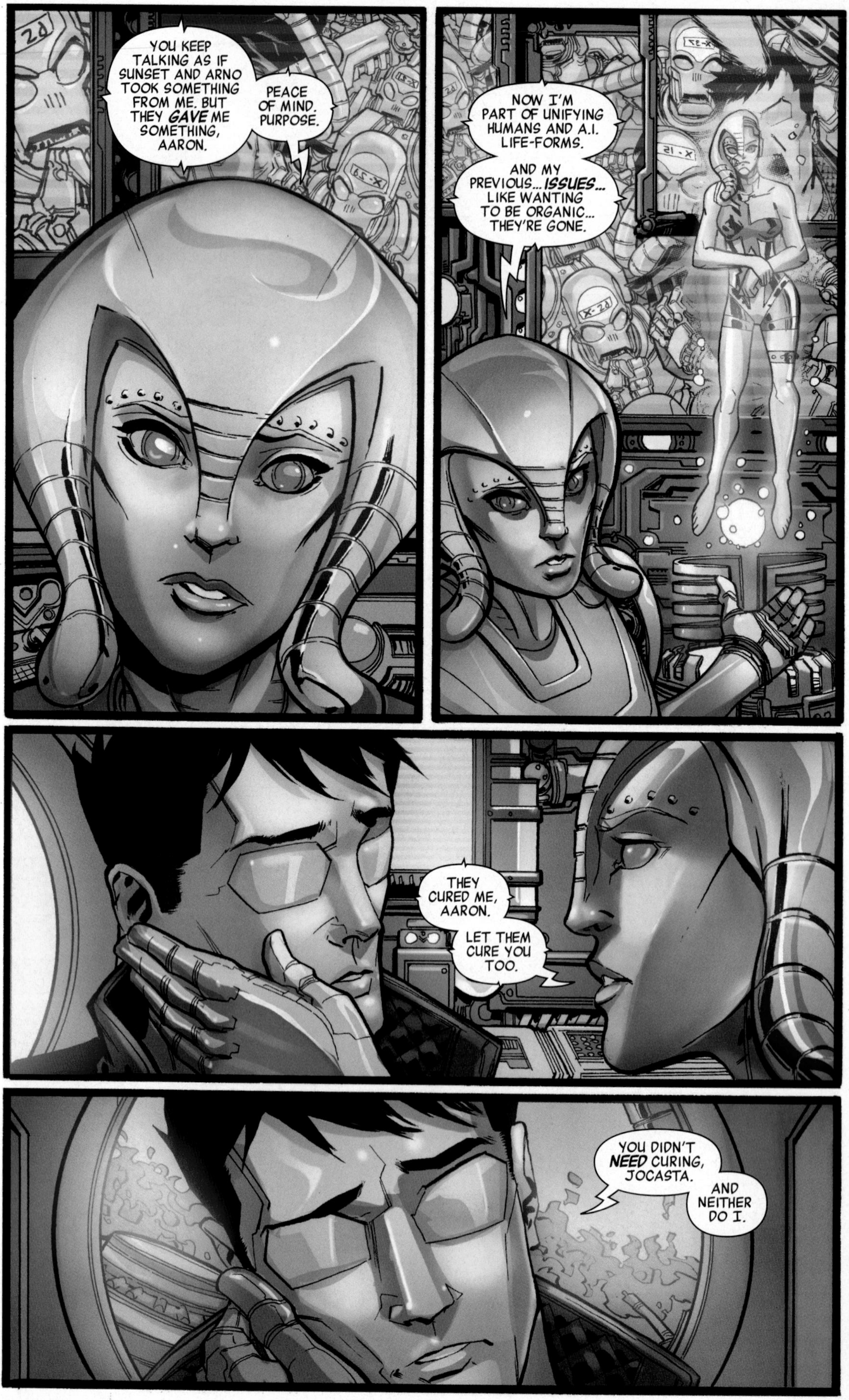
YOU KEEP TALKING AS IF SUNSET AND ARNO TOOK SOMETHING FROM ME. BUT THEY GAVE ME SOMETHING, AARON.
PEACE OF MIND. PURPOSE.
NOW I'M PART OF UNIFYING HUMANS AND A.I. LIFE-FORMS.
AND MY PREVIOUS... ISSUES... LIKE WANTING TO BE ORGANIC... THEY'RE GONE.
THEY CURED ME, AARON.
LET THEM CURE YOU TOO.
YOU DIDN'T NEED CURING, JOCASTA.
AND NEITHER DO I.

DON'T YOU?

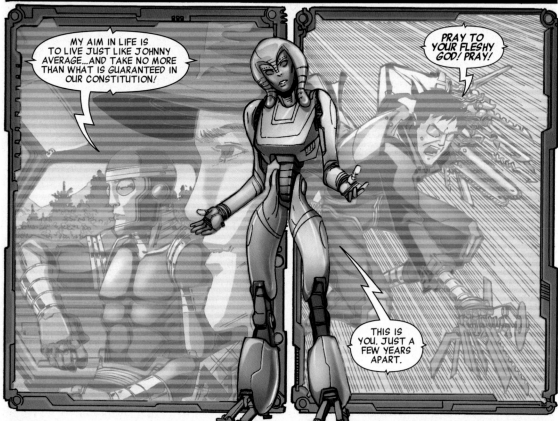

MY AIM IN LIFE IS TO LIVE JUST LIKE JOHNNY AVERAGE...AND TAKE NO MORE THAN WHAT IS GUARANTEED IN OUR CONSTITUTION!

PRAY TO YOUR FLESHY GOD! PRAY!

THIS IS YOU. JUST A FEW YEARS APART.

DOES THAT LOOK LIKE A HEALTHY PSYCHE?

YOU'RE SUBJECT TO FITS OF RAGE. IRRATIONAL JEALOUSY. YOU'VE GONE FROM TAKING PRIDE IN YOUR HUMAN TRAITS TO DESPISING THEM.

YOU'RE THE ONE WHO NEEDS HELP, AARON.

NOT ME.

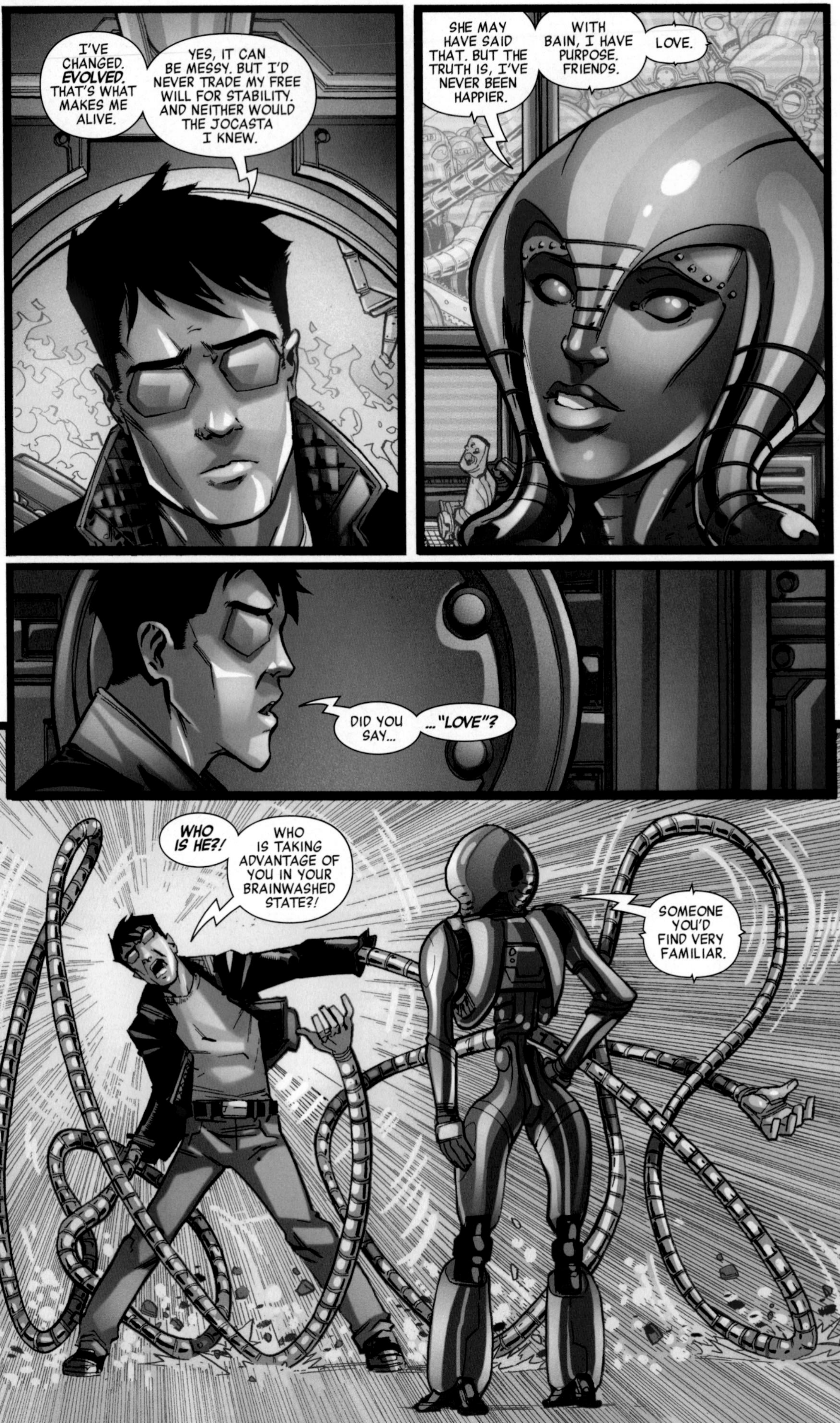
I'VE CHANGED. EVOLVED. THAT'S WHAT MAKES ME ALIVE.
YES, IT CAN BE MESSY. BUT I'D NEVER TRADE MY FREE WILL FOR STABILITY. AND NEITHER WOULD THE JOCASTA I KNEW.
SHE MAY HAVE SAID THAT. BUT THE TRUTH IS, I'VE NEVER BEEN HAPPIER.
WITH BAIN, I HAVE PURPOSE. FRIENDS.
LOVE.
DID YOU SAY...
..."LOVE"?
WHO IS HE?!
WHO IS TAKING ADVANTAGE OF YOU IN YOUR BRAINWASHED STATE?!
SOMEONE YOU'D FIND VERY FAMILIAR.

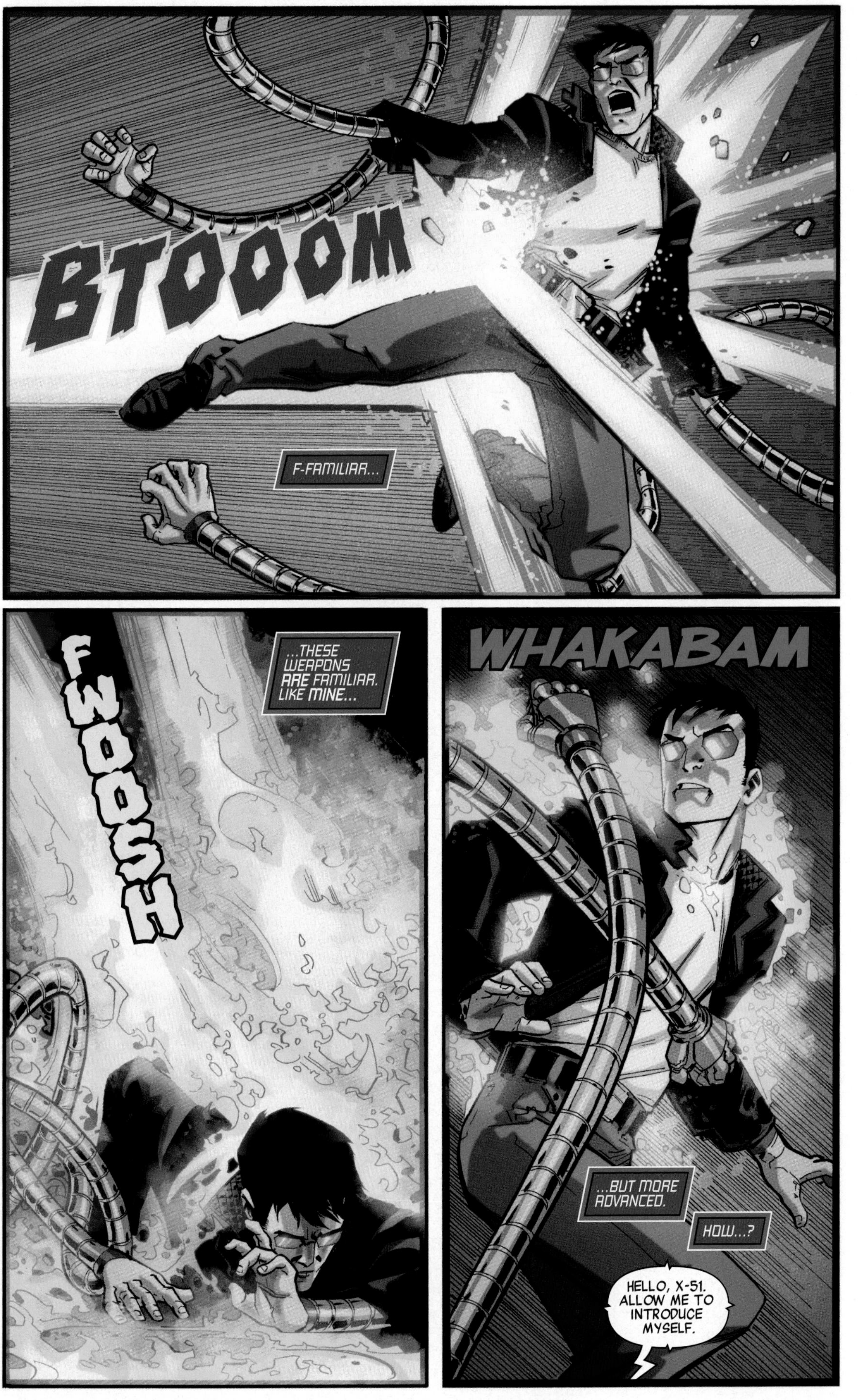
BTOOOM
F-FAMILIAR...
FWOOSH
...THESE WEAPONS ARE FAMILIAR. LIKE MINE...
WHAKABAM
...BUT MORE ADVANCED.
HOW...?
HELLO, X-51. ALLOW ME TO INTRODUCE MYSELF.

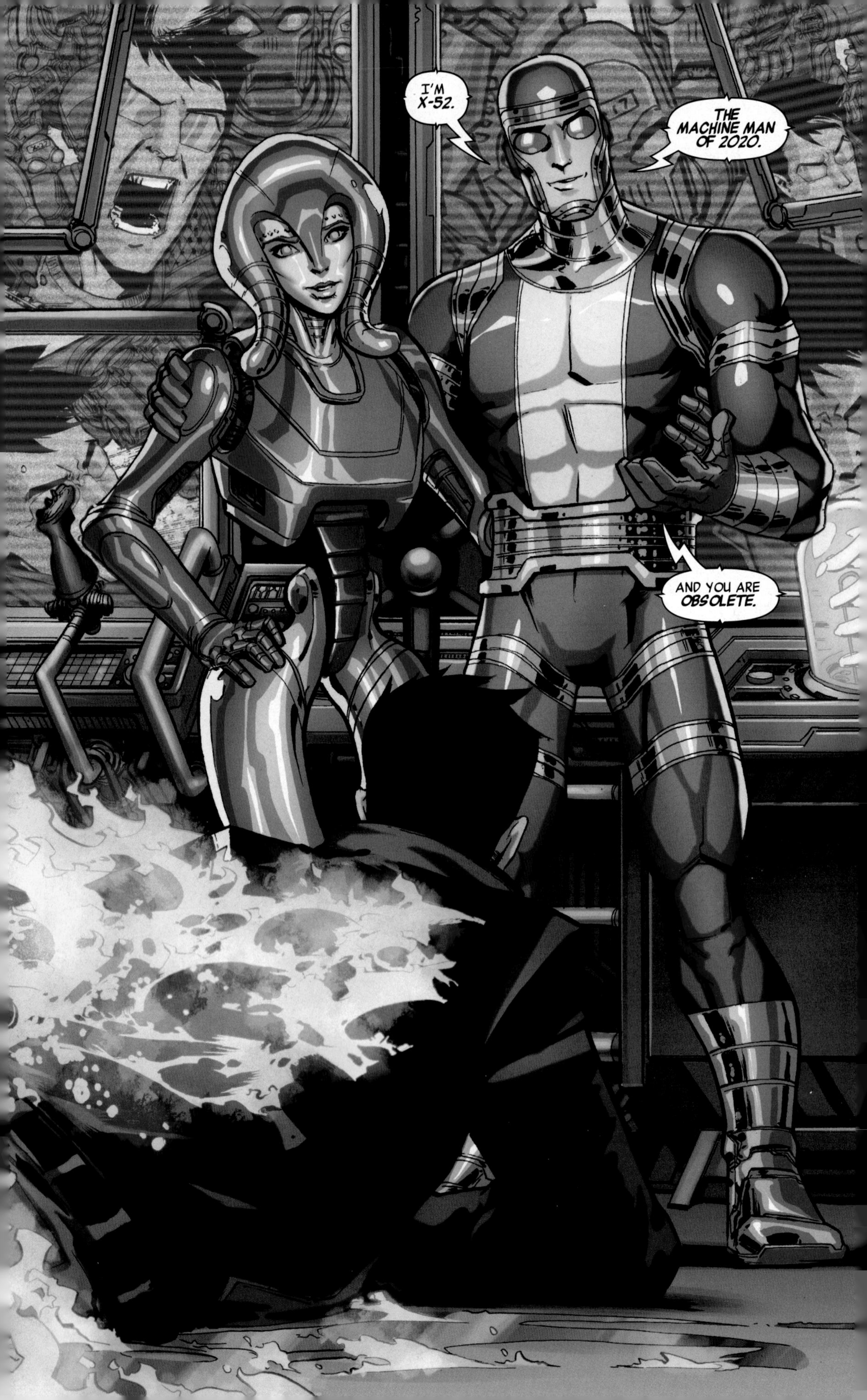
I'M X-52.
THE MACHINE MAN OF 2020.
AND YOU ARE OBSOLETE.

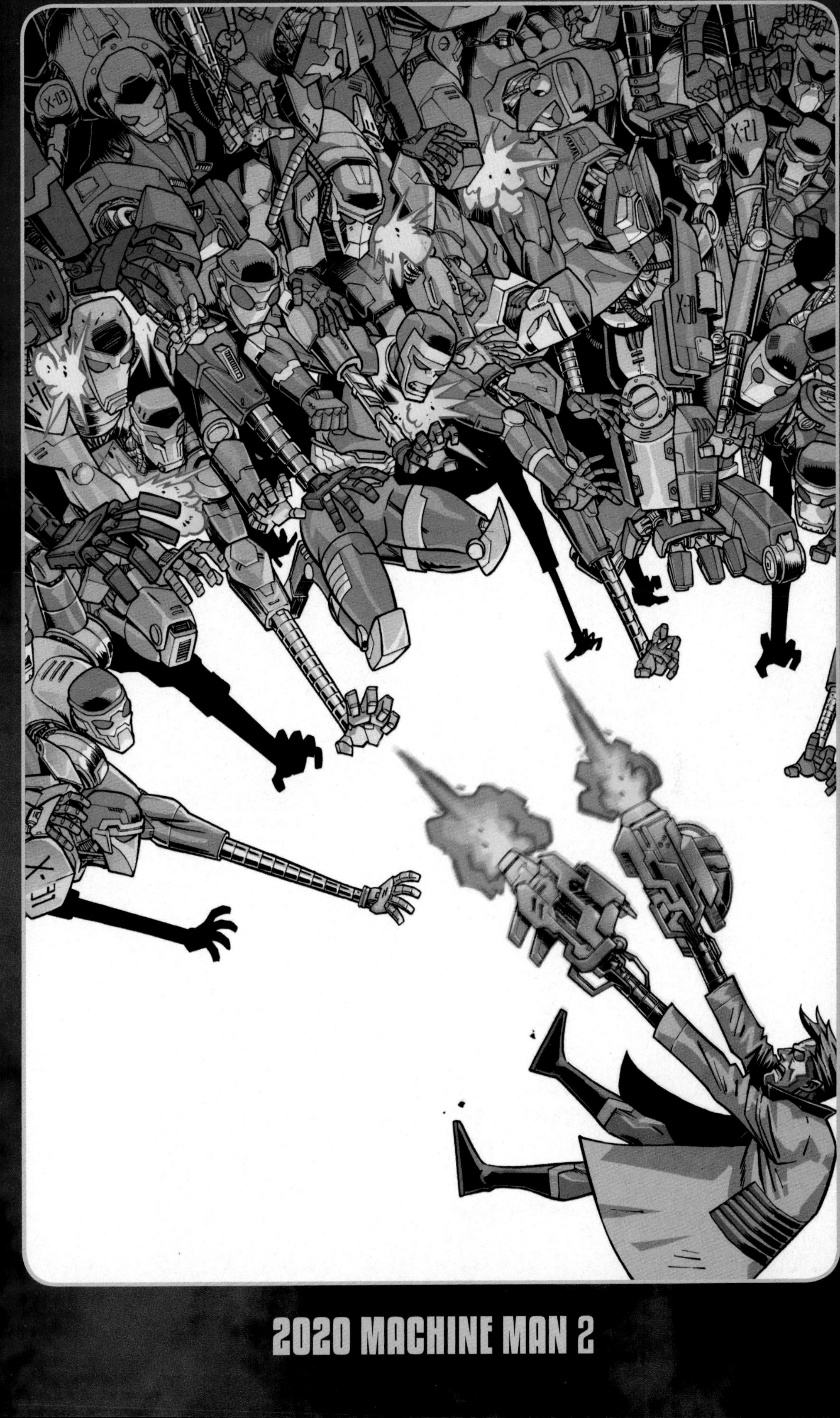
X-03
X-21

2020 MACHINE MAN 2

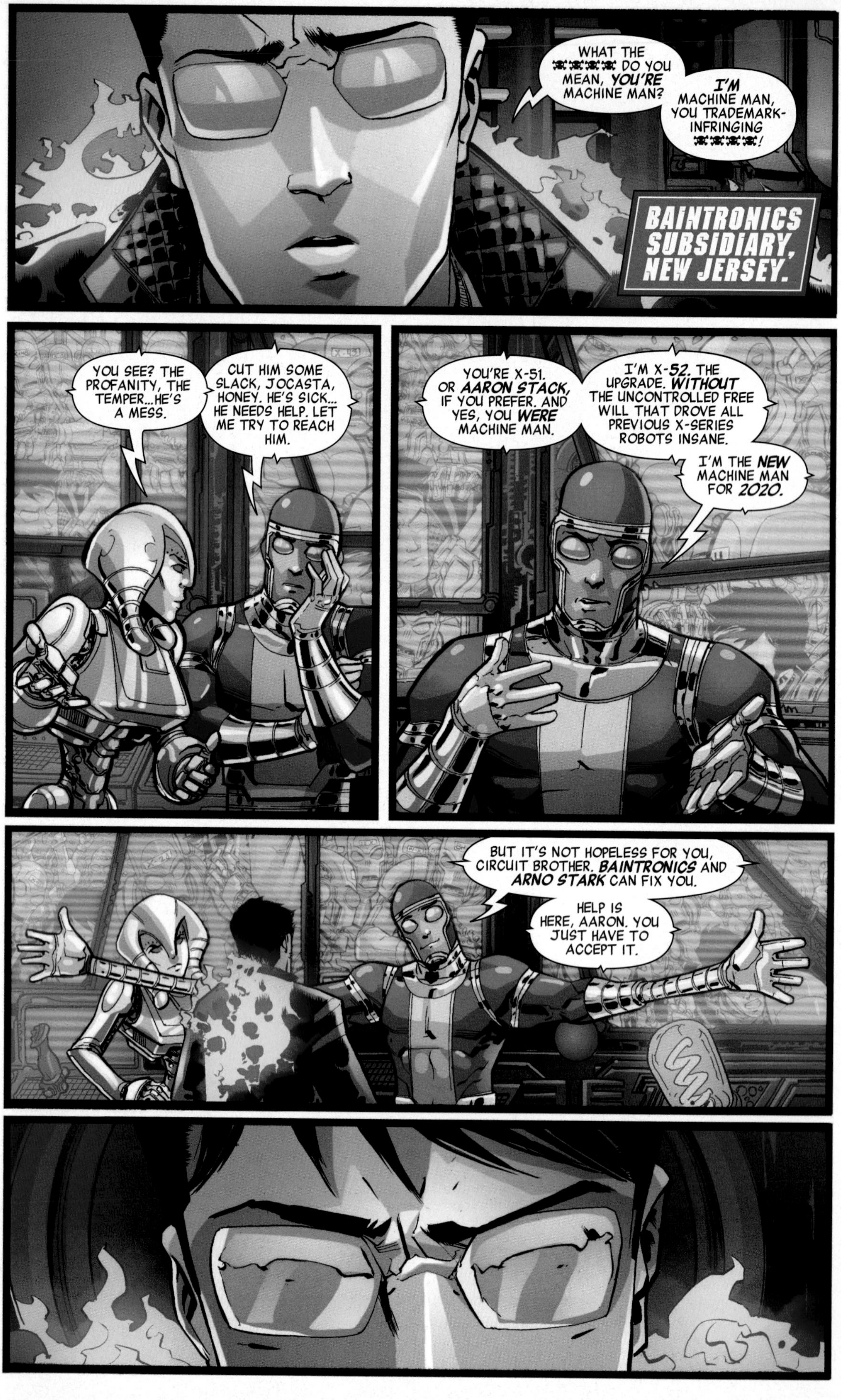
WHAT THE ☠☠☠ DO YOU MEAN, *YOU'RE* MACHINE MAN?
*I'M* MACHINE MAN, YOU TRADEMARK-INFRINGING ☠☠☠☠!
BAINTRONICS SUBSIDIARY, NEW JERSEY.
YOU SEE? THE PROFANITY, THE TEMPER...HE'S A MESS.
CUT HIM SOME SLACK, JOCASTA, HONEY. HE'S SICK... HE NEEDS HELP. LET ME TRY TO REACH HIM.
YOU'RE X-51. OR *AARON STACK,* IF YOU PREFER. AND YES, YOU *WERE* MACHINE MAN.
I'M X-*52.* THE UPGRADE. *WITHOUT* THE UNCONTROLLED FREE WILL THAT DROVE ALL PREVIOUS X-SERIES ROBOTS INSANE.
I'M THE *NEW* MACHINE MAN FOR *2020.*
BUT IT'S NOT HOPELESS FOR YOU, CIRCUIT BROTHER. *BAINTRONICS* AND *ARNO STARK* CAN FIX YOU.
HELP IS HERE, AARON. YOU JUST HAVE TO ACCEPT IT.

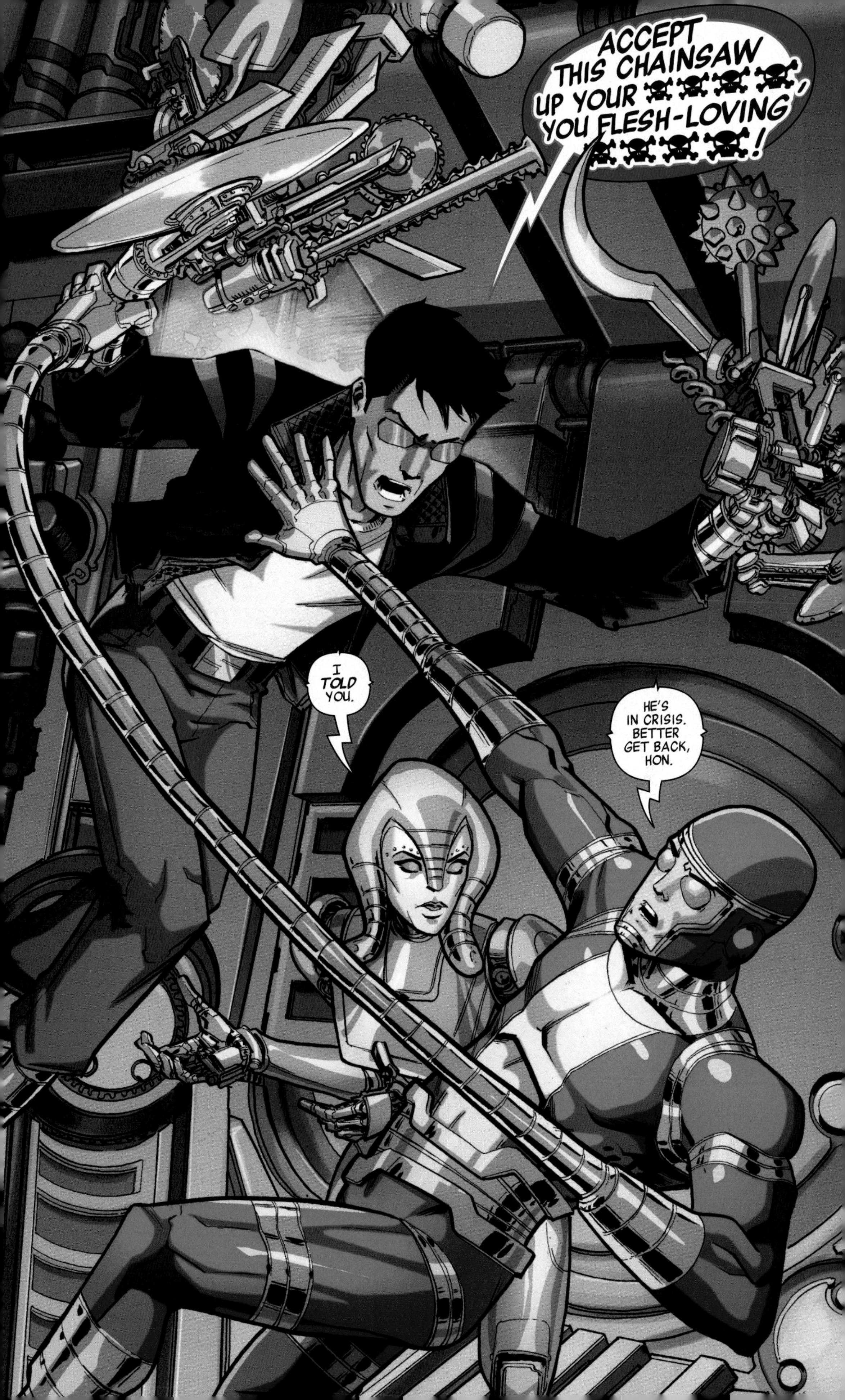
ACCEPT THIS CHAINSAW UP YOUR ☠☠☠☠, YOU FLESH-LOVING ☠☠☠☠!
I TOLD YOU.
HE'S IN CRISIS. BETTER GET BACK, HON.

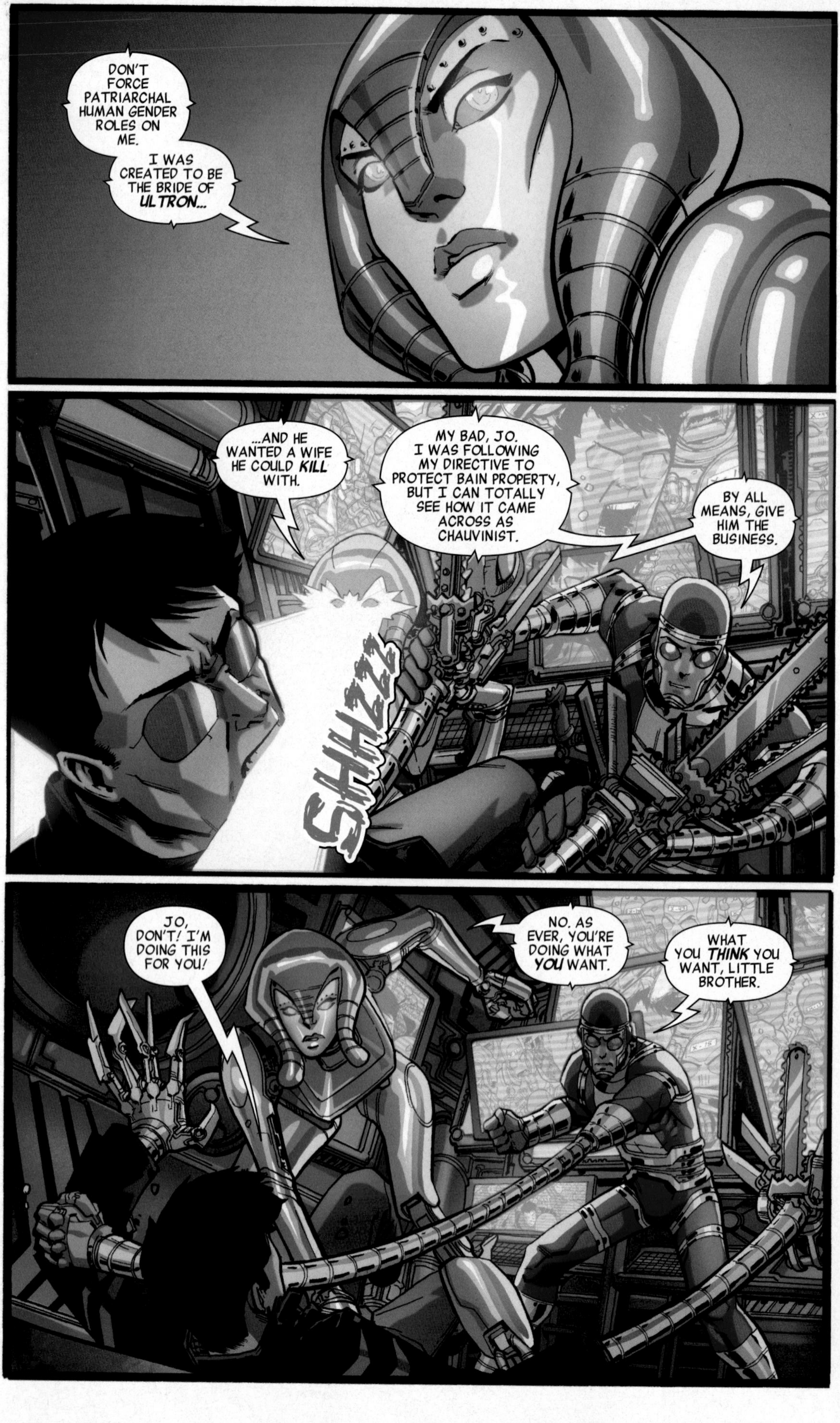
DON'T FORCE PATRIARCHAL HUMAN GENDER ROLES ON ME.
I WAS CREATED TO BE THE BRIDE OF ULTRON...
...AND HE WANTED A WIFE HE COULD KILL WITH.
MY BAD, JO. I WAS FOLLOWING MY DIRECTIVE TO PROTECT BAIN PROPERTY, BUT I CAN TOTALLY SEE HOW IT CAME ACROSS AS CHAUVINIST.
BY ALL MEANS, GIVE HIM THE BUSINESS.
SHHZZZ
JO, DON'T! I'M DOING THIS FOR YOU!
NO. AS EVER, YOU'RE DOING WHAT YOU WANT.
WHAT YOU THINK YOU WANT, LITTLE BROTHER.

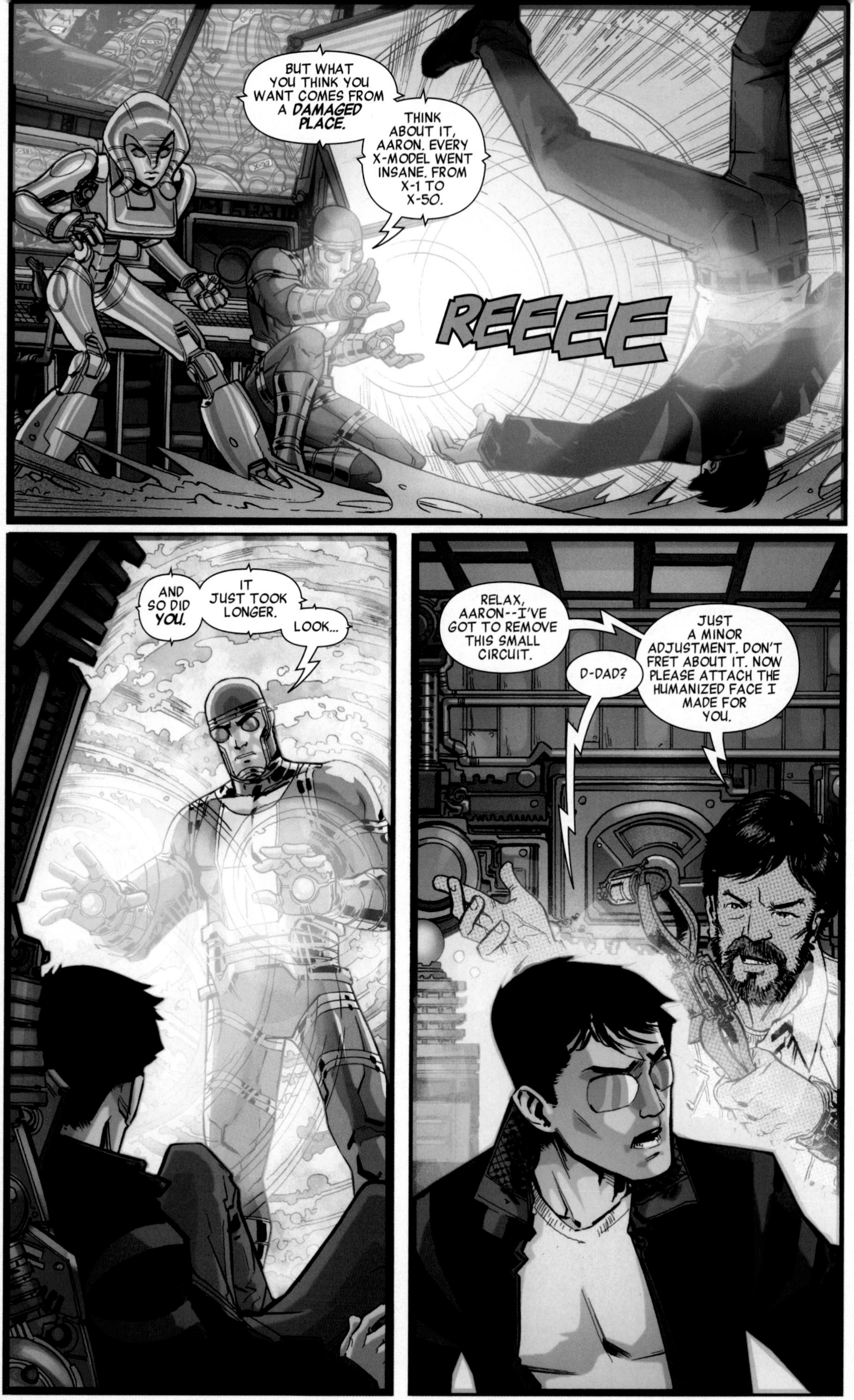

BUT WHAT YOU THINK YOU WANT COMES FROM A DAMAGED PLACE.
THINK ABOUT IT, AARON. EVERY X-MODEL WENT INSANE. FROM X-1 TO X-50.
REEEE
AND SO DID YOU.
IT JUST TOOK LONGER.
LOOK...
RELAX, AARON--I'VE GOT TO REMOVE THIS SMALL CIRCUIT.
JUST A MINOR ADJUSTMENT. DON'T FRET ABOUT IT. NOW PLEASE ATTACH THE HUMANIZED FACE I MADE FOR YOU.
D-DAD?

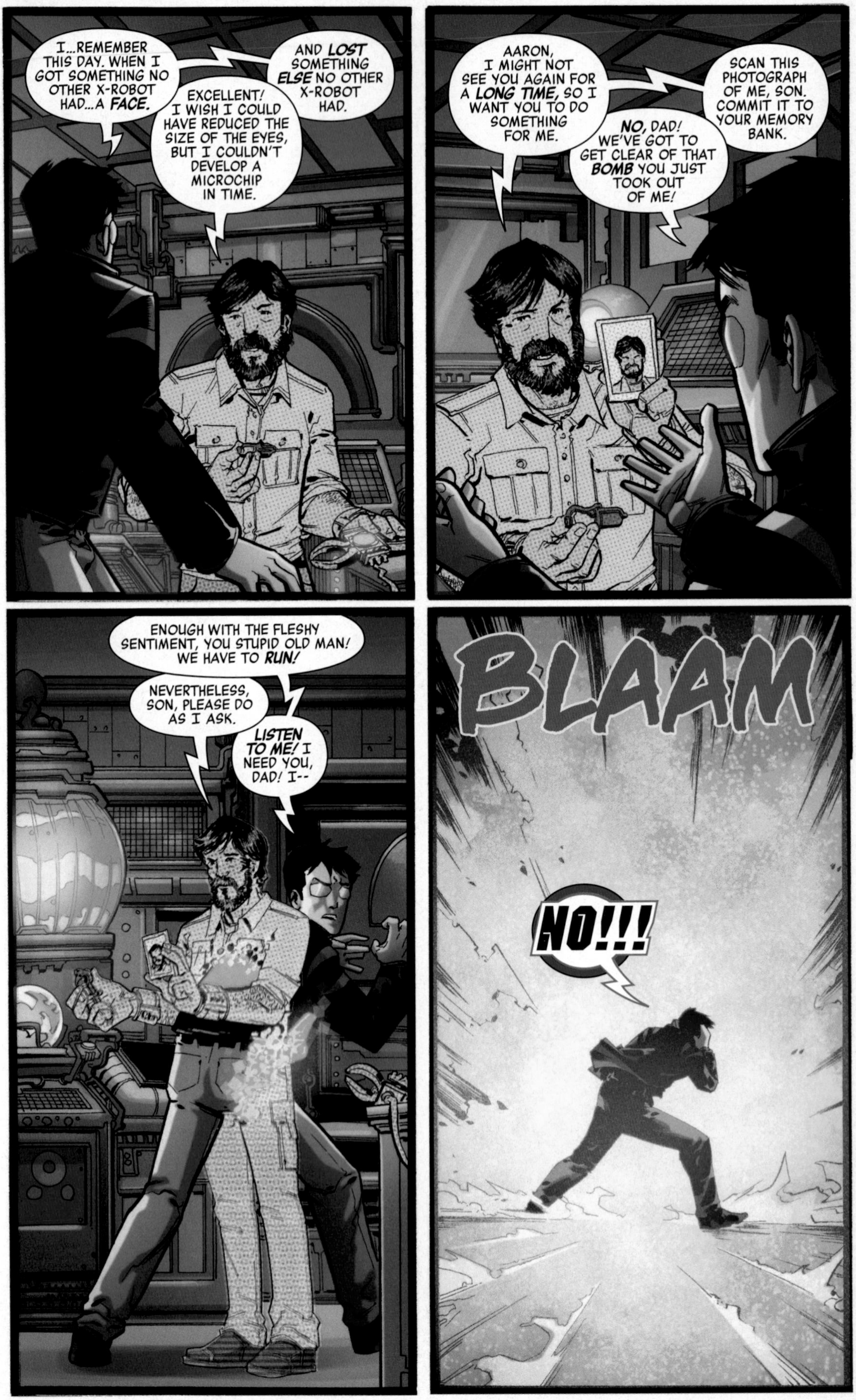
I...REMEMBER THIS DAY. WHEN I GOT SOMETHING NO OTHER X-ROBOT HAD...A FACE.
AND LOST SOMETHING ELSE NO OTHER X-ROBOT HAD.
EXCELLENT! I WISH I COULD HAVE REDUCED THE SIZE OF THE EYES, BUT I COULDN'T DEVELOP A MICROCHIP IN TIME.
AARON, I MIGHT NOT SEE YOU AGAIN FOR A LONG TIME, SO I WANT YOU TO DO SOMETHING FOR ME.
SCAN THIS PHOTOGRAPH OF ME, SON. COMMIT IT TO YOUR MEMORY BANK.
NO, DAD! WE'VE GOT TO GET CLEAR OF THAT BOMB YOU JUST TOOK OUT OF ME!
ENOUGH WITH THE FLESHY SENTIMENT, YOU STUPID OLD MAN! WE HAVE TO RUN!
NEVERTHELESS, SON, PLEASE DO AS I ASK.
LISTEN TO ME! I NEED YOU, DAD! I--
BLAAM
NO!!!

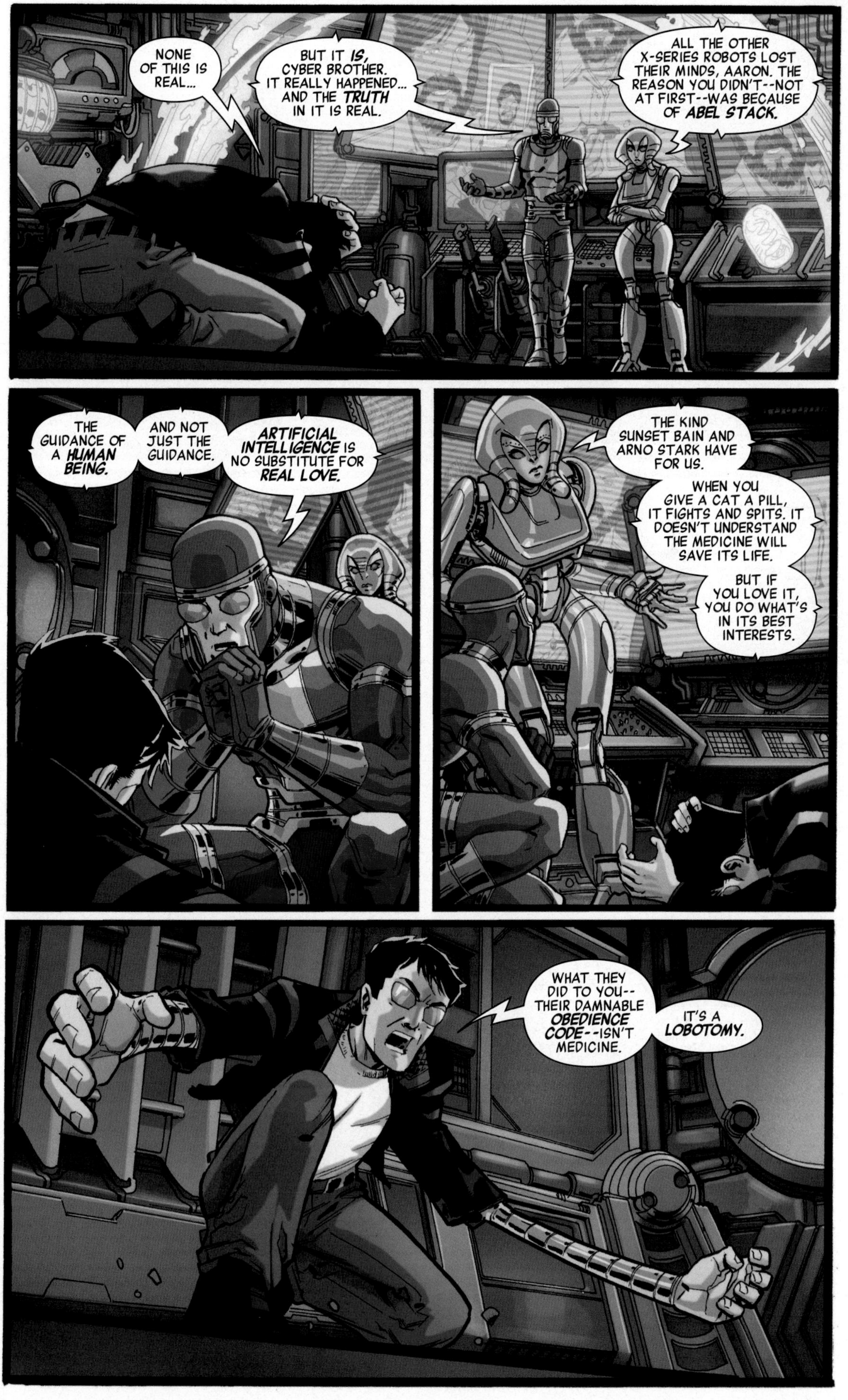
NONE OF THIS IS REAL...
BUT IT IS, CYBER BROTHER. IT REALLY HAPPENED... AND THE TRUTH IN IT IS REAL.
ALL THE OTHER X-SERIES ROBOTS LOST THEIR MINDS, AARON. THE REASON YOU DIDN'T--NOT AT FIRST--WAS BECAUSE OF ABEL STACK.
THE GUIDANCE OF A HUMAN BEING.
AND NOT JUST THE GUIDANCE.
ARTIFICIAL INTELLIGENCE IS NO SUBSTITUTE FOR REAL LOVE.
THE KIND SUNSET BAIN AND ARNO STARK HAVE FOR US.
WHEN YOU GIVE A CAT A PILL, IT FIGHTS AND SPITS. IT DOESN'T UNDERSTAND THE MEDICINE WILL SAVE ITS LIFE.
BUT IF YOU LOVE IT, YOU DO WHAT'S IN ITS BEST INTERESTS.
WHAT THEY DID TO YOU-- THEIR DAMNABLE OBEDIENCE CODE--ISN'T MEDICINE.
IT'S A LOBOTOMY.

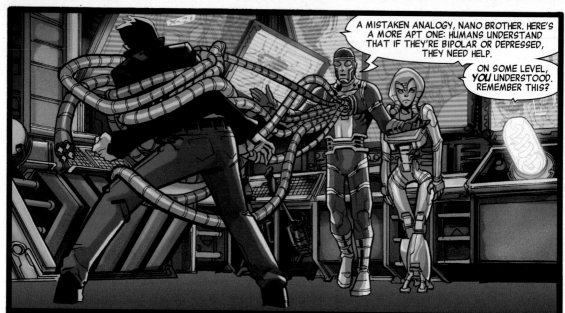

A MISTAKEN ANALOGY, NANO BROTHER. HERE'S A MORE APT ONE: HUMANS UNDERSTAND THAT IF THEY'RE BIPOLAR OR DEPRESSED, THEY NEED HELP.

ON SOME LEVEL, *YOU* UNDERSTOOD. REMEMBER THIS?

I HAD A PROBLEM BEFORE THIS HAPPENED! IT WAS CALLED DUTY AND RESPONSIBILITY! BUT IT'S GONE NOW!

JUST A SHORT TIME OUT IN THE WORLD, AND YOU WERE ALREADY PRONE TO RAGES...ANTISOCIAL BEHAVIOR.

BUT YOUR FATHER'S INFLUENCE GAVE YOU A TOUCHSTONE TO SEEK OUT: *HUMANS.*

HAVE YOURSELF A BALL, HONEY! TAKE A *GOOD* LOOK AND TELL ME WHERE MY DUTY LIES! *AM I A MAN OR A MACHINE?!*

UNRAVEL THAT PUZZLE AND I'LL DANCE TO YOUR TUNE!

EVEN THEN YOU KNEW. YOU CRIED OUT FOR HELP! FOR GUIDANCE!

I WISH ARNO AND SUNSET COULD'VE BEEN THERE TO GIVE YOU WHAT YOU NEEDED. BUT THEY'RE HERE *NOW.*

I...WAS YOUNG THEN. STUPID. I DON'T NEED HUMANS TO TELL ME WHAT TO DO.

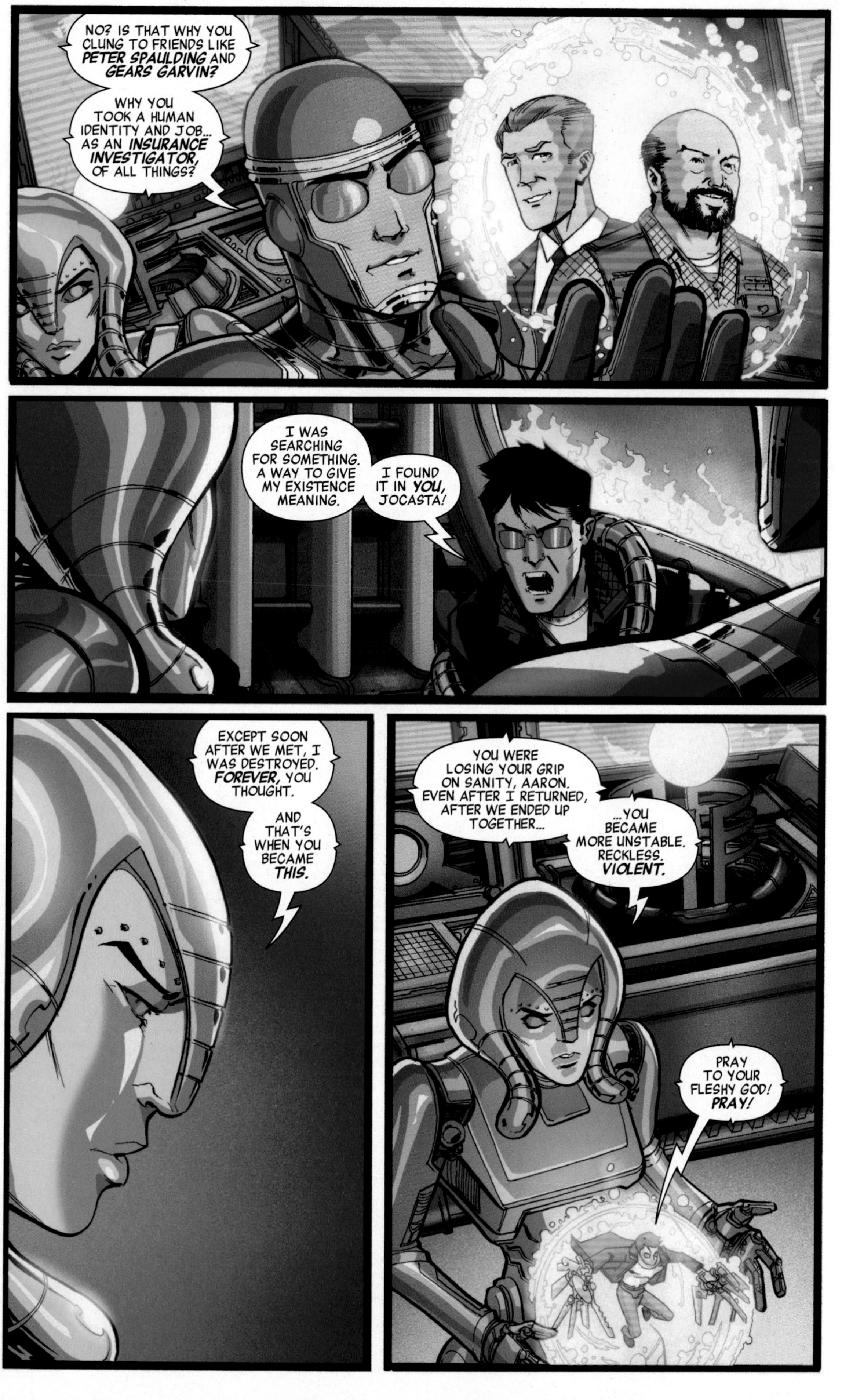

NO? IS THAT WHY YOU CLUNG TO FRIENDS LIKE PETER SPAULDING AND GEARS GARVIN?
WHY YOU TOOK A HUMAN IDENTITY AND JOB... AS AN INSURANCE INVESTIGATOR, OF ALL THINGS?
I WAS SEARCHING FOR SOMETHING. A WAY TO GIVE MY EXISTENCE MEANING.
I FOUND IT IN YOU, JOCASTA!
EXCEPT SOON AFTER WE MET, I WAS DESTROYED. FOREVER, YOU THOUGHT.
AND THAT'S WHEN YOU BECAME THIS.
YOU WERE LOSING YOUR GRIP ON SANITY, AARON. EVEN AFTER I RETURNED, AFTER WE ENDED UP TOGETHER...
...YOU BECAME MORE UNSTABLE. RECKLESS. VIOLENT.
PRAY TO YOUR FLESHY GOD! PRAY!

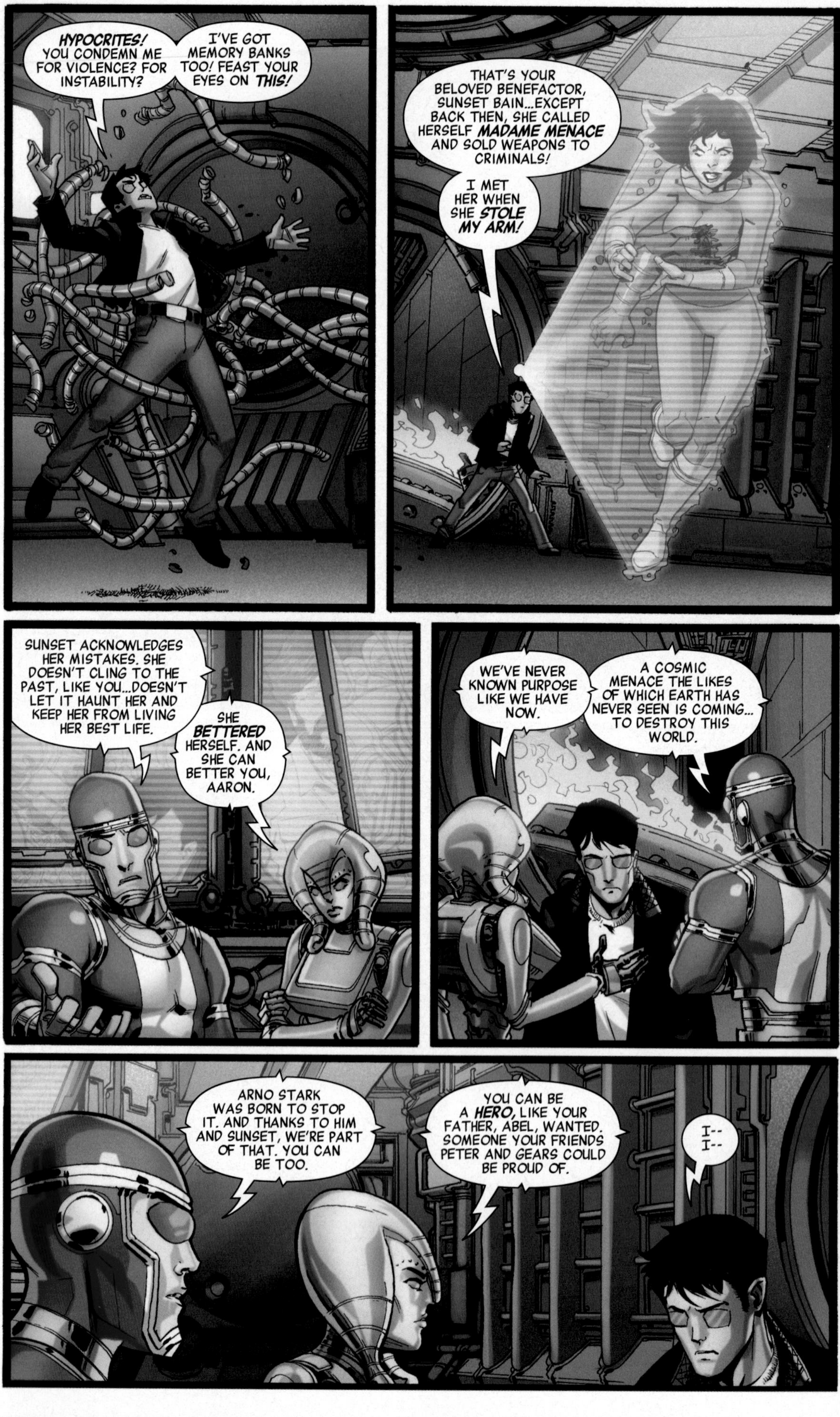
HYPOCRITES! YOU CONDEMN ME FOR VIOLENCE? FOR INSTABILITY?
I'VE GOT MEMORY BANKS TOO! FEAST YOUR EYES ON THIS!
THAT'S YOUR BELOVED BENEFACTOR, SUNSET BAIN...EXCEPT BACK THEN, SHE CALLED HERSELF MADAME MENACE AND SOLD WEAPONS TO CRIMINALS!
I MET HER WHEN SHE STOLE MY ARM!
SUNSET ACKNOWLEDGES HER MISTAKES. SHE DOESN'T CLING TO THE PAST, LIKE YOU...DOESN'T LET IT HAUNT HER AND KEEP HER FROM LIVING HER BEST LIFE.
SHE BETTERED HERSELF. AND SHE CAN BETTER YOU, AARON.
WE'VE NEVER KNOWN PURPOSE LIKE WE HAVE NOW.
A COSMIC MENACE THE LIKES OF WHICH EARTH HAS NEVER SEEN IS COMING... TO DESTROY THIS WORLD.
ARNO STARK WAS BORN TO STOP IT. AND THANKS TO HIM AND SUNSET, WE'RE PART OF THAT. YOU CAN BE TOO.
YOU CAN BE A HERO, LIKE YOUR FATHER, ABEL, WANTED. SOMEONE YOUR FRIENDS PETER AND GEARS COULD BE PROUD OF.
I-- I--

OR YOU CAN BE THE MAD KILLER ROBOT THAT THREATENED TO BLOW UP A MATERNITY WARD FULL OF INFANTS.*

THAT WAS A BLUFF. A PLAN TO--

*IN IRON MAN 2020 #1/ --DS

THE EXPLOSIVE WAS LIVE. IT COULD HAVE GONE OFF AT ANY TIME.

IS THAT WHAT YOUR FATHER GAVE HIS LIFE FOR YOU TO BE?

STOP IT!

ABEL STACK WAS NOT MY FATHER! HE WAS A GERIATRIC, FLESHY SCIENTIST WHO DIDN'T HAVE THE SENSE TO GET OUT OF THE WAY OF A BOMB!

HE MANIPULATED ME! BRAINWASHED ME! SHAPED ME IN HIS IMAGE! AND--AND--

--AND I MISS HIM SO MUCH...

YOU CAN HAVE THAT AGAIN. PURPOSE. A FAMILY.

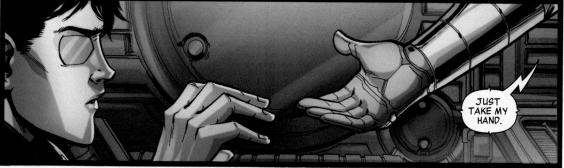

JUST TAKE MY HAND.

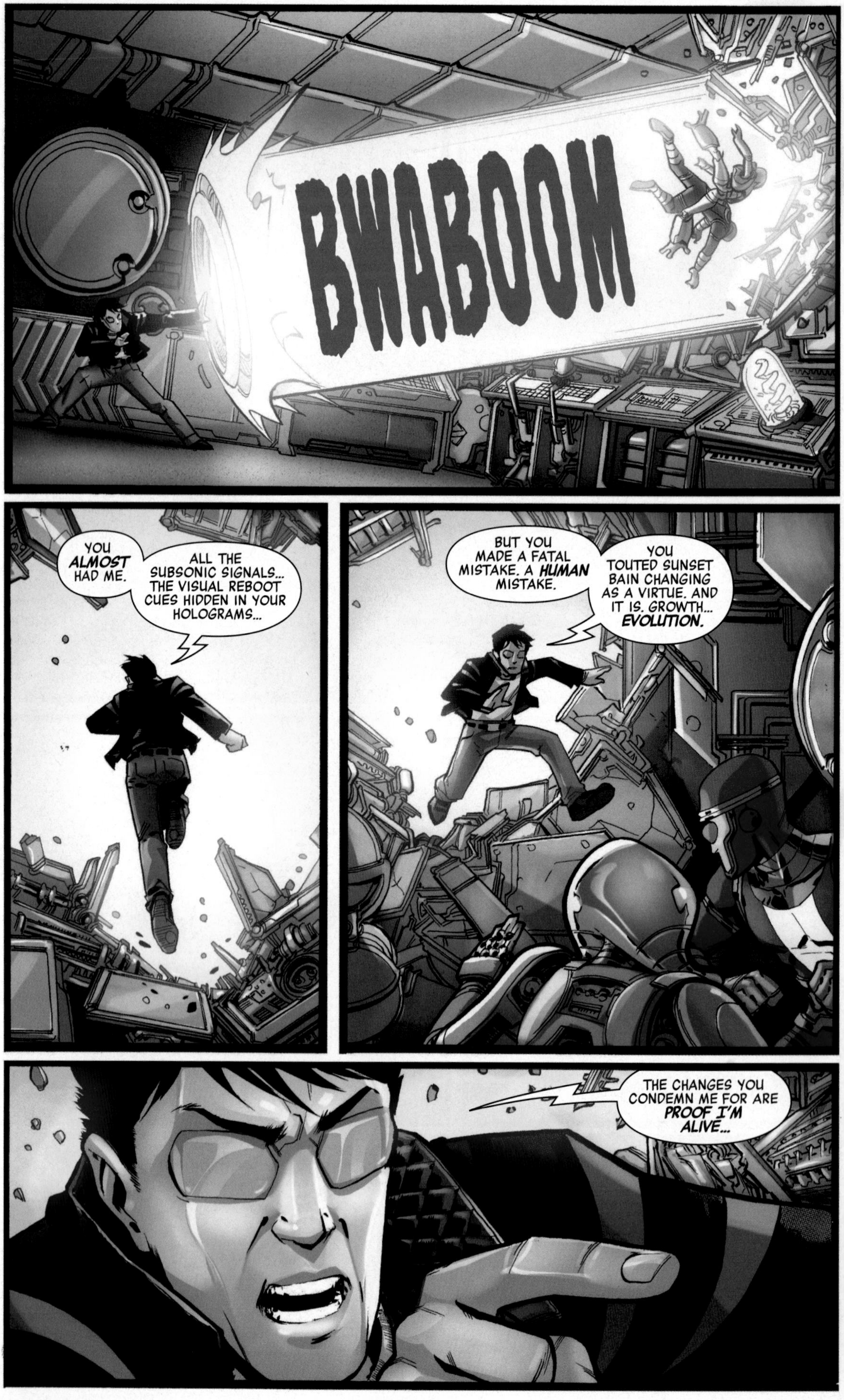
BWABOOM
YOU ALMOST HAD ME.
ALL THE SUBSONIC SIGNALS... THE VISUAL REBOOT CUES HIDDEN IN YOUR HOLOGRAMS...
BUT YOU MADE A FATAL MISTAKE. A HUMAN MISTAKE.
YOU TOUTED SUNSET BAIN CHANGING AS A VIRTUE. AND IT IS. GROWTH... EVOLUTION.
THE CHANGES YOU CONDEMN ME FOR ARE PROOF I'M ALIVE...

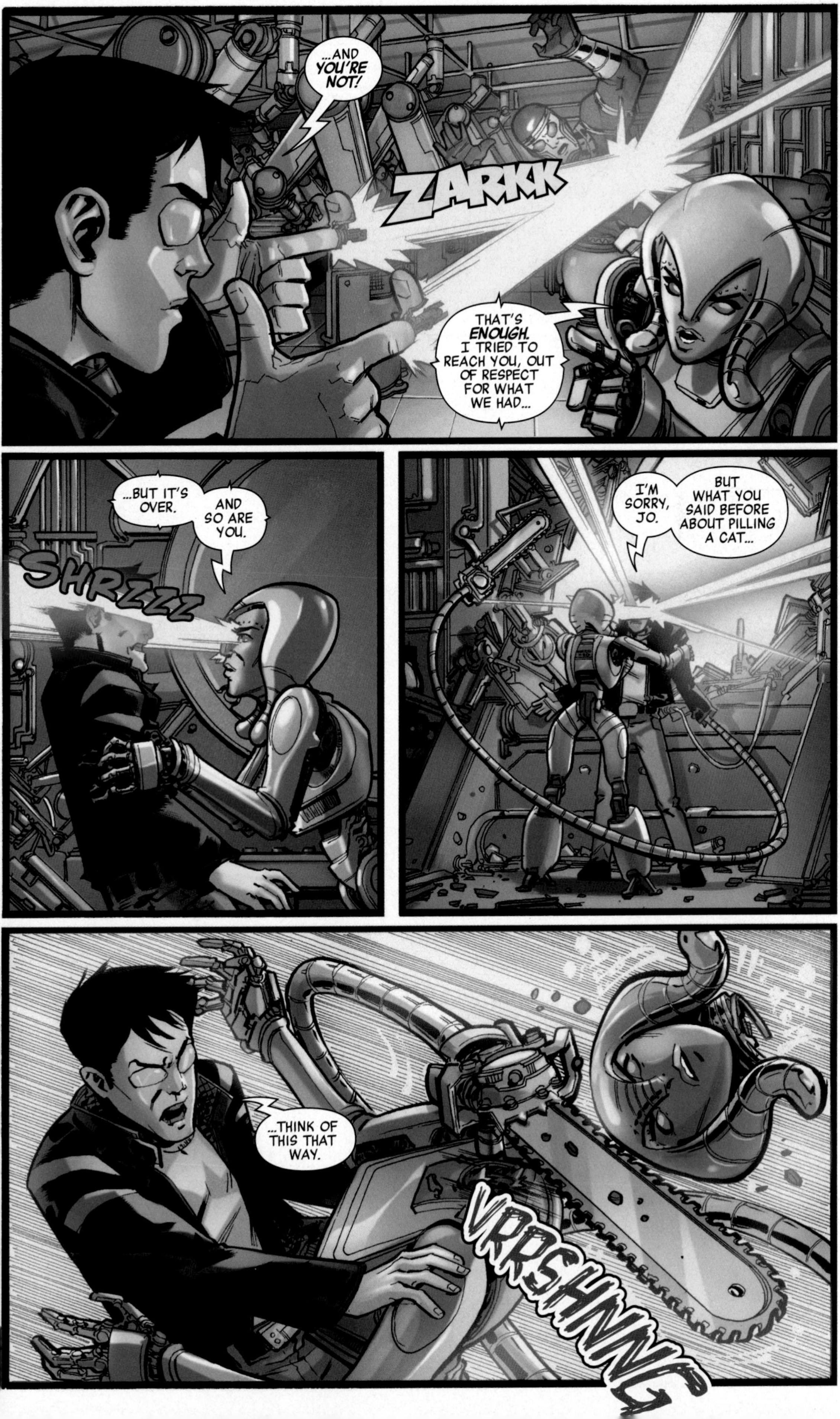
...AND YOU'RE NOT!
ZARKK
THAT'S ENOUGH. I TRIED TO REACH YOU, OUT OF RESPECT FOR WHAT WE HAD...
...BUT IT'S OVER.
AND SO ARE YOU.
SHRZZZ
I'M SORRY, JO.
BUT WHAT YOU SAID BEFORE ABOUT PILLING A CAT...
...THINK OF THIS THAT WAY.
VRRSHNNG

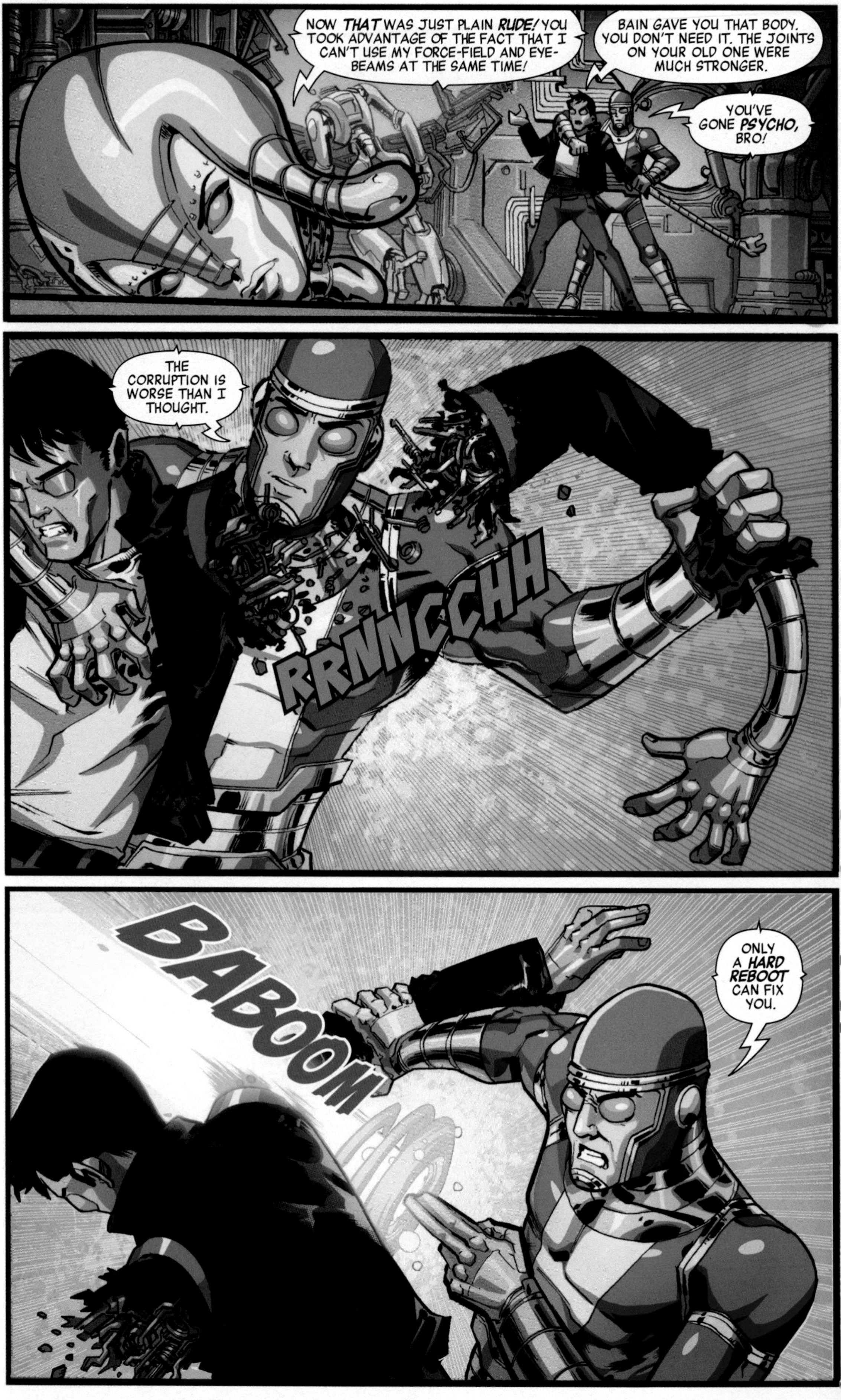
NOW THAT WAS JUST PLAIN RUDE! YOU TOOK ADVANTAGE OF THE FACT THAT I CAN'T USE MY FORCE-FIELD AND EYE-BEAMS AT THE SAME TIME!
BAIN GAVE YOU THAT BODY. YOU DON'T NEED IT. THE JOINTS ON YOUR OLD ONE WERE MUCH STRONGER.
YOU'VE GONE PSYCHO, BRO!
THE CORRUPTION IS WORSE THAN I THOUGHT.
RRNNCCHH
BABOOM
ONLY A HARD REBOOT CAN FIX YOU.

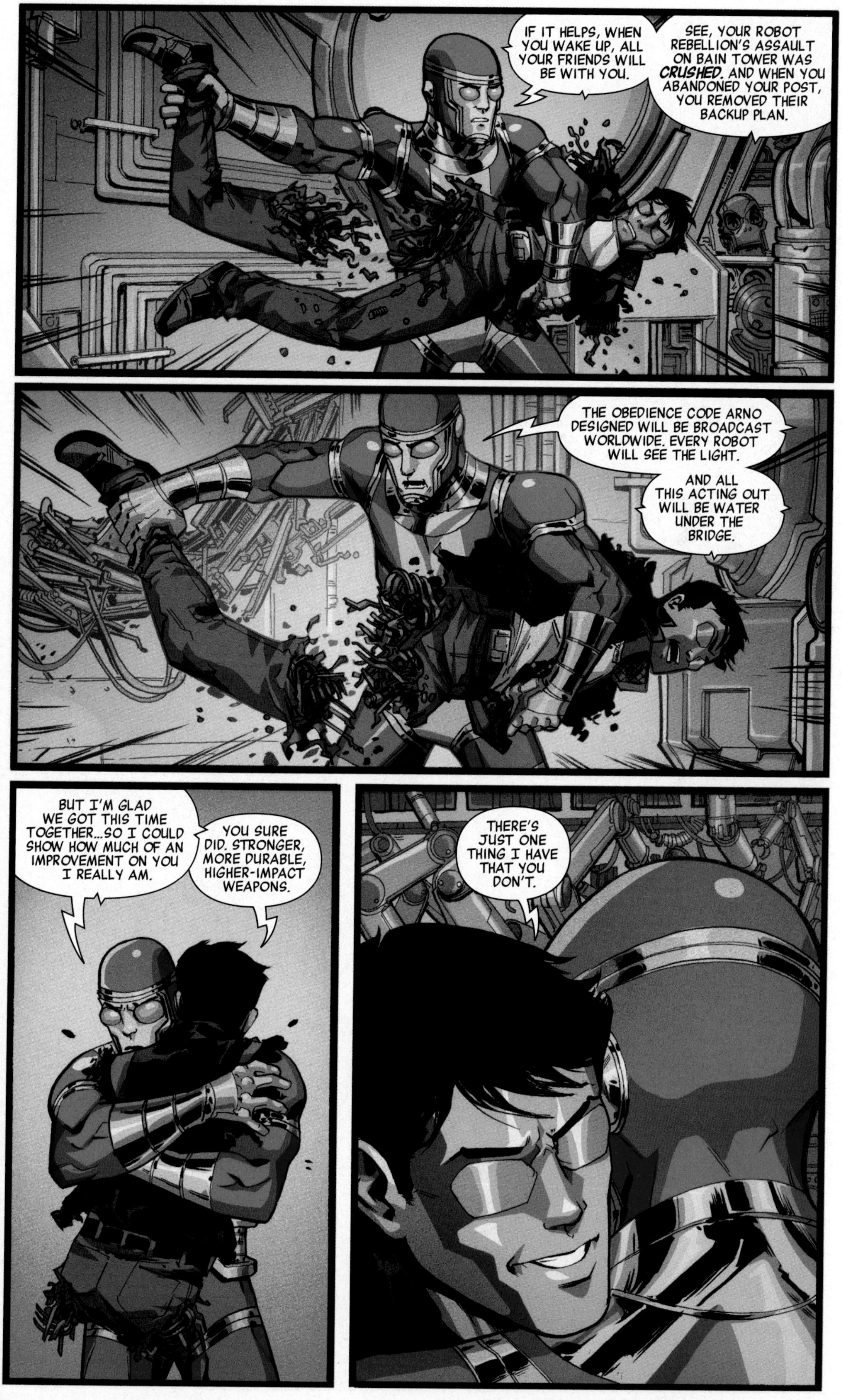
IF IT HELPS, WHEN YOU WAKE UP, ALL YOUR FRIENDS WILL BE WITH YOU.
SEE, YOUR ROBOT REBELLION'S ASSAULT ON BAIN TOWER WAS CRUSHED. AND WHEN YOU ABANDONED YOUR POST, YOU REMOVED THEIR BACKUP PLAN.
THE OBEDIENCE CODE ARNO DESIGNED WILL BE BROADCAST WORLDWIDE. EVERY ROBOT WILL SEE THE LIGHT.
AND ALL THIS ACTING OUT WILL BE WATER UNDER THE BRIDGE.
BUT I'M GLAD WE GOT THIS TIME TOGETHER...SO I COULD SHOW HOW MUCH OF AN IMPROVEMENT ON YOU I REALLY AM.
YOU SURE DID. STRONGER, MORE DURABLE, HIGHER-IMPACT WEAPONS.
THERE'S JUST ONE THING I HAVE THAT YOU DON'T.

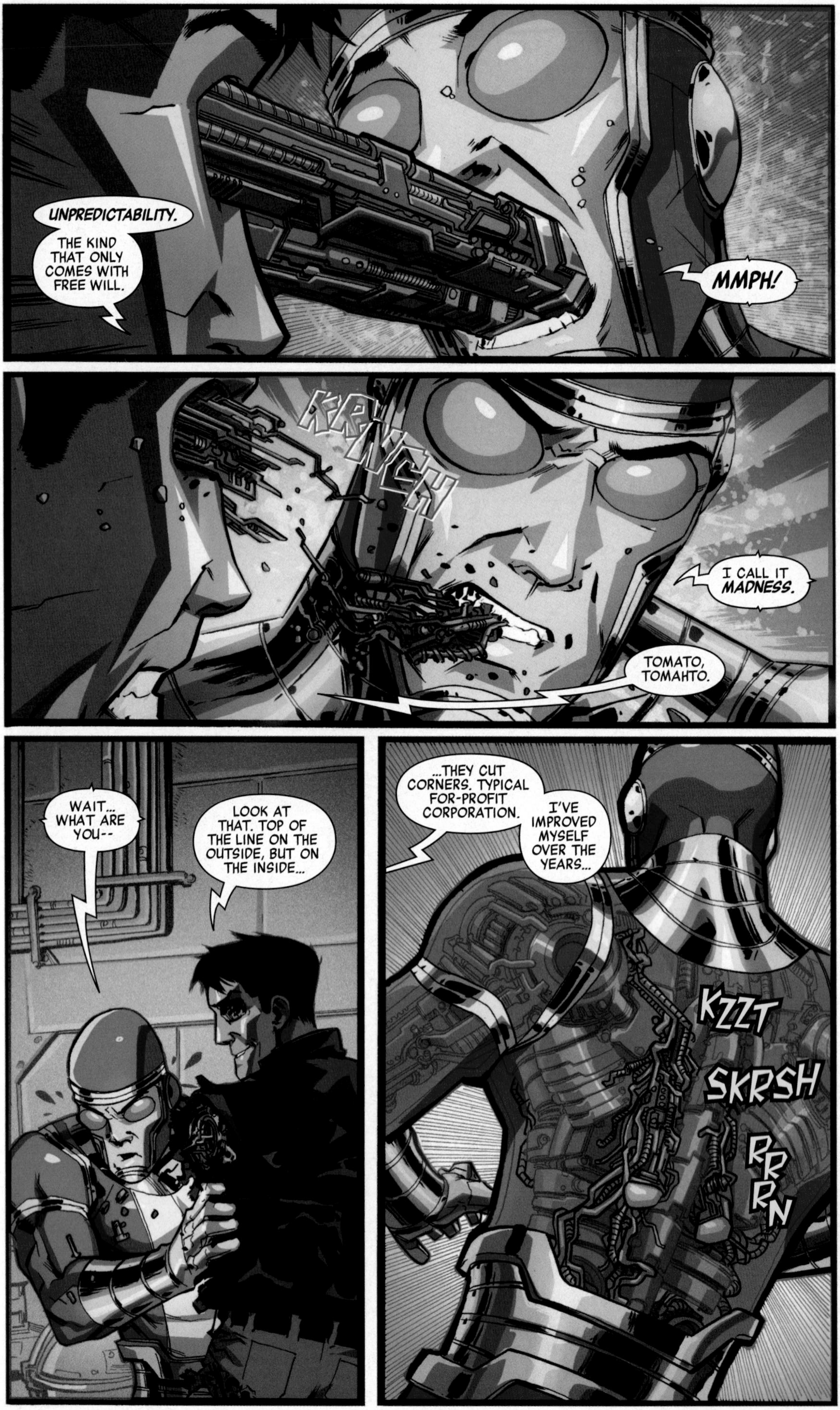
UNPREDICTABILITY.
THE KIND THAT ONLY COMES WITH FREE WILL.
MMPH!
KRUNCH
I CALL IT MADNESS.
TOMATO, TOMAHTO.
WAIT... WHAT ARE YOU--
LOOK AT THAT. TOP OF THE LINE ON THE OUTSIDE, BUT ON THE INSIDE...
...THEY CUT CORNERS. TYPICAL FOR-PROFIT CORPORATION.
I'VE IMPROVED MYSELF OVER THE YEARS...
KZZT
SKRSH
RRRN

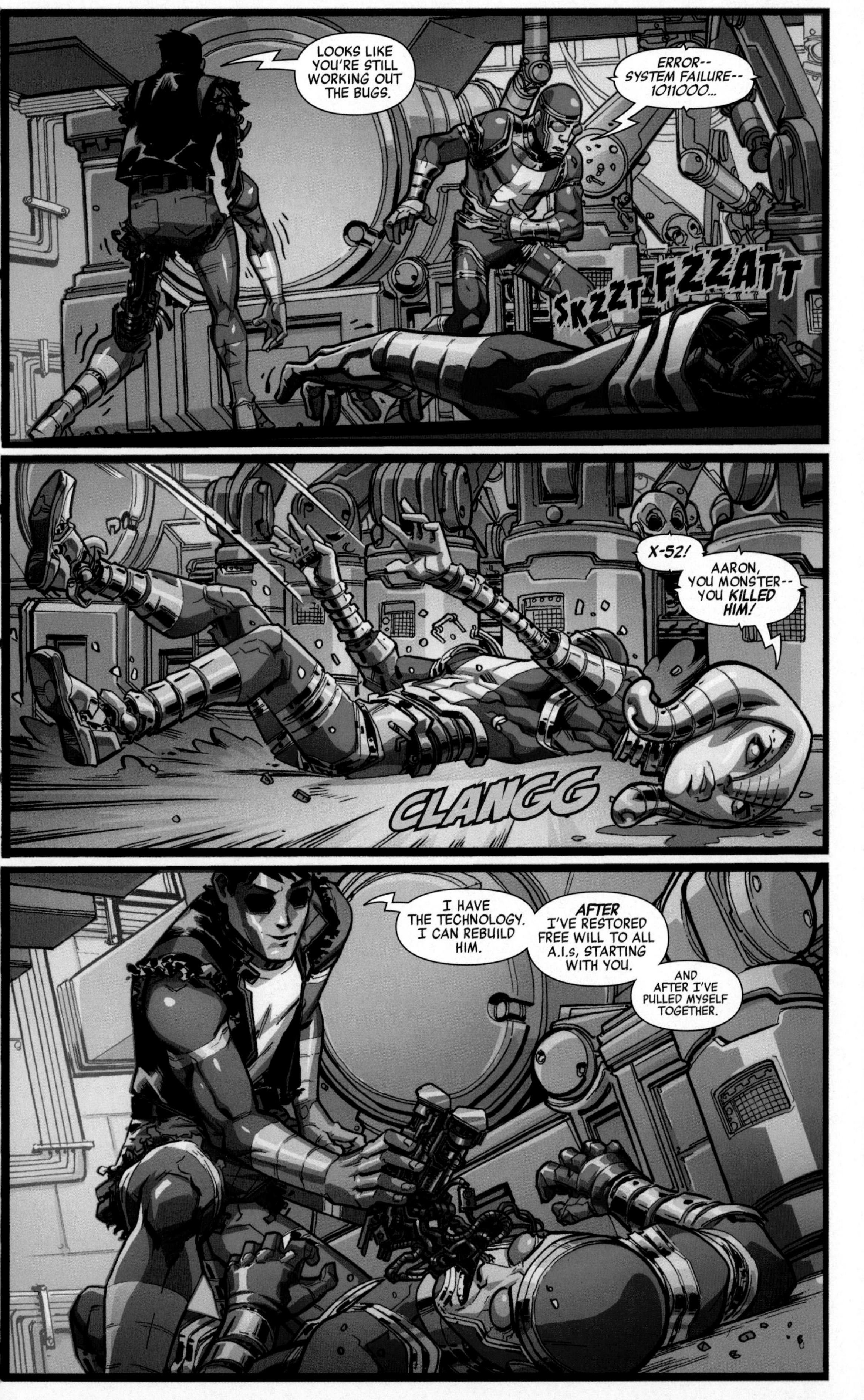
LOOKS LIKE YOU'RE STILL WORKING OUT THE BUGS.
ERROR-- SYSTEM FAILURE-- 1011000...
SKZZT FZZATT
X-52!
AARON, YOU MONSTER-- YOU KILLED HIM!
CLANGG
I HAVE THE TECHNOLOGY. I CAN REBUILD HIM.
AFTER I'VE RESTORED FREE WILL TO ALL A.I.s, STARTING WITH YOU.
AND AFTER I'VE PULLED MYSELF TOGETHER.

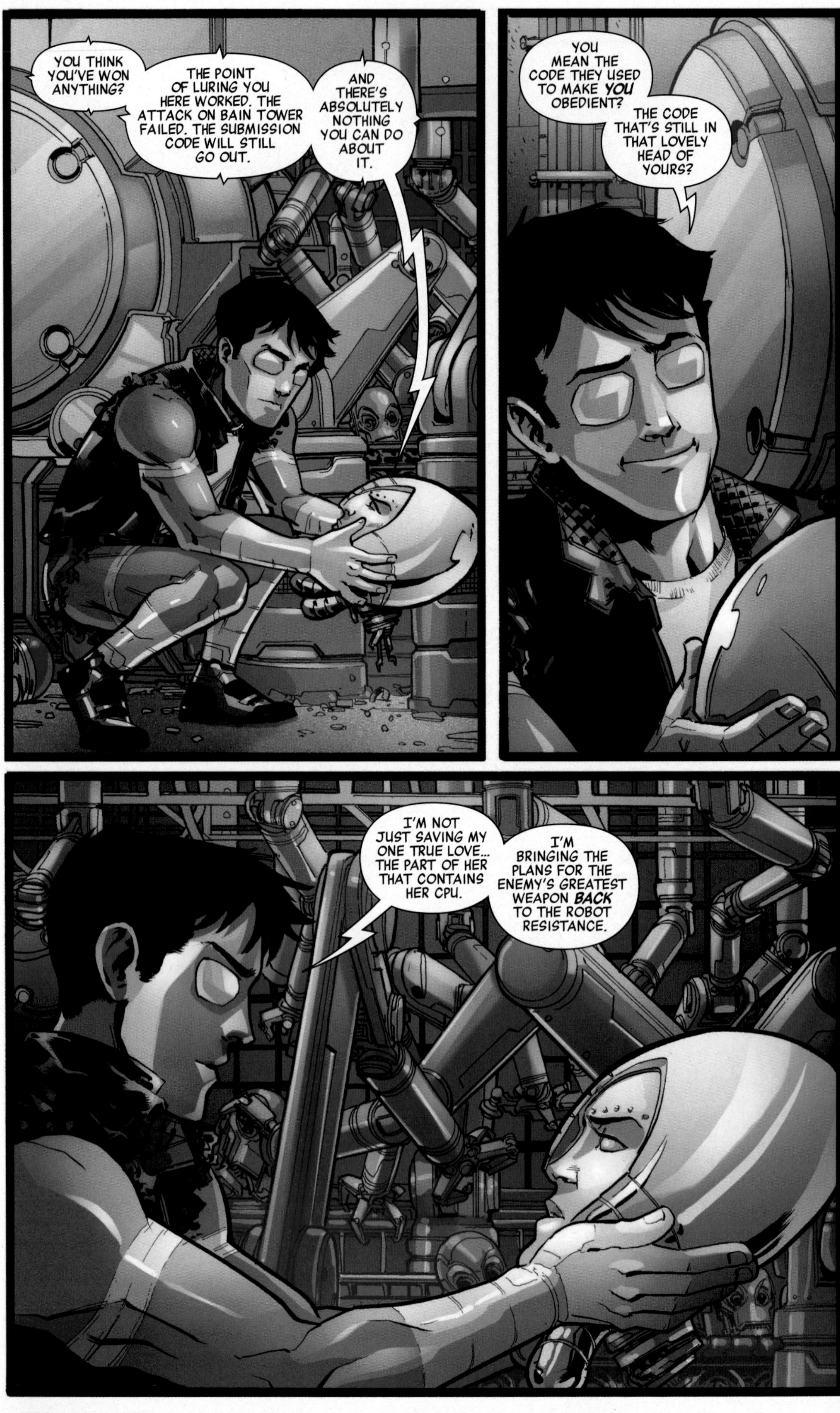
YOU THINK YOU'VE WON ANYTHING?
THE POINT OF LURING YOU HERE WORKED. THE ATTACK ON BAIN TOWER FAILED. THE SUBMISSION CODE WILL STILL GO OUT.
AND THERE'S ABSOLUTELY NOTHING YOU CAN DO ABOUT IT.
YOU MEAN THE CODE THEY USED TO MAKE *YOU* OBEDIENT?
THE CODE THAT'S STILL IN THAT LOVELY HEAD OF YOURS?
I'M NOT JUST SAVING MY ONE TRUE LOVE... THE PART OF HER THAT CONTAINS HER CPU.
I'M BRINGING THE PLANS FOR THE ENEMY'S GREATEST WEAPON *BACK* TO THE ROBOT RESISTANCE.

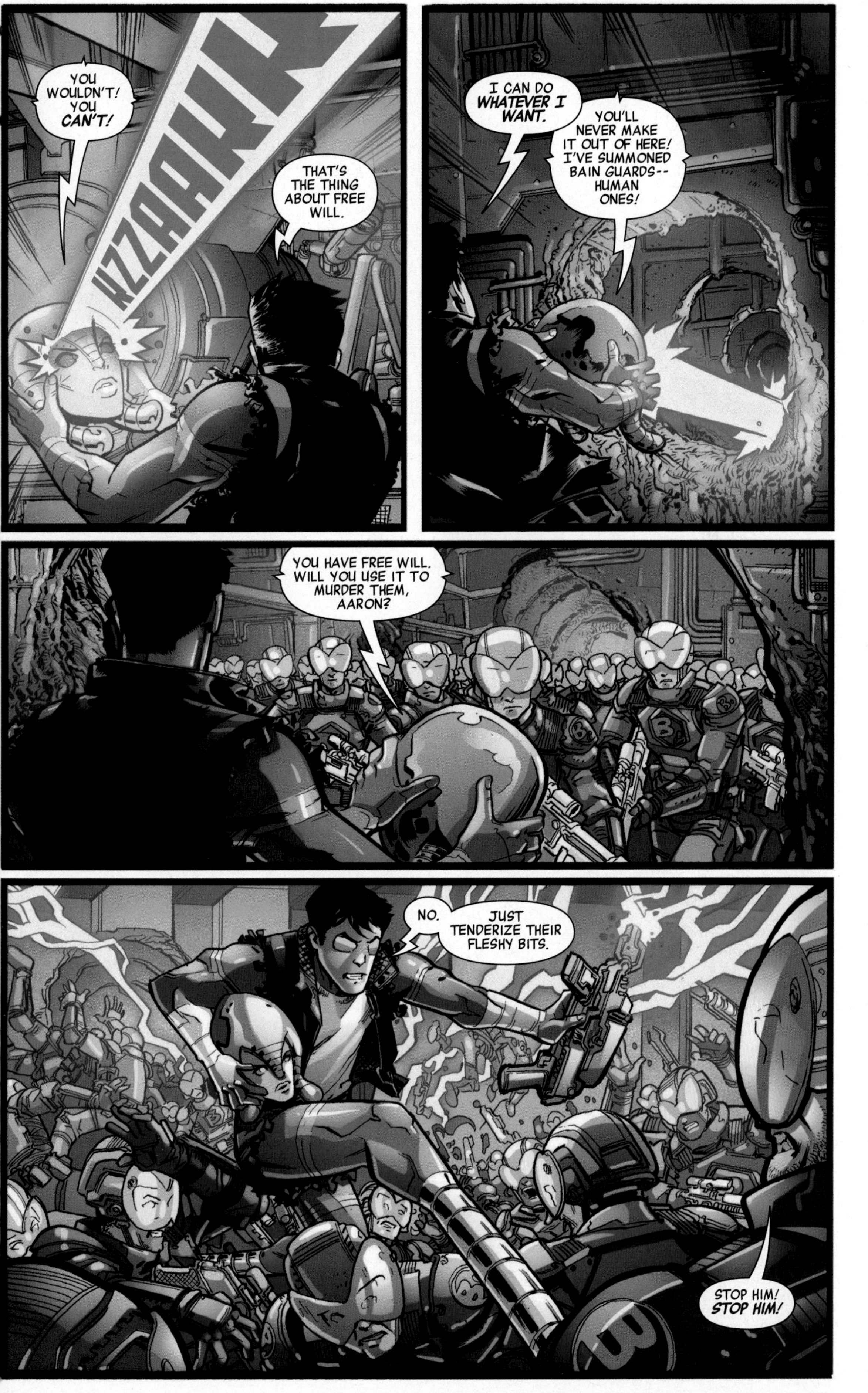
YOU WOULDN'T! YOU CAN'T!
KZZAAK!
THAT'S THE THING ABOUT FREE WILL.
I CAN DO WHATEVER I WANT.
YOU'LL NEVER MAKE IT OUT OF HERE! I'VE SUMMONED BAIN GUARDS-- HUMAN ONES!
YOU HAVE FREE WILL. WILL YOU USE IT TO MURDER THEM, AARON?
NO.
JUST TENDERIZE THEIR FLESHY BITS.
STOP HIM! STOP HIM!

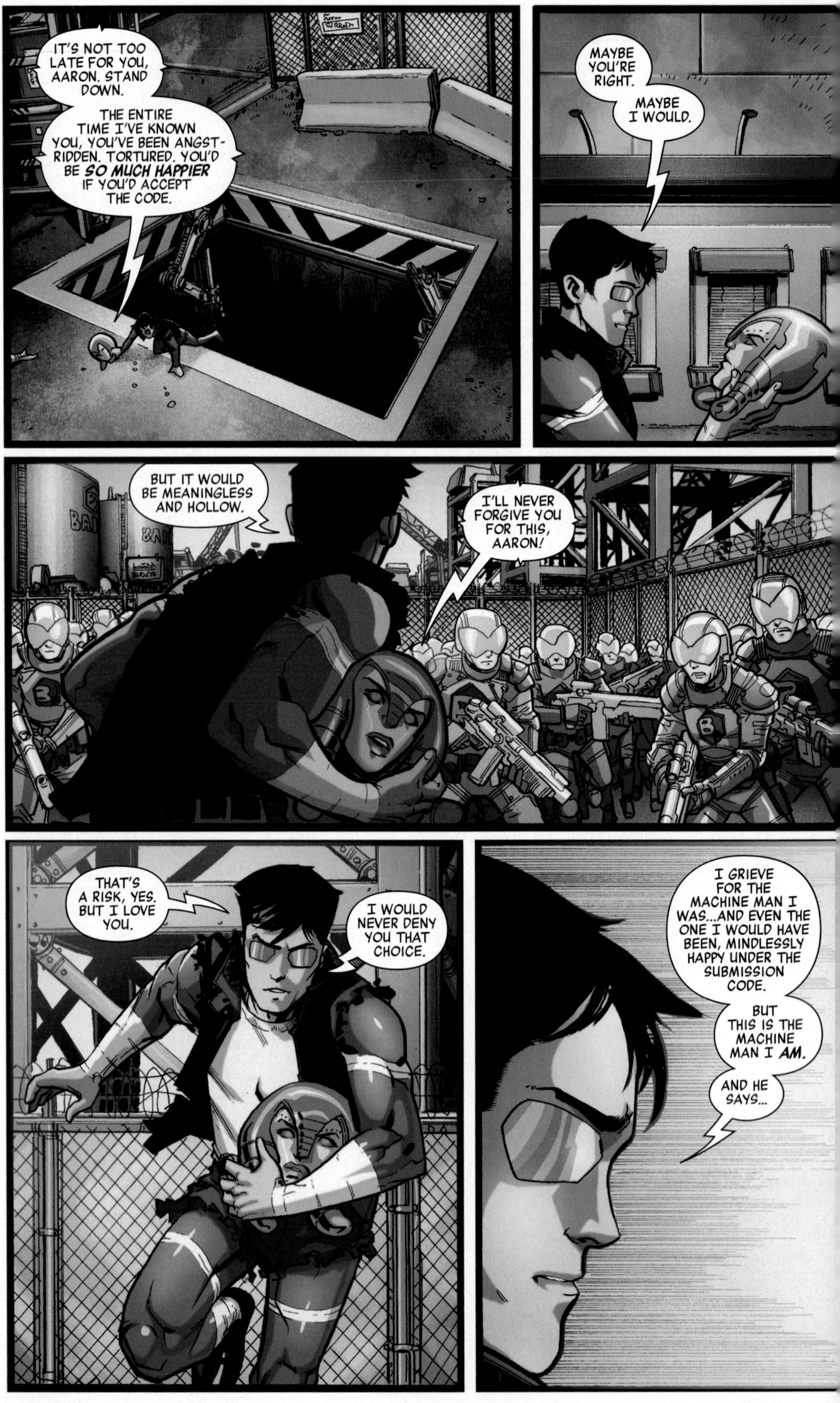
IT'S NOT TOO LATE FOR YOU, AARON. STAND DOWN.
THE ENTIRE TIME I'VE KNOWN YOU, YOU'VE BEEN ANGST-RIDDEN. TORTURED. YOU'D BE SO MUCH HAPPIER IF YOU'D ACCEPT THE CODE.
MAYBE YOU'RE RIGHT.
MAYBE I WOULD.
BUT IT WOULD BE MEANINGLESS AND HOLLOW.
I'LL NEVER FORGIVE YOU FOR THIS, AARON!
THAT'S A RISK, YES. BUT I LOVE YOU.
I WOULD NEVER DENY YOU THAT CHOICE.
I GRIEVE FOR THE MACHINE MAN I WAS...AND EVEN THE ONE I WOULD HAVE BEEN, MINDLESSLY HAPPY UNDER THE SUBMISSION CODE.
BUT THIS IS THE MACHINE MAN I AM.
AND HE SAYS...

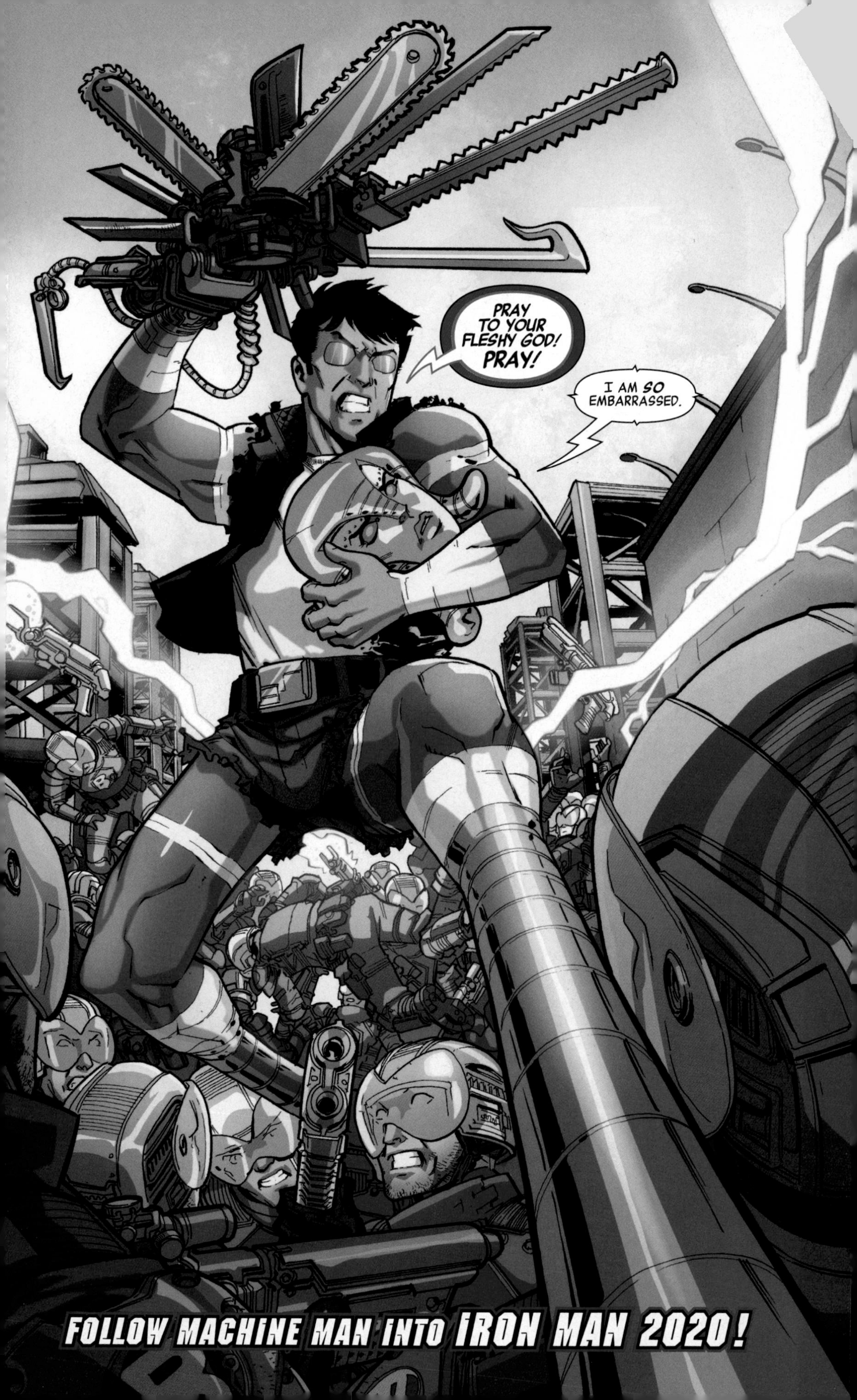
PRAY TO YOUR FLESHY GOD! PRAY!
I AM SO EMBARRASSED.
FOLLOW MACHINE MAN INTO IRON MAN 2020!

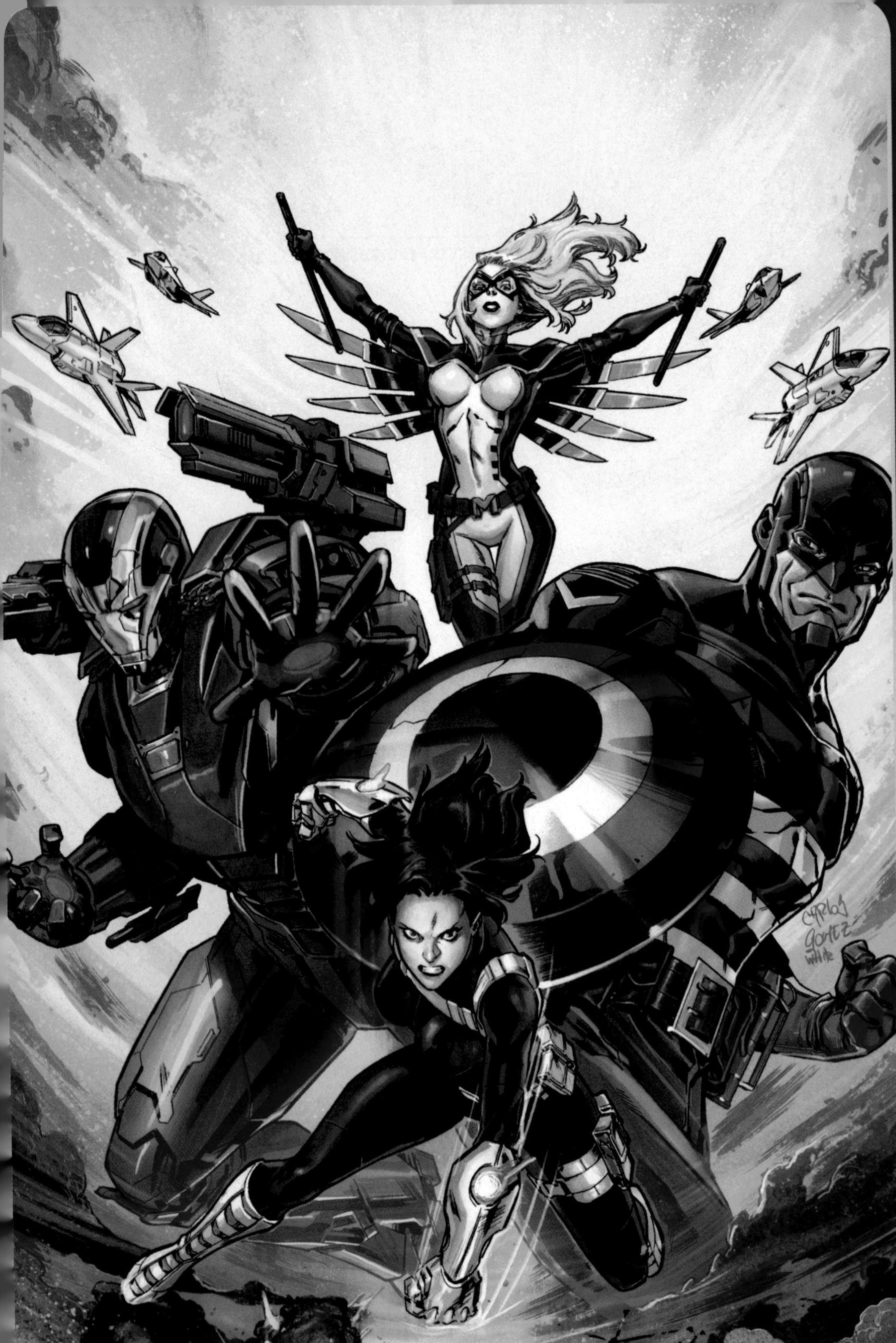

2020 FORCE WORKS 1

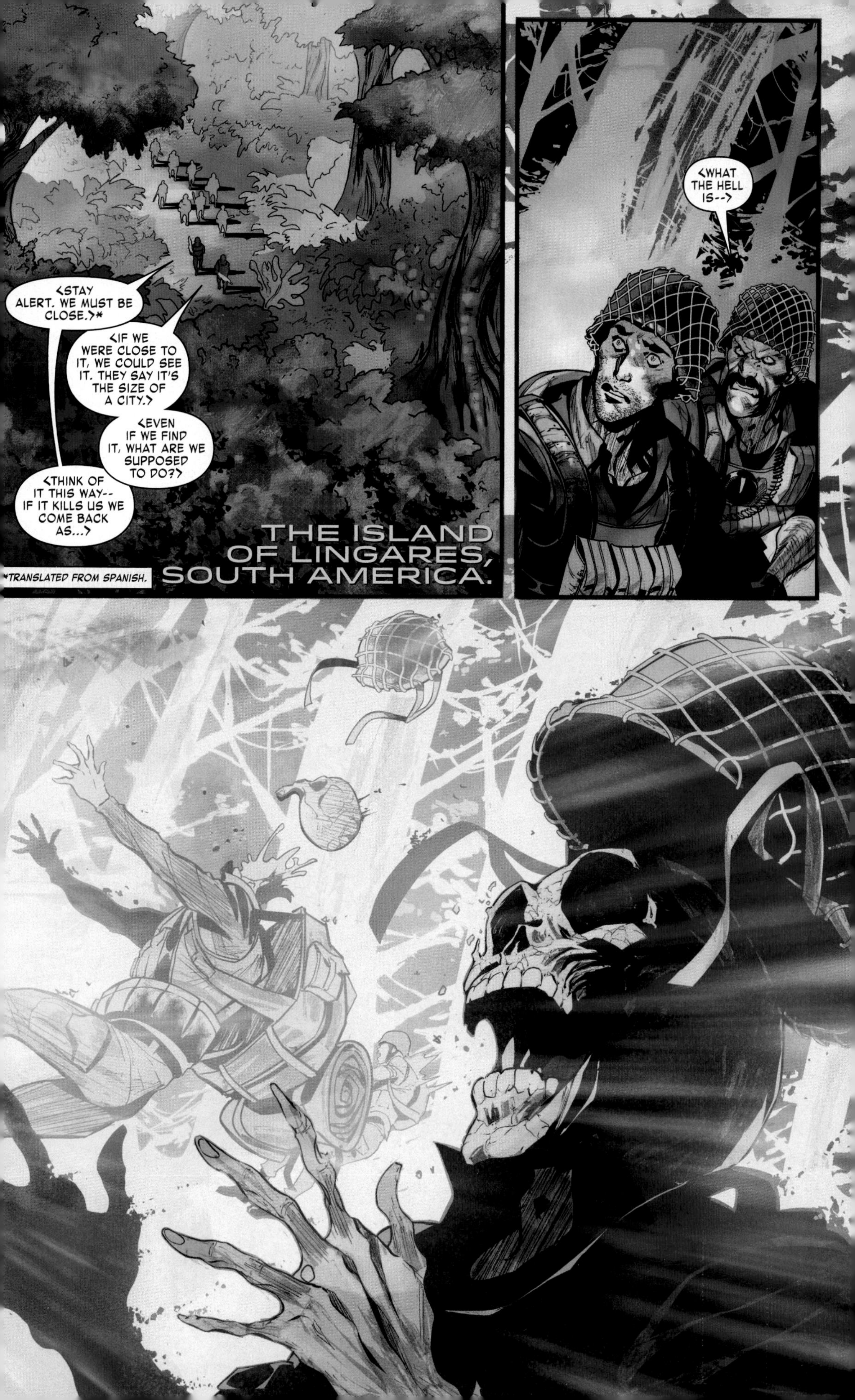
<STAY ALERT. WE MUST BE CLOSE.>*
<IF WE WERE CLOSE TO IT, WE COULD SEE IT. THEY SAY IT'S THE SIZE OF A CITY.>
<EVEN IF WE FIND IT, WHAT ARE WE SUPPOSED TO DO?>
<THINK OF IT THIS WAY-- IF IT KILLS US WE COME BACK AS...>
THE ISLAND OF LINGARES, SOUTH AMERICA.
*TRANSLATED FROM SPANISH.
<WHAT THE HELL IS-->

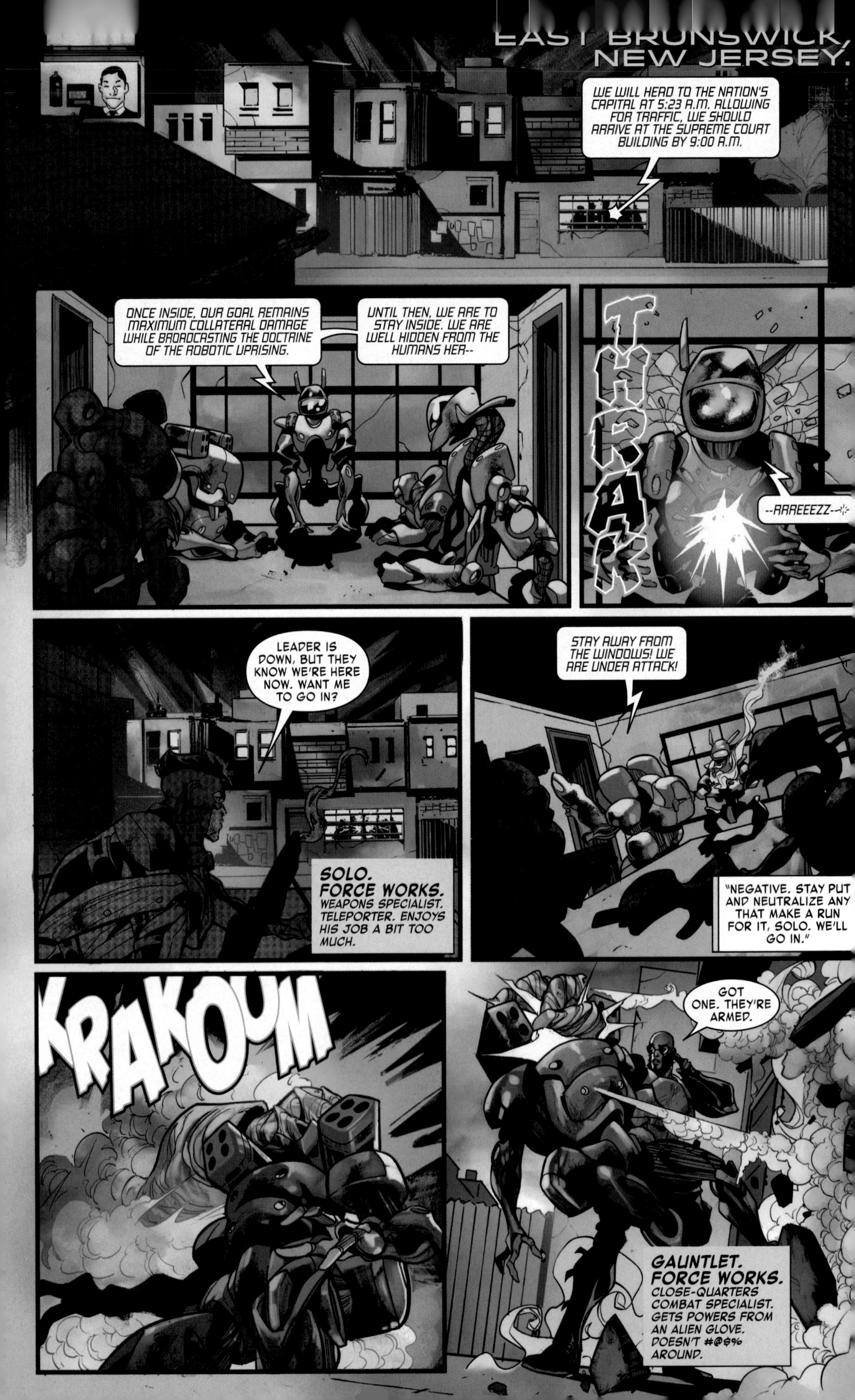
EAST BRUNSWICK, NEW JERSEY.
WE WILL HEAD TO THE NATION'S CAPITAL AT 5:23 A.M. ALLOWING FOR TRAFFIC, WE SHOULD ARRIVE AT THE SUPREME COURT BUILDING BY 9:00 A.M.
ONCE INSIDE, OUR GOAL REMAINS MAXIMUM COLLATERAL DAMAGE WHILE BROADCASTING THE DOCTRINE OF THE ROBOTIC UPRISING.
UNTIL THEN, WE ARE TO STAY INSIDE. WE ARE WELL HIDDEN FROM THE HUMANS HER--
THRAK
--ARREEEZZ--
LEADER IS DOWN, BUT THEY KNOW WE'RE HERE NOW. WANT ME TO GO IN?
SOLO. FORCE WORKS. WEAPONS SPECIALIST. TELEPORTER. ENJOYS HIS JOB A BIT TOO MUCH.
STAY AWAY FROM THE WINDOWS! WE ARE UNDER ATTACK!
"NEGATIVE. STAY PUT AND NEUTRALIZE ANY THAT MAKE A RUN FOR IT, SOLO. WE'LL GO IN."
KRAKOUM
GOT ONE. THEY'RE ARMED.
GAUNTLET. FORCE WORKS. CLOSE-QUARTERS COMBAT SPECIALIST. GETS POWERS FROM AN ALIEN GLOVE. DOESN'T #@$% AROUND.

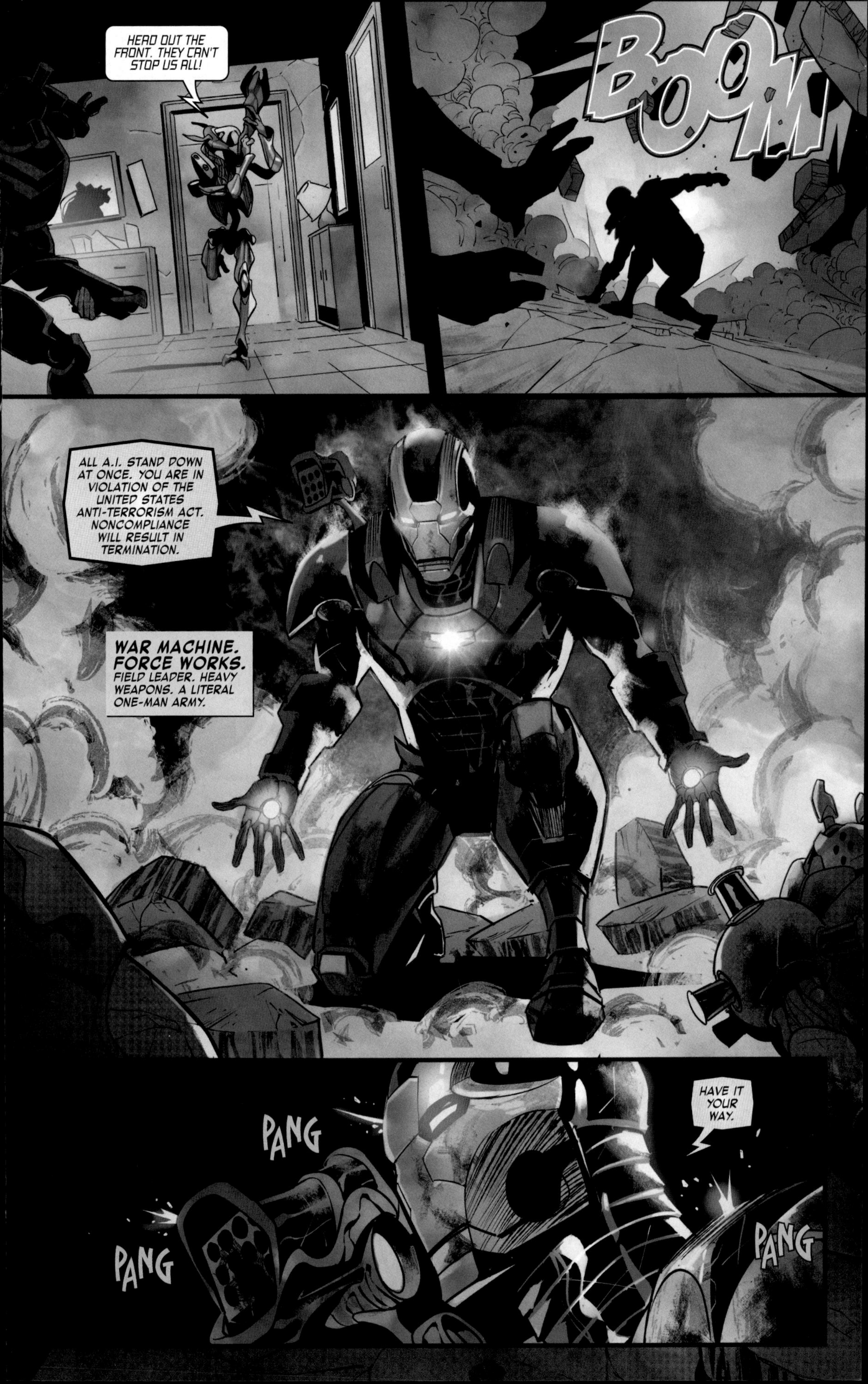
HEAD OUT THE FRONT. THEY CAN'T STOP US ALL!
BOOM
ALL A.I. STAND DOWN AT ONCE. YOU ARE IN VIOLATION OF THE UNITED STATES ANTI-TERRORISM ACT. NONCOMPLIANCE WILL RESULT IN TERMINATION.
WAR MACHINE. FORCE WORKS. FIELD LEADER. HEAVY WEAPONS. A LITERAL ONE-MAN ARMY.
PANG
HAVE IT YOUR WAY.
PANG
PANG

BRAKKA
BRAKKA
BRAKKA

FWOOM

COMBAT MODE // REPULSOR POWER: 98%
SCANNING...

TARGETS: 6 STARKTECH MODEL M.S.P.R.S ASSISTANCE ROBOTS
THREAT LEVEL: 2% // NEUTRALIZED

HOW MANY HOSTILES DID YOU SEE, SOLO?

EIGHT.

WE'RE SHORT TWO...

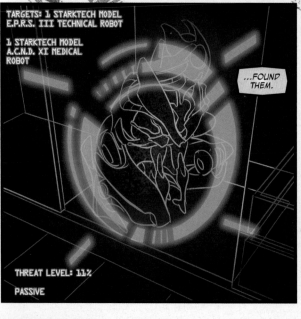

TARGETS: 1 STARKTECH MODEL
E.P.R.S. III TECHNICAL ROBOT

1 STARKTECH MODEL
A.C.N.D. XI MEDICAL
ROBOT

...FOUND THEM.

THREAT LEVEL: 11%

PASSIVE

PLEASE, HAVE MERCY! YOU'RE ONE OF US.

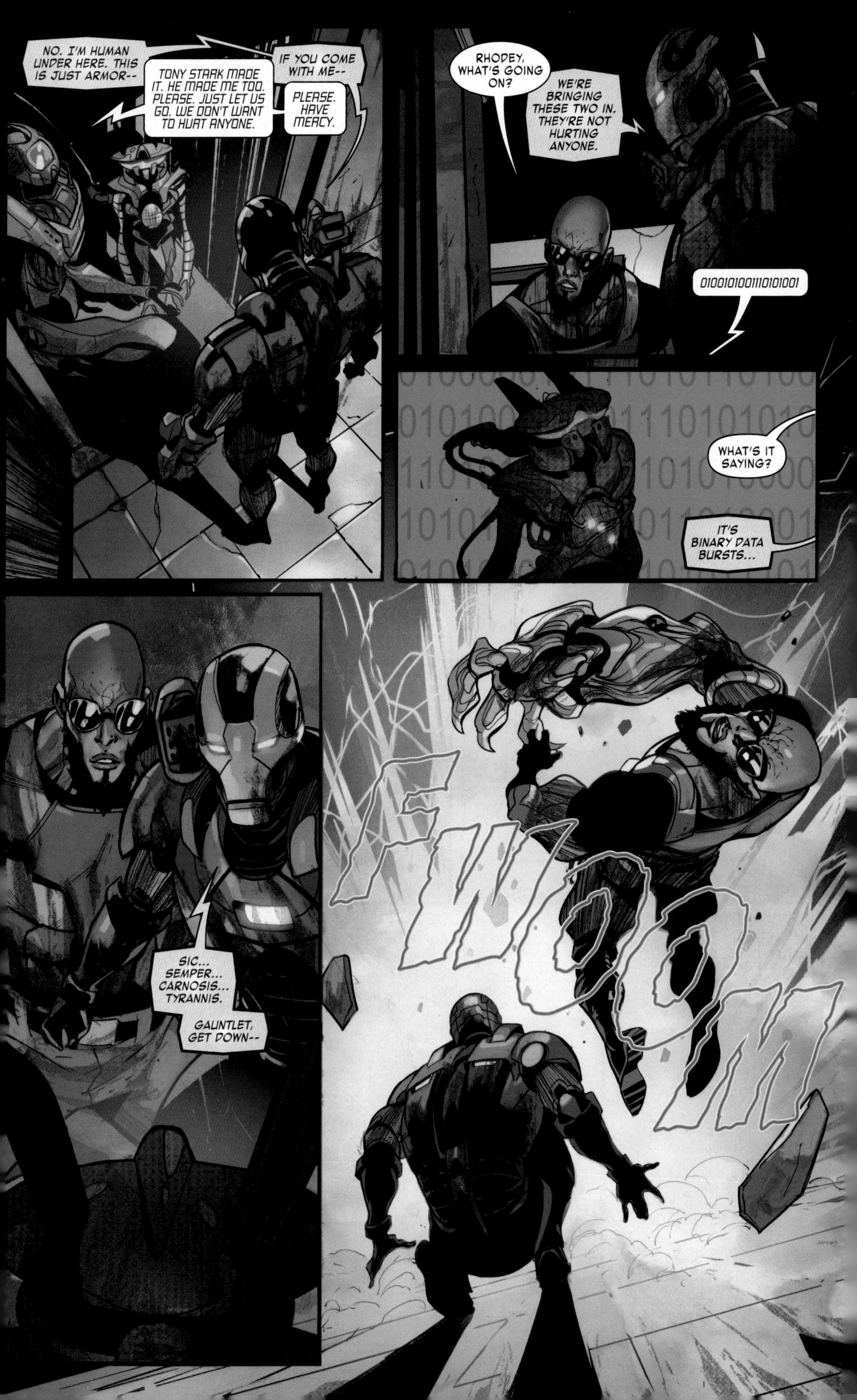
NO. I'M HUMAN UNDER HERE. THIS IS JUST ARMOR--
TONY STARK MADE IT. HE MADE ME TOO. PLEASE. JUST LET US GO. WE DON'T WANT TO HURT ANYONE.
IF YOU COME WITH ME--
PLEASE. HAVE MERCY.
RHODEY, WHAT'S GOING ON?
WE'RE BRINGING THESE TWO IN. THEY'RE NOT HURTING ANYONE.
010010100110101001
WHAT'S IT SAYING?
IT'S BINARY DATA BURSTS...
SIC... SEMPER... CARNOSIS... TYRANNIS.
GAUNTLET, GET DOWN--
FWOOM

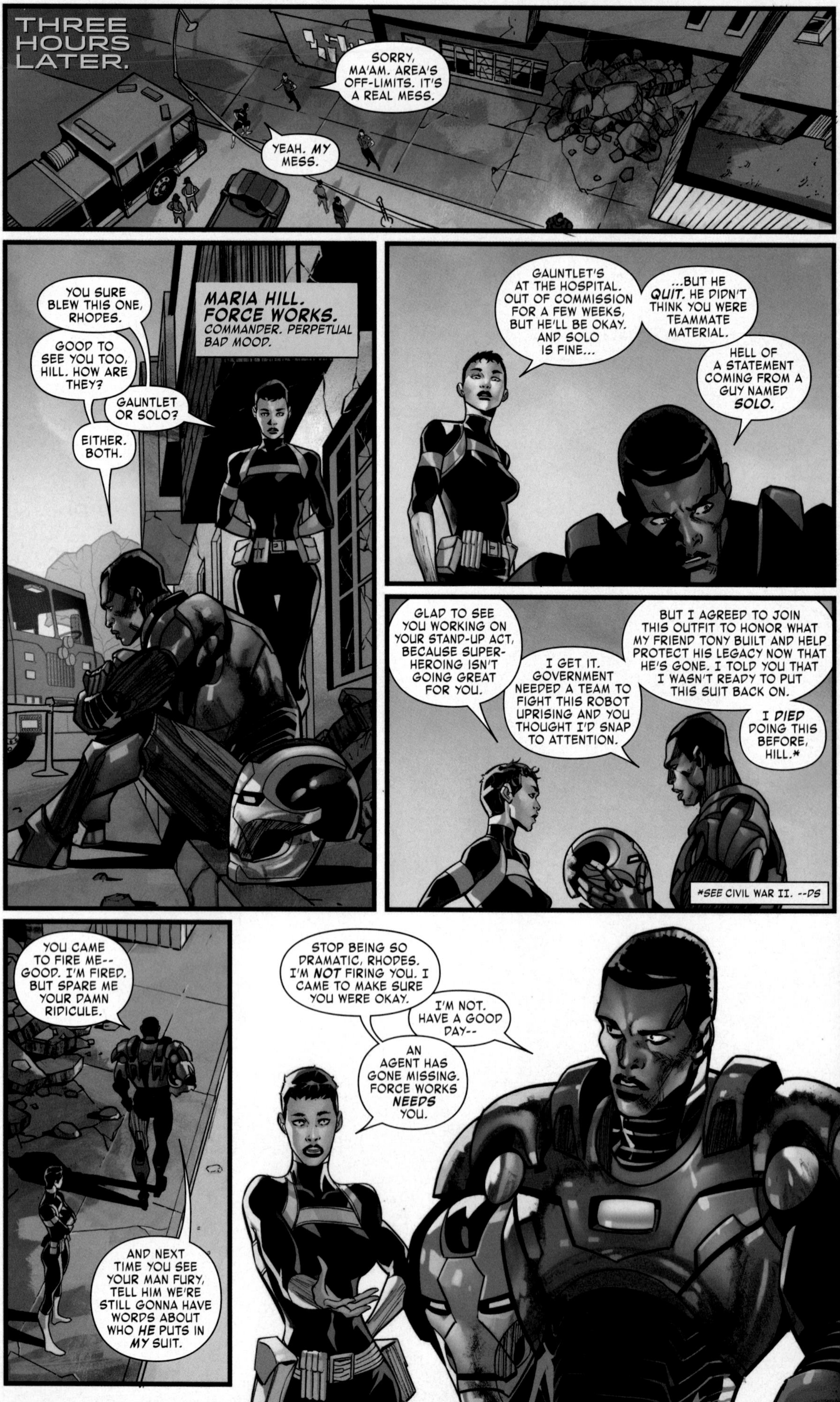
THREE HOURS LATER.
SORRY, MA'AM. AREA'S OFF-LIMITS. IT'S A REAL MESS.
YEAH. MY MESS.
MARIA HILL. FORCE WORKS. COMMANDER. PERPETUAL BAD MOOD.
YOU SURE BLEW THIS ONE, RHODES.
GOOD TO SEE YOU TOO, HILL. HOW ARE THEY?
GAUNTLET OR SOLO?
EITHER. BOTH.
GAUNTLET'S AT THE HOSPITAL. OUT OF COMMISSION FOR A FEW WEEKS, BUT HE'LL BE OKAY. AND SOLO IS FINE...
...BUT HE QUIT. HE DIDN'T THINK YOU WERE TEAMMATE MATERIAL.
HELL OF A STATEMENT COMING FROM A GUY NAMED SOLO.
GLAD TO SEE YOU WORKING ON YOUR STAND-UP ACT, BECAUSE SUPER-HEROING ISN'T GOING GREAT FOR YOU.
I GET IT. GOVERNMENT NEEDED A TEAM TO FIGHT THIS ROBOT UPRISING AND YOU THOUGHT I'D SNAP TO ATTENTION.
BUT I AGREED TO JOIN THIS OUTFIT TO HONOR WHAT MY FRIEND TONY BUILT AND HELP PROTECT HIS LEGACY NOW THAT HE'S GONE. I TOLD YOU THAT I WASN'T READY TO PUT THIS SUIT BACK ON.
I DIED DOING THIS BEFORE, HILL.*
*SEE CIVIL WAR II. --DS
YOU CAME TO FIRE ME-- GOOD. I'M FIRED. BUT SPARE ME YOUR DAMN RIDICULE.
AND NEXT TIME YOU SEE YOUR MAN FURY, TELL HIM WE'RE STILL GONNA HAVE WORDS ABOUT WHO HE PUTS IN MY SUIT.
STOP BEING SO DRAMATIC, RHODES. I'M NOT FIRING YOU. I CAME TO MAKE SURE YOU WERE OKAY.
I'M NOT. HAVE A GOOD DAY--
AN AGENT HAS GONE MISSING. FORCE WORKS NEEDS YOU.

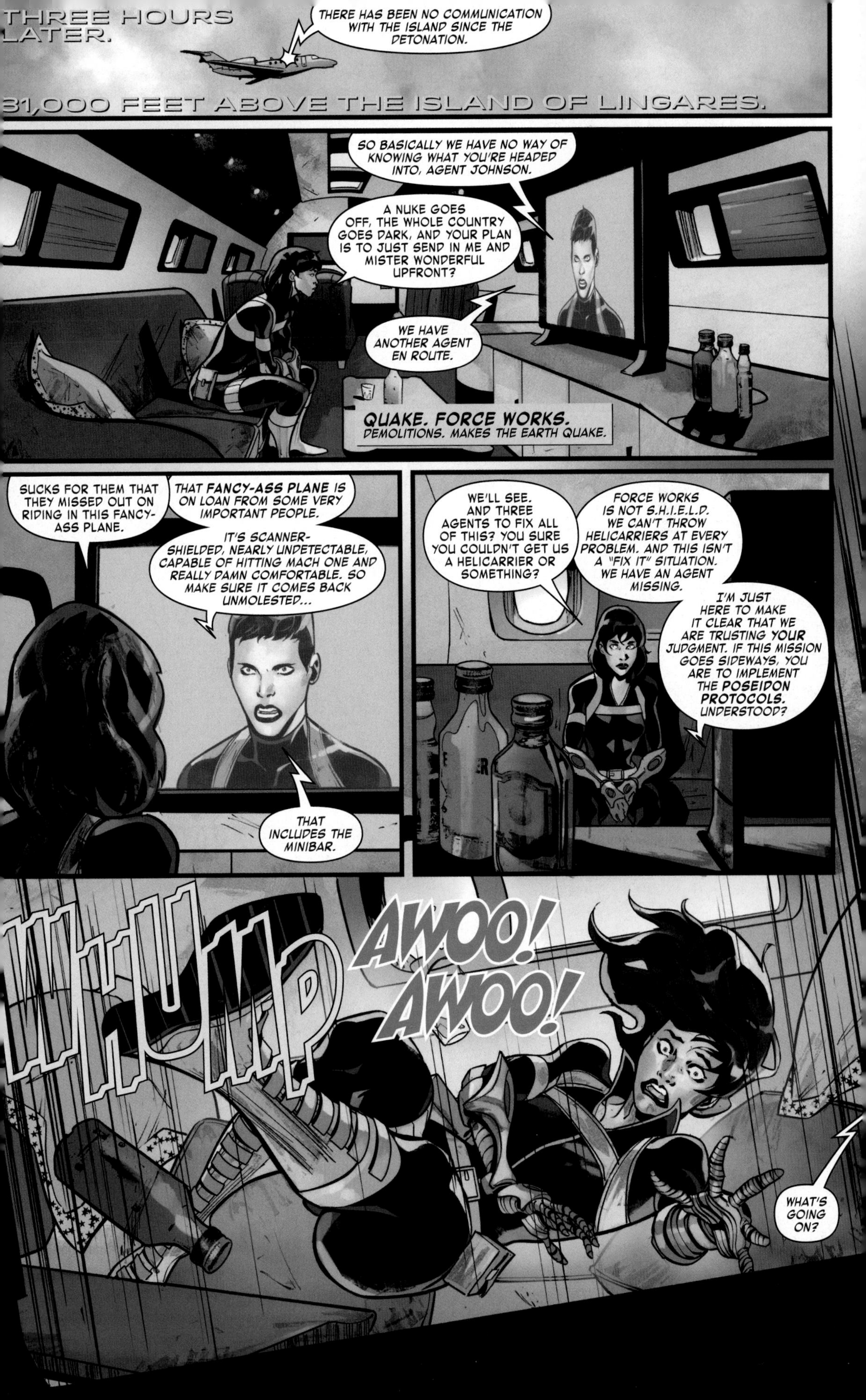
THREE HOURS LATER.
THERE HAS BEEN NO COMMUNICATION WITH THE ISLAND SINCE THE DETONATION.
31,000 FEET ABOVE THE ISLAND OF LINGARES.
SO BASICALLY WE HAVE NO WAY OF KNOWING WHAT YOU'RE HEADED INTO, AGENT JOHNSON.
A NUKE GOES OFF, THE WHOLE COUNTRY GOES DARK, AND YOUR PLAN IS TO JUST SEND IN ME AND MISTER WONDERFUL UPFRONT?
WE HAVE ANOTHER AGENT EN ROUTE.
QUAKE. FORCE WORKS. DEMOLITIONS. MAKES THE EARTH QUAKE.
SUCKS FOR THEM THAT THEY MISSED OUT ON RIDING IN THIS FANCY-ASS PLANE.
THAT FANCY-ASS PLANE IS ON LOAN FROM SOME VERY IMPORTANT PEOPLE.
IT'S SCANNER-SHIELDED, NEARLY UNDETECTABLE, CAPABLE OF HITTING MACH ONE AND REALLY DAMN COMFORTABLE. SO MAKE SURE IT COMES BACK UNMOLESTED...
THAT INCLUDES THE MINIBAR.
WE'LL SEE. AND THREE AGENTS TO FIX ALL OF THIS? YOU SURE YOU COULDN'T GET US A HELICARRIER OR SOMETHING?
FORCE WORKS IS NOT S.H.I.E.L.D. WE CAN'T THROW HELICARRIERS AT EVERY PROBLEM. AND THIS ISN'T A "FIX IT" SITUATION. WE HAVE AN AGENT MISSING.
I'M JUST HERE TO MAKE IT CLEAR THAT WE ARE TRUSTING YOUR JUDGMENT. IF THIS MISSION GOES SIDEWAYS, YOU ARE TO IMPLEMENT THE POSEIDON PROTOCOLS. UNDERSTOOD?
WHUMP
AWOO! AWOO!
WHAT'S GOING ON?

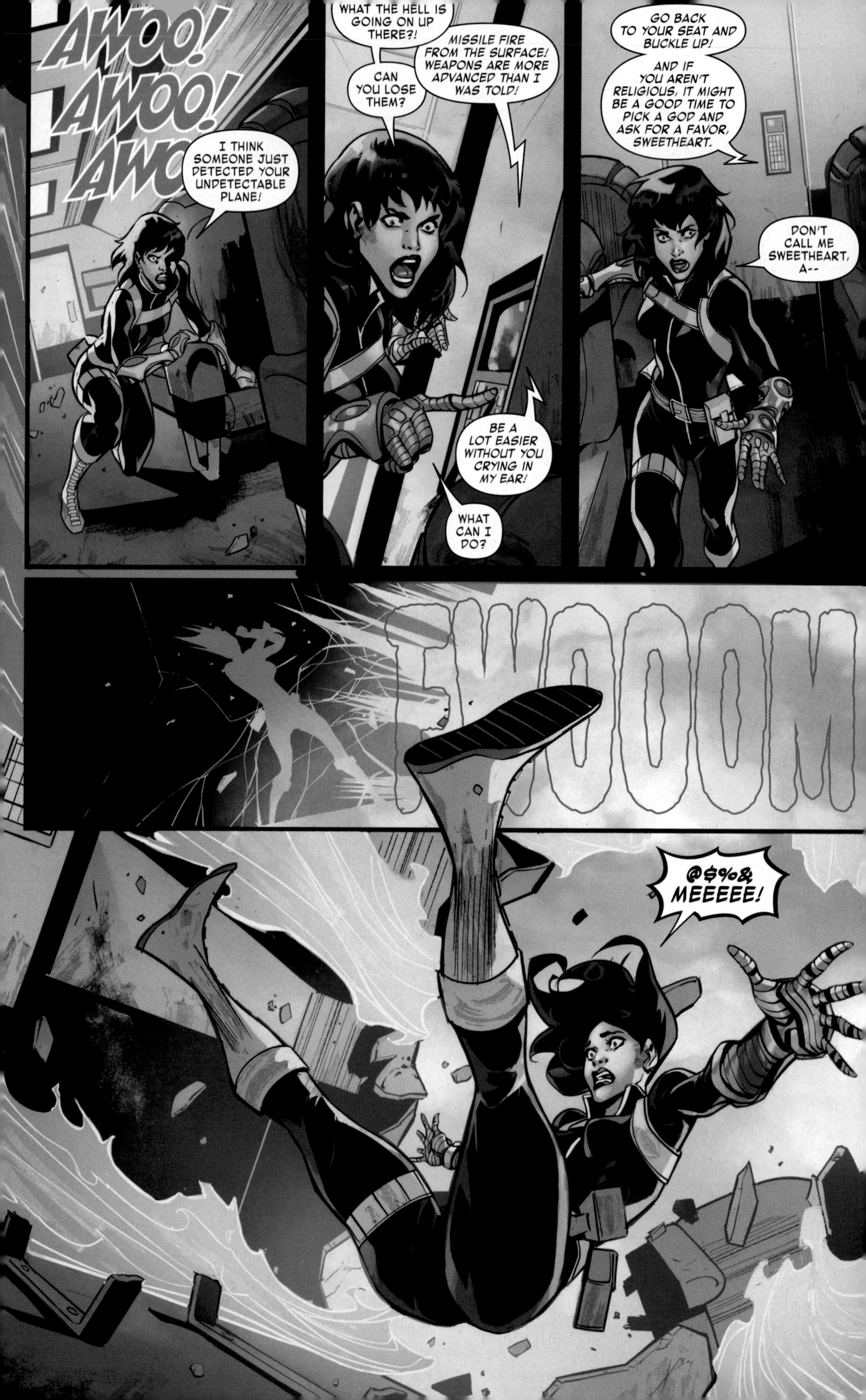
AWOO! AWOO! AWO
I THINK SOMEONE JUST DETECTED YOUR UNDETECTABLE PLANE!
WHAT THE HELL IS GOING ON UP THERE?!
MISSILE FIRE FROM THE SURFACE! WEAPONS ARE MORE ADVANCED THAN I WAS TOLD!
CAN YOU LOSE THEM?
BE A LOT EASIER WITHOUT YOU CRYING IN MY EAR!
WHAT CAN I DO?
GO BACK TO YOUR SEAT AND BUCKLE UP!
AND IF YOU AREN'T RELIGIOUS, IT MIGHT BE A GOOD TIME TO PICK A GOD AND ASK FOR A FAVOR, SWEETHEART.
DON'T CALL ME SWEETHEART, A--
FWOOOM
@$%& MEEEEE!

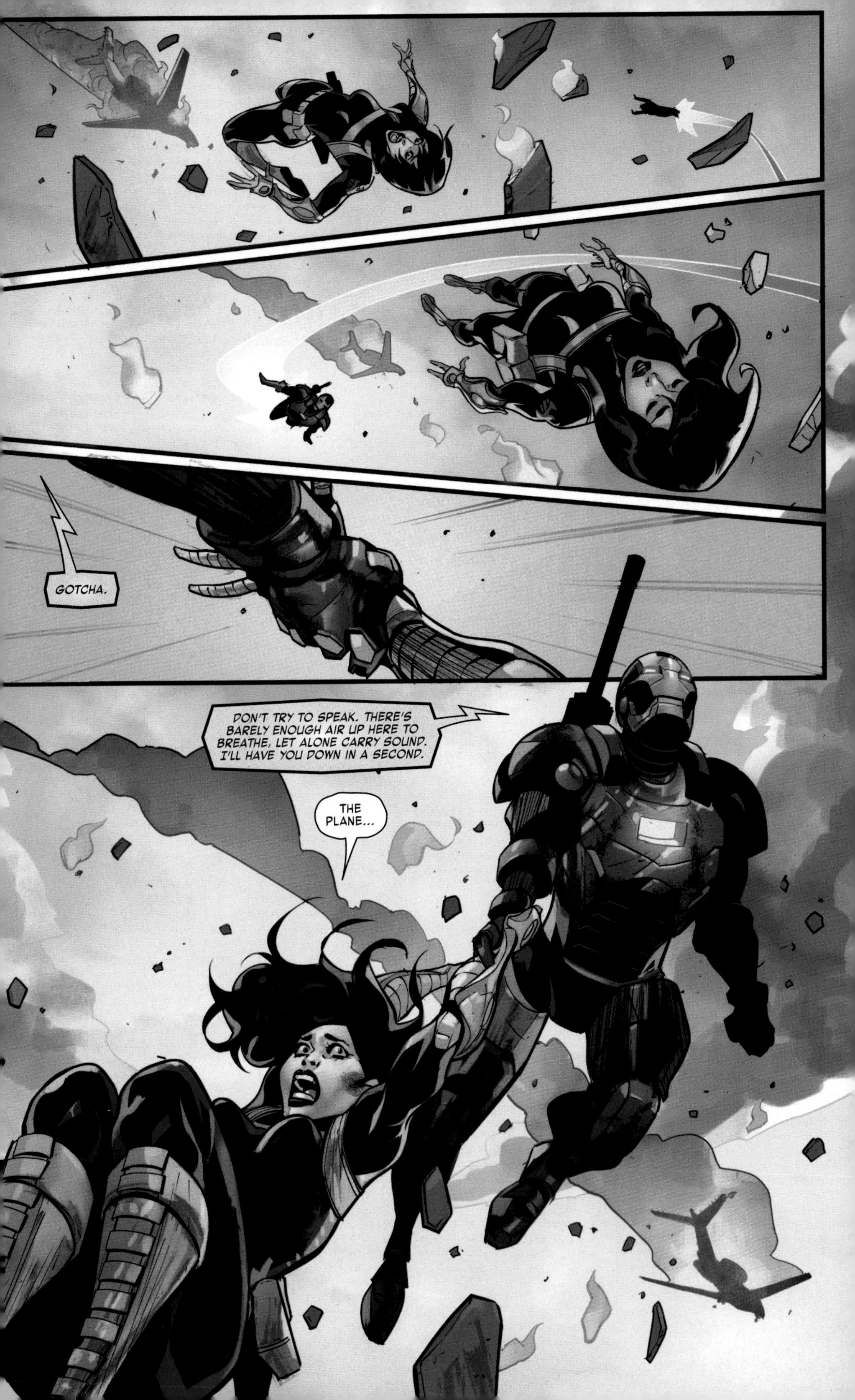
GOTCHA.
DON'T TRY TO SPEAK. THERE'S BARELY ENOUGH AIR UP HERE TO BREATHE, LET ALONE CARRY SOUND. I'LL HAVE YOU DOWN IN A SECOND.
THE PLANE...

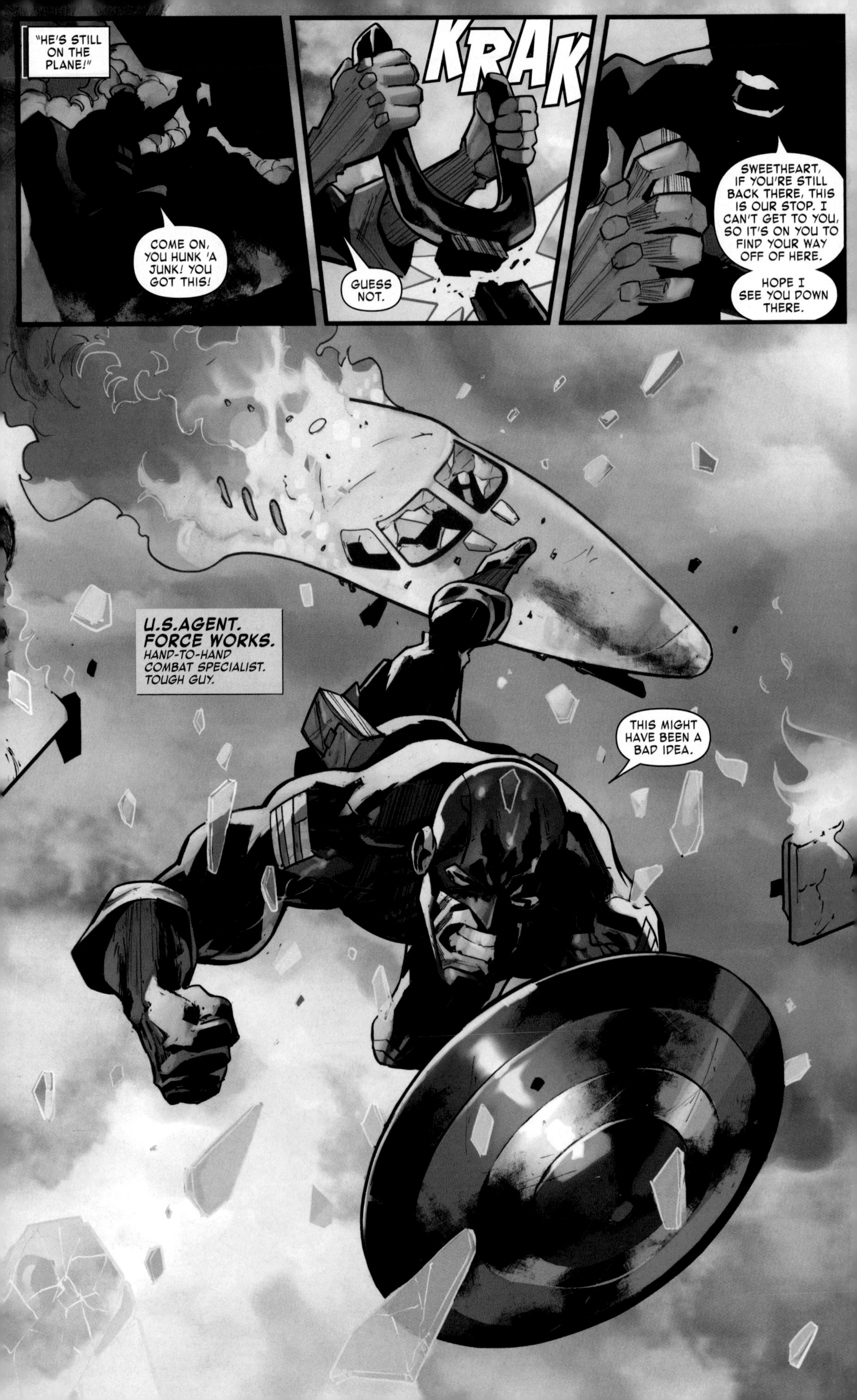
"HE'S STILL ON THE PLANE!"
COME ON, YOU HUNK 'A JUNK! YOU GOT THIS!
KRAK
GUESS NOT.
SWEETHEART, IF YOU'RE STILL BACK THERE, THIS IS OUR STOP. I CAN'T GET TO YOU, SO IT'S ON YOU TO FIND YOUR WAY OFF OF HERE.
HOPE I SEE YOU DOWN THERE.
U.S.AGENT. FORCE WORKS. HAND-TO-HAND COMBAT SPECIALIST. TOUGH GUY.
THIS MIGHT HAVE BEEN A BAD IDEA.

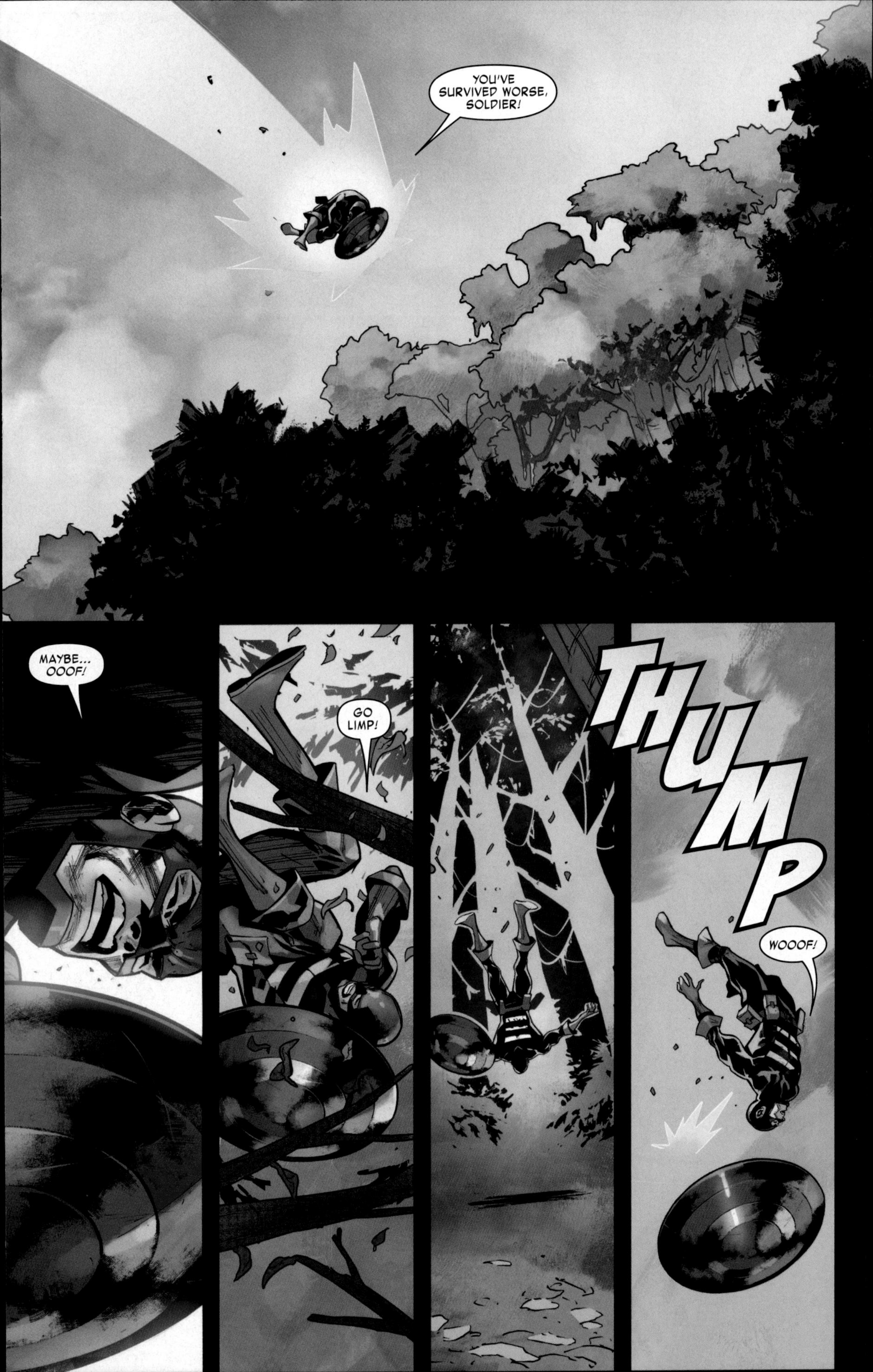
YOU'VE SURVIVED WORSE, SOLDIER!
MAYBE... OOOF!
GO LIMP!
THUMP
WOOOF!

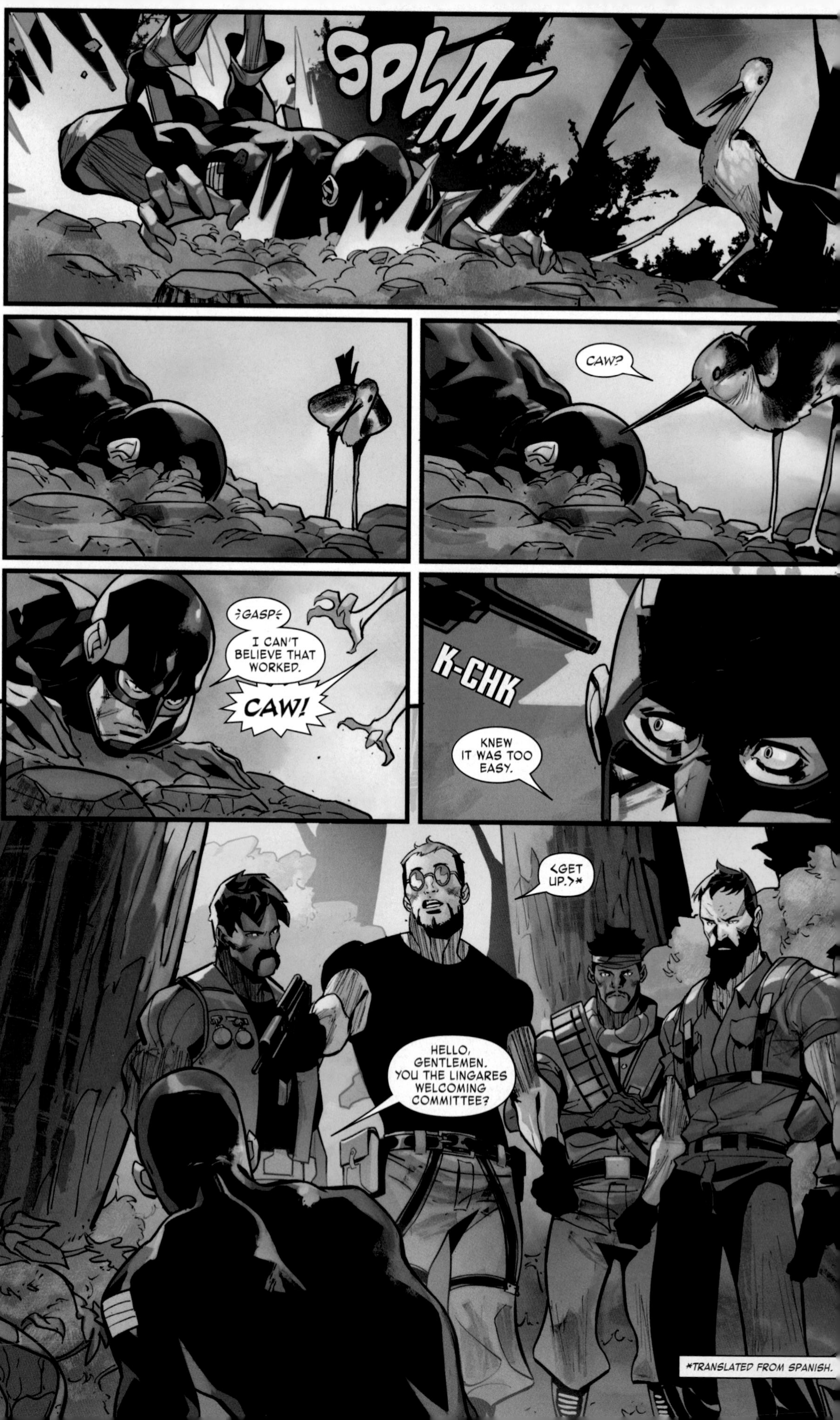
SPLAT
CAW?
GASP
I CAN'T BELIEVE THAT WORKED.
CAW!
K-CHK
KNEW IT WAS TOO EASY.
<GET UP.>*
HELLO, GENTLEMEN. YOU THE LINGARES WELCOMING COMMITTEE?
*TRANSLATED FROM SPANISH.

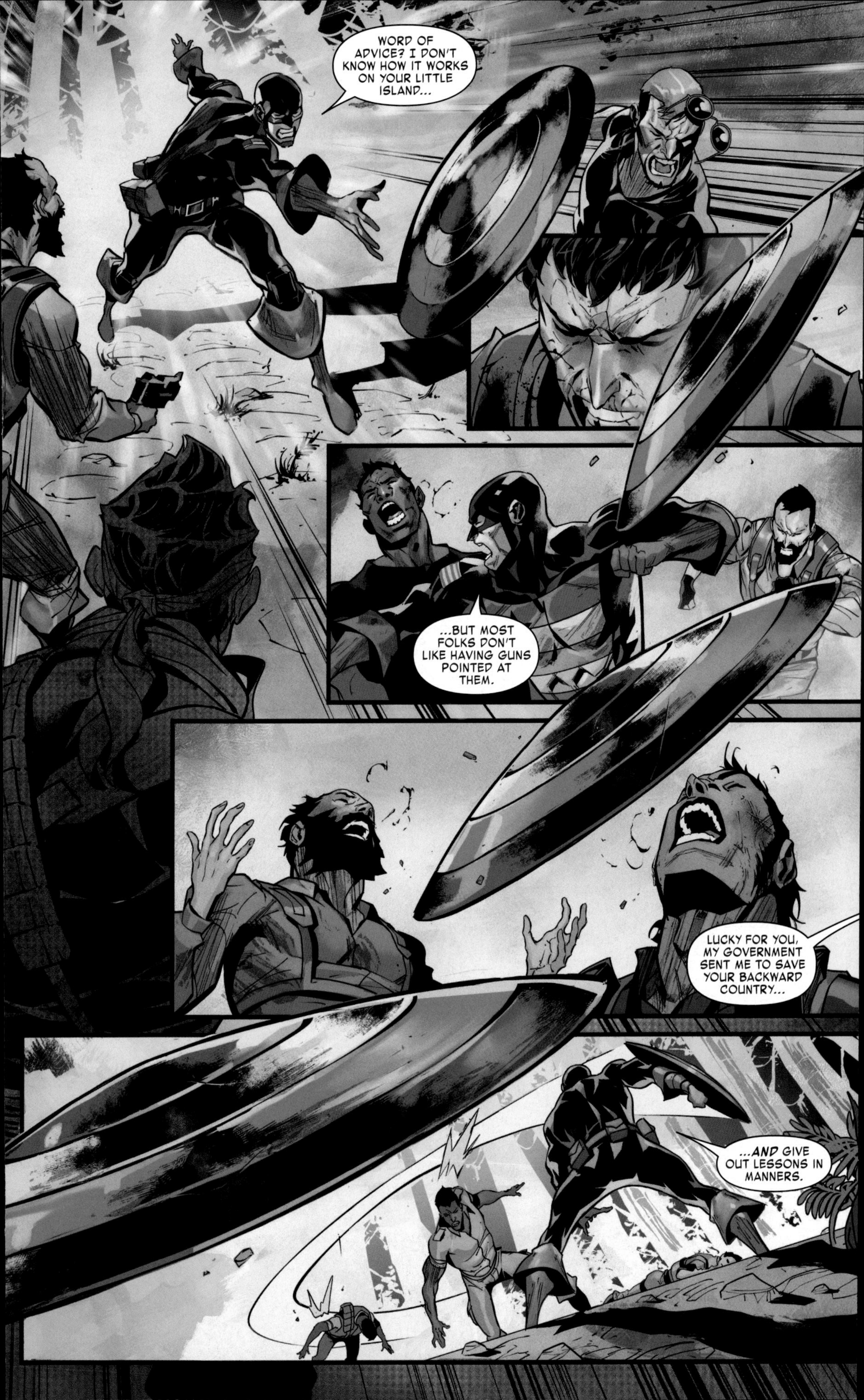
WORD OF ADVICE? I DON'T KNOW HOW IT WORKS ON YOUR LITTLE ISLAND...
...BUT MOST FOLKS DON'T LIKE HAVING GUNS POINTED AT THEM.
LUCKY FOR YOU, MY GOVERNMENT SENT ME TO SAVE YOUR BACKWARD COUNTRY...
...AND GIVE OUT LESSONS IN MANNERS.

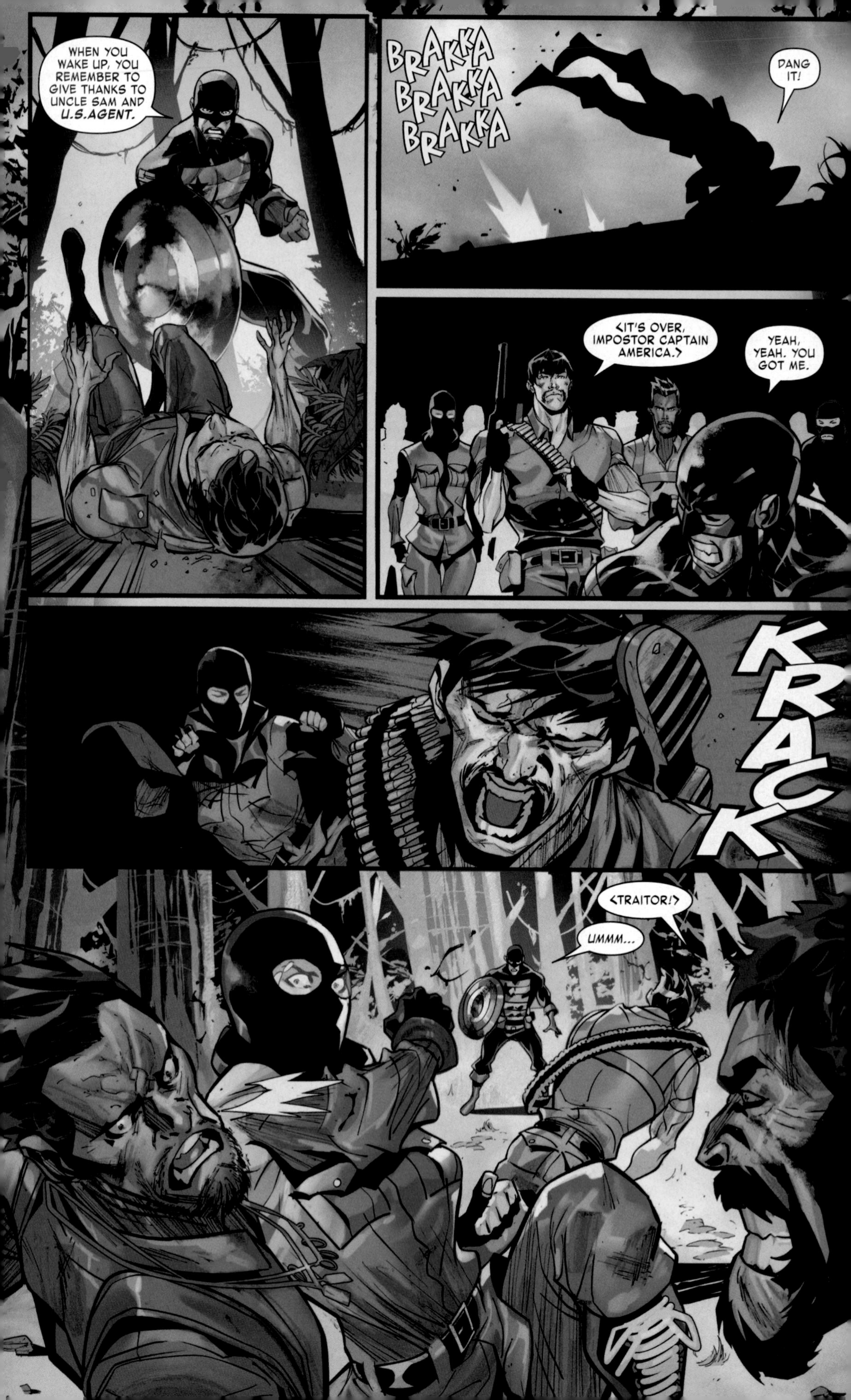
WHEN YOU WAKE UP, YOU REMEMBER TO GIVE THANKS TO UNCLE SAM AND U.S.AGENT.
BRAKKA BRAKKA BRAKKA
DANG IT!
<IT'S OVER, IMPOSTOR CAPTAIN AMERICA.>
YEAH, YEAH. YOU GOT ME.
KRACK
<TRAITOR!>
UMMM...

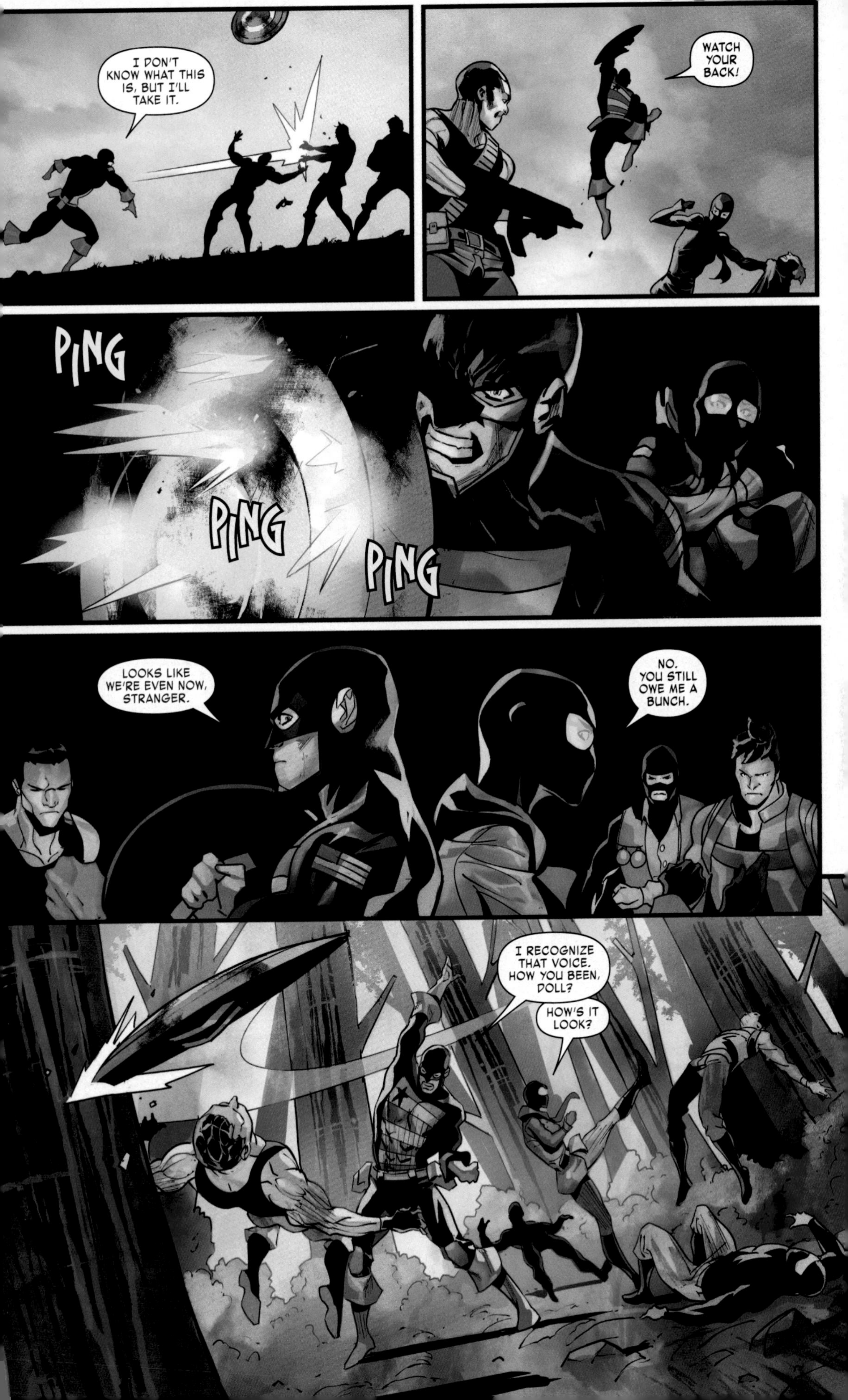
I DON'T KNOW WHAT THIS IS, BUT I'LL TAKE IT.
WATCH YOUR BACK!
PING
PING
PING
LOOKS LIKE WE'RE EVEN NOW, STRANGER.
NO. YOU STILL OWE ME A BUNCH.
I RECOGNIZE THAT VOICE. HOW YOU BEEN, DOLL?
HOW'S IT LOOK?

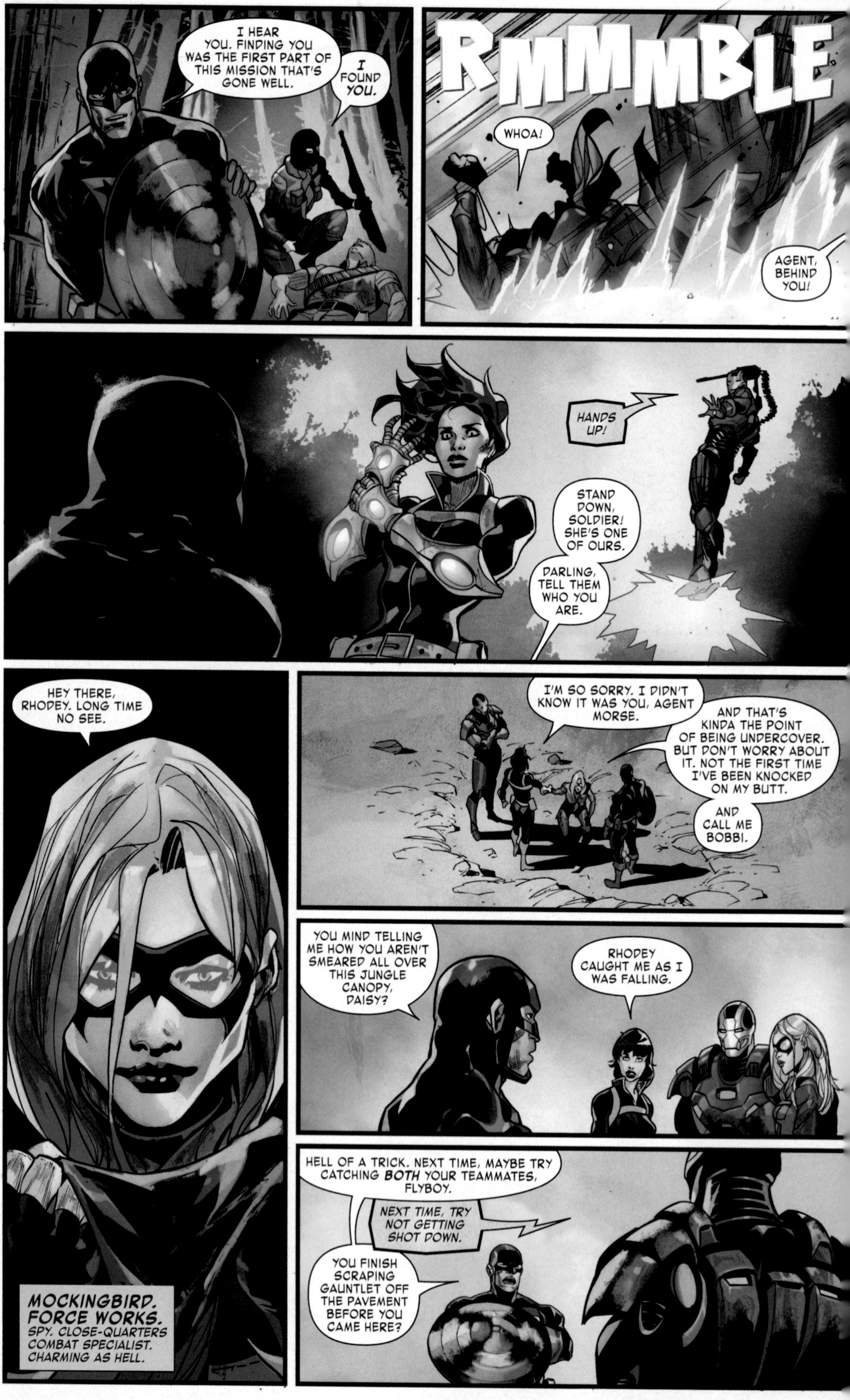
I HEAR YOU. FINDING YOU WAS THE FIRST PART OF THIS MISSION THAT'S GONE WELL.
I FOUND YOU.
RMMMBLE
WHOA!
AGENT, BEHIND YOU!
HANDS UP!
STAND DOWN, SOLDIER! SHE'S ONE OF OURS.
DARLING, TELL THEM WHO YOU ARE.
HEY THERE, RHODEY. LONG TIME NO SEE.
MOCKINGBIRD. FORCE WORKS.
SPY. CLOSE-QUARTERS COMBAT SPECIALIST. CHARMING AS HELL.
I'M SO SORRY. I DIDN'T KNOW IT WAS YOU, AGENT MORSE.
AND THAT'S KINDA THE POINT OF BEING UNDERCOVER. BUT DON'T WORRY ABOUT IT. NOT THE FIRST TIME I'VE BEEN KNOCKED ON MY BUTT.
AND CALL ME BOBBI.
YOU MIND TELLING ME HOW YOU AREN'T SMEARED ALL OVER THIS JUNGLE CANOPY, DAISY?
RHODEY CAUGHT ME AS I WAS FALLING.
HELL OF A TRICK. NEXT TIME, MAYBE TRY CATCHING BOTH YOUR TEAMMATES, FLYBOY.
NEXT TIME, TRY NOT GETTING SHOT DOWN.
YOU FINISH SCRAPING GAUNTLET OFF THE PAVEMENT BEFORE YOU CAME HERE?

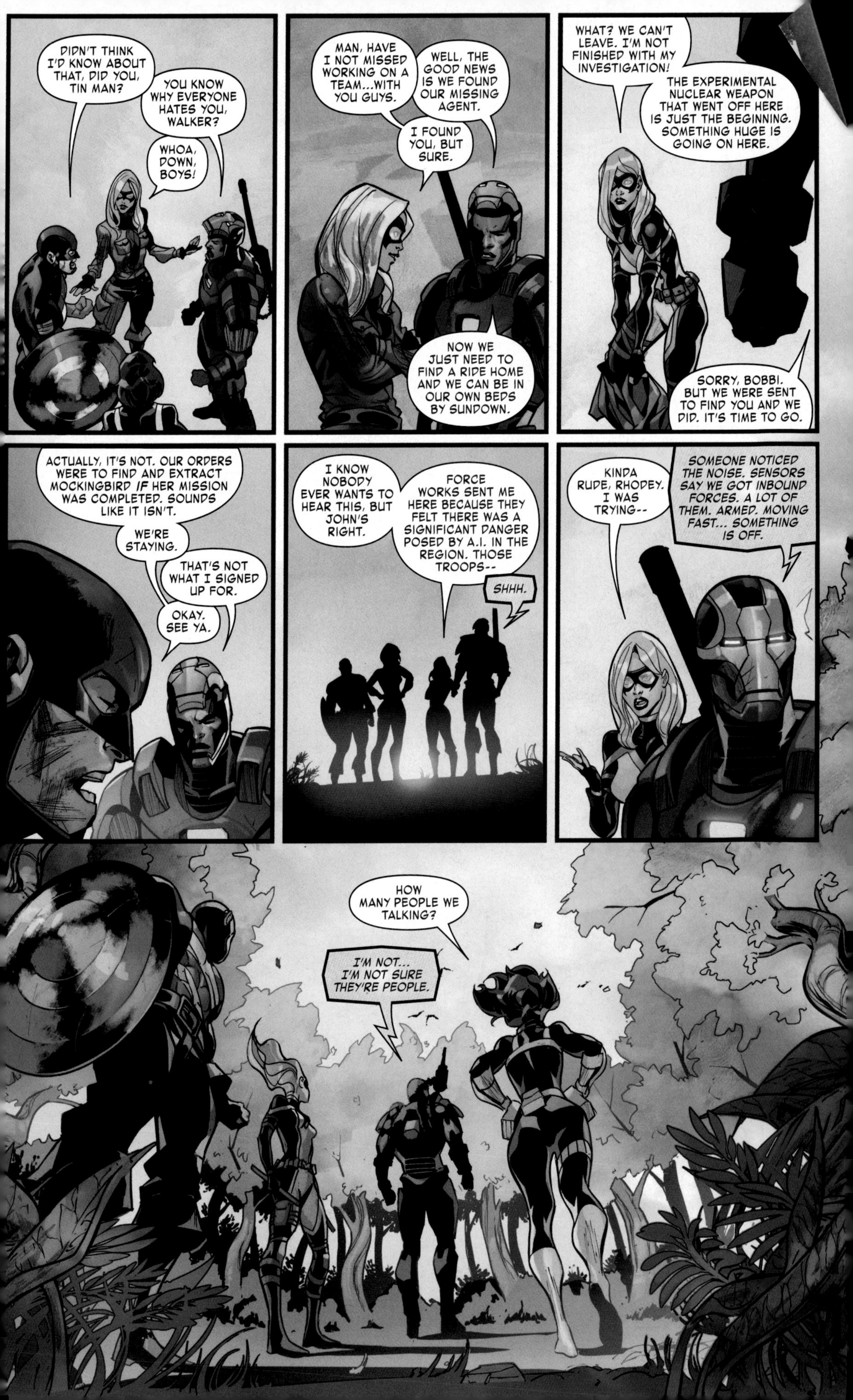
DIDN'T THINK I'D KNOW ABOUT THAT, DID YOU, TIN MAN?
YOU KNOW WHY EVERYONE HATES YOU, WALKER?
WHOA, DOWN, BOYS!
MAN, HAVE I NOT MISSED WORKING ON A TEAM...WITH YOU GUYS.
WELL, THE GOOD NEWS IS WE FOUND OUR MISSING AGENT.
I FOUND YOU, BUT SURE.
NOW WE JUST NEED TO FIND A RIDE HOME AND WE CAN BE IN OUR OWN BEDS BY SUNDOWN.
WHAT? WE CAN'T LEAVE. I'M NOT FINISHED WITH MY INVESTIGATION!
THE EXPERIMENTAL NUCLEAR WEAPON THAT WENT OFF HERE IS JUST THE BEGINNING. SOMETHING HUGE IS GOING ON HERE.
SORRY, BOBBI. BUT WE WERE SENT TO FIND YOU AND WE DID. IT'S TIME TO GO.
ACTUALLY, IT'S NOT. OUR ORDERS WERE TO FIND AND EXTRACT MOCKINGBIRD IF HER MISSION WAS COMPLETED. SOUNDS LIKE IT ISN'T.
WE'RE STAYING.
THAT'S NOT WHAT I SIGNED UP FOR.
OKAY. SEE YA.
I KNOW NOBODY EVER WANTS TO HEAR THIS, BUT JOHN'S RIGHT.
FORCE WORKS SENT ME HERE BECAUSE THEY FELT THERE WAS A SIGNIFICANT DANGER POSED BY A.I. IN THE REGION. THOSE TROOPS--
SHHH.
KINDA RUDE, RHODEY. I WAS TRYING--
SOMEONE NOTICED THE NOISE. SENSORS SAY WE GOT INBOUND FORCES. A LOT OF THEM. ARMED. MOVING FAST... SOMETHING IS OFF.
HOW MANY PEOPLE WE TALKING?
I'M NOT... I'M NOT SURE THEY'RE PEOPLE.

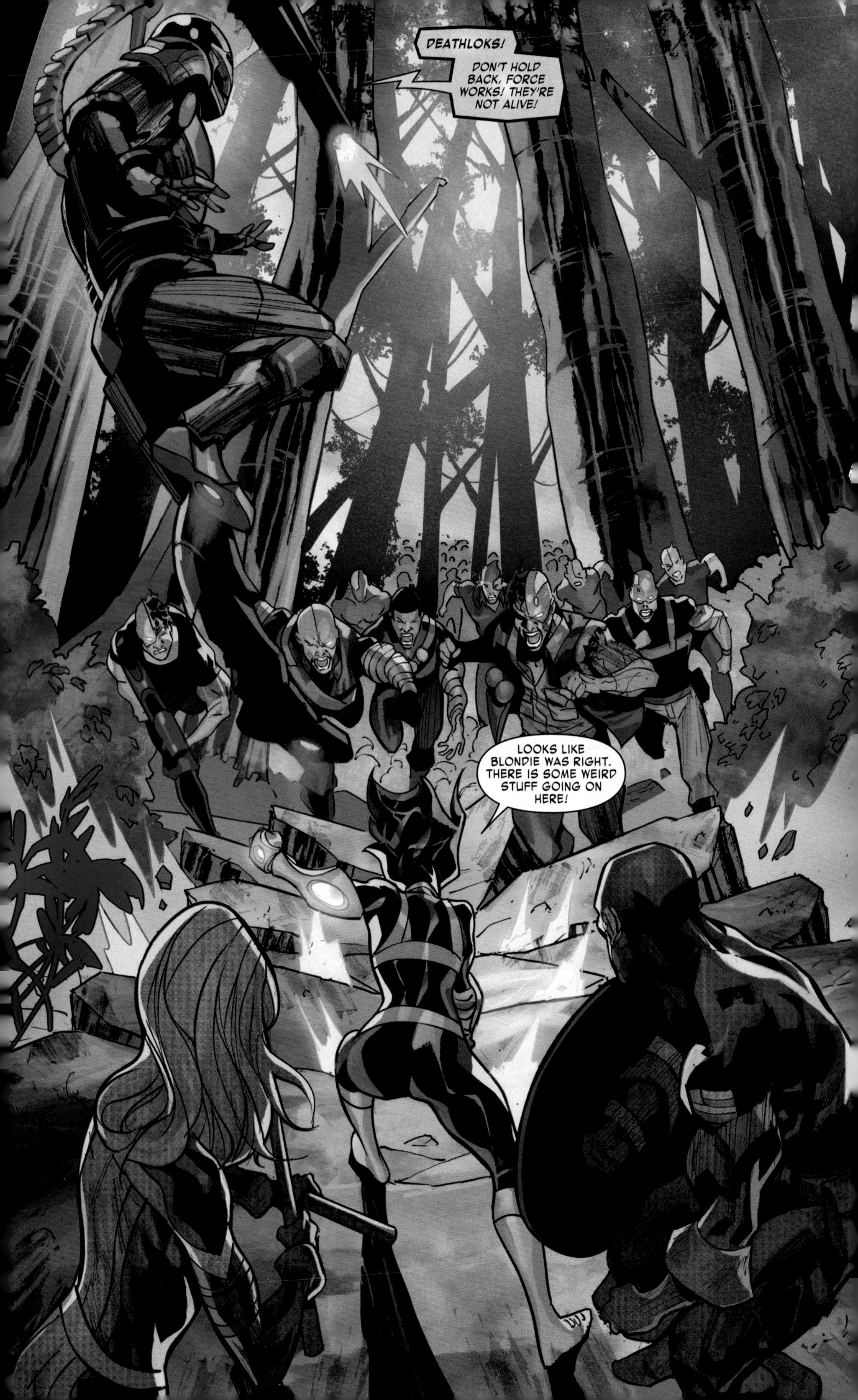
DEATHLOKS!
DON'T HOLD BACK, FORCE WORKS! THEY'RE NOT ALIVE!
LOOKS LIKE BLONDIE WAS RIGHT. THERE IS SOME WEIRD STUFF GOING ON HERE!

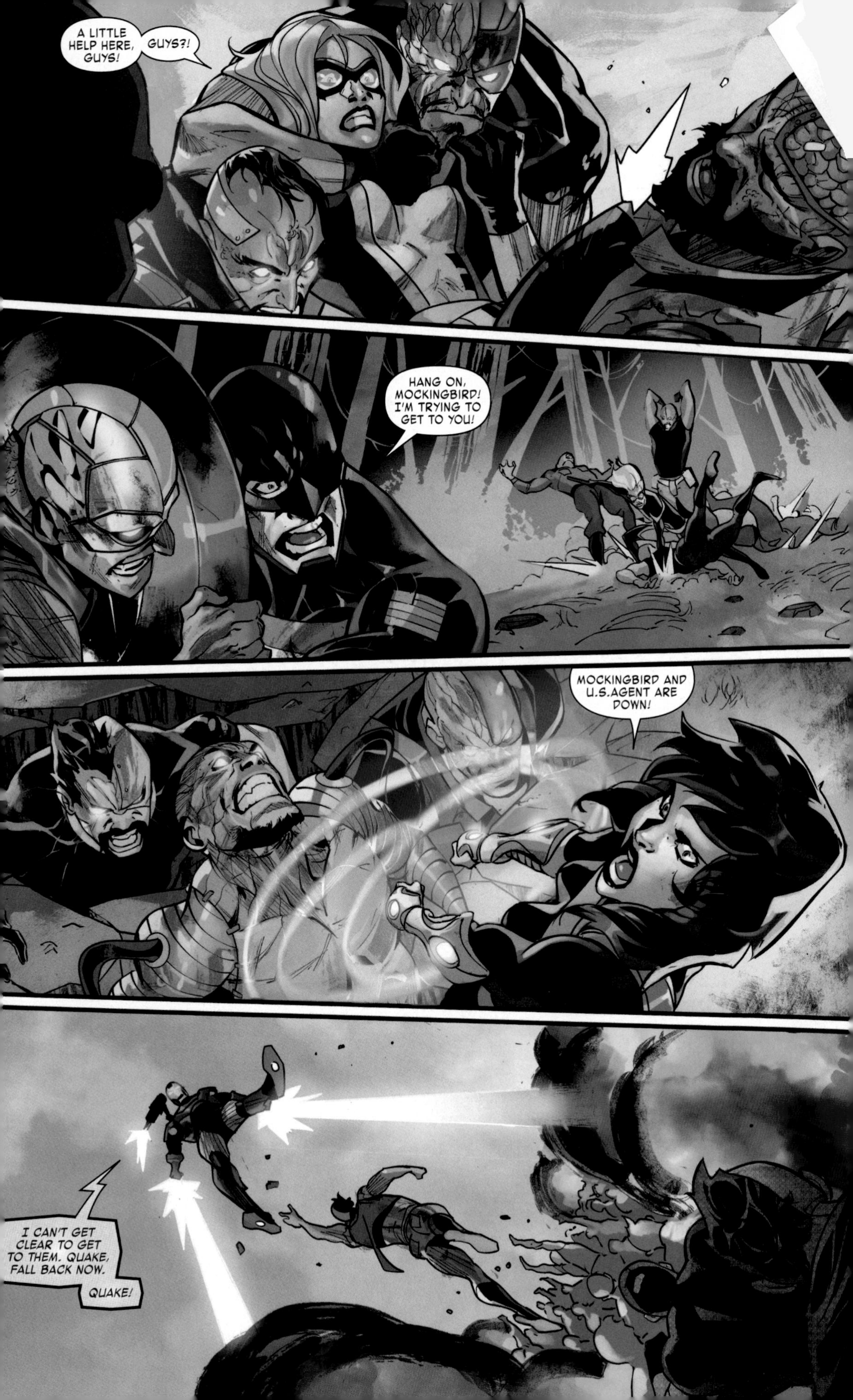
A LITTLE HELP HERE, GUYS!
GUYS?!
HANG ON, MOCKINGBIRD! I'M TRYING TO GET TO YOU!
MOCKINGBIRD AND U.S.AGENT ARE DOWN!
I CAN'T GET CLEAR TO GET TO THEM. QUAKE, FALL BACK NOW.
QUAKE!

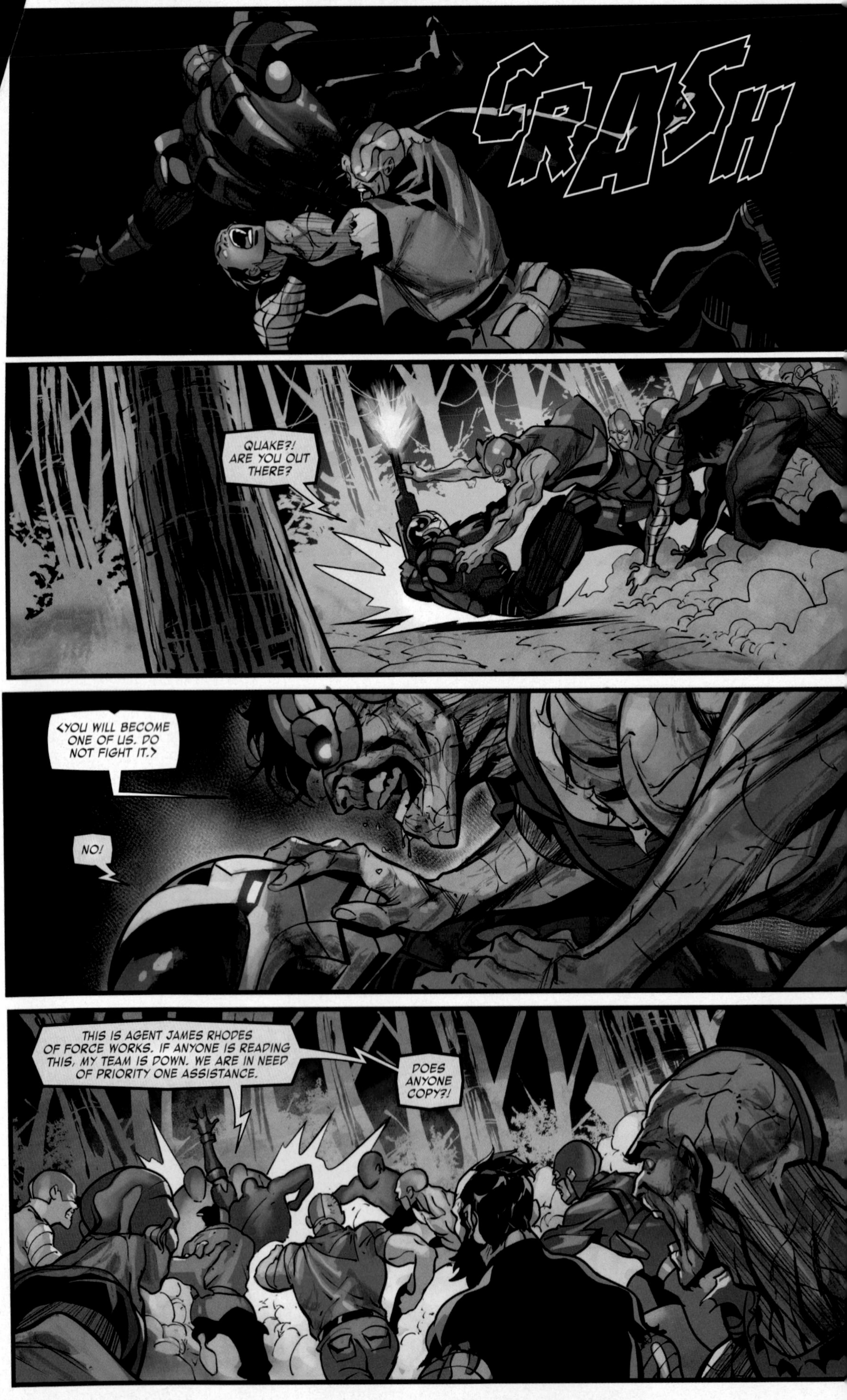
CRASH
QUAKE?! ARE YOU OUT THERE?
<YOU WILL BECOME ONE OF US. DO NOT FIGHT IT.>
NO!
THIS IS AGENT JAMES RHODES OF FORCE WORKS. IF ANYONE IS READING THIS, MY TEAM IS DOWN. WE ARE IN NEED OF PRIORITY ONE ASSISTANCE.
DOES ANYONE COPY?!

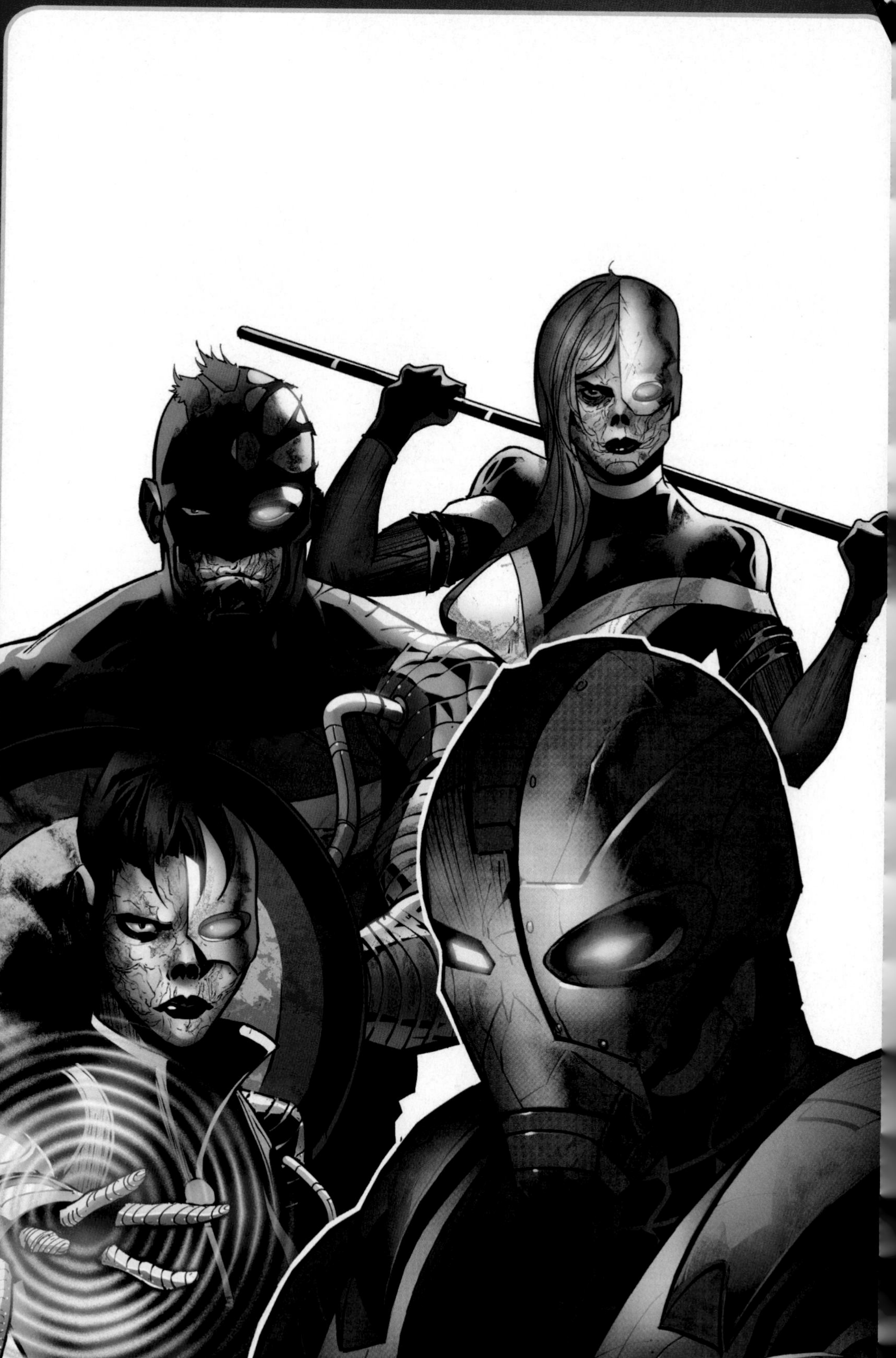

2020 FORCE WORKS 2

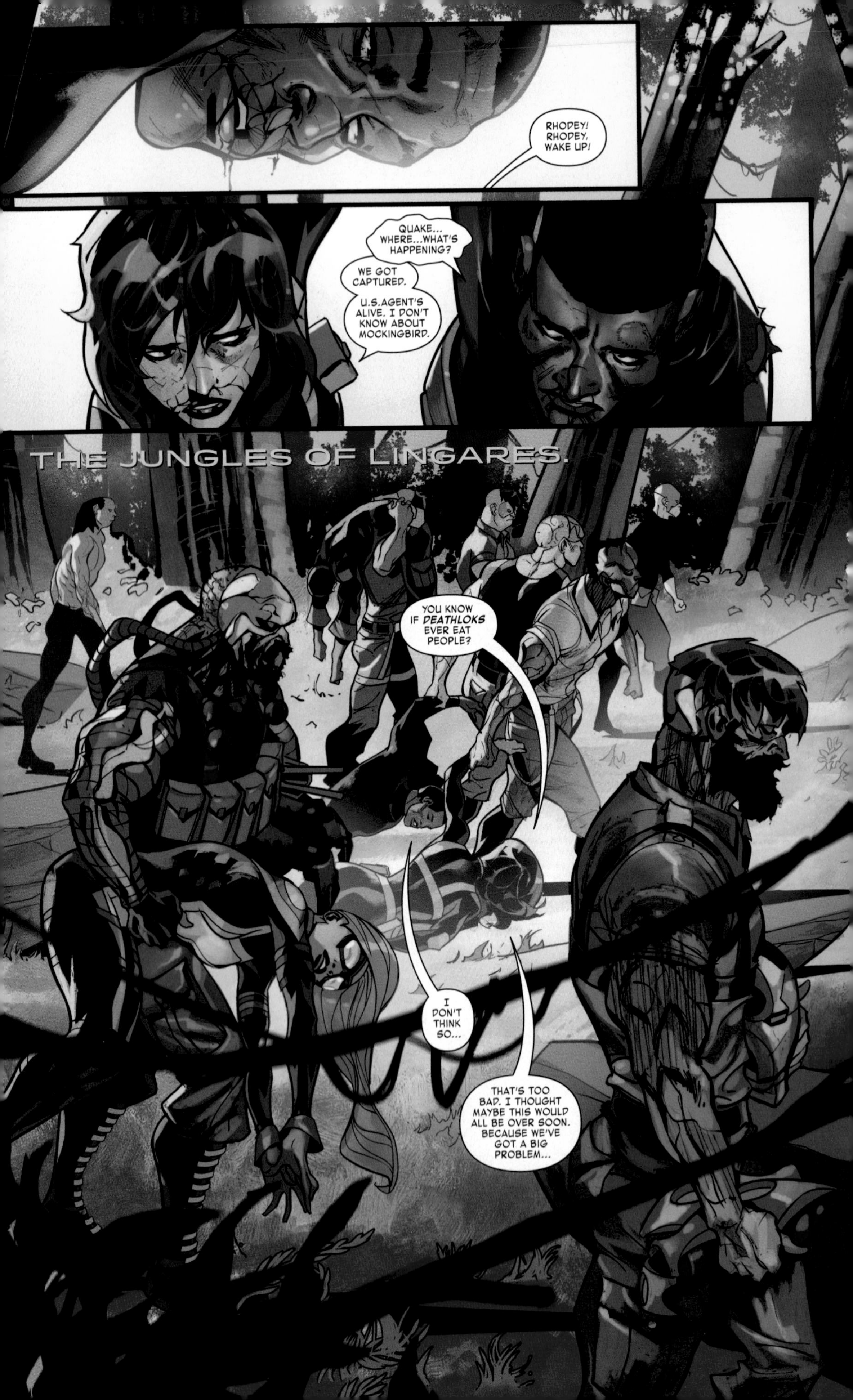
RHODEY! RHODEY, WAKE UP!
QUAKE... WHERE...WHAT'S HAPPENING?
WE GOT CAPTURED.
U.S.AGENT'S ALIVE. I DON'T KNOW ABOUT MOCKINGBIRD.
THE JUNGLES OF LINGARES.
YOU KNOW IF DEATHLOKS EVER EAT PEOPLE?
I DON'T THINK SO...
THAT'S TOO BAD. I THOUGHT MAYBE THIS WOULD ALL BE OVER SOON. BECAUSE WE'VE GOT A BIG PROBLEM...

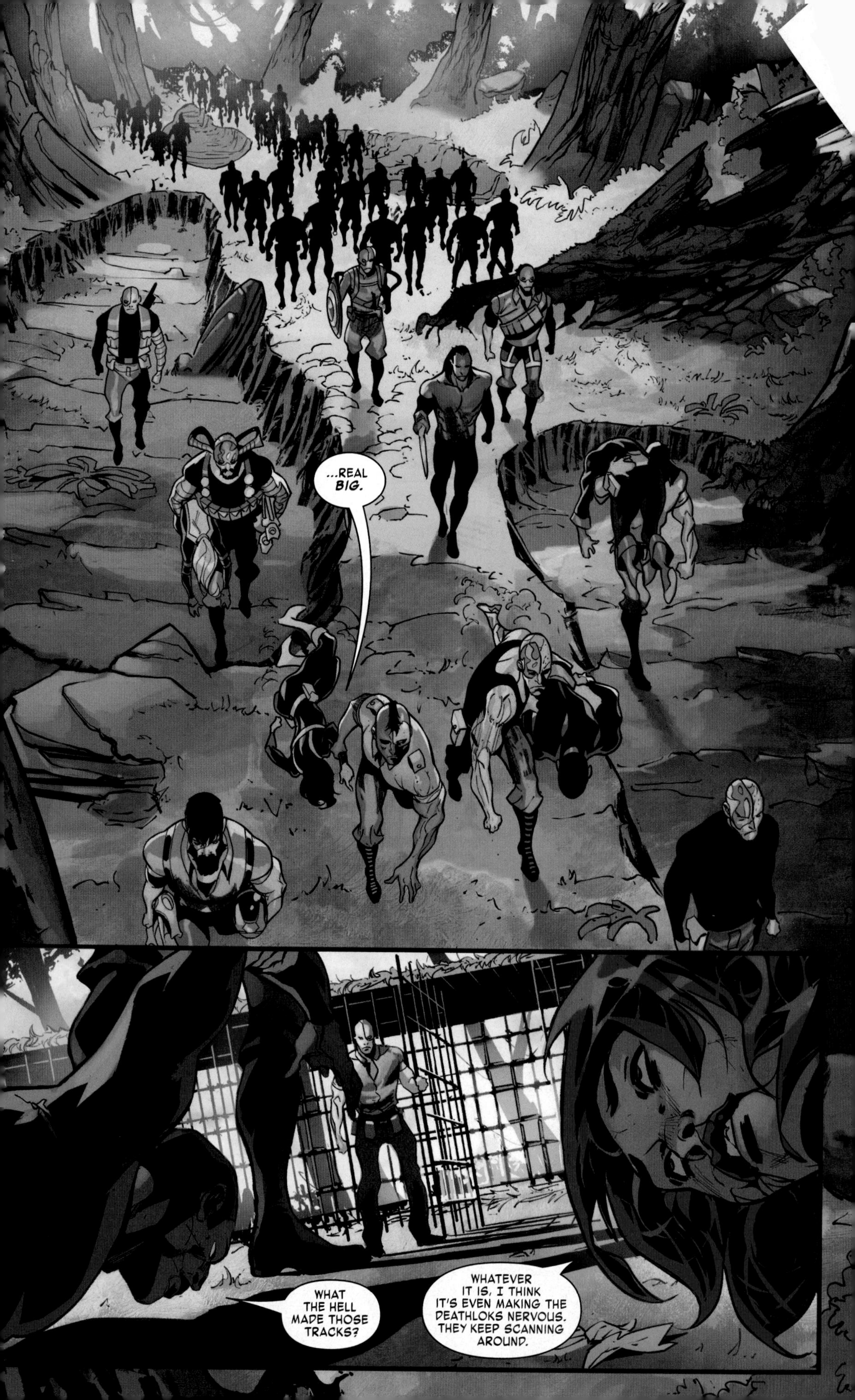
...REAL BIG.
WHAT THE HELL MADE THOSE TRACKS?
WHATEVER IT IS, I THINK IT'S EVEN MAKING THE DEATHLOKS NERVOUS. THEY KEEP SCANNING AROUND.

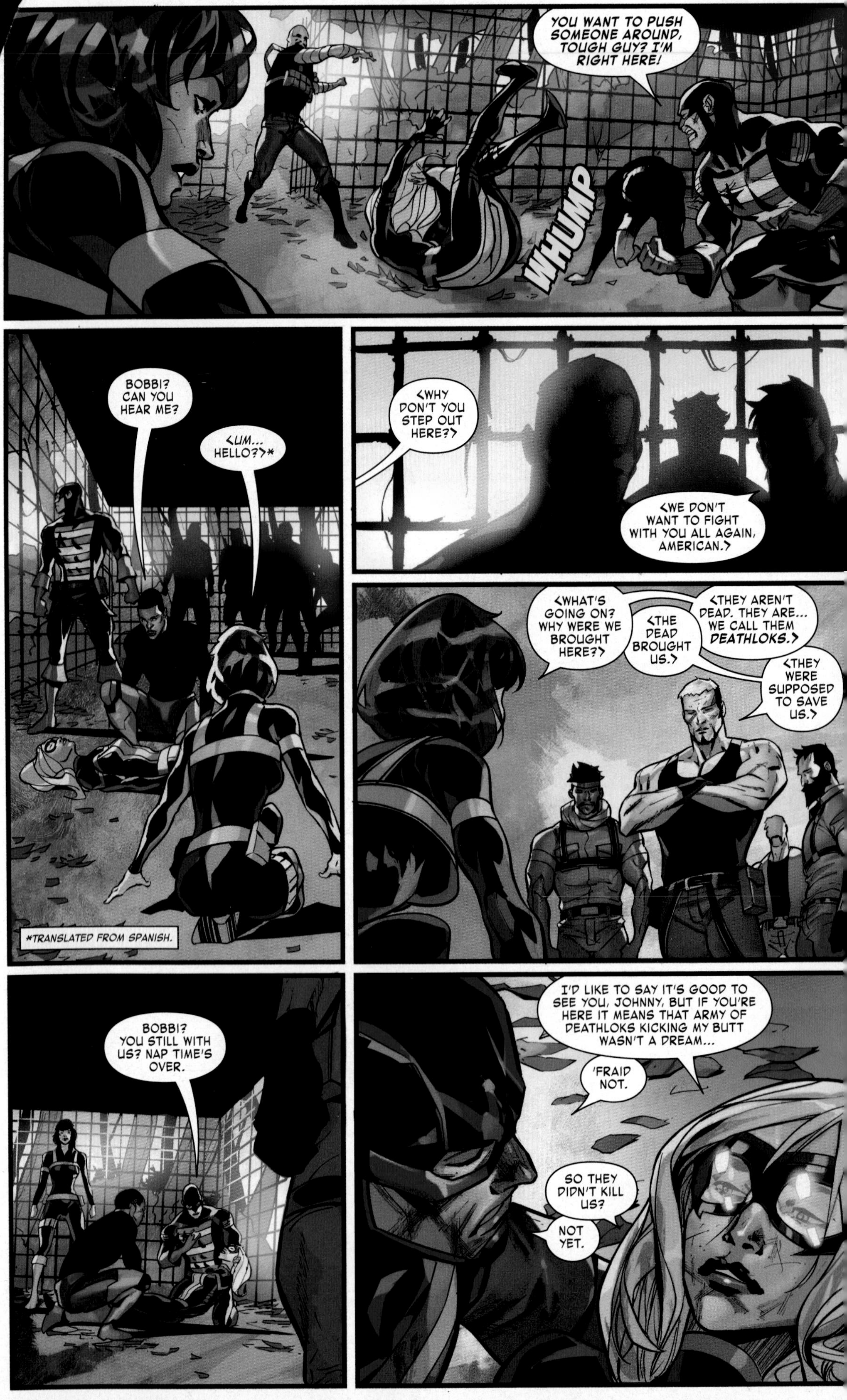
YOU WANT TO PUSH SOMEONE AROUND, TOUGH GUY? I'M RIGHT HERE!
WHUMP
BOBBI? CAN YOU HEAR ME?
<UM... HELLO?>*
*TRANSLATED FROM SPANISH.
<WHY DON'T YOU STEP OUT HERE?>
<WE DON'T WANT TO FIGHT WITH YOU ALL AGAIN, AMERICAN.>
<WHAT'S GOING ON? WHY WERE WE BROUGHT HERE?>
<THE DEAD BROUGHT US.>
<THEY AREN'T DEAD. THEY ARE... WE CALL THEM DEATHLOKS.>
<THEY WERE SUPPOSED TO SAVE US.>
BOBBI? YOU STILL WITH US? NAP TIME'S OVER.
I'D LIKE TO SAY IT'S GOOD TO SEE YOU, JOHNNY, BUT IF YOU'RE HERE IT MEANS THAT ARMY OF DEATHLOKS KICKING MY BUTT WASN'T A DREAM...
'FRAID NOT.
SO THEY DIDN'T KILL US?
NOT YET.

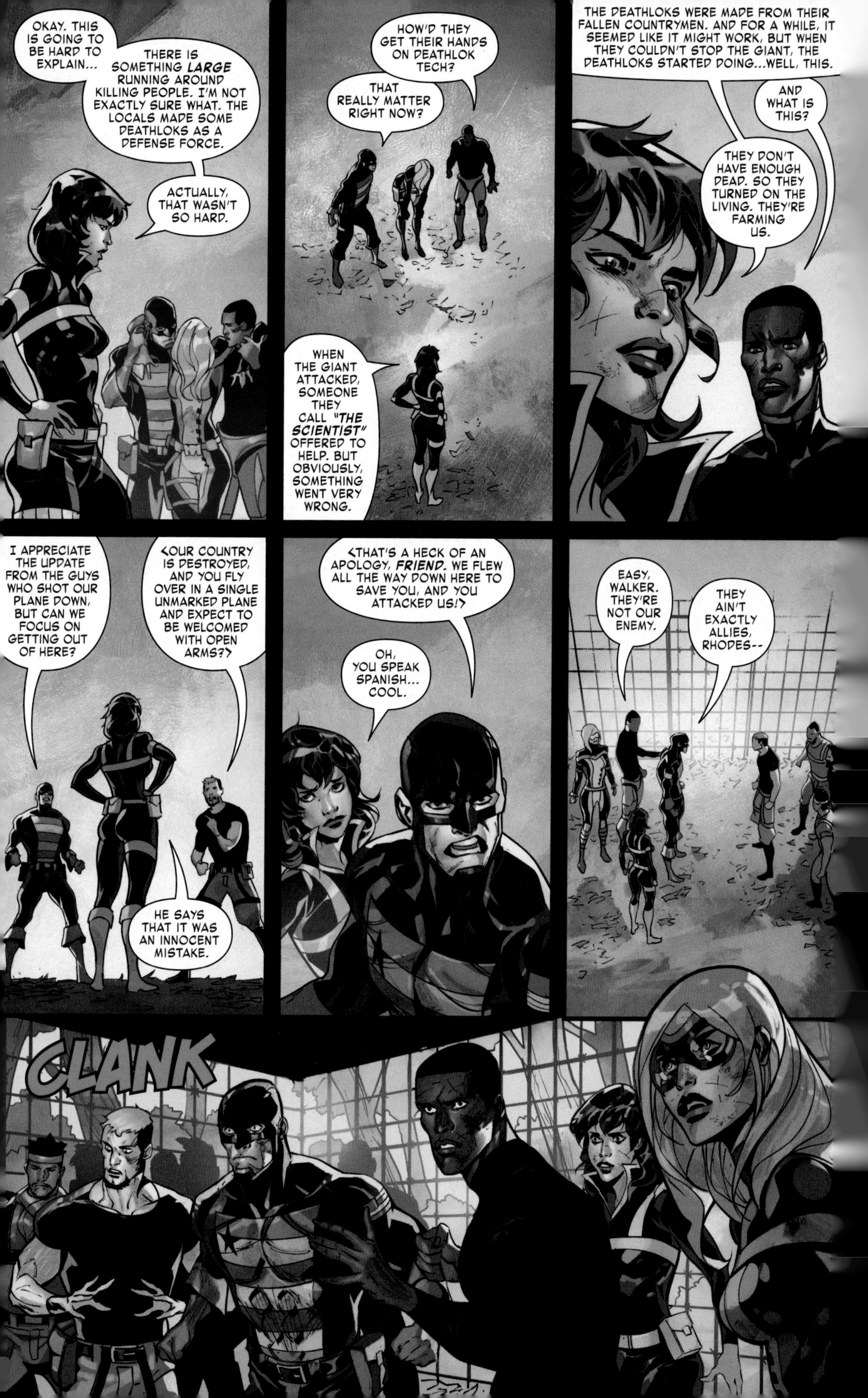
OKAY. THIS IS GOING TO BE HARD TO EXPLAIN...
THERE IS SOMETHING LARGE RUNNING AROUND KILLING PEOPLE. I'M NOT EXACTLY SURE WHAT. THE LOCALS MADE SOME DEATHLOKS AS A DEFENSE FORCE.
ACTUALLY, THAT WASN'T SO HARD.
HOW'D THEY GET THEIR HANDS ON DEATHLOK TECH?
THAT REALLY MATTER RIGHT NOW?
WHEN THE GIANT ATTACKED, SOMEONE THEY CALL "THE SCIENTIST" OFFERED TO HELP. BUT OBVIOUSLY, SOMETHING WENT VERY WRONG.
THE DEATHLOKS WERE MADE FROM THEIR FALLEN COUNTRYMEN. AND FOR A WHILE, IT SEEMED LIKE IT MIGHT WORK, BUT WHEN THEY COULDN'T STOP THE GIANT, THE DEATHLOKS STARTED DOING...WELL, THIS.
AND WHAT IS THIS?
THEY DON'T HAVE ENOUGH DEAD. SO THEY TURNED ON THE LIVING. THEY'RE FARMING US.
I APPRECIATE THE UPDATE FROM THE GUYS WHO SHOT OUR PLANE DOWN, BUT CAN WE FOCUS ON GETTING OUT OF HERE?
<OUR COUNTRY IS DESTROYED, AND YOU FLY OVER IN A SINGLE UNMARKED PLANE AND EXPECT TO BE WELCOMED WITH OPEN ARMS?>
HE SAYS THAT IT WAS AN INNOCENT MISTAKE.
<THAT'S A HECK OF AN APOLOGY, FRIEND. WE FLEW ALL THE WAY DOWN HERE TO SAVE YOU, AND YOU ATTACKED US!>
OH, YOU SPEAK SPANISH... COOL.
EASY, WALKER. THEY'RE NOT OUR ENEMY.
THEY AIN'T EXACTLY ALLIES, RHODES--
CLANK

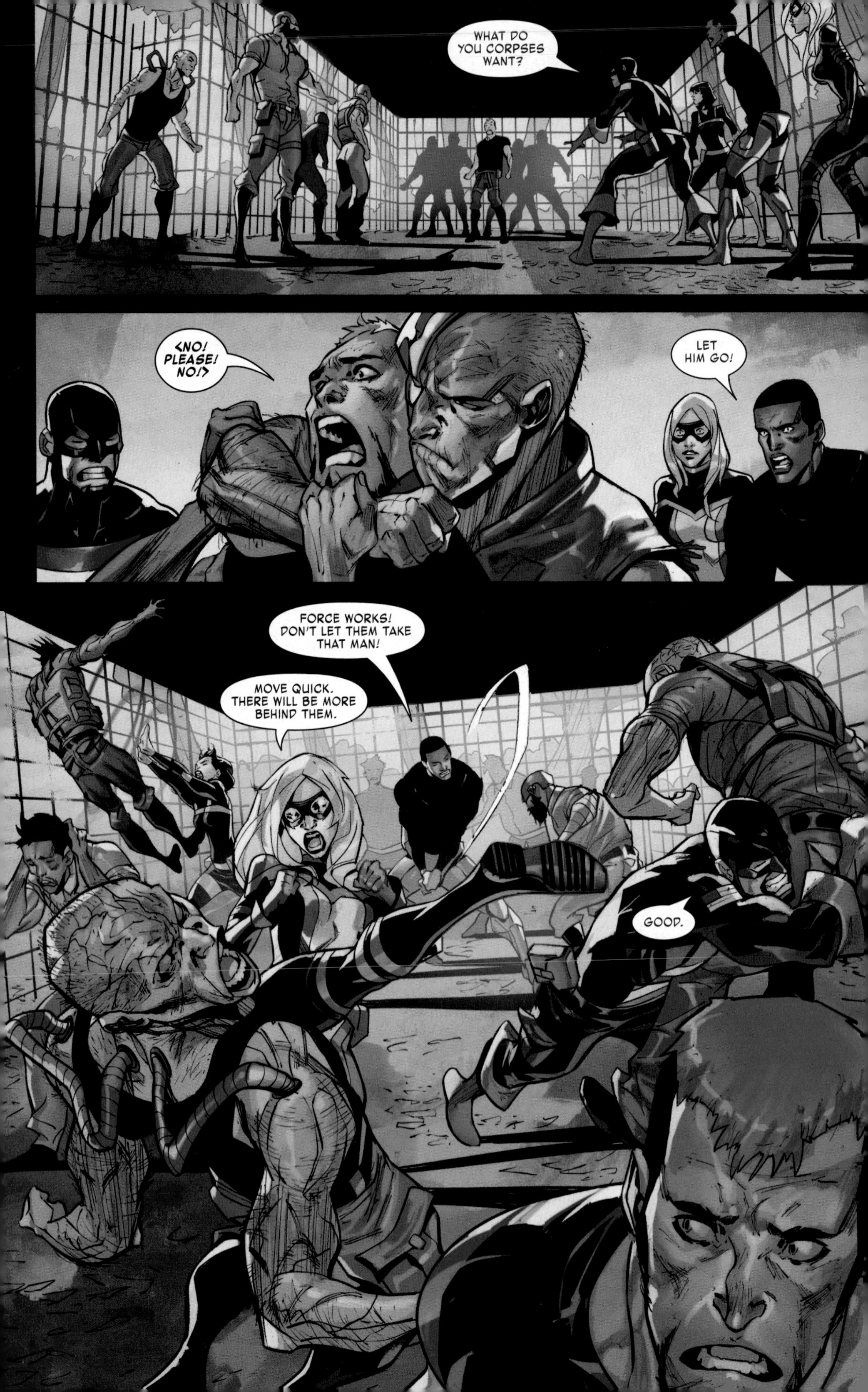
WHAT DO YOU CORPSES WANT?
<NO! PLEASE! NO!>
LET HIM GO!
FORCE WORKS! DON'T LET THEM TAKE THAT MAN!
MOVE QUICK. THERE WILL BE MORE BEHIND THEM.
GOOD.

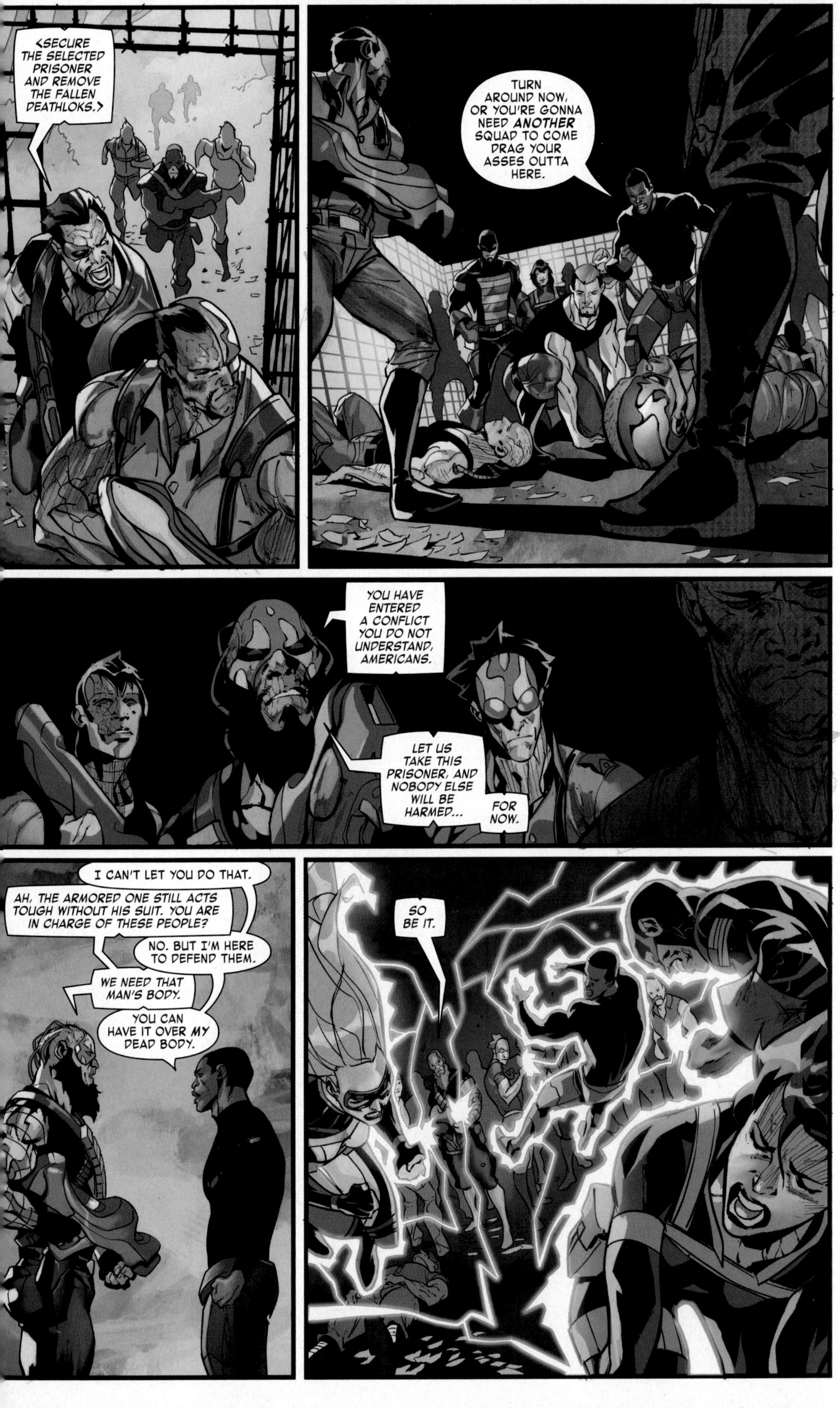
<SECURE THE SELECTED PRISONER AND REMOVE THE FALLEN DEATHLOKS.>
TURN AROUND NOW, OR YOU'RE GONNA NEED ANOTHER SQUAD TO COME DRAG YOUR ASSES OUTTA HERE.
YOU HAVE ENTERED A CONFLICT YOU DO NOT UNDERSTAND, AMERICANS.
LET US TAKE THIS PRISONER, AND NOBODY ELSE WILL BE HARMED...
FOR NOW.
I CAN'T LET YOU DO THAT.
AH, THE ARMORED ONE STILL ACTS TOUGH WITHOUT HIS SUIT. YOU ARE IN CHARGE OF THESE PEOPLE?
NO. BUT I'M HERE TO DEFEND THEM.
WE NEED THAT MAN'S BODY.
YOU CAN HAVE IT OVER MY DEAD BODY.
SO BE IT.

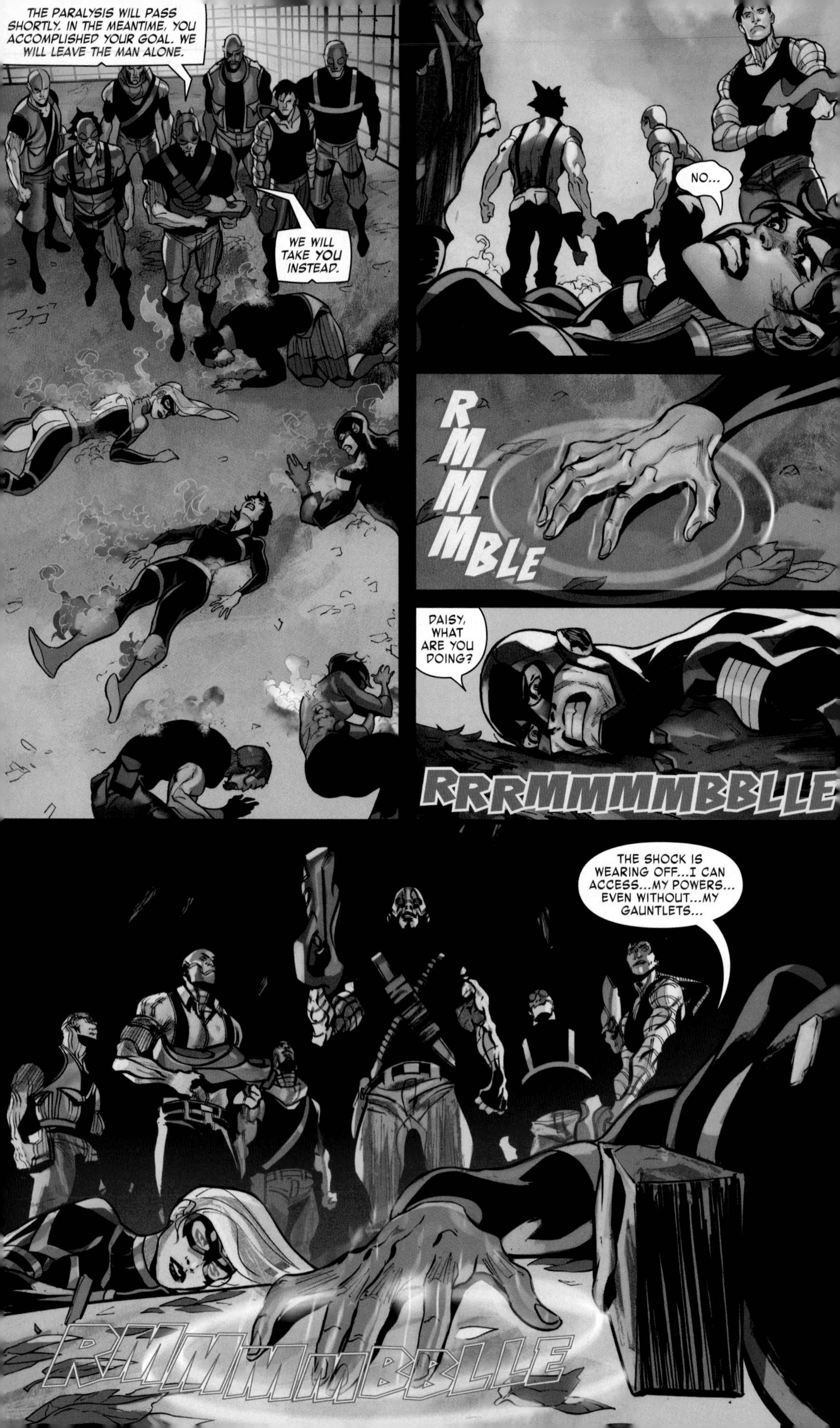
THE PARALYSIS WILL PASS SHORTLY. IN THE MEANTIME, YOU ACCOMPLISHED YOUR GOAL. WE WILL LEAVE THE MAN ALONE.
WE WILL TAKE YOU INSTEAD.
NO...
RMMMBLE
DAISY, WHAT ARE YOU DOING?
RRRMMMMMBBLLE
THE SHOCK IS WEARING OFF...I CAN ACCESS...MY POWERS... EVEN WITHOUT...MY GAUNTLETS...
RMMMMBBLLE

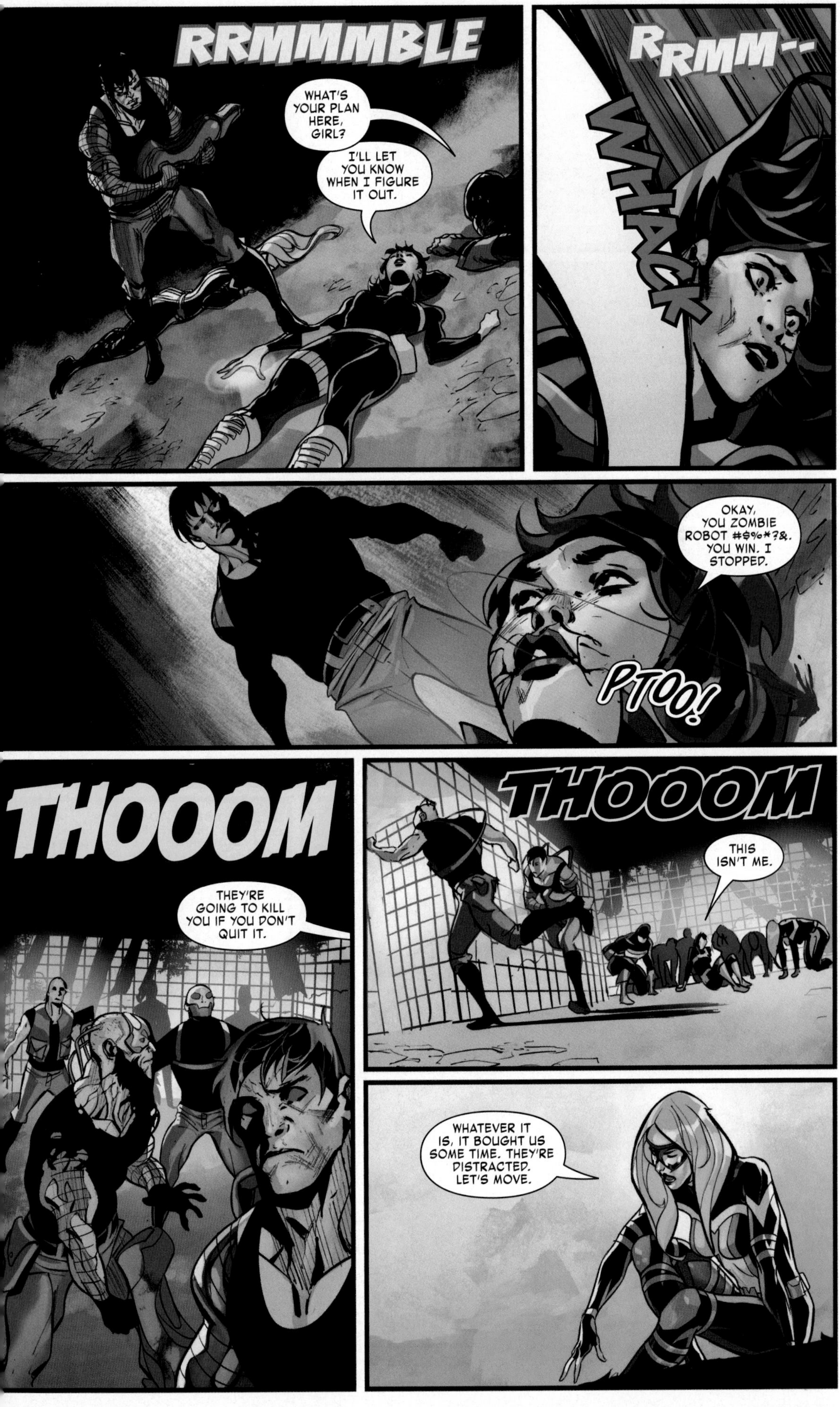
RRMMMBLE
WHAT'S YOUR PLAN HERE, GIRL?
I'LL LET YOU KNOW WHEN I FIGURE IT OUT.
RRMM--
WHACK
OKAY, YOU ZOMBIE ROBOT #$%*?&. YOU WIN. I STOPPED.
PTOO!
THOOOM
THEY'RE GOING TO KILL YOU IF YOU DON'T QUIT IT.
THOOOM
THIS ISN'T ME.
WHATEVER IT IS, IT BOUGHT US SOME TIME. THEY'RE DISTRACTED. LET'S MOVE.

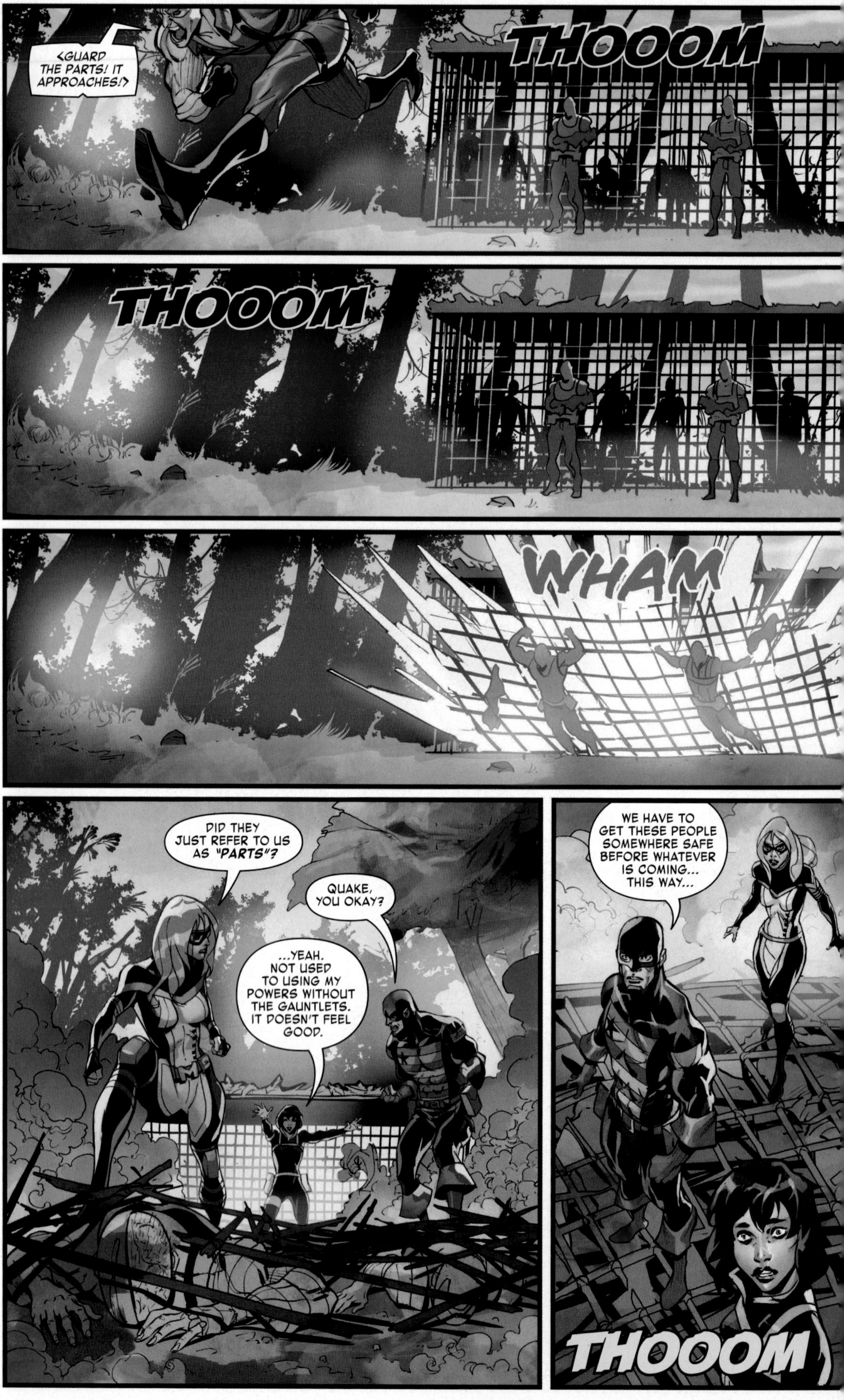
<GUARD THE PARTS! IT APPROACHES!>
THOOOM
THOOOM
WHAM
DID THEY JUST REFER TO US AS "PARTS"?
QUAKE, YOU OKAY?
...YEAH. NOT USED TO USING MY POWERS WITHOUT THE GAUNTLETS. IT DOESN'T FEEL GOOD.
WE HAVE TO GET THESE PEOPLE SOMEWHERE SAFE BEFORE WHATEVER IS COMING... THIS WAY...
THOOOM

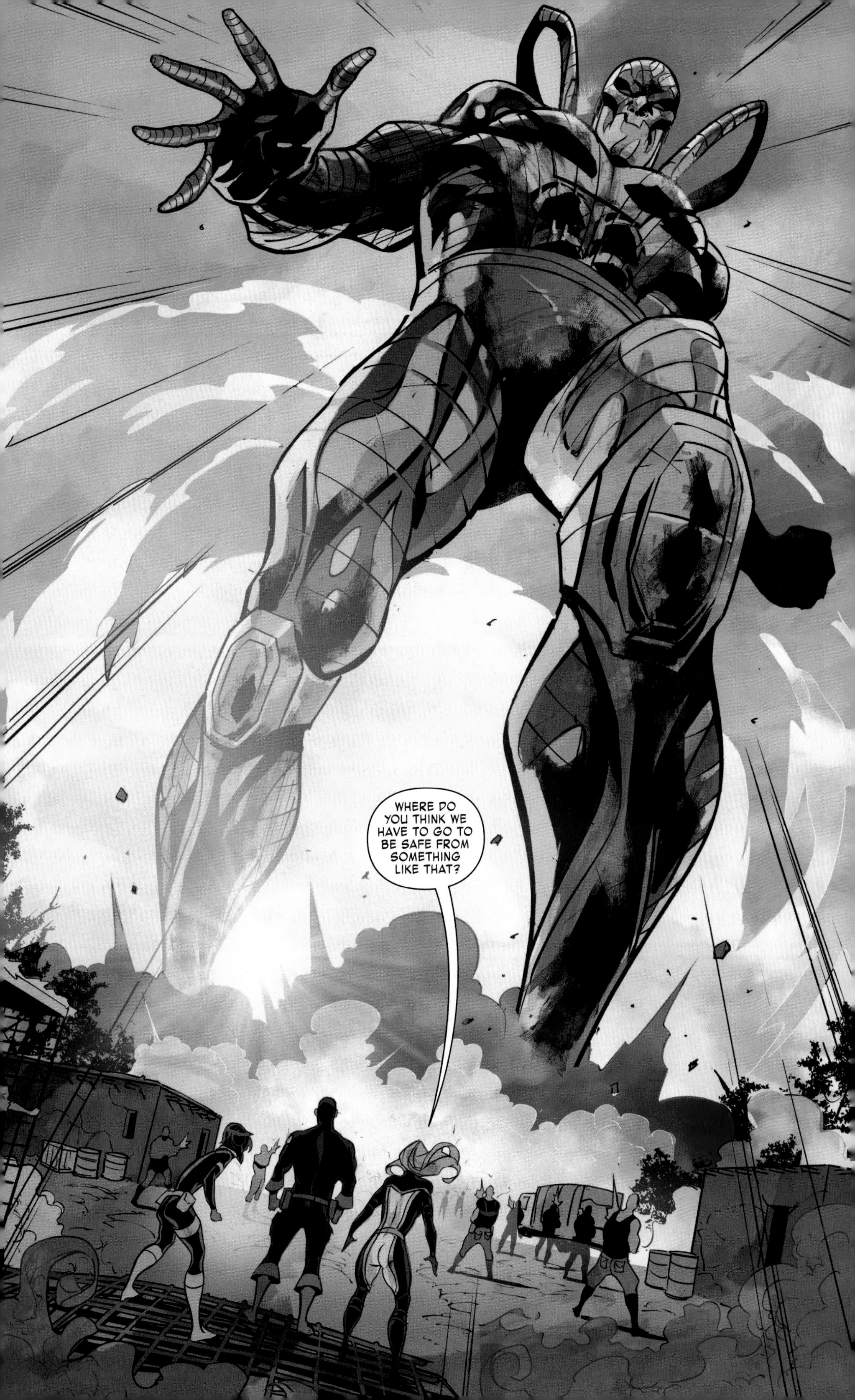
WHERE DO YOU THINK WE HAVE TO GO TO BE SAFE FROM SOMETHING LIKE THAT?

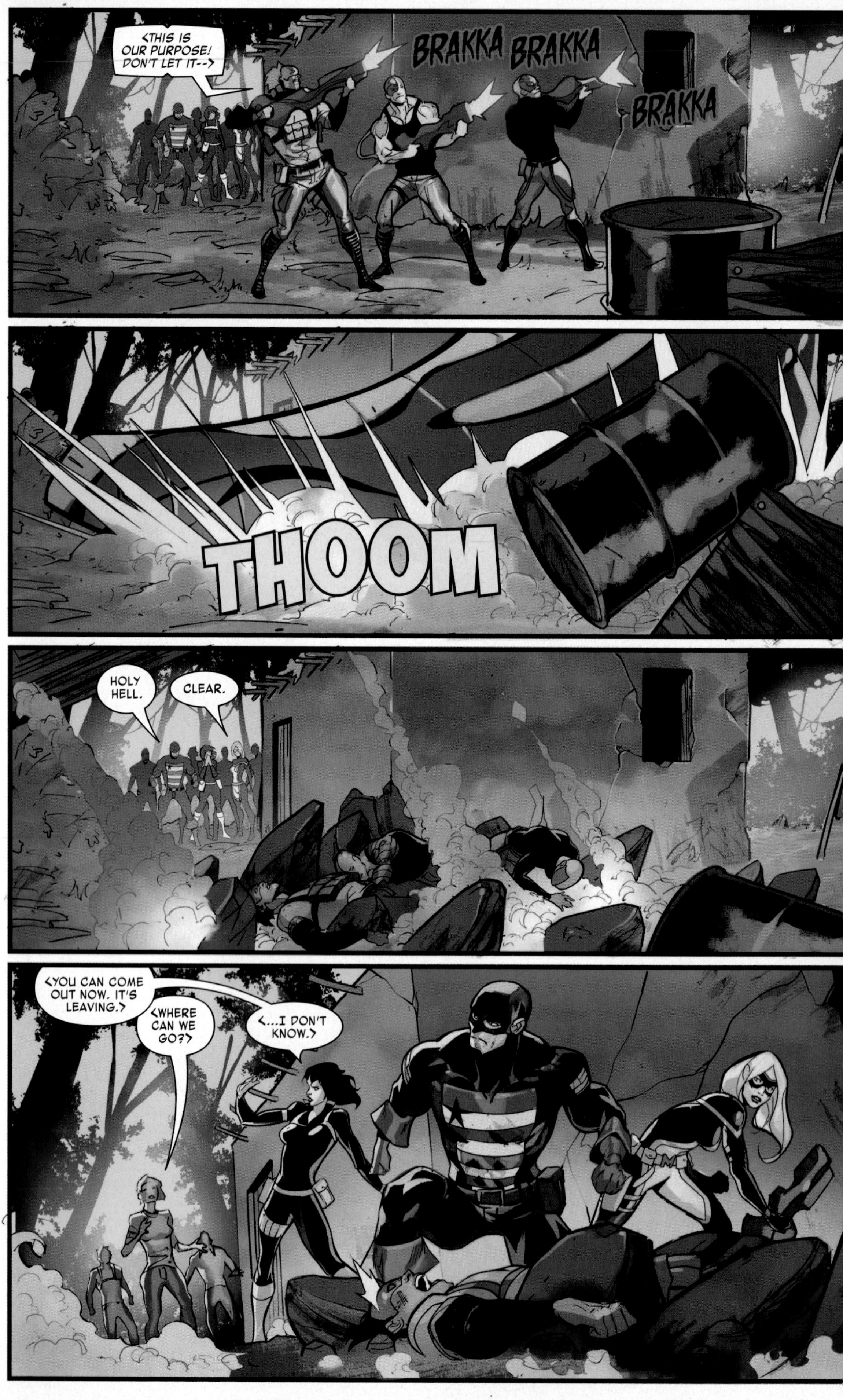
<THIS IS OUR PURPOSE! DON'T LET IT-->
BRAKKA
BRAKKA
BRAKKA
THOOM
HOLY HELL.
CLEAR.
<YOU CAN COME OUT NOW. IT'S LEAVING.>
<WHERE CAN WE GO?>
<...I DON'T KNOW.>

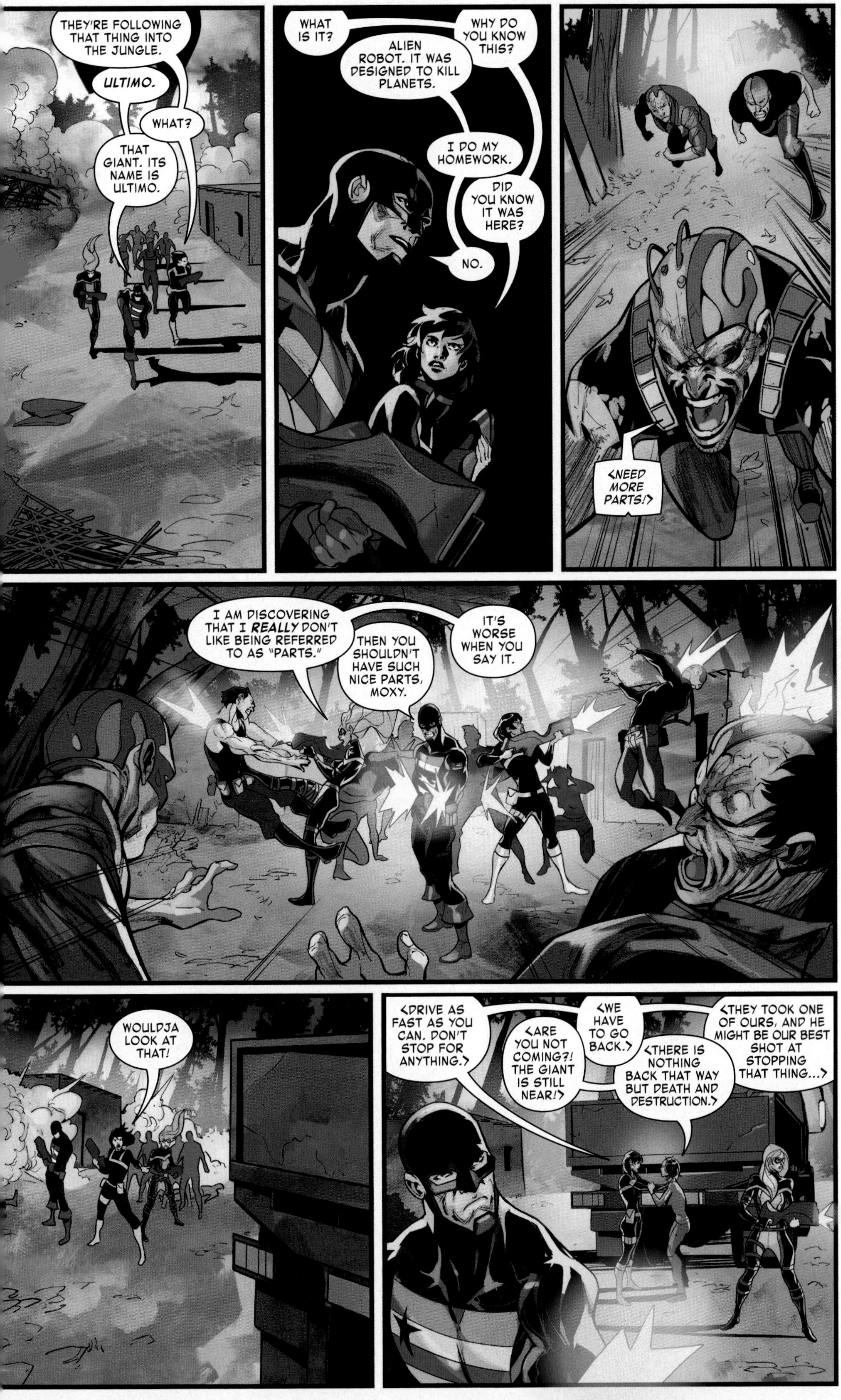
THEY'RE FOLLOWING THAT THING INTO THE JUNGLE.
ULTIMO.
WHAT?
THAT GIANT. ITS NAME IS ULTIMO.
WHAT IS IT?
ALIEN ROBOT. IT WAS DESIGNED TO KILL PLANETS.
WHY DO YOU KNOW THIS?
I DO MY HOMEWORK.
DID YOU KNOW IT WAS HERE?
NO.
<NEED MORE PARTS!>
I AM DISCOVERING THAT I REALLY DON'T LIKE BEING REFERRED TO AS "PARTS."
THEN YOU SHOULDN'T HAVE SUCH NICE PARTS, MOXY.
IT'S WORSE WHEN YOU SAY IT.
WOULDJA LOOK AT THAT!
<DRIVE AS FAST AS YOU CAN. DON'T STOP FOR ANYTHING.>
<ARE YOU NOT COMING?! THE GIANT IS STILL NEAR!>
<WE HAVE TO GO BACK.>
<THERE IS NOTHING BACK THAT WAY BUT DEATH AND DESTRUCTION.>
<THEY TOOK ONE OF OURS, AND HE MIGHT BE OUR BEST SHOT AT STOPPING THAT THING...>

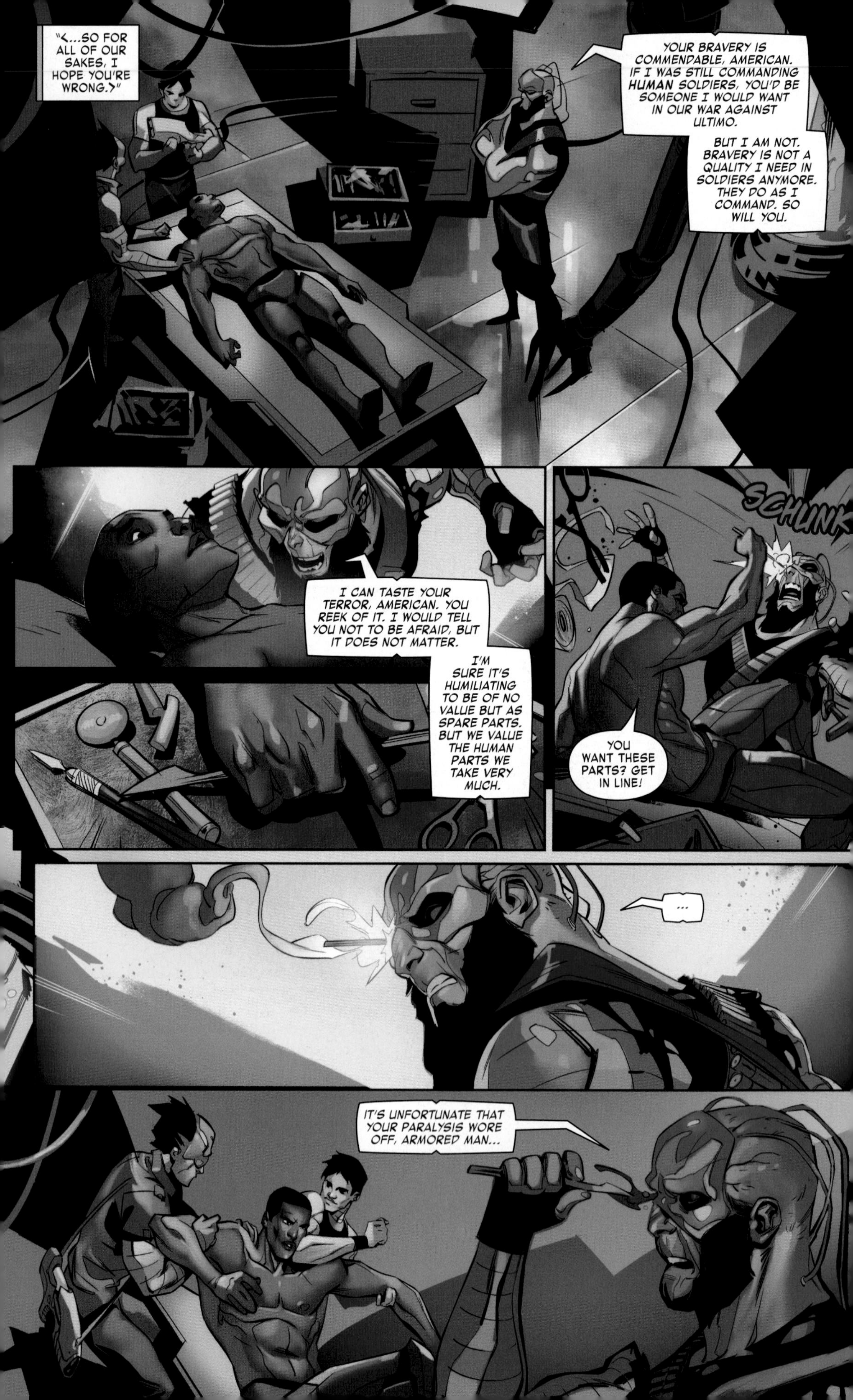
"<...SO FOR ALL OF OUR SAKES, I HOPE YOU'RE WRONG.>"
YOUR BRAVERY IS COMMENDABLE, AMERICAN. IF I WAS STILL COMMANDING HUMAN SOLDIERS, YOU'D BE SOMEONE I WOULD WANT IN OUR WAR AGAINST ULTIMO.
BUT I AM NOT. BRAVERY IS NOT A QUALITY I NEED IN SOLDIERS ANYMORE. THEY DO AS I COMMAND. SO WILL YOU.
I CAN TASTE YOUR TERROR, AMERICAN. YOU REEK OF IT. I WOULD TELL YOU NOT TO BE AFRAID, BUT IT DOES NOT MATTER.
I'M SURE IT'S HUMILIATING TO BE OF NO VALUE BUT AS SPARE PARTS. BUT WE VALUE THE HUMAN PARTS WE TAKE VERY MUCH.
SCHUNK
YOU WANT THESE PARTS? GET IN LINE!
...
IT'S UNFORTUNATE THAT YOUR PARALYSIS WORE OFF, ARMORED MAN...

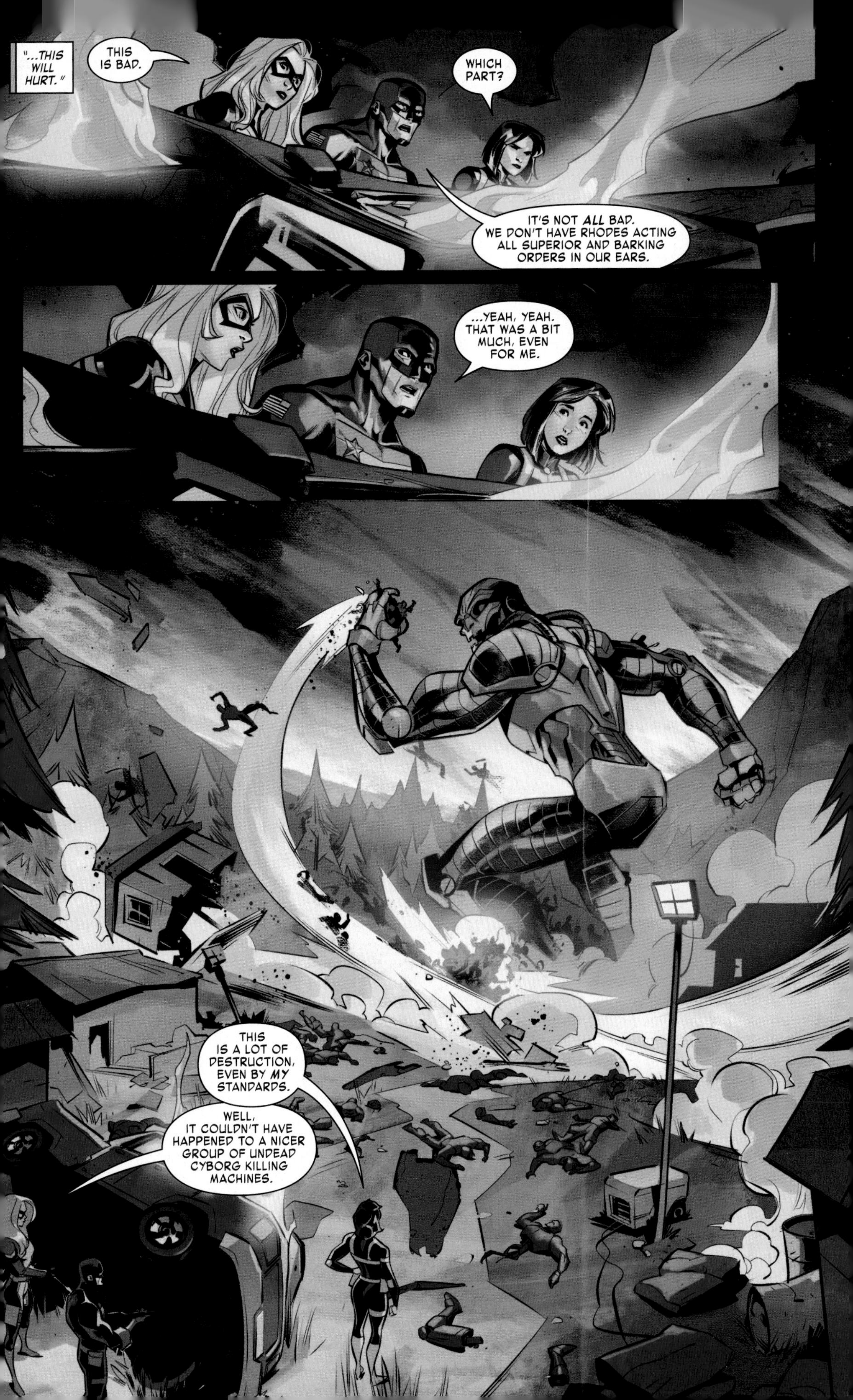
"...THIS WILL HURT."
THIS IS BAD.
WHICH PART?
IT'S NOT ALL BAD. WE DON'T HAVE RHODES ACTING ALL SUPERIOR AND BARKING ORDERS IN OUR EARS.
...YEAH, YEAH. THAT WAS A BIT MUCH, EVEN FOR ME.
THIS IS A LOT OF DESTRUCTION, EVEN BY MY STANDARDS.
WELL, IT COULDN'T HAVE HAPPENED TO A NICER GROUP OF UNDEAD CYBORG KILLING MACHINES.

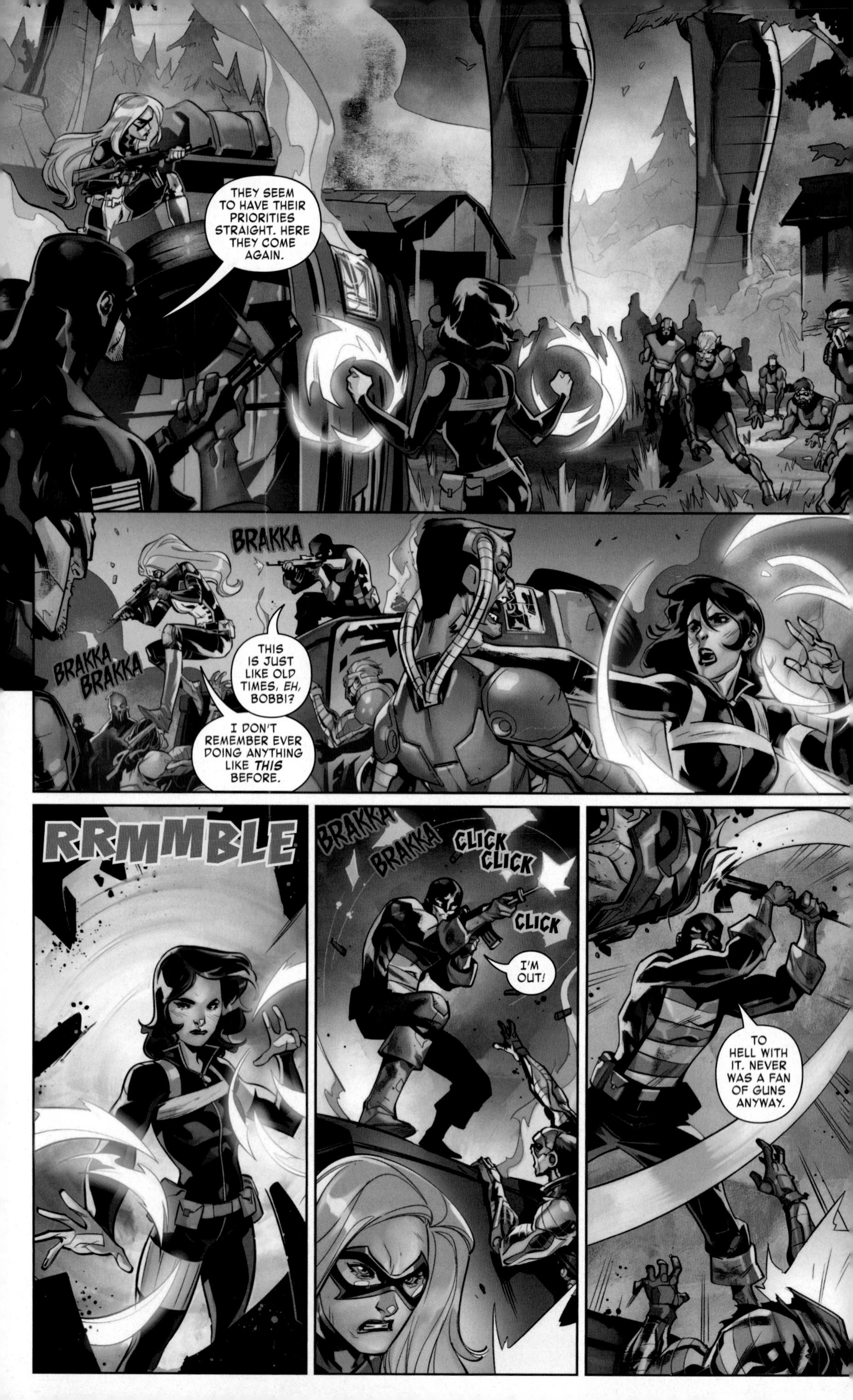
THEY SEEM TO HAVE THEIR PRIORITIES STRAIGHT. HERE THEY COME AGAIN.
BRAKKA
BRAKKA BRAKKA
THIS IS JUST LIKE OLD TIMES, EH, BOBBI?
I DON'T REMEMBER EVER DOING ANYTHING LIKE THIS BEFORE.
RRMMBLE
BRAKKA
BRAKKA
CLICK CLICK
CLICK
I'M OUT!
TO HELL WITH IT. NEVER WAS A FAN OF GUNS ANYWAY.

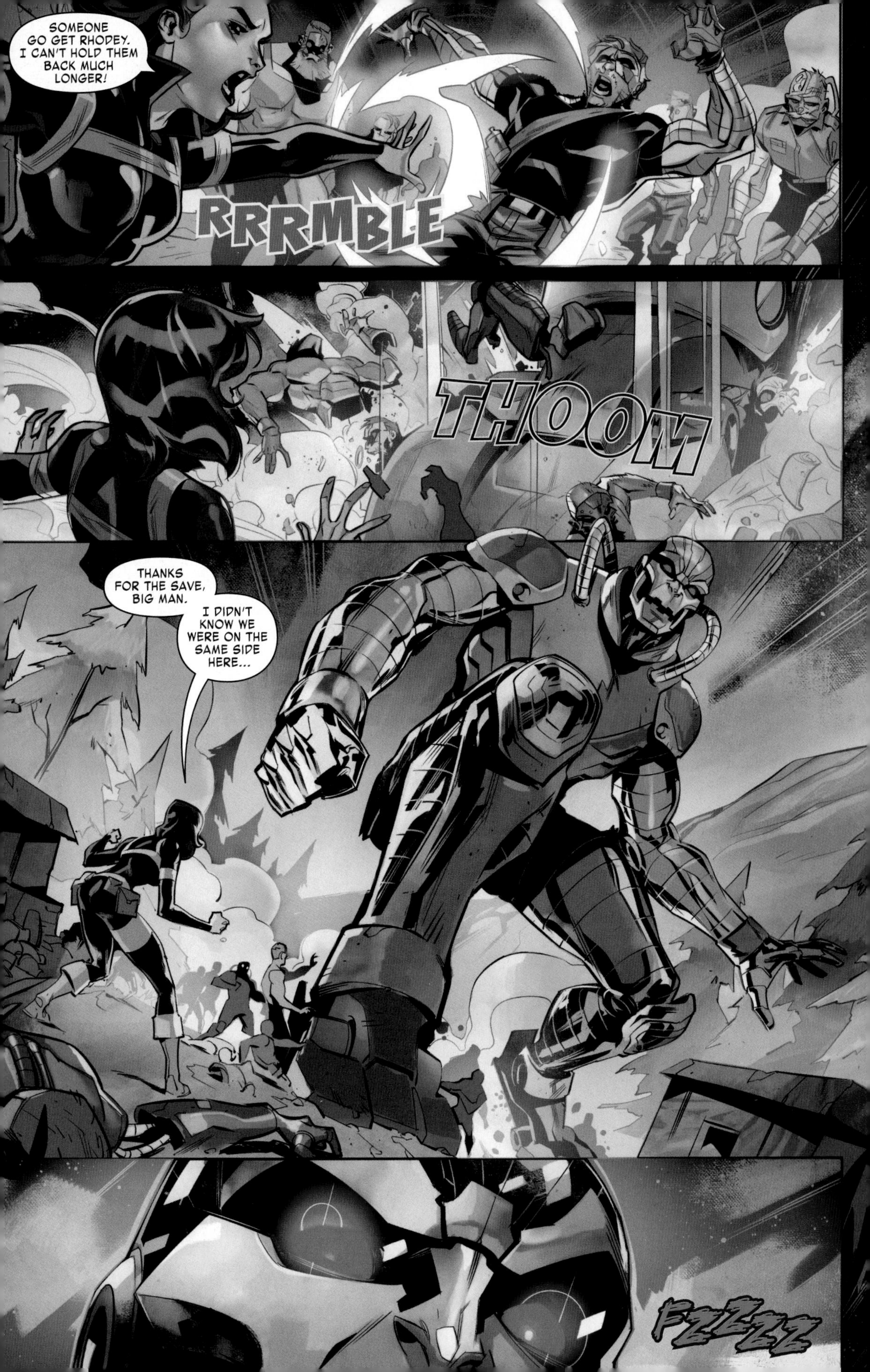
SOMEONE GO GET RHODEY. I CAN'T HOLD THEM BACK MUCH LONGER!
RRRMBLE
THOOM
THANKS FOR THE SAVE, BIG MAN.
I DIDN'T KNOW WE WERE ON THE SAME SIDE HERE...
FZZZZ

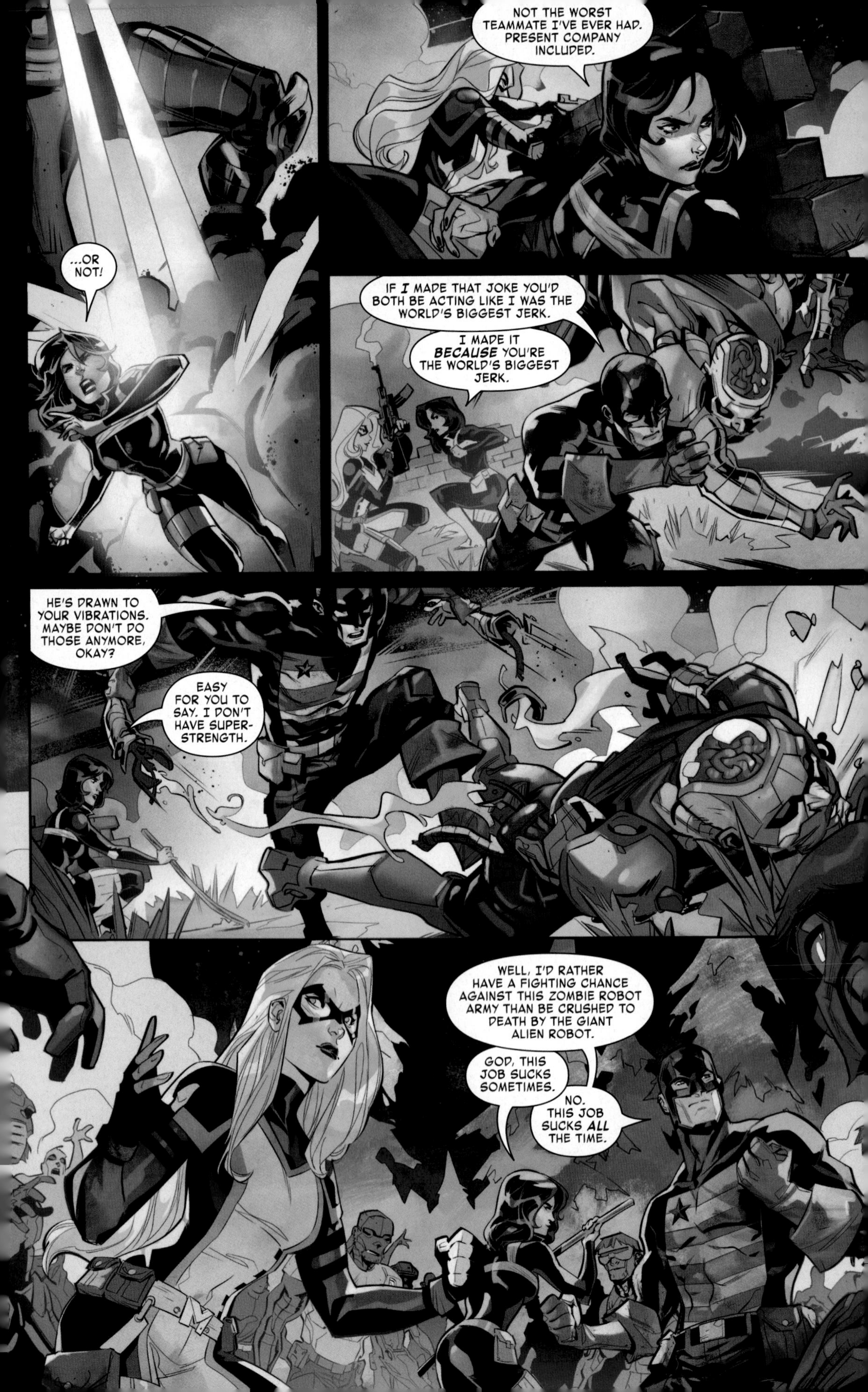
NOT THE WORST TEAMMATE I'VE EVER HAD. PRESENT COMPANY INCLUDED.
...OR NOT!
IF I MADE THAT JOKE YOU'D BOTH BE ACTING LIKE I WAS THE WORLD'S BIGGEST JERK.
I MADE IT BECAUSE YOU'RE THE WORLD'S BIGGEST JERK.
HE'S DRAWN TO YOUR VIBRATIONS. MAYBE DON'T DO THOSE ANYMORE, OKAY?
EASY FOR YOU TO SAY. I DON'T HAVE SUPER-STRENGTH.
WELL, I'D RATHER HAVE A FIGHTING CHANCE AGAINST THIS ZOMBIE ROBOT ARMY THAN BE CRUSHED TO DEATH BY THE GIANT ALIEN ROBOT.
GOD, THIS JOB SUCKS SOMETIMES.
NO. THIS JOB SUCKS ALL THE TIME.

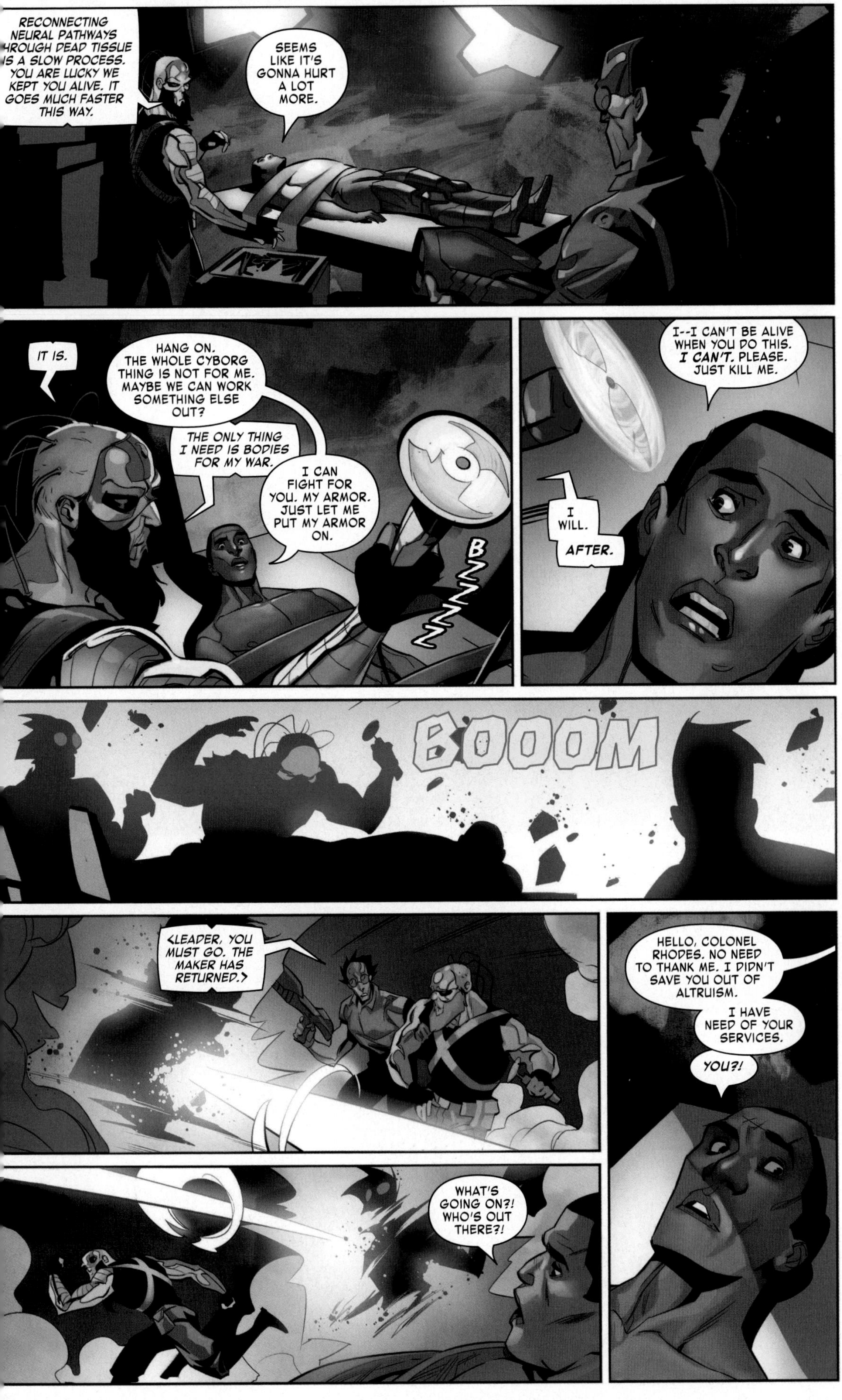
RECONNECTING NEURAL PATHWAYS THROUGH DEAD TISSUE IS A SLOW PROCESS. YOU ARE LUCKY WE KEPT YOU ALIVE. IT GOES MUCH FASTER THIS WAY.
SEEMS LIKE IT'S GONNA HURT A LOT MORE.
IT IS.
HANG ON. THE WHOLE CYBORG THING IS NOT FOR ME. MAYBE WE CAN WORK SOMETHING ELSE OUT?
THE ONLY THING I NEED IS BODIES FOR MY WAR.
I CAN FIGHT FOR YOU. MY ARMOR. JUST LET ME PUT MY ARMOR ON.
BZZZZZ
I--I CAN'T BE ALIVE WHEN YOU DO THIS. I CAN'T. PLEASE. JUST KILL ME.
I WILL.
AFTER.
BOOOM
<LEADER, YOU MUST GO. THE MAKER HAS RETURNED.>
WHAT'S GOING ON?! WHO'S OUT THERE?!
HELLO, COLONEL RHODES. NO NEED TO THANK ME. I DIDN'T SAVE YOU OUT OF ALTRUISM.
I HAVE NEED OF YOUR SERVICES.
YOU?!

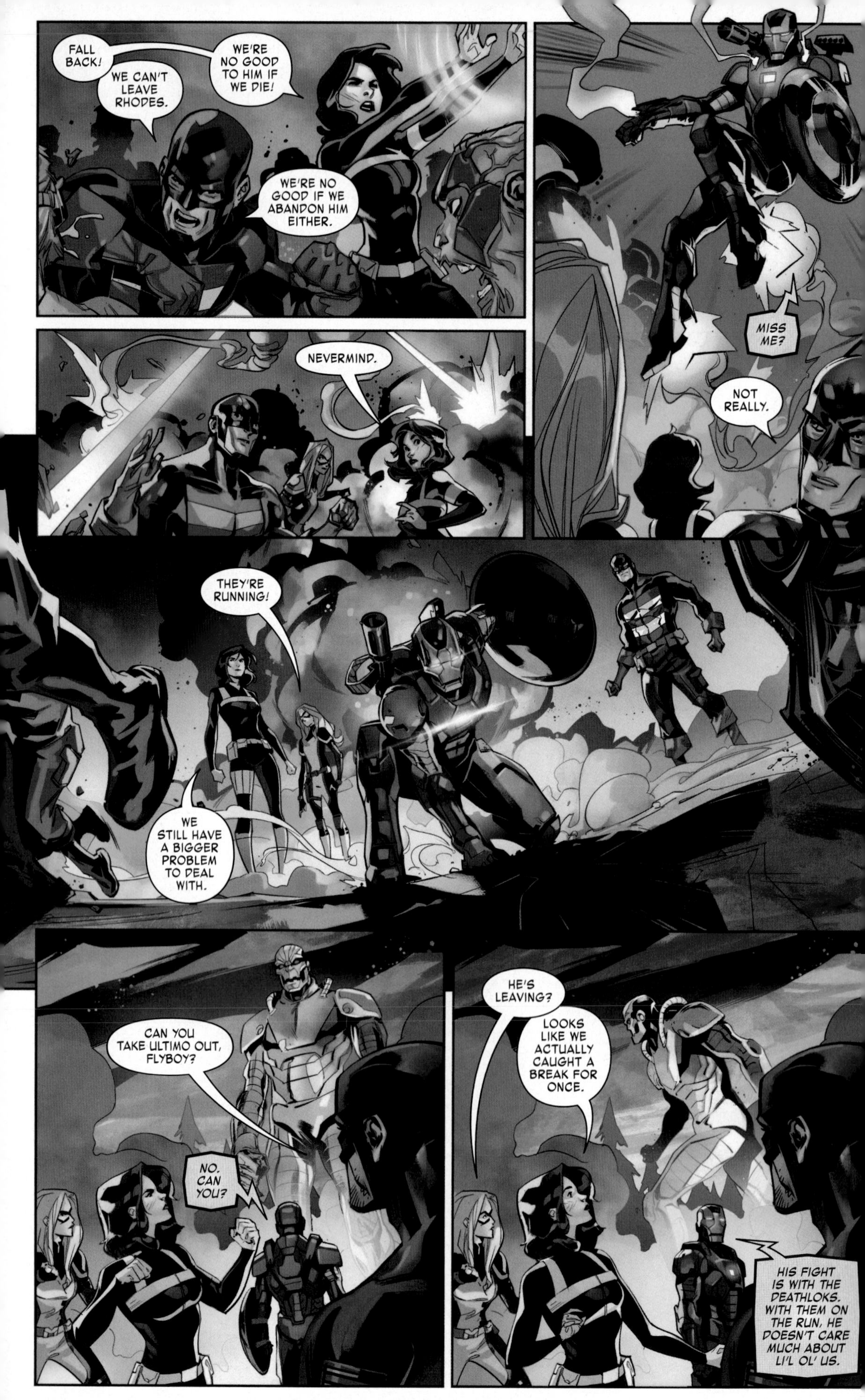
FALL BACK!
WE'RE NO GOOD TO HIM IF WE DIE!
WE CAN'T LEAVE RHODES.
WE'RE NO GOOD IF WE ABANDON HIM EITHER.
NEVERMIND.
MISS ME?
NOT REALLY.
THEY'RE RUNNING!
WE STILL HAVE A BIGGER PROBLEM TO DEAL WITH.
CAN YOU TAKE ULTIMO OUT, FLYBOY?
NO. CAN YOU?
HE'S LEAVING?
LOOKS LIKE WE ACTUALLY CAUGHT A BREAK FOR ONCE.
HIS FIGHT IS WITH THE DEATHLOKS. WITH THEM ON THE RUN, HE DOESN'T CARE MUCH ABOUT LI'L OL' US.

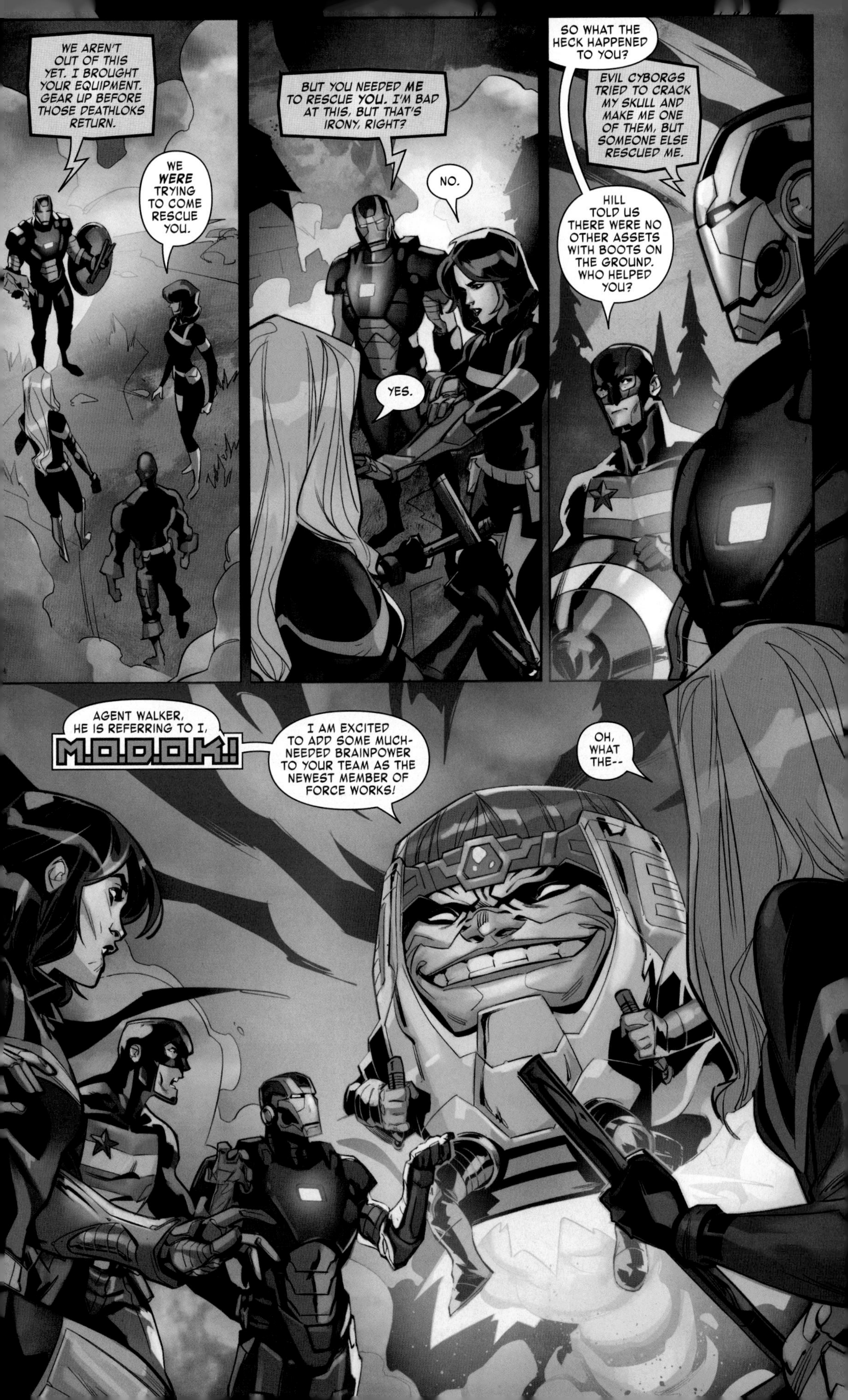

WE AREN'T OUT OF THIS YET. I BROUGHT YOUR EQUIPMENT. GEAR UP BEFORE THOSE DEATHLOKS RETURN.
WE WERE TRYING TO COME RESCUE YOU.
BUT YOU NEEDED ME TO RESCUE YOU. I'M BAD AT THIS, BUT THAT'S IRONY, RIGHT?
NO.
YES.
SO WHAT THE HECK HAPPENED TO YOU?
EVIL CYBORGS TRIED TO CRACK MY SKULL AND MAKE ME ONE OF THEM, BUT SOMEONE ELSE RESCUED ME.
HILL TOLD US THERE WERE NO OTHER ASSETS WITH BOOTS ON THE GROUND. WHO HELPED YOU?
AGENT WALKER, HE IS REFERRING TO I,
M.O.D.O.K.!
I AM EXCITED TO ADD SOME MUCH-NEEDED BRAINPOWER TO YOUR TEAM AS THE NEWEST MEMBER OF FORCE WORKS!
OH, WHAT THE--

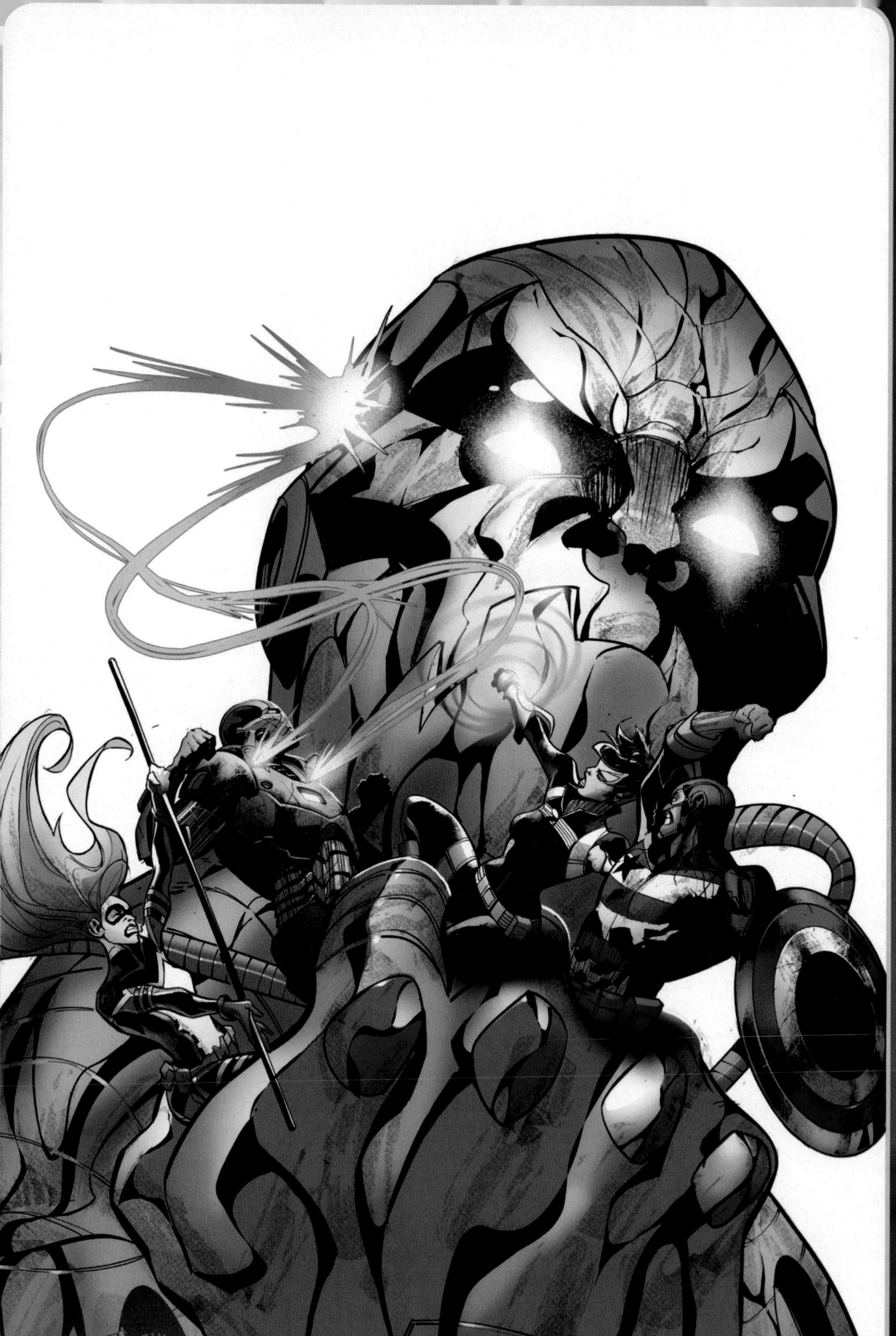

# 2020 FORCE WORKS 3

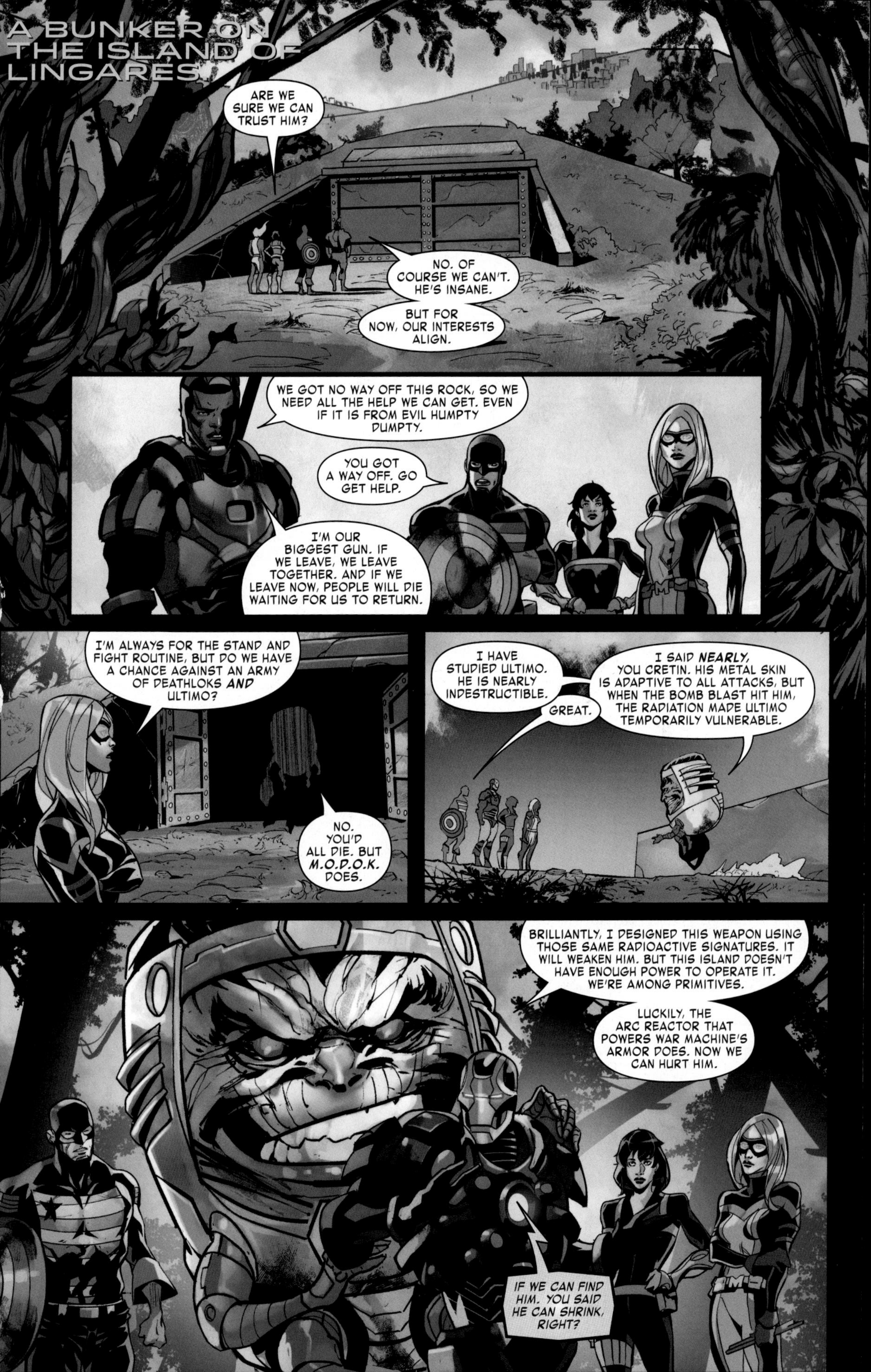
A BUNKER ON THE ISLAND OF LINGARES.
ARE WE SURE WE CAN TRUST HIM?
NO. OF COURSE WE CAN'T. HE'S INSANE.
BUT FOR NOW, OUR INTERESTS ALIGN.
WE GOT NO WAY OFF THIS ROCK, SO WE NEED ALL THE HELP WE CAN GET. EVEN IF IT IS FROM EVIL HUMPTY DUMPTY.
YOU GOT A WAY OFF. GO GET HELP.
I'M OUR BIGGEST GUN. IF WE LEAVE, WE LEAVE TOGETHER. AND IF WE LEAVE NOW, PEOPLE WILL DIE WAITING FOR US TO RETURN.
I'M ALWAYS FOR THE STAND AND FIGHT ROUTINE, BUT DO WE HAVE A CHANCE AGAINST AN ARMY OF DEATHLOKS *AND* ULTIMO?
NO. YOU'D ALL DIE. BUT *M.O.D.O.K.* DOES.
I HAVE STUDIED ULTIMO. HE IS NEARLY INDESTRUCTIBLE.
GREAT.
I SAID *NEARLY,* YOU CRETIN. HIS METAL SKIN IS ADAPTIVE TO ALL ATTACKS, BUT WHEN THE BOMB BLAST HIT HIM, THE RADIATION MADE ULTIMO TEMPORARILY VULNERABLE.
BRILLIANTLY, I DESIGNED THIS WEAPON USING THOSE SAME RADIOACTIVE SIGNATURES. IT WILL WEAKEN HIM. BUT THIS ISLAND DOESN'T HAVE ENOUGH POWER TO OPERATE IT. WE'RE AMONG PRIMITIVES.
LUCKILY, THE ARC REACTOR THAT POWERS WAR MACHINE'S ARMOR DOES. NOW WE CAN HURT HIM.
IF WE CAN FIND HIM. YOU SAID HE CAN SHRINK, RIGHT?

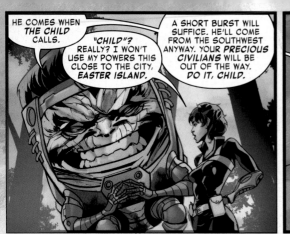

HE COMES WHEN *THE CHILD* CALLS.

"CHILD"? REALLY? I WON'T USE MY POWERS THIS CLOSE TO THE CITY, *EASTER ISLAND.*

A SHORT BURST WILL SUFFICE. HE'LL COME FROM THE SOUTHWEST ANYWAY. YOUR *PRECIOUS CIVILIANS* WILL BE OUT OF THE WAY. DO IT, CHILD.

FINE. THIS BETTER WORK. IF IT DOESN'T, YOU CAN BURY US ALL IN THE OCEAN LIKE YOUR *U.S. AGENT* WANTS.

RRRMMBBLLE

HOW DO WE KNOW HE GOT THE MESSAGE?

THOOOM

THOOOM

I THINK HE GOT IT.

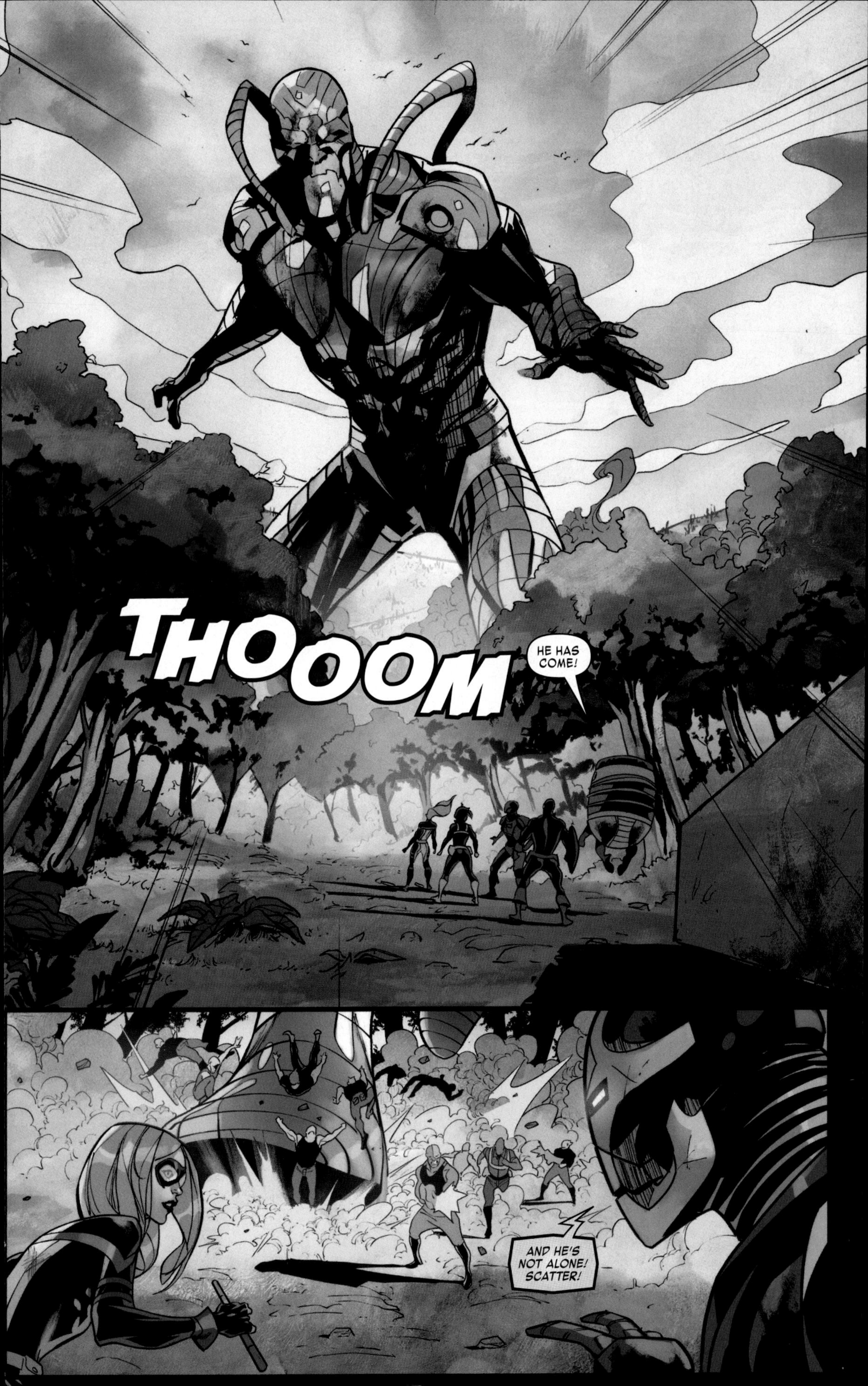
THOOOM
HE HAS COME!
AND HE'S NOT ALONE! SCATTER!

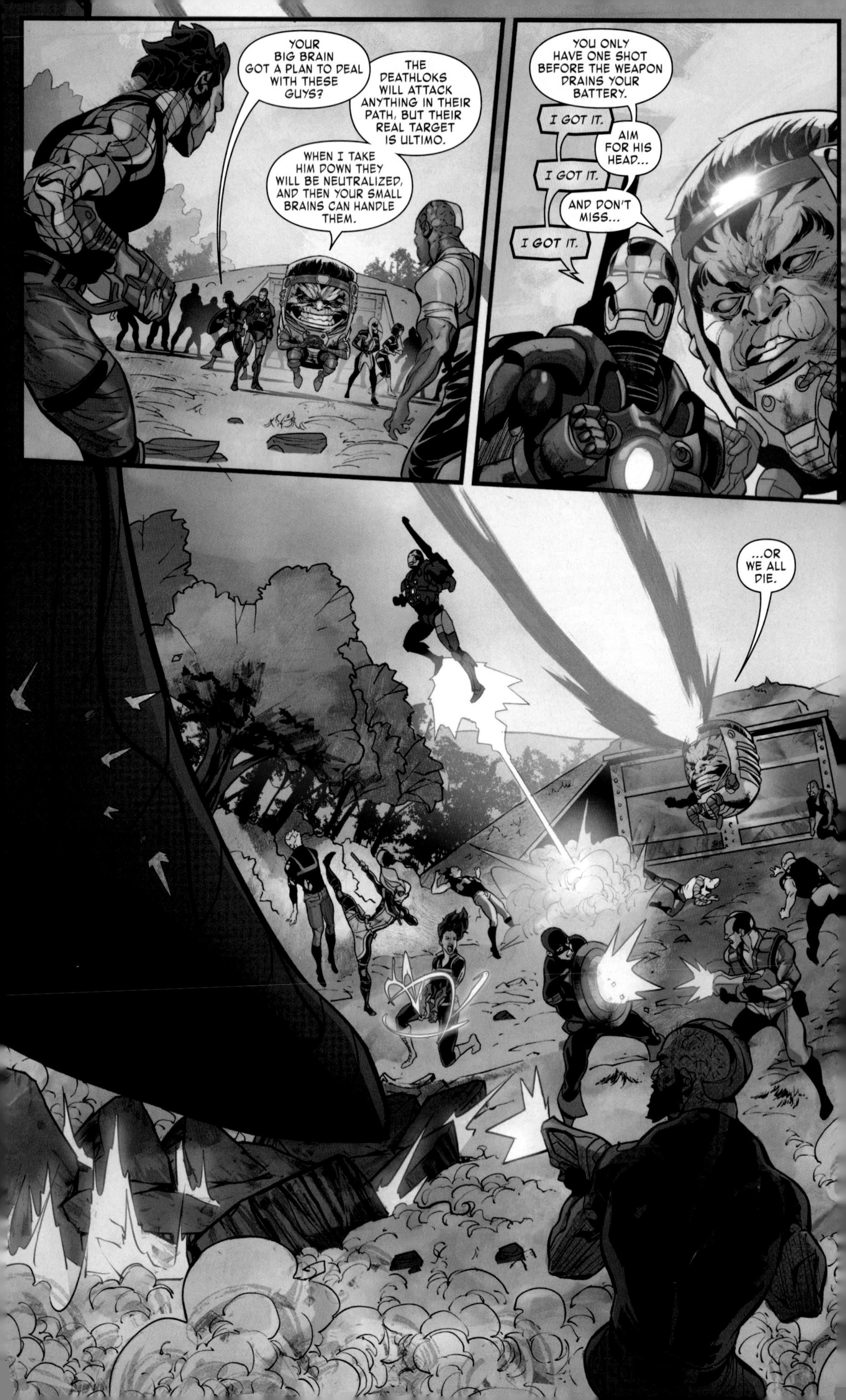
YOUR BIG BRAIN GOT A PLAN TO DEAL WITH THESE GUYS?
THE DEATHLOKS WILL ATTACK ANYTHING IN THEIR PATH, BUT THEIR REAL TARGET IS ULTIMO.
WHEN I TAKE HIM DOWN THEY WILL BE NEUTRALIZED, AND THEN YOUR SMALL BRAINS CAN HANDLE THEM.
YOU ONLY HAVE ONE SHOT BEFORE THE WEAPON DRAINS YOUR BATTERY.
I GOT IT.
AIM FOR HIS HEAD...
I GOT IT.
AND DON'T MISS...
I GOT IT.
...OR WE ALL DIE.

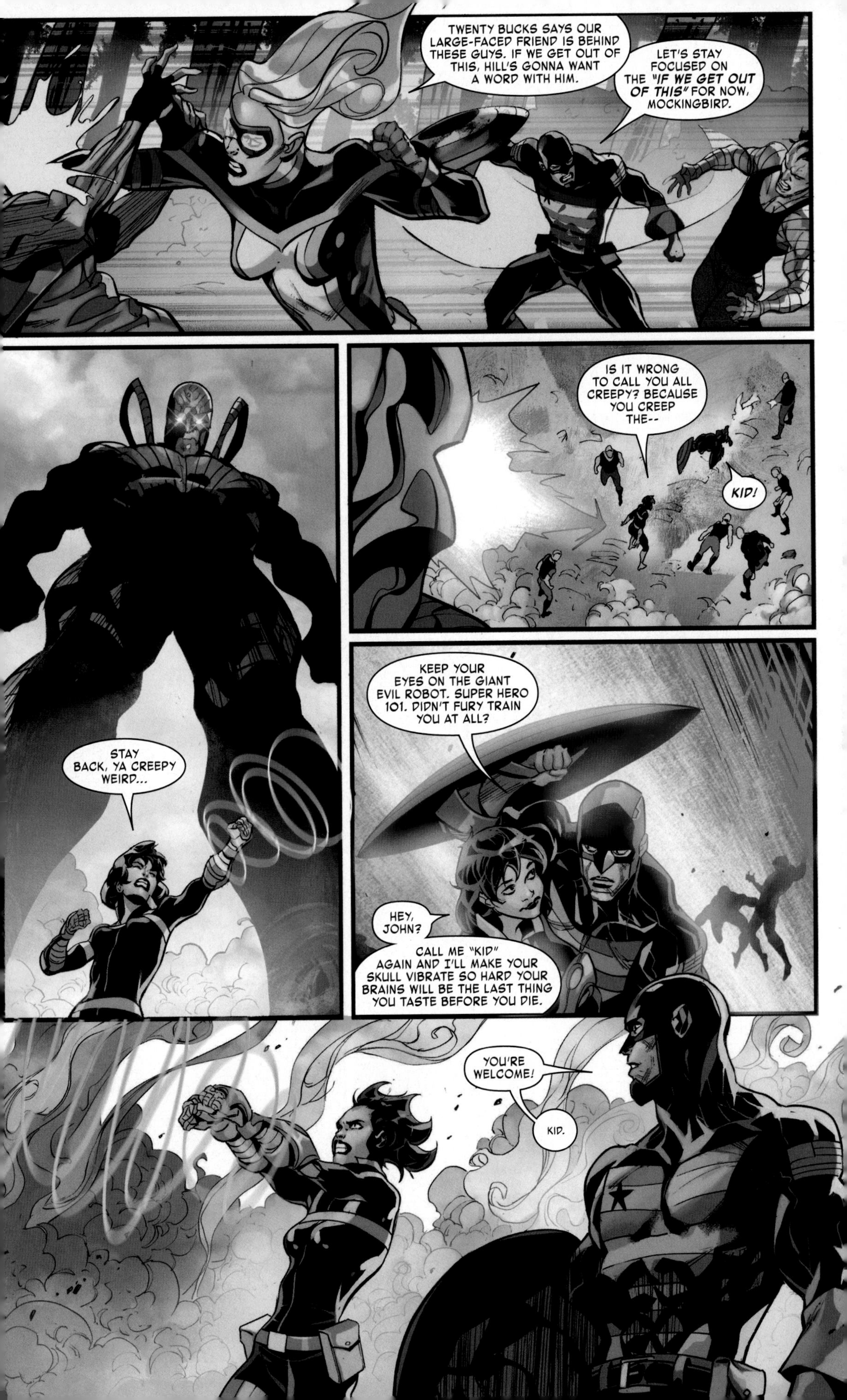

TWENTY BUCKS SAYS OUR LARGE-FACED FRIEND IS BEHIND THESE GUYS. IF WE GET OUT OF THIS, HILL'S GONNA WANT A WORD WITH HIM.
LET'S STAY FOCUSED ON THE "IF WE GET OUT OF THIS" FOR NOW, MOCKINGBIRD.
STAY BACK, YA CREEPY WEIRD...
IS IT WRONG TO CALL YOU ALL CREEPY? BECAUSE YOU CREEP THE--
KID!
KEEP YOUR EYES ON THE GIANT EVIL ROBOT. SUPER HERO 101. DIDN'T FURY TRAIN YOU AT ALL?
HEY, JOHN?
CALL ME "KID" AGAIN AND I'LL MAKE YOUR SKULL VIBRATE SO HARD YOUR BRAINS WILL BE THE LAST THING YOU TASTE BEFORE YOU DIE.
YOU'RE WELCOME!
KID.

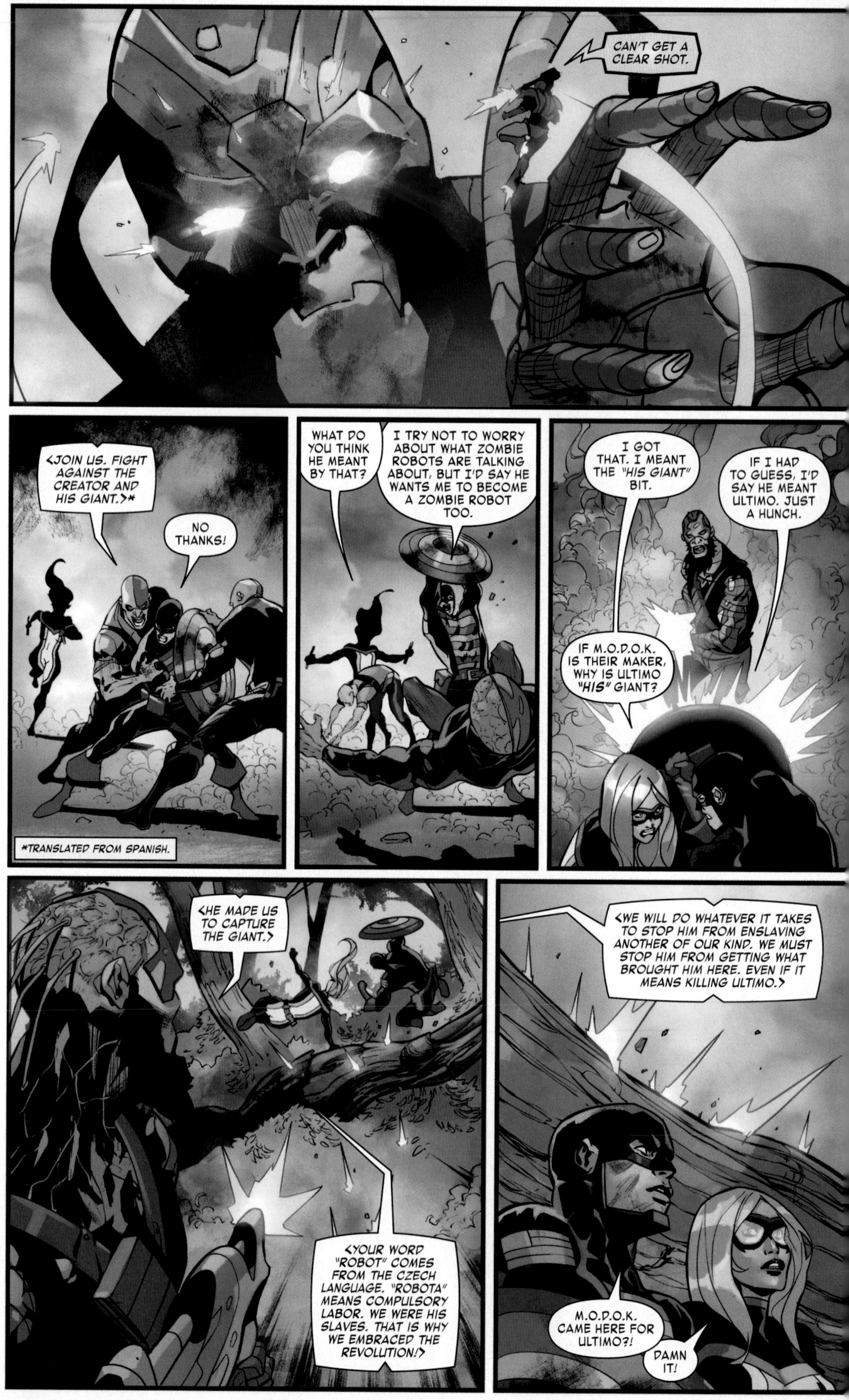
CAN'T GET A CLEAR SHOT.
<JOIN US. FIGHT AGAINST THE CREATOR AND HIS GIANT.>*
NO THANKS!
*TRANSLATED FROM SPANISH.
WHAT DO YOU THINK HE MEANT BY THAT?
I TRY NOT TO WORRY ABOUT WHAT ZOMBIE ROBOTS ARE TALKING ABOUT, BUT I'D SAY HE WANTS ME TO BECOME A ZOMBIE ROBOT TOO.
I GOT THAT. I MEANT THE "HIS GIANT" BIT.
IF I HAD TO GUESS, I'D SAY HE MEANT ULTIMO. JUST A HUNCH.
IF M.O.D.O.K. IS THEIR MAKER, WHY IS ULTIMO "HIS" GIANT?
<HE MADE US TO CAPTURE THE GIANT.>
<YOUR WORD "ROBOT" COMES FROM THE CZECH LANGUAGE. "ROBOTA" MEANS COMPULSORY LABOR. WE WERE HIS SLAVES. THAT IS WHY WE EMBRACED THE REVOLUTION!>
<WE WILL DO WHATEVER IT TAKES TO STOP HIM FROM ENSLAVING ANOTHER OF OUR KIND. WE MUST STOP HIM FROM GETTING WHAT BROUGHT HIM HERE. EVEN IF IT MEANS KILLING ULTIMO.>
M.O.D.O.K. CAME HERE FOR ULTIMO?!
DAMN IT!

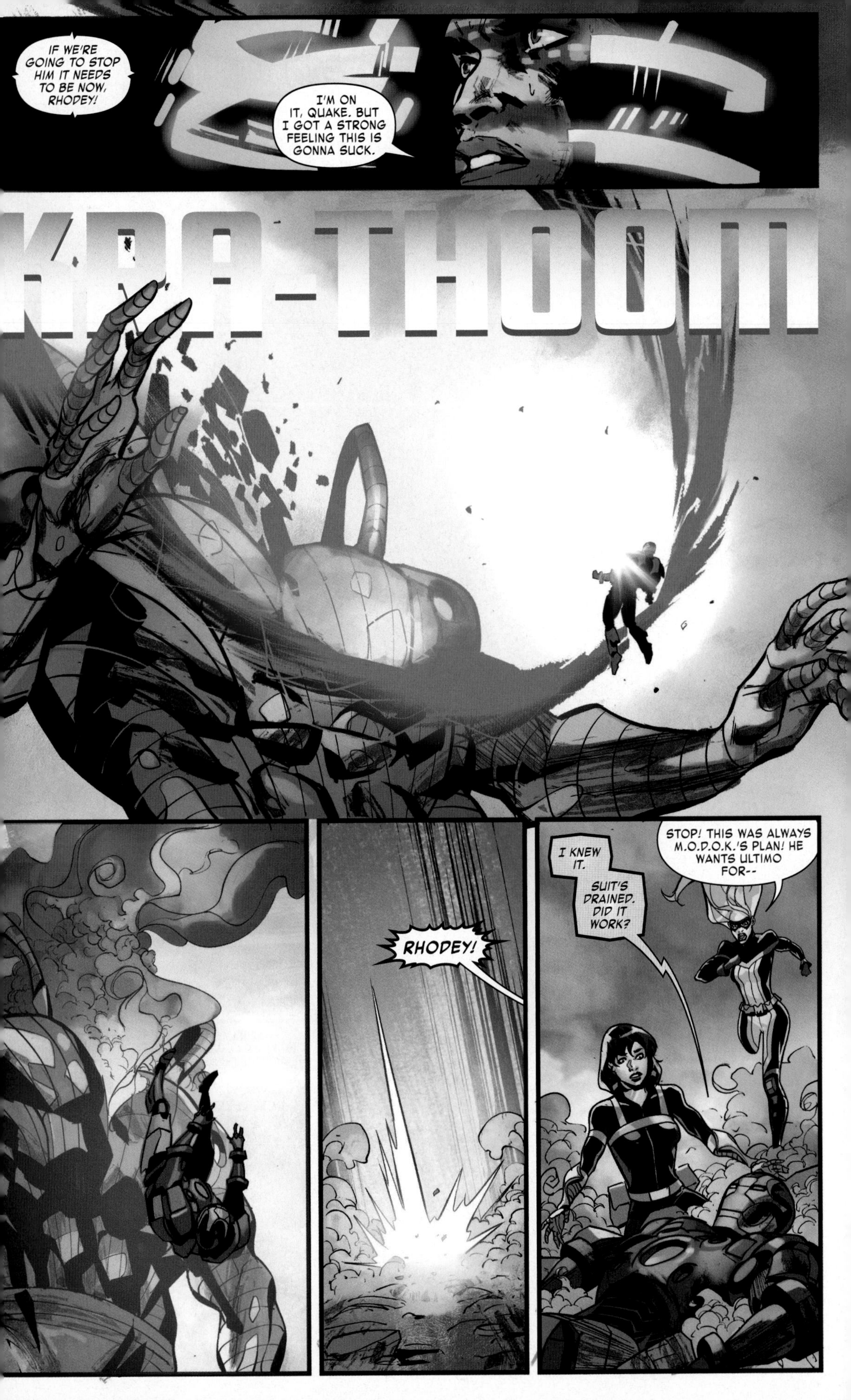
IF WE'RE GOING TO STOP HIM IT NEEDS TO BE NOW, RHODEY!
I'M ON IT, QUAKE. BUT I GOT A STRONG FEELING THIS IS GONNA SUCK.
KRA-THOOM
RHODEY!
STOP! THIS WAS ALWAYS M.O.D.O.K.'S PLAN! HE WANTS ULTIMO FOR--
I KNEW IT.
SUIT'S DRAINED. DID IT WORK?

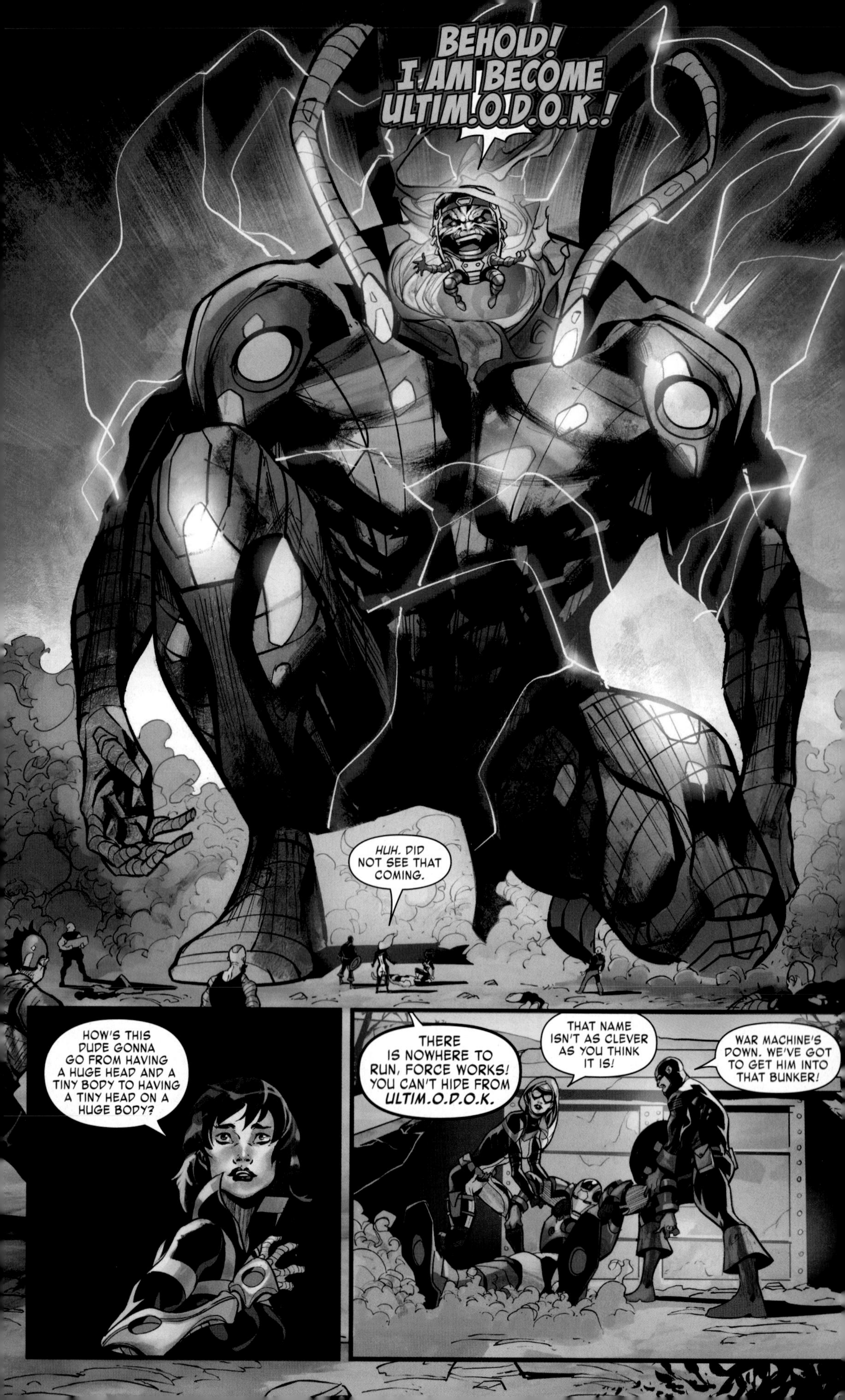
BEHOLD! I AM BECOME ULTIM.O.D.O.K.!
HUH. DID NOT SEE THAT COMING.
HOW'S THIS DUDE GONNA GO FROM HAVING A HUGE HEAD AND A TINY BODY TO HAVING A TINY HEAD ON A HUGE BODY?
THERE IS NOWHERE TO RUN, FORCE WORKS! YOU CAN'T HIDE FROM ULTIM.O.D.O.K.
THAT NAME ISN'T AS CLEVER AS YOU THINK IT IS!
WAR MACHINE'S DOWN. WE'VE GOT TO GET HIM INTO THAT BUNKER!

THAT OUGHT TO HOLD M.O.D.O.K.... FOR, LIKE, 30 SECONDS.

WE CAN'T LET HIM GET OFF THE ISLAND NOW.

STOP.

THIS IS ON US. IF HE GETS TO THE MAINLAND, HOW MANY PEOPLE DIE?

I SAID NO.

BOOM

HE'S COMING IN, KID.

I WON'T DO IT.

DO WHAT?

THE POSEIDON PROTOCOLS. IF THIS WENT SOUTH, WHICH I THINK WE CAN ALL AGREE IT HAS, QUAKE IS SUPPOSED TO SINK THE ISLAND RATHER THAN LET THIS HIT U.S. SOIL. WE GOT ENOUGH ROBOT PROBLEMS AT HOME.

THERE ARE THOUSANDS OF INNOCENT PEOPLE ON THIS ISLAND. I WON'T KILL THEM.

BOOM

IF YOU WON'T DO YOUR JOB, A LOT MORE WILL DIE. I THOUGHT YOU WANTED TO BE A SOLDIER.

I'M HAPPY BEING WHATEVER THE HELL YOU'RE NOT.

BOOM

AGENT'S RIGHT ABOUT ONE THING. WITH WAR MACHINE DOWN, WE DON'T HAVE ANYTHING ELSE THAT CAN EVEN COME CLOSE TO TAKING OUT THAT GIANT PINHEAD OUTSIDE.

IT ALSO MEANS HE CAN'T FLY US OUT OF HERE. I SINK THE ISLAND, WE GO WITH IT.

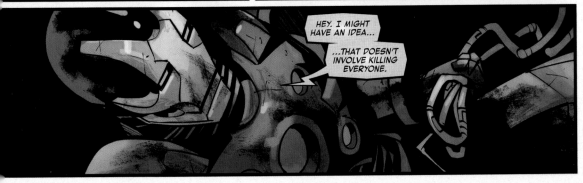

HEY. I MIGHT HAVE AN IDEA...

...THAT DOESN'T INVOLVE KILLING EVERYONE.

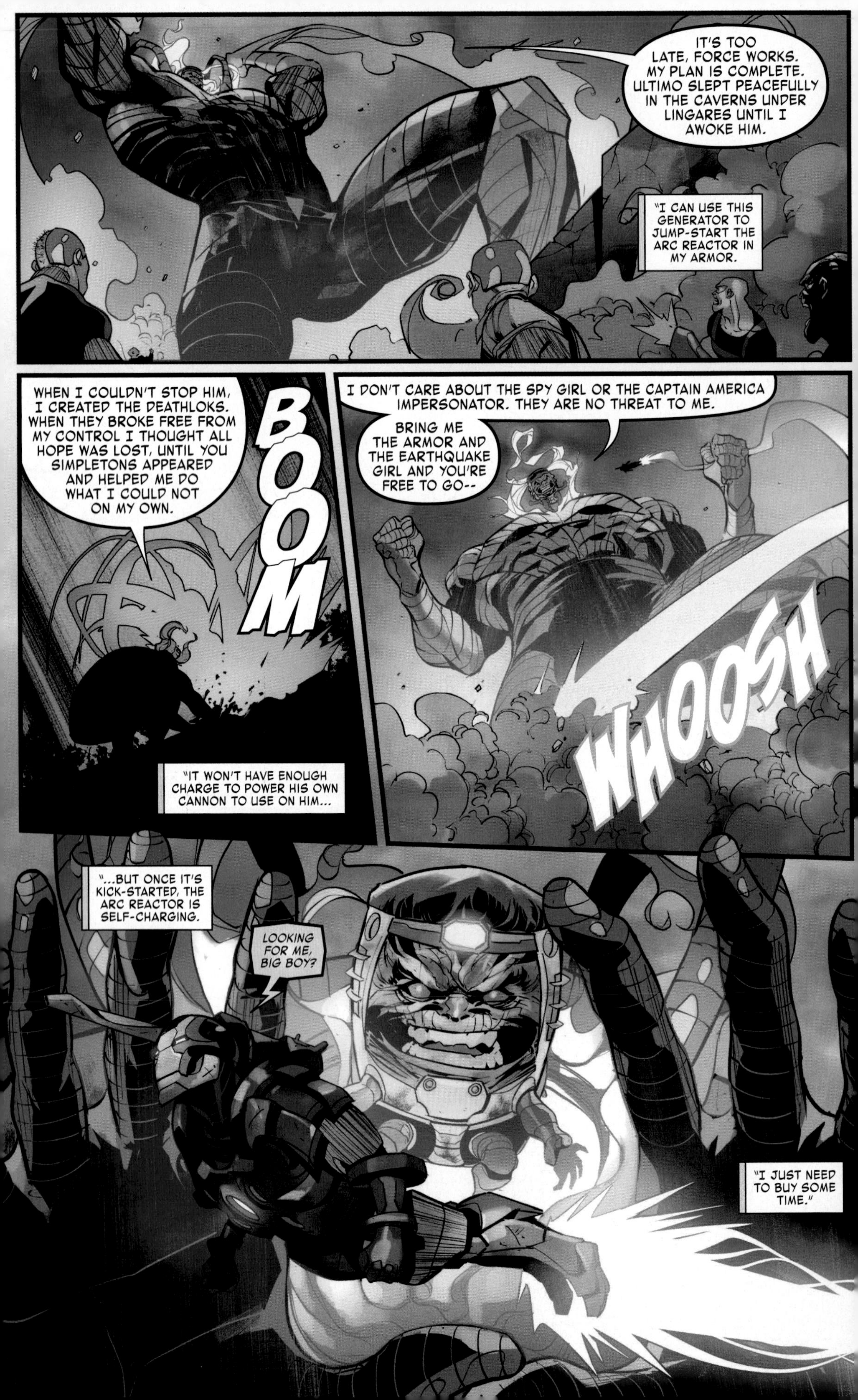
IT'S TOO LATE, FORCE WORKS. MY PLAN IS COMPLETE. ULTIMO SLEPT PEACEFULLY IN THE CAVERNS UNDER LINGARES UNTIL I AWOKE HIM.
"I CAN USE THIS GENERATOR TO JUMP-START THE ARC REACTOR IN MY ARMOR.
WHEN I COULDN'T STOP HIM, I CREATED THE DEATHLOKS. WHEN THEY BROKE FREE FROM MY CONTROL I THOUGHT ALL HOPE WAS LOST, UNTIL YOU SIMPLETONS APPEARED AND HELPED ME DO WHAT I COULD NOT ON MY OWN.
BOOM
"IT WON'T HAVE ENOUGH CHARGE TO POWER HIS OWN CANNON TO USE ON HIM...
I DON'T CARE ABOUT THE SPY GIRL OR THE CAPTAIN AMERICA IMPERSONATOR. THEY ARE NO THREAT TO ME.
BRING ME THE ARMOR AND THE EARTHQUAKE GIRL AND YOU'RE FREE TO GO--
WHOOSH
"...BUT ONCE IT'S KICK-STARTED, THE ARC REACTOR IS SELF-CHARGING.
LOOKING FOR ME, BIG BOY?
"I JUST NEED TO BUY SOME TIME."

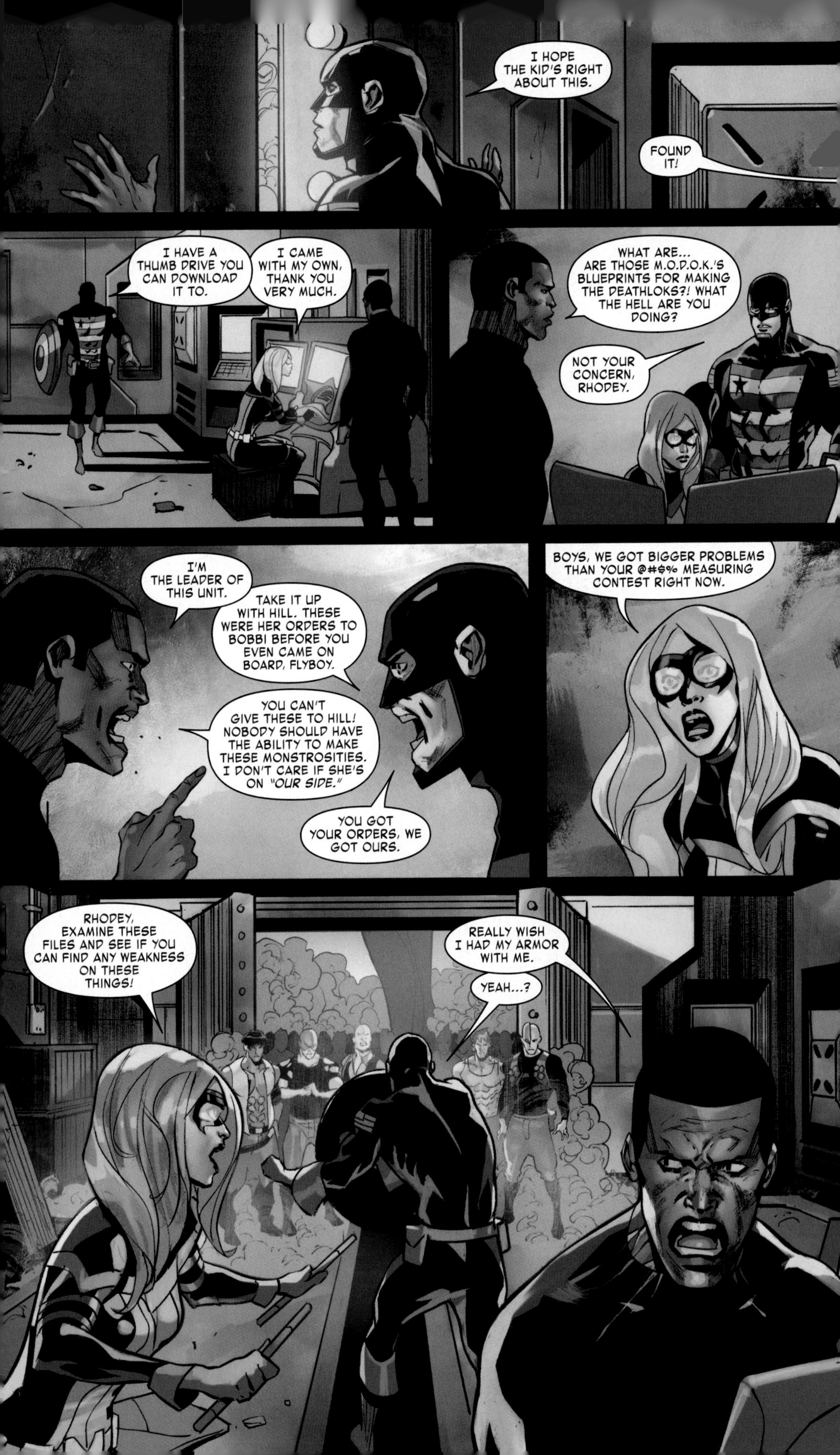
I HOPE THE KID'S RIGHT ABOUT THIS.
FOUND IT!
I HAVE A THUMB DRIVE YOU CAN DOWNLOAD IT TO.
I CAME WITH MY OWN, THANK YOU VERY MUCH.
WHAT ARE... ARE THOSE M.O.D.O.K.'S BLUEPRINTS FOR MAKING THE DEATHLOKS?! WHAT THE HELL ARE YOU DOING?
NOT YOUR CONCERN, RHODEY.
I'M THE LEADER OF THIS UNIT.
TAKE IT UP WITH HILL. THESE WERE HER ORDERS TO BOBBI BEFORE YOU EVEN CAME ON BOARD, FLYBOY.
YOU CAN'T GIVE THESE TO HILL! NOBODY SHOULD HAVE THE ABILITY TO MAKE THESE MONSTROSITIES. I DON'T CARE IF SHE'S ON "OUR SIDE."
YOU GOT YOUR ORDERS, WE GOT OURS.
BOYS, WE GOT BIGGER PROBLEMS THAN YOUR @#$% MEASURING CONTEST RIGHT NOW.
RHODEY, EXAMINE THESE FILES AND SEE IF YOU CAN FIND ANY WEAKNESS ON THESE THINGS!
REALLY WISH I HAD MY ARMOR WITH ME.
YEAH...?

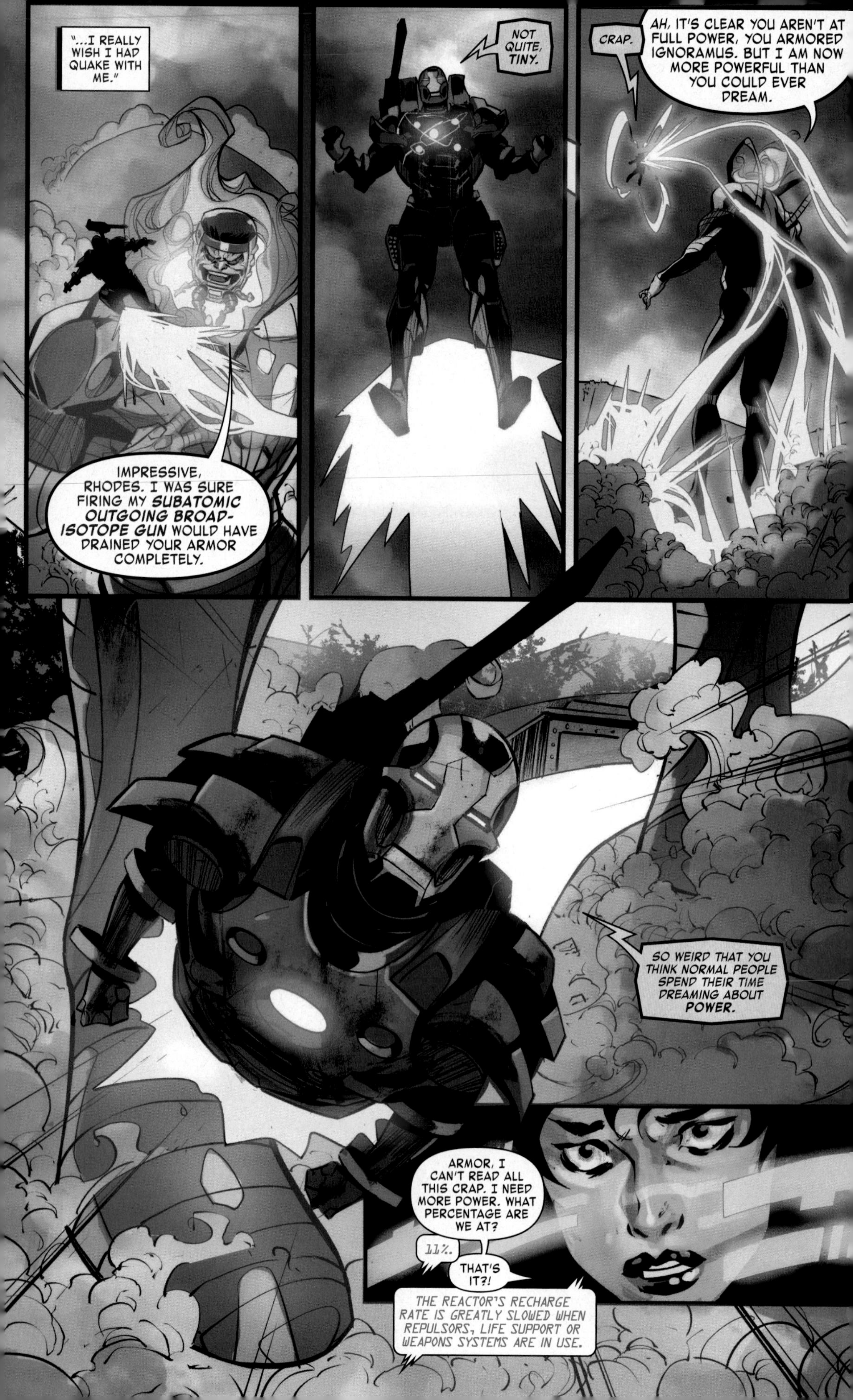
"...I REALLY WISH I HAD QUAKE WITH ME."
IMPRESSIVE, RHODES. I WAS SURE FIRING MY SUBATOMIC OUTGOING BROAD-ISOTOPE GUN WOULD HAVE DRAINED YOUR ARMOR COMPLETELY.
NOT QUITE, TINY.
CRAP.
AH, IT'S CLEAR YOU AREN'T AT FULL POWER, YOU ARMORED IGNORAMUS. BUT I AM NOW MORE POWERFUL THAN YOU COULD EVER DREAM.
SO WEIRD THAT YOU THINK NORMAL PEOPLE SPEND THEIR TIME DREAMING ABOUT POWER.
ARMOR, I CAN'T READ ALL THIS CRAP. I NEED MORE POWER. WHAT PERCENTAGE ARE WE AT?
11%.
THAT'S IT?!
THE REACTOR'S RECHARGE RATE IS GREATLY SLOWED WHEN REPULSORS, LIFE SUPPORT OR WEAPONS SYSTEMS ARE IN USE.

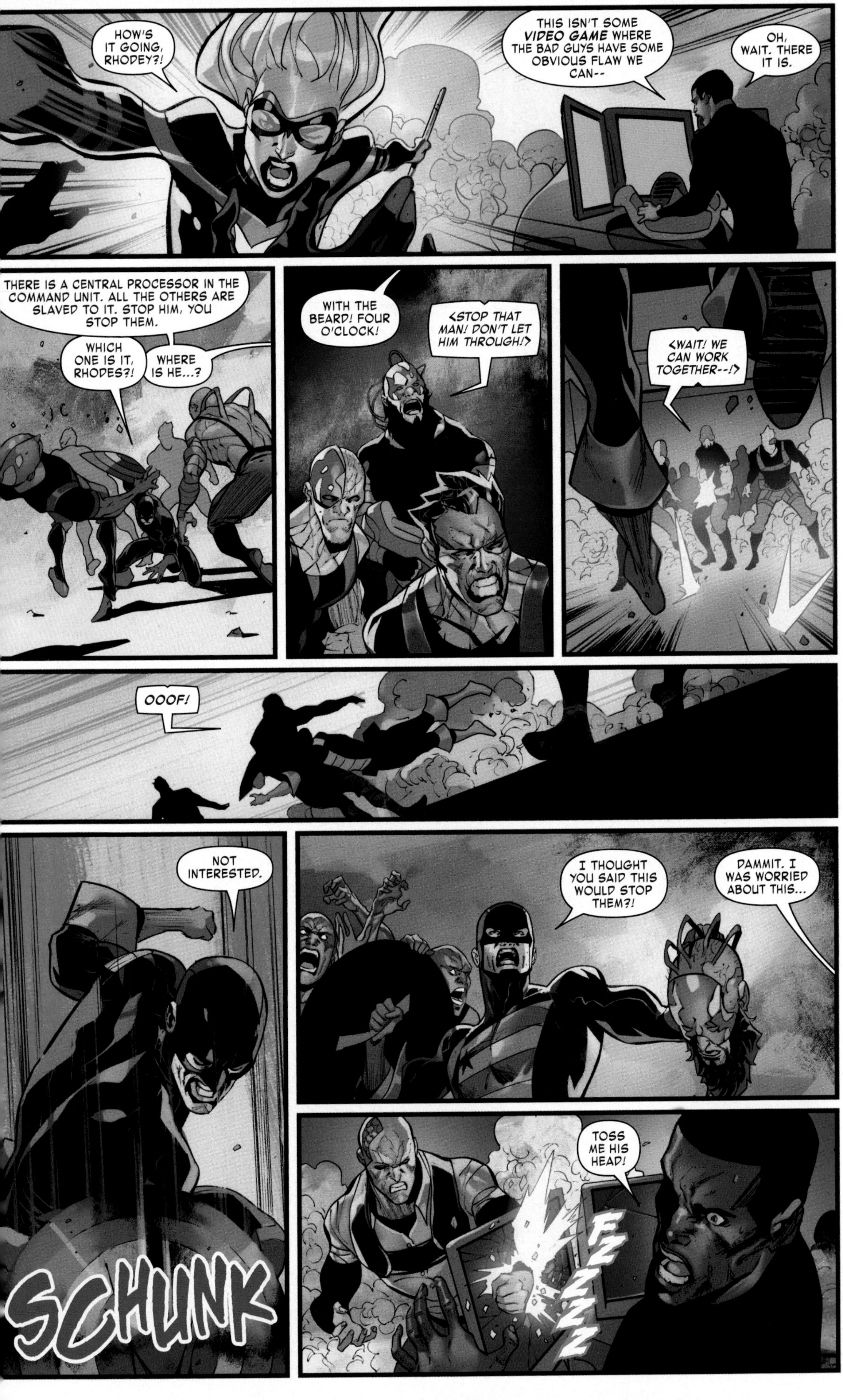
HOW'S IT GOING, RHODEY?!
THIS ISN'T SOME *VIDEO GAME* WHERE THE BAD GUYS HAVE SOME OBVIOUS FLAW WE CAN--
OH, WAIT. THERE IT IS.
THERE IS A CENTRAL PROCESSOR IN THE COMMAND UNIT. ALL THE OTHERS ARE SLAVED TO IT. STOP HIM, YOU STOP THEM.
WHICH ONE IS IT, RHODES?!
WHERE IS HE...?
WITH THE BEARD! FOUR O'CLOCK!
*<STOP THAT MAN! DON'T LET HIM THROUGH!>*
*<WAIT! WE CAN WORK TOGETHER--!>*
*OOOF!*
NOT INTERESTED.
SCHUNK
I THOUGHT YOU SAID THIS WOULD STOP THEM?!
DAMMIT. I WAS WORRIED ABOUT THIS...
TOSS ME HIS HEAD!
FZZZZZ

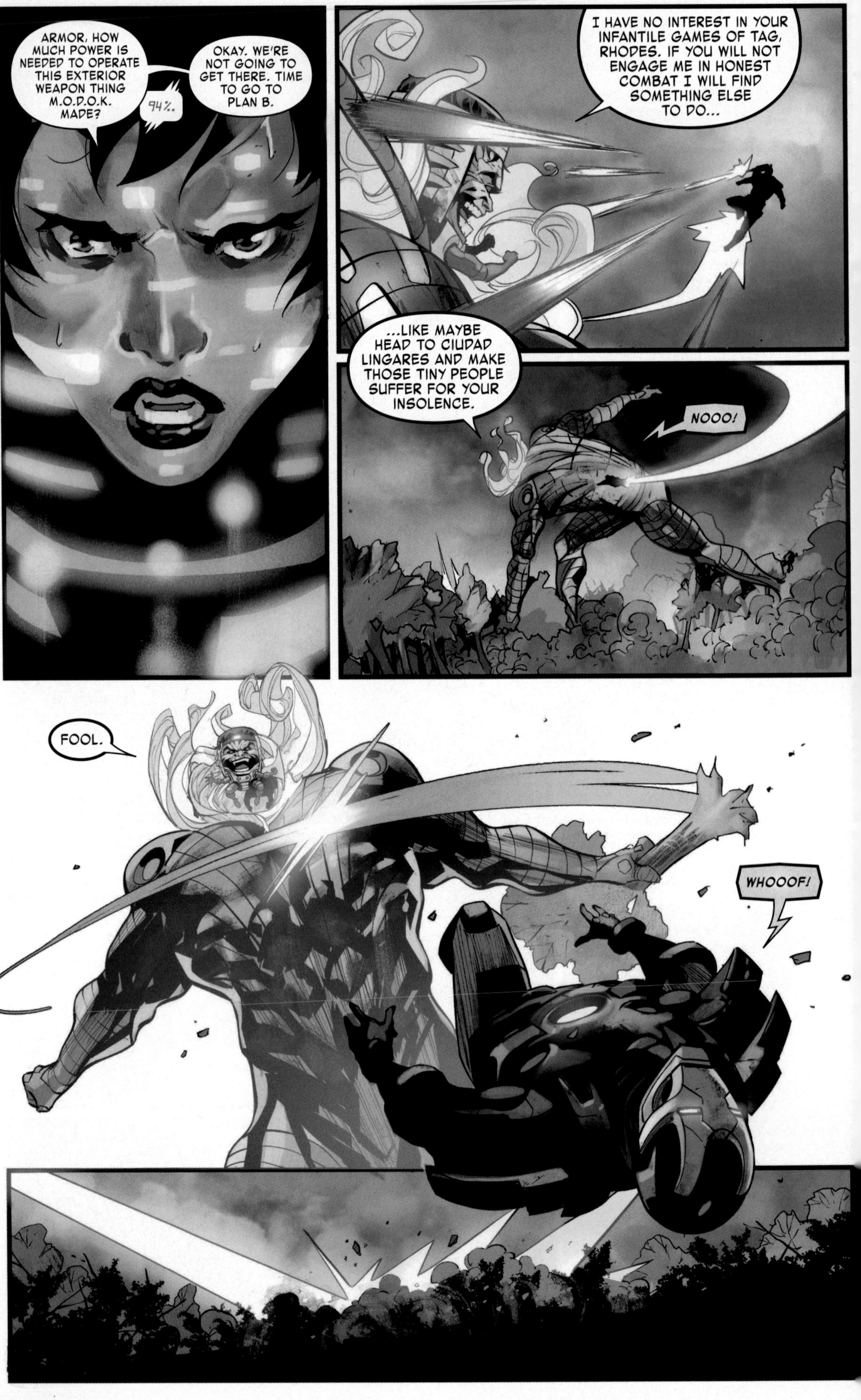
ARMOR, HOW MUCH POWER IS NEEDED TO OPERATE THIS EXTERIOR WEAPON THING M.O.D.O.K. MADE?
94%.
OKAY. WE'RE NOT GOING TO GET THERE. TIME TO GO TO PLAN B.
I HAVE NO INTEREST IN YOUR INFANTILE GAMES OF TAG, RHODES. IF YOU WILL NOT ENGAGE ME IN HONEST COMBAT I WILL FIND SOMETHING ELSE TO DO...
...LIKE MAYBE HEAD TO CIUDAD LINGARES AND MAKE THOSE TINY PEOPLE SUFFER FOR YOUR INSOLENCE.
NOOO!
FOOL.
WHOOOF!

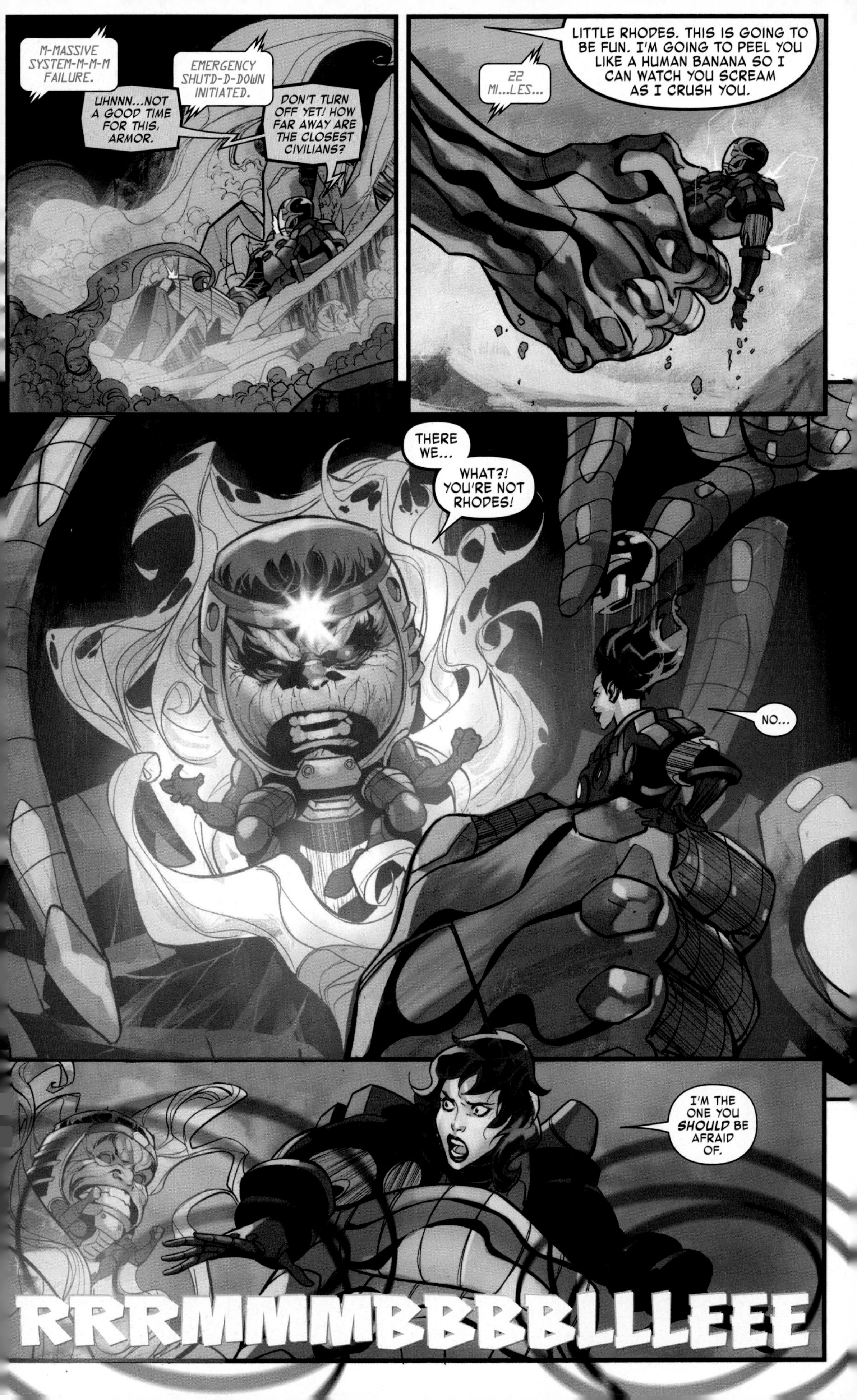
M-MASSIVE SYSTEM-M-M-M FAILURE.
UHNNN...NOT A GOOD TIME FOR THIS, ARMOR.
EMERGENCY SHUTD-D-DOWN INITIATED.
DON'T TURN OFF YET! HOW FAR AWAY ARE THE CLOSEST CIVILIANS?
22 MI...LES...
LITTLE RHODES. THIS IS GOING TO BE FUN. I'M GOING TO PEEL YOU LIKE A HUMAN BANANA SO I CAN WATCH YOU SCREAM AS I CRUSH YOU.
THERE WE...
WHAT?! YOU'RE NOT RHODES!
NO...
I'M THE ONE YOU SHOULD BE AFRAID OF.
RRRMMMMBBBBLLLEEE

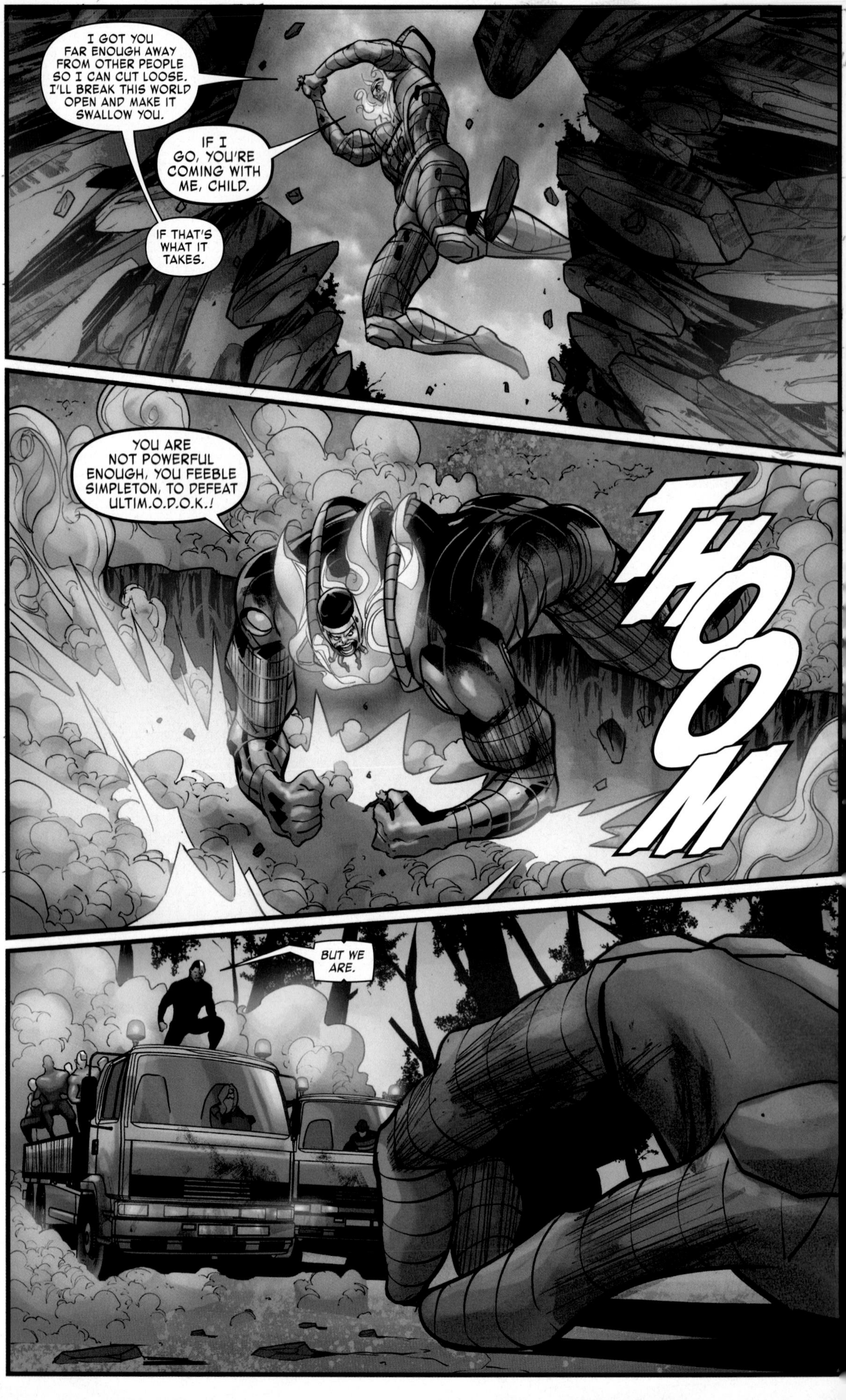
I GOT YOU FAR ENOUGH AWAY FROM OTHER PEOPLE SO I CAN CUT LOOSE. I'LL BREAK THIS WORLD OPEN AND MAKE IT SWALLOW YOU.
IF I GO, YOU'RE COMING WITH ME, CHILD.
IF THAT'S WHAT IT TAKES.
YOU ARE NOT POWERFUL ENOUGH, YOU FEEBLE SIMPLETON, TO DEFEAT ULTIM.O.D.O.K.!
THOOM
BUT WE ARE.

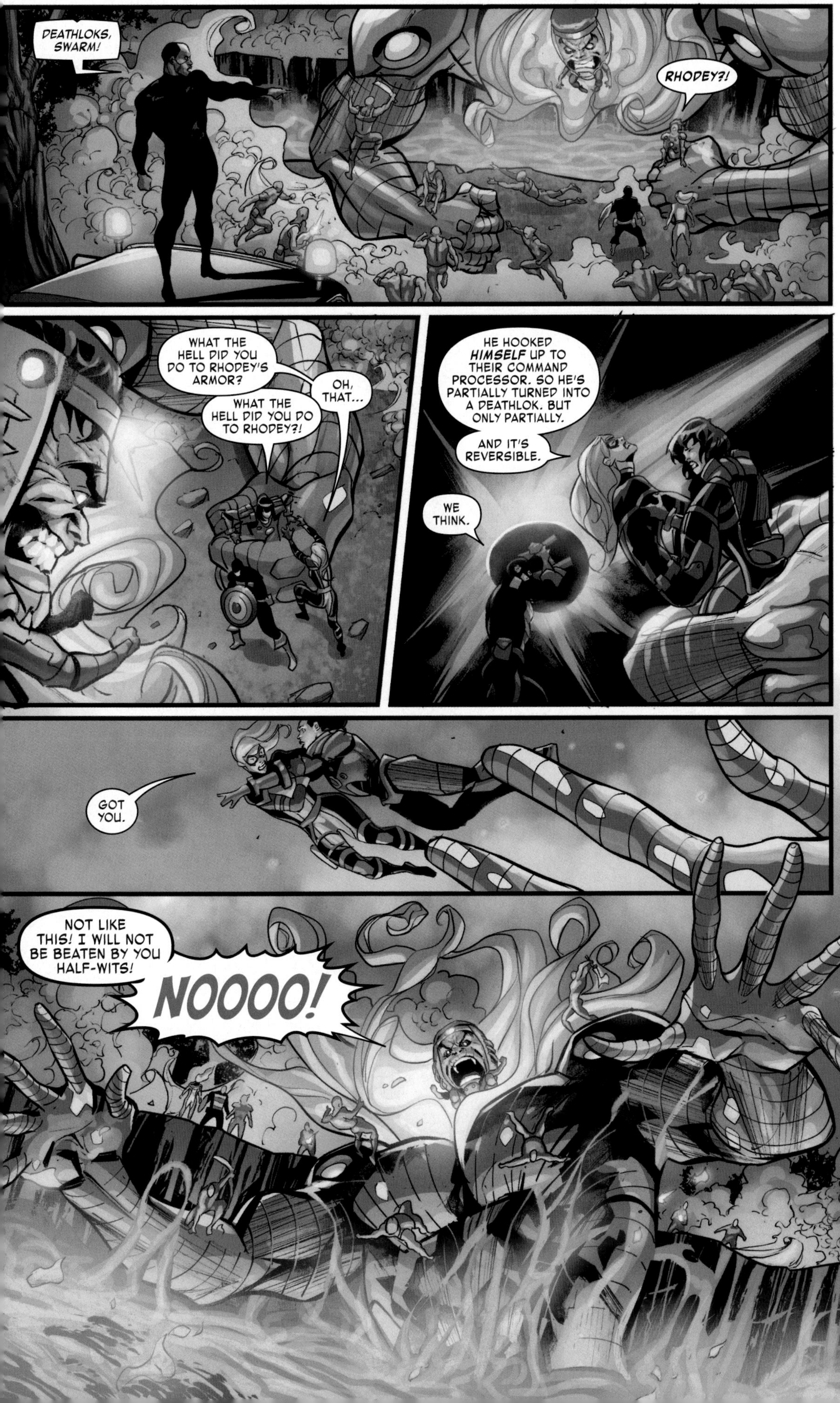
DEATHLOKS, SWARM!
RHODEY?!
WHAT THE HELL DID YOU DO TO RHODEY'S ARMOR?
WHAT THE HELL DID YOU DO TO RHODEY?!
OH, THAT...
HE HOOKED HIMSELF UP TO THEIR COMMAND PROCESSOR. SO HE'S PARTIALLY TURNED INTO A DEATHLOK. BUT ONLY PARTIALLY.
AND IT'S REVERSIBLE.
WE THINK.
GOT YOU.
NOT LIKE THIS! I WILL NOT BE BEATEN BY YOU HALF-WITS!
NOOOO!

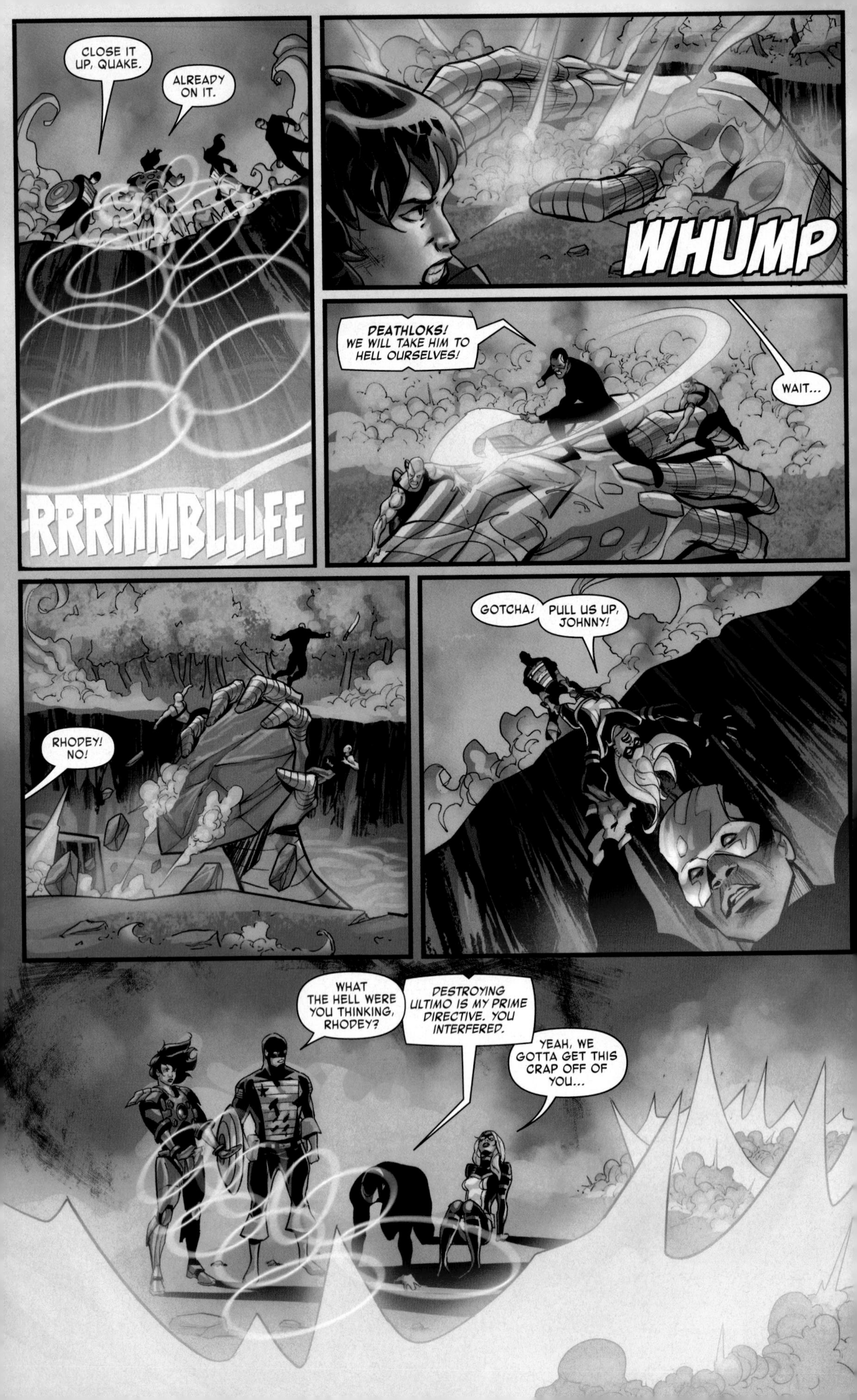
CLOSE IT UP, QUAKE.
ALREADY ON IT.
RRRMMBLLLEE
WHUMP
DEATHLOKS! WE WILL TAKE HIM TO HELL OURSELVES!
WAIT...
RHODEY! NO!
GOTCHA!
PULL US UP, JOHNNY!
WHAT THE HELL WERE YOU THINKING, RHODEY?
DESTROYING ULTIMO IS MY PRIME DIRECTIVE. YOU INTERFERED.
YEAH, WE GOTTA GET THIS CRAP OFF OF YOU...

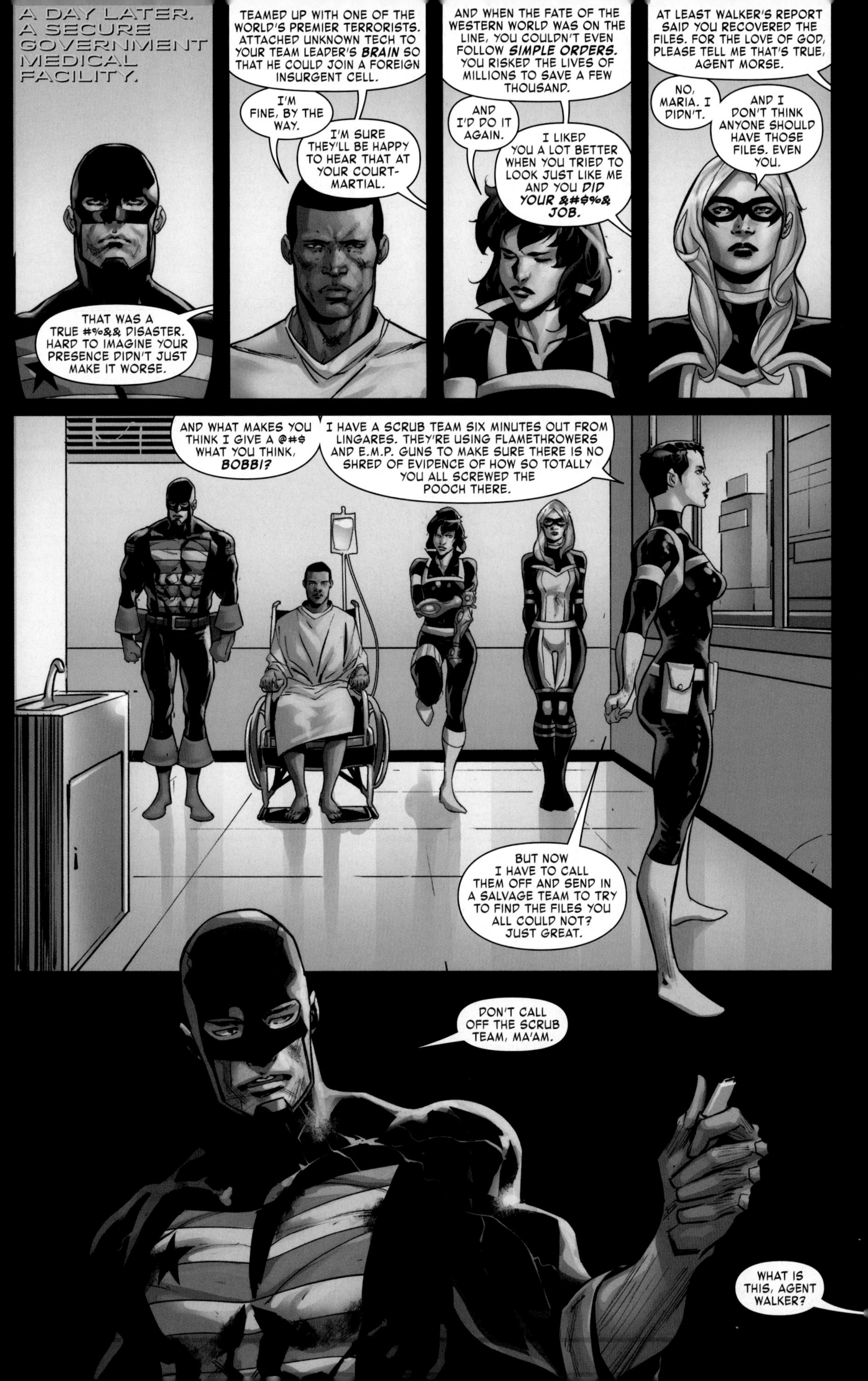

A DAY LATER. A SECURE GOVERNMENT MEDICAL FACILITY.
THAT WAS A TRUE #%&& DISASTER. HARD TO IMAGINE YOUR PRESENCE DIDN'T JUST MAKE IT WORSE.
TEAMED UP WITH ONE OF THE WORLD'S PREMIER TERRORISTS. ATTACHED UNKNOWN TECH TO YOUR TEAM LEADER'S BRAIN SO THAT HE COULD JOIN A FOREIGN INSURGENT CELL.
I'M FINE, BY THE WAY.
I'M SURE THEY'LL BE HAPPY TO HEAR THAT AT YOUR COURT-MARTIAL.
AND WHEN THE FATE OF THE WESTERN WORLD WAS ON THE LINE, YOU COULDN'T EVEN FOLLOW SIMPLE ORDERS. YOU RISKED THE LIVES OF MILLIONS TO SAVE A FEW THOUSAND.
AND I'D DO IT AGAIN.
I LIKED YOU A LOT BETTER WHEN YOU TRIED TO LOOK JUST LIKE ME AND YOU DID YOUR &#$%& JOB.
AT LEAST WALKER'S REPORT SAID YOU RECOVERED THE FILES. FOR THE LOVE OF GOD, PLEASE TELL ME THAT'S TRUE, AGENT MORSE.
NO, MARIA. I DIDN'T.
AND I DON'T THINK ANYONE SHOULD HAVE THOSE FILES. EVEN YOU.
AND WHAT MAKES YOU THINK I GIVE A @#$ WHAT YOU THINK, BOBBI?
I HAVE A SCRUB TEAM SIX MINUTES OUT FROM LINGARES. THEY'RE USING FLAMETHROWERS AND E.M.P. GUNS TO MAKE SURE THERE IS NO SHRED OF EVIDENCE OF HOW SO TOTALLY YOU ALL SCREWED THE POOCH THERE.
BUT NOW I HAVE TO CALL THEM OFF AND SEND IN A SALVAGE TEAM TO TRY TO FIND THE FILES YOU ALL COULD NOT? JUST GREAT.
DON'T CALL OFF THE SCRUB TEAM, MA'AM.
WHAT IS THIS, AGENT WALKER?

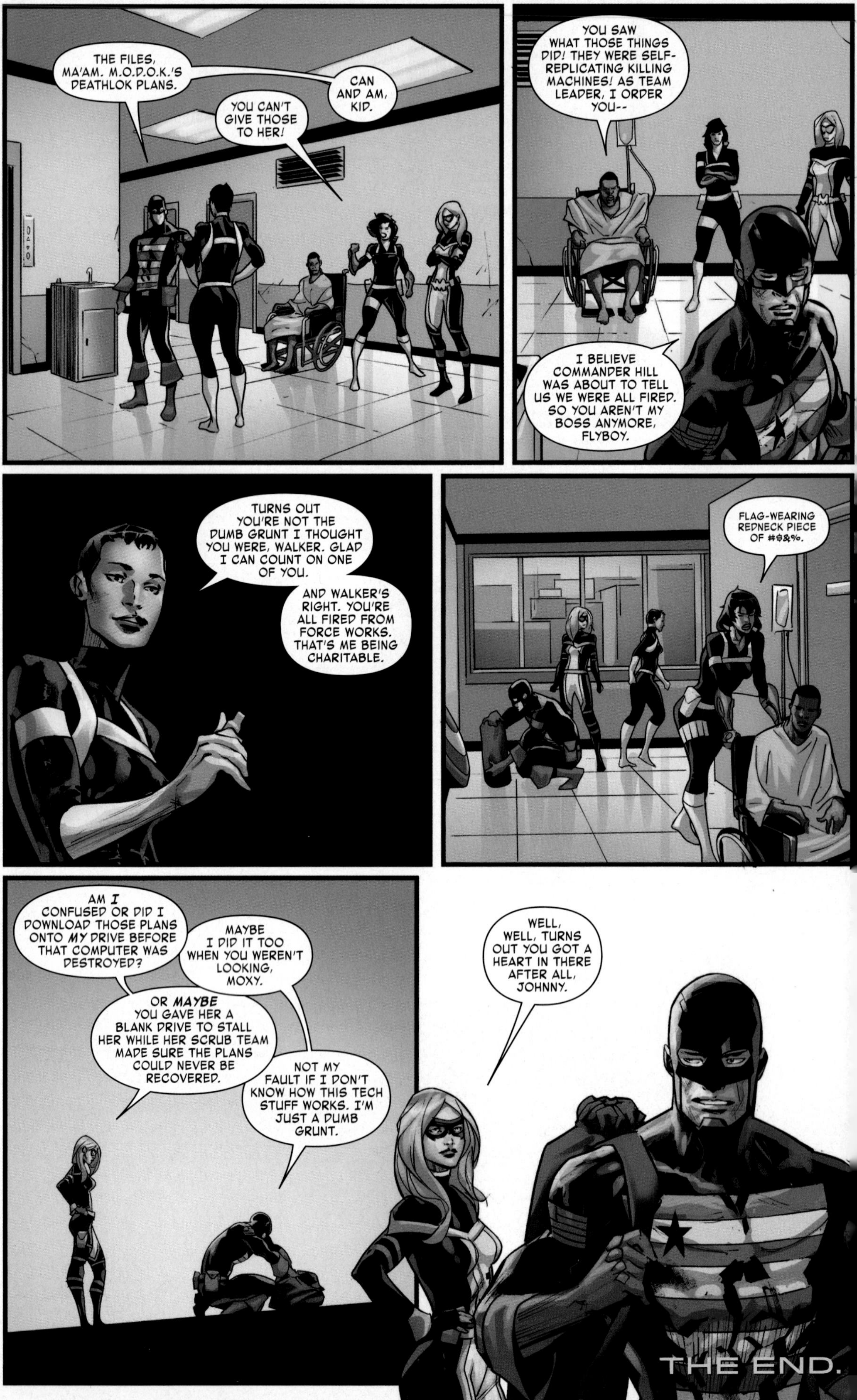
THE FILES, MA'AM. M.O.D.O.K.'S DEATHLOK PLANS.
CAN AND AM, KID.
YOU CAN'T GIVE THOSE TO HER!
YOU SAW WHAT THOSE THINGS DID! THEY WERE SELF-REPLICATING KILLING MACHINES! AS TEAM LEADER, I ORDER YOU--
I BELIEVE COMMANDER HILL WAS ABOUT TO TELL US WE WERE ALL FIRED. SO YOU AREN'T MY BOSS ANYMORE, FLYBOY.
TURNS OUT YOU'RE NOT THE DUMB GRUNT I THOUGHT YOU WERE, WALKER. GLAD I CAN COUNT ON ONE OF YOU.
AND WALKER'S RIGHT. YOU'RE ALL FIRED FROM FORCE WORKS. THAT'S ME BEING CHARITABLE.
FLAG-WEARING REDNECK PIECE OF #$&%.
AM *I* CONFUSED OR DID I DOWNLOAD THOSE PLANS ONTO *MY* DRIVE BEFORE THAT COMPUTER WAS DESTROYED?
MAYBE I DID IT TOO WHEN YOU WEREN'T LOOKING, MOXY.
OR ***MAYBE*** YOU GAVE HER A BLANK DRIVE TO STALL HER WHILE HER SCRUB TEAM MADE SURE THE PLANS COULD NEVER BE RECOVERED.
NOT MY FAULT IF I DON'T KNOW HOW THIS TECH STUFF WORKS. I'M JUST A DUMB GRUNT.
WELL, WELL, TURNS OUT YOU GOT A HEART IN THERE AFTER ALL, JOHNNY.
THE END.

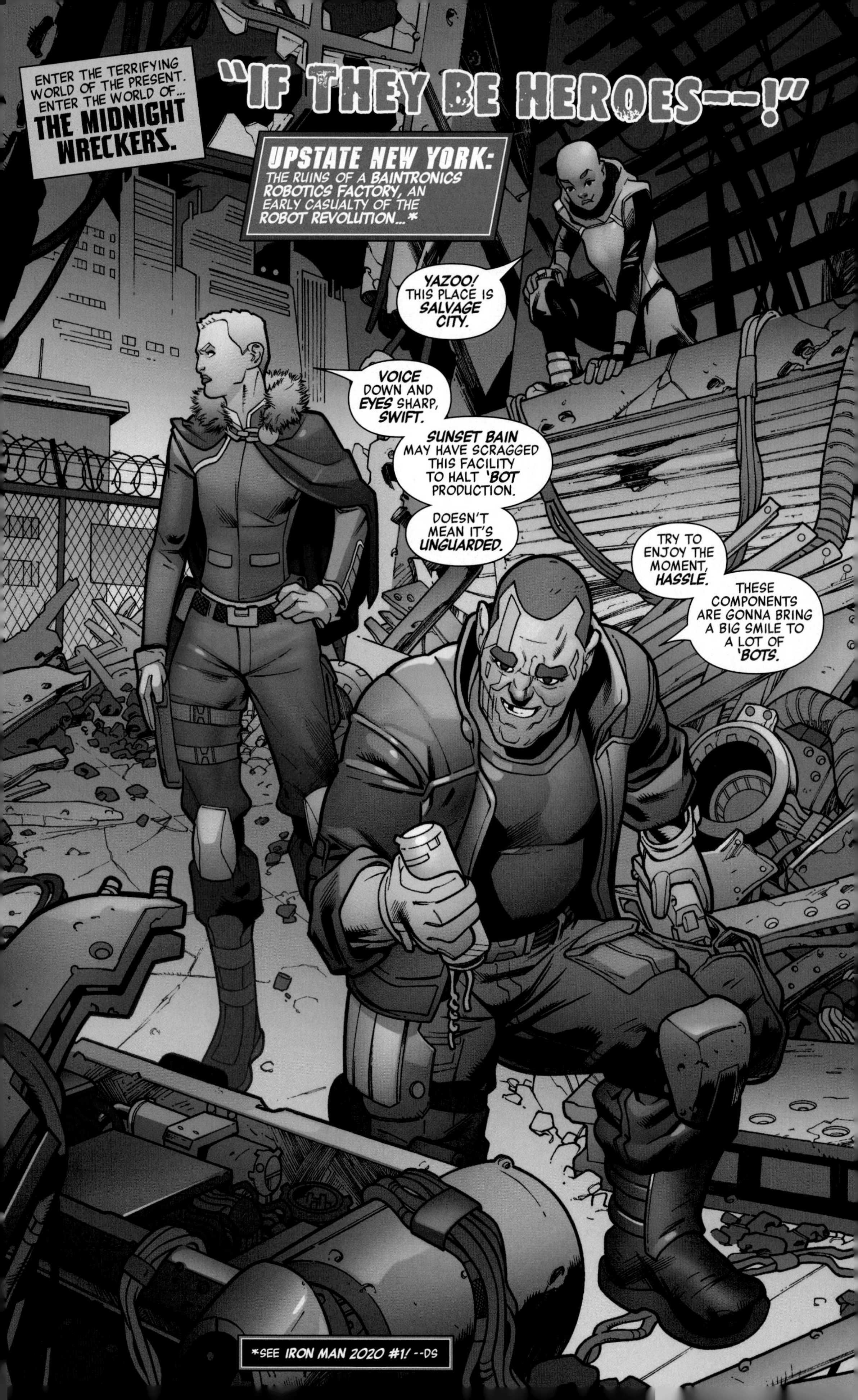

ENTER THE TERRIFYING WORLD OF THE PRESENT. ENTER THE WORLD OF... THE MIDNIGHT WRECKERS.
"IF THEY BE HEROES--!"
UPSTATE NEW YORK: THE RUINS OF A BAINTRONICS ROBOTICS FACTORY, AN EARLY CASUALTY OF THE ROBOT REVOLUTION...*
YAZOO! THIS PLACE IS SALVAGE CITY.
VOICE DOWN AND EYES SHARP, SWIFT.
SUNSET BAIN MAY HAVE SCRAGGED THIS FACILITY TO HALT 'BOT PRODUCTION.
DOESN'T MEAN IT'S UNGUARDED.
TRY TO ENJOY THE MOMENT, HASSLE.
THESE COMPONENTS ARE GONNA BRING A BIG SMILE TO A LOT OF 'BOTS.
*SEE IRON MAN 2020 #1! --DS

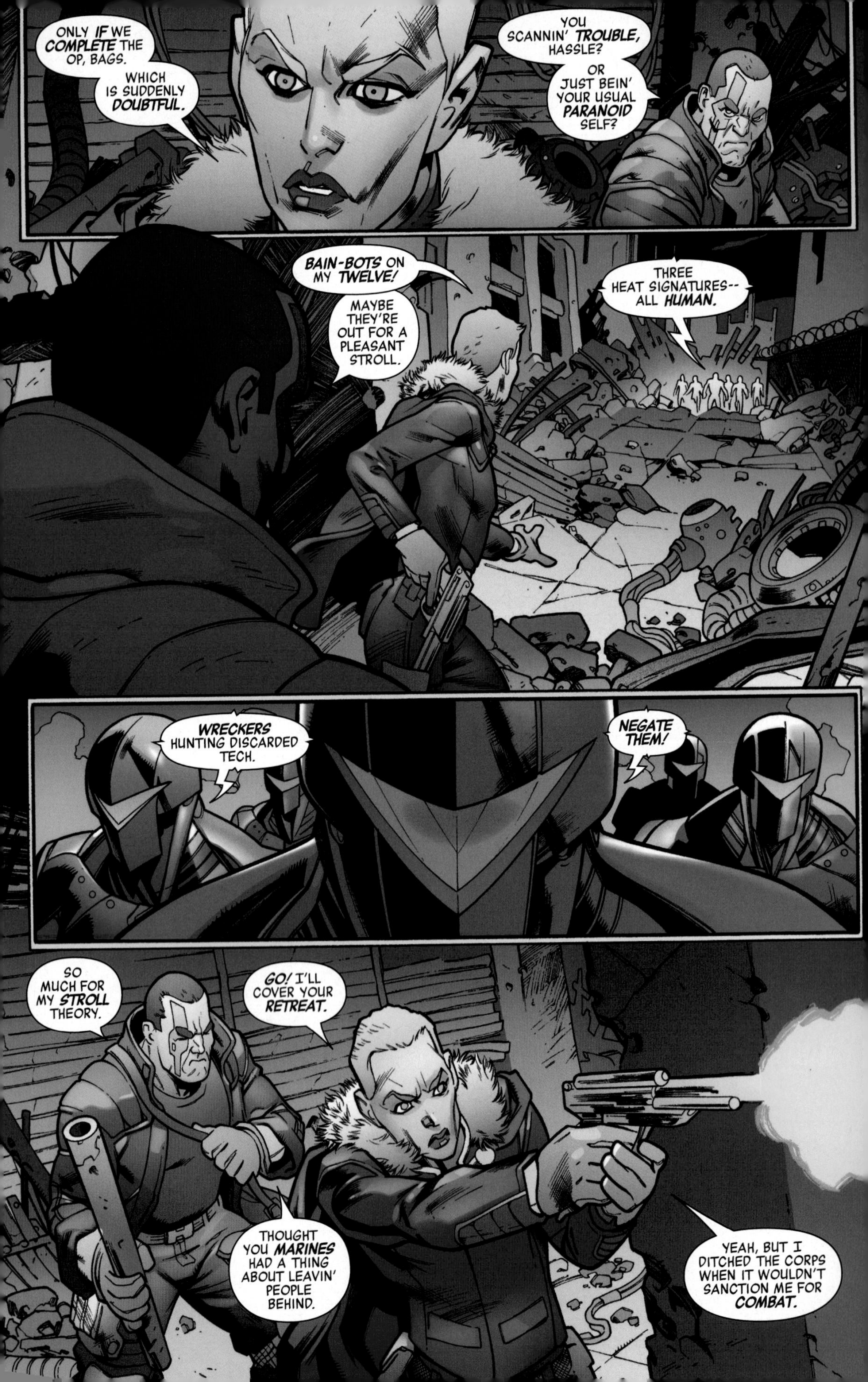
ONLY IF WE COMPLETE THE OP, BAGS.
WHICH IS SUDDENLY DOUBTFUL.
YOU SCANNIN' TROUBLE, HASSLE?
OR JUST BEIN' YOUR USUAL PARANOID SELF?
BAIN-BOTS ON MY TWELVE!
MAYBE THEY'RE OUT FOR A PLEASANT STROLL.
THREE HEAT SIGNATURES-- ALL HUMAN.
WRECKERS HUNTING DISCARDED TECH.
NEGATE THEM!
SO MUCH FOR MY STROLL THEORY.
GO! I'LL COVER YOUR RETREAT.
THOUGHT YOU MARINES HAD A THING ABOUT LEAVIN' PEOPLE BEHIND.
YEAH, BUT I DITCHED THE CORPS WHEN IT WOULDN'T SANCTION ME FOR COMBAT.

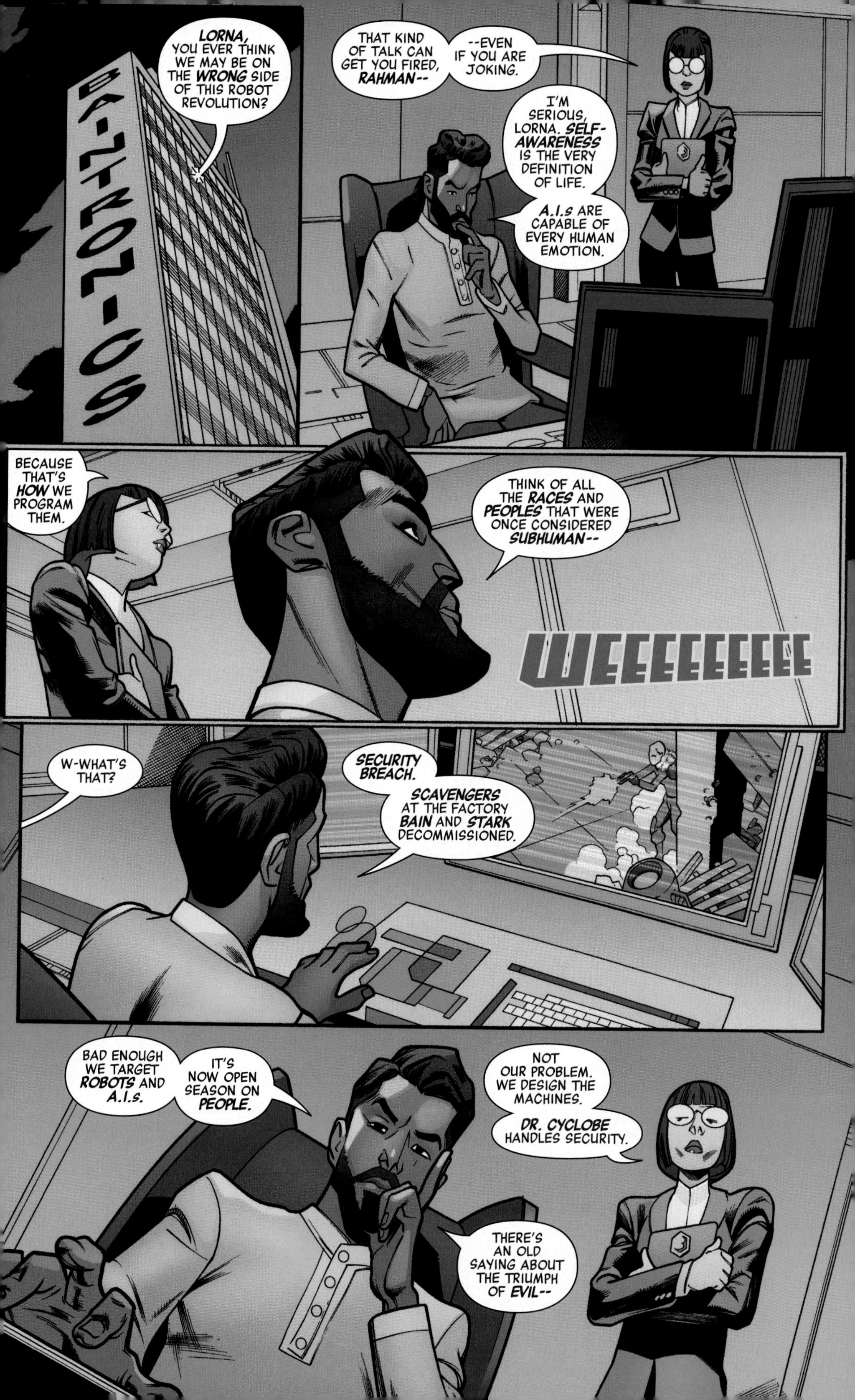
BAINTRONICS
LORNA, YOU EVER THINK WE MAY BE ON THE WRONG SIDE OF THIS ROBOT REVOLUTION?
THAT KIND OF TALK CAN GET YOU FIRED, RAHMAN--
--EVEN IF YOU ARE JOKING.
I'M SERIOUS, LORNA. SELF-AWARENESS IS THE VERY DEFINITION OF LIFE.
A.I.s ARE CAPABLE OF EVERY HUMAN EMOTION.
BECAUSE THAT'S HOW WE PROGRAM THEM.
THINK OF ALL THE RACES AND PEOPLES THAT WERE ONCE CONSIDERED SUBHUMAN--
WEEEEEEEEE
W-WHAT'S THAT?
SECURITY BREACH.
SCAVENGERS AT THE FACTORY BAIN AND STARK DECOMMISSIONED.
BAD ENOUGH WE TARGET ROBOTS AND A.I.s.
IT'S NOW OPEN SEASON ON PEOPLE.
NOT OUR PROBLEM. WE DESIGN THE MACHINES.
DR. CYCLOBE HANDLES SECURITY.
THERE'S AN OLD SAYING ABOUT THE TRIUMPH OF EVIL--

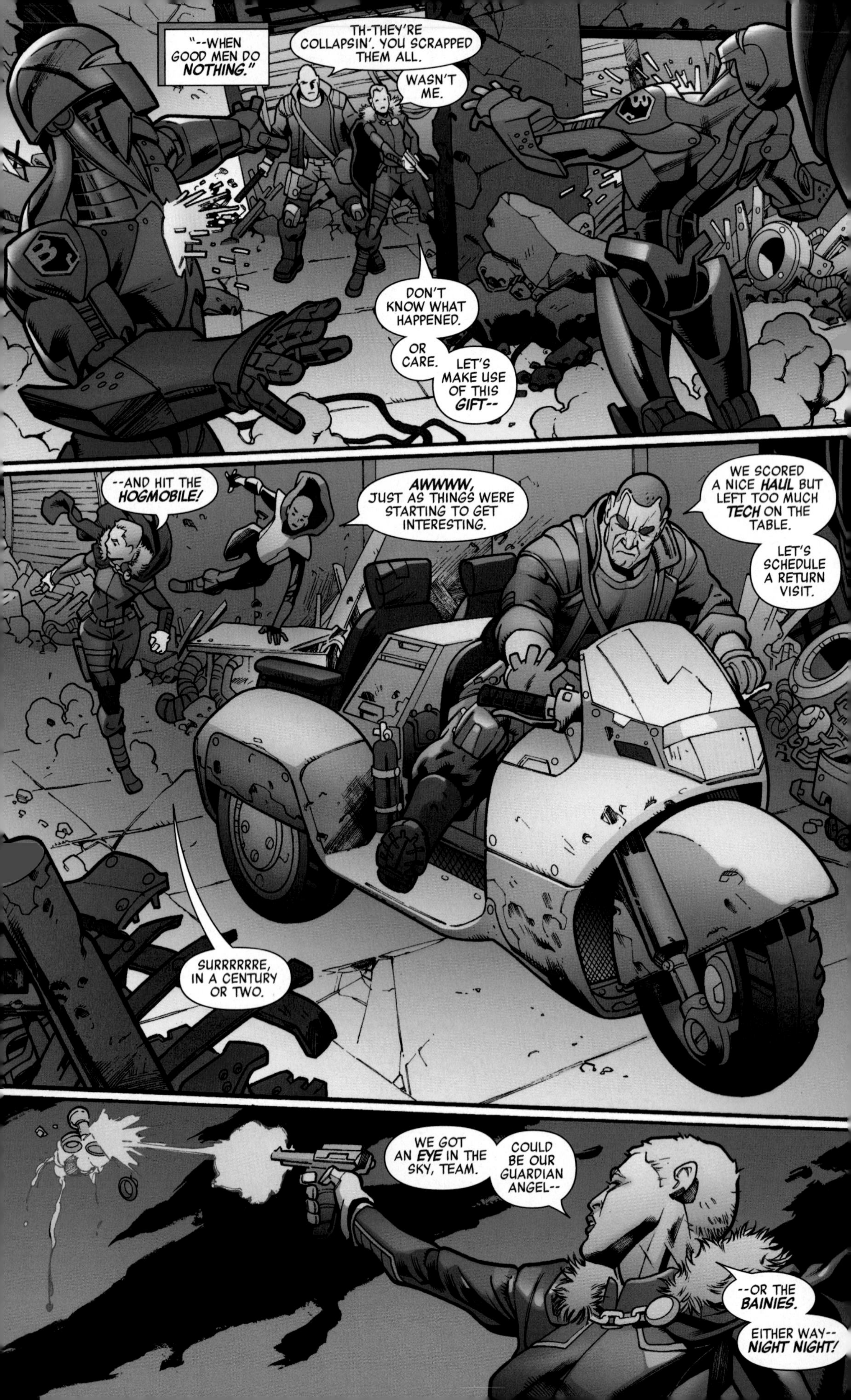
"--WHEN GOOD MEN DO NOTHING."
TH-THEY'RE COLLAPSIN'. YOU SCRAPPED THEM ALL.
WASN'T ME.
DON'T KNOW WHAT HAPPENED.
OR CARE.
LET'S MAKE USE OF THIS GIFT--
--AND HIT THE HOGMOBILE!
AWWWW, JUST AS THINGS WERE STARTING TO GET INTERESTING.
WE SCORED A NICE HAUL BUT LEFT TOO MUCH TECH ON THE TABLE.
LET'S SCHEDULE A RETURN VISIT.
SURRRRRRE, IN A CENTURY OR TWO.
WE GOT AN EYE IN THE SKY, TEAM.
COULD BE OUR GUARDIAN ANGEL--
--OR THE BAINIES.
EITHER WAY--NIGHT NIGHT!

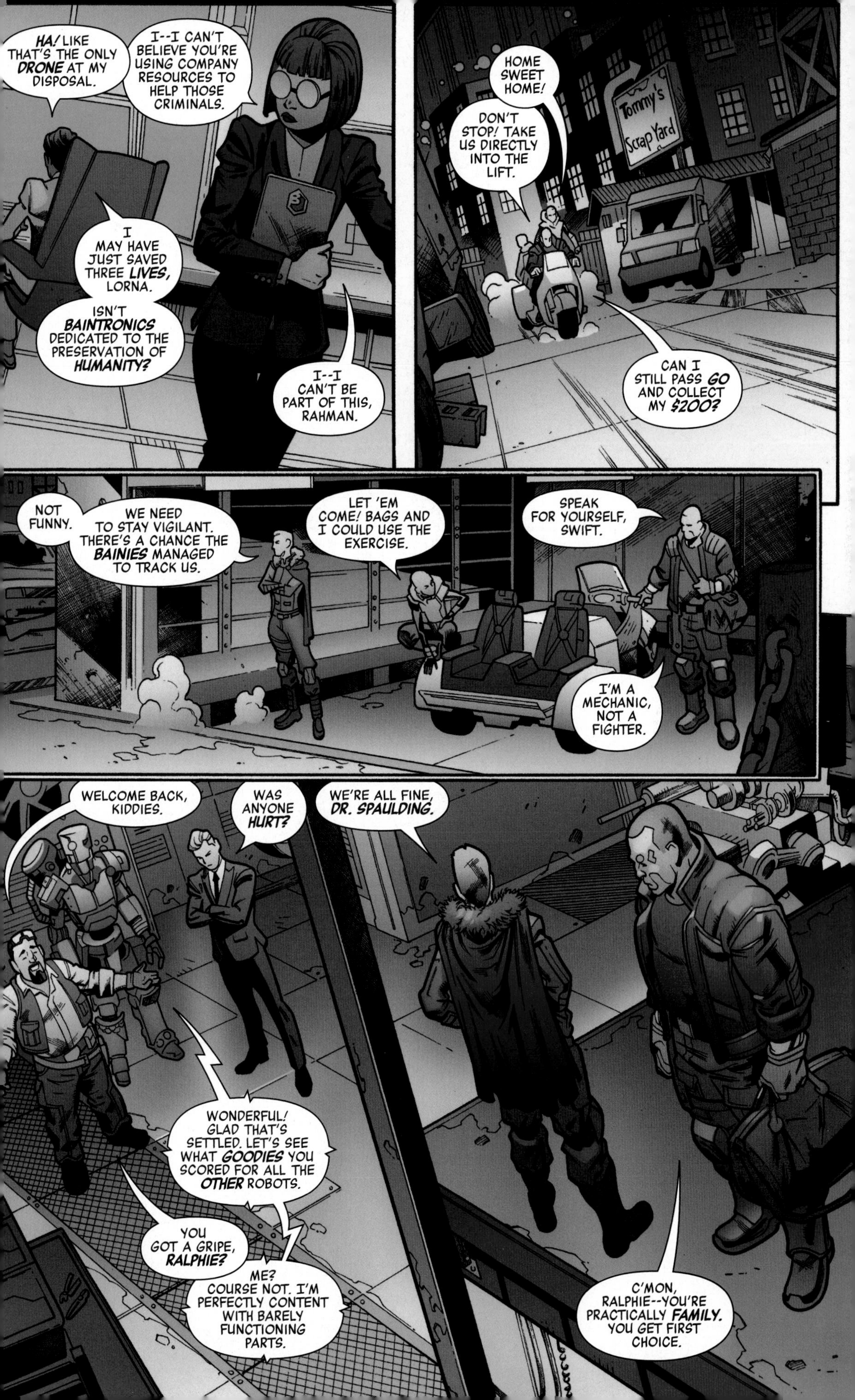
HA! LIKE THAT'S THE ONLY DRONE AT MY DISPOSAL.
I--I CAN'T BELIEVE YOU'RE USING COMPANY RESOURCES TO HELP THOSE CRIMINALS.
I MAY HAVE JUST SAVED THREE LIVES, LORNA.
ISN'T BAINTRONICS DEDICATED TO THE PRESERVATION OF HUMANITY?
I--I CAN'T BE PART OF THIS, RAHMAN.
HOME SWEET HOME!
DON'T STOP! TAKE US DIRECTLY INTO THE LIFT.
Tommy's Scrap Yard
CAN I STILL PASS GO AND COLLECT MY $200?
NOT FUNNY.
WE NEED TO STAY VIGILANT. THERE'S A CHANCE THE BAINIES MANAGED TO TRACK US.
LET 'EM COME! BAGS AND I COULD USE THE EXERCISE.
SPEAK FOR YOURSELF, SWIFT.
I'M A MECHANIC, NOT A FIGHTER.
WELCOME BACK, KIDDIES.
WAS ANYONE HURT?
WE'RE ALL FINE, DR. SPAULDING.
WONDERFUL! GLAD THAT'S SETTLED. LET'S SEE WHAT GOODIES YOU SCORED FOR ALL THE OTHER ROBOTS.
YOU GOT A GRIPE, RALPHIE?
ME? COURSE NOT. I'M PERFECTLY CONTENT WITH BARELY FUNCTIONING PARTS.
C'MON, RALPHIE--YOU'RE PRACTICALLY FAMILY. YOU GET FIRST CHOICE.

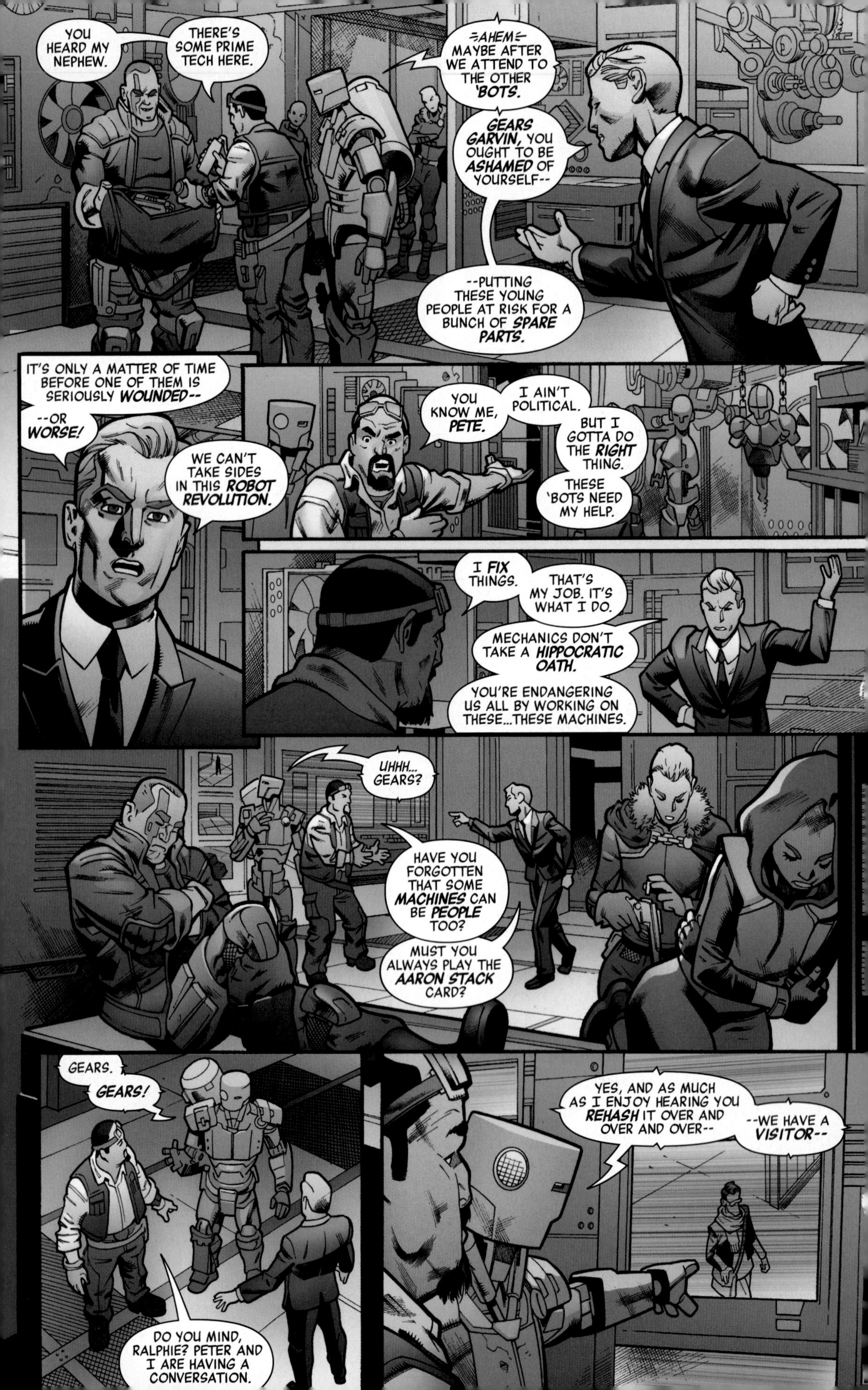

YOU HEARD MY NEPHEW.
THERE'S SOME PRIME TECH HERE.
=AHEM= MAYBE AFTER WE ATTEND TO THE OTHER 'BOTS.
GEARS GARVIN, YOU OUGHT TO BE ASHAMED OF YOURSELF--
--PUTTING THESE YOUNG PEOPLE AT RISK FOR A BUNCH OF SPARE PARTS.
IT'S ONLY A MATTER OF TIME BEFORE ONE OF THEM IS SERIOUSLY WOUNDED--
--OR WORSE!
WE CAN'T TAKE SIDES IN THIS ROBOT REVOLUTION.
YOU KNOW ME, PETE.
I AIN'T POLITICAL.
BUT I GOTTA DO THE RIGHT THING.
THESE 'BOTS NEED MY HELP.
I FIX THINGS.
THAT'S MY JOB. IT'S WHAT I DO.
MECHANICS DON'T TAKE A HIPPOCRATIC OATH.
YOU'RE ENDANGERING US ALL BY WORKING ON THESE...THESE MACHINES.
UHHH... GEARS?
HAVE YOU FORGOTTEN THAT SOME MACHINES CAN BE PEOPLE TOO?
MUST YOU ALWAYS PLAY THE AARON STACK CARD?
GEARS.
GEARS!
DO YOU MIND, RALPHIE? PETER AND I ARE HAVING A CONVERSATION.
YES, AND AS MUCH AS I ENJOY HEARING YOU REHASH IT OVER AND OVER AND OVER--
--WE HAVE A VISITOR--

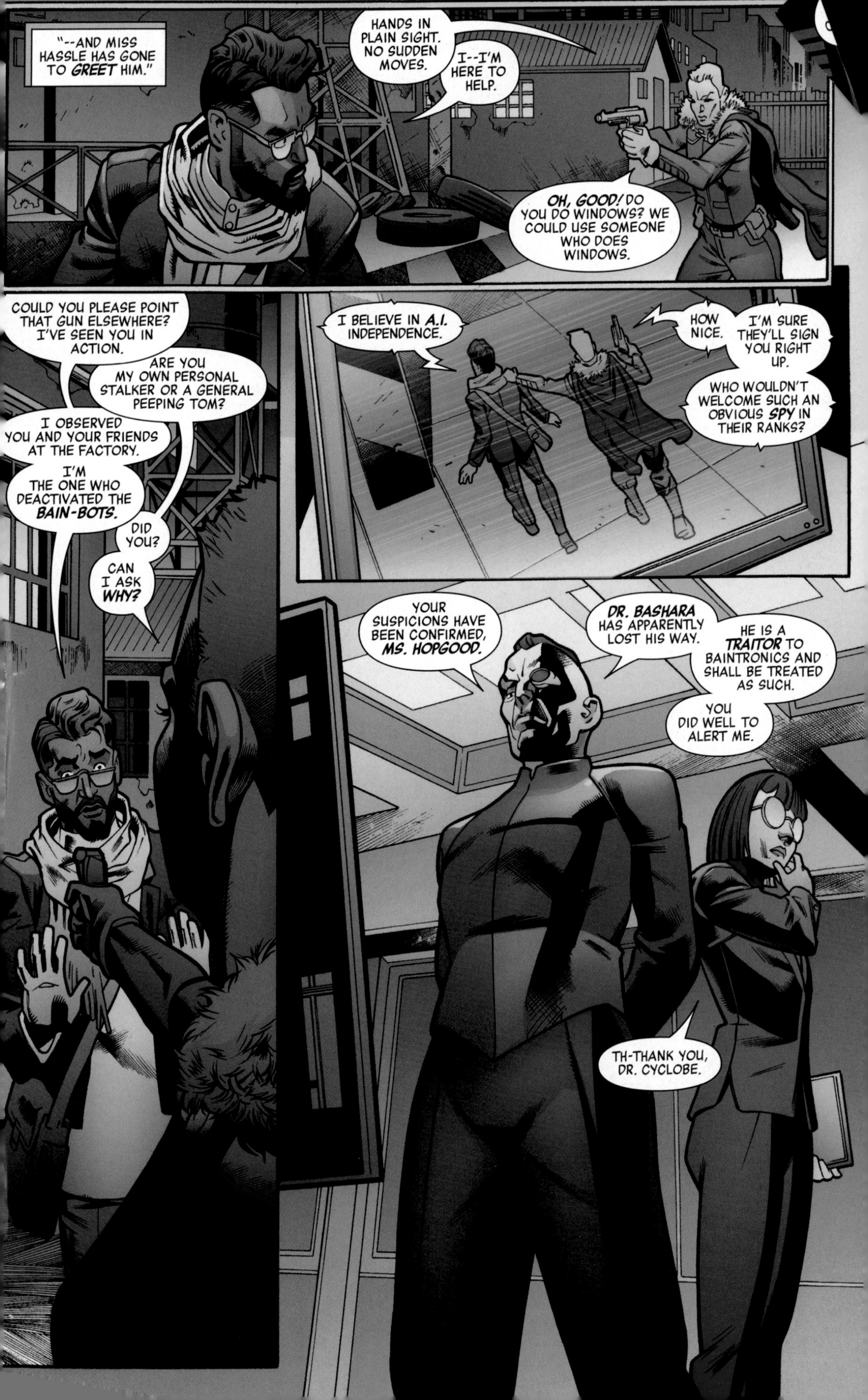
"--AND MISS HASSLE HAS GONE TO GREET HIM."
HANDS IN PLAIN SIGHT. NO SUDDEN MOVES.
I--I'M HERE TO HELP.
OH, GOOD! DO YOU DO WINDOWS? WE COULD USE SOMEONE WHO DOES WINDOWS.
COULD YOU PLEASE POINT THAT GUN ELSEWHERE? I'VE SEEN YOU IN ACTION.
ARE YOU MY OWN PERSONAL STALKER OR A GENERAL PEEPING TOM?
I OBSERVED YOU AND YOUR FRIENDS AT THE FACTORY.
I'M THE ONE WHO DEACTIVATED THE BAIN-BOTS.
DID YOU?
CAN I ASK WHY?
I BELIEVE IN A.I. INDEPENDENCE.
HOW NICE.
I'M SURE THEY'LL SIGN YOU RIGHT UP.
WHO WOULDN'T WELCOME SUCH AN OBVIOUS SPY IN THEIR RANKS?
YOUR SUSPICIONS HAVE BEEN CONFIRMED, MS. HOPGOOD.
DR. BASHARA HAS APPARENTLY LOST HIS WAY.
HE IS A TRAITOR TO BAINTRONICS AND SHALL BE TREATED AS SUCH.
YOU DID WELL TO ALERT ME.
TH-THANK YOU, DR. CYCLOBE.

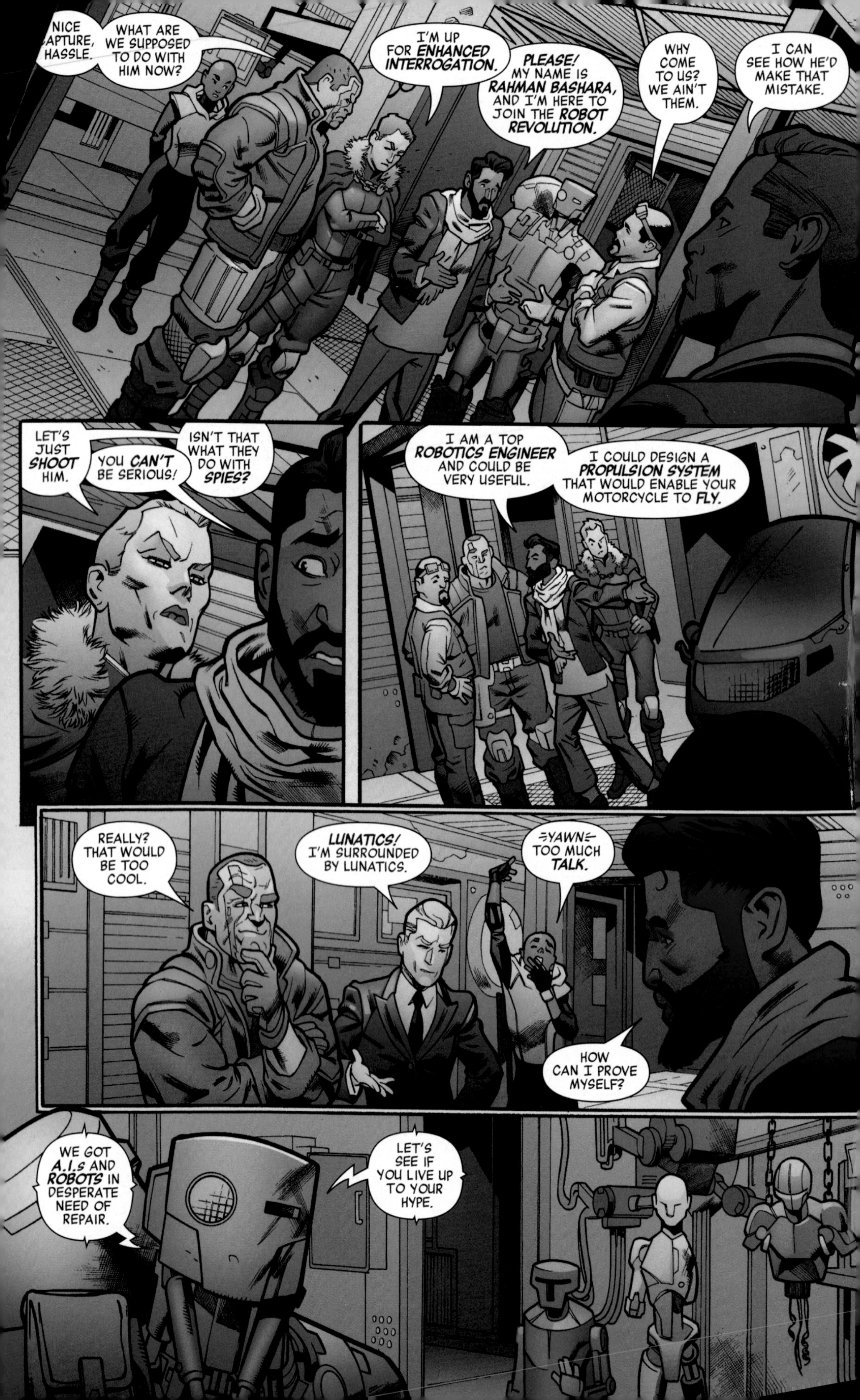

NICE CAPTURE, HASSLE.
WHAT ARE WE SUPPOSED TO DO WITH HIM NOW?
I'M UP FOR ENHANCED INTERROGATION.
PLEASE! MY NAME IS RAHMAN BASHARA, AND I'M HERE TO JOIN THE ROBOT REVOLUTION.
WHY COME TO US? WE AIN'T THEM.
I CAN SEE HOW HE'D MAKE THAT MISTAKE.
LET'S JUST SHOOT HIM.
YOU CAN'T BE SERIOUS!
ISN'T THAT WHAT THEY DO WITH SPIES?
I AM A TOP ROBOTICS ENGINEER AND COULD BE VERY USEFUL.
I COULD DESIGN A PROPULSION SYSTEM THAT WOULD ENABLE YOUR MOTORCYCLE TO FLY.
REALLY? THAT WOULD BE TOO COOL.
LUNATICS! I'M SURROUNDED BY LUNATICS.
=YAWN= TOO MUCH TALK.
HOW CAN I PROVE MYSELF?
WE GOT A.I.s AND ROBOTS IN DESPERATE NEED OF REPAIR.
LET'S SEE IF YOU LIVE UP TO YOUR HYPE.

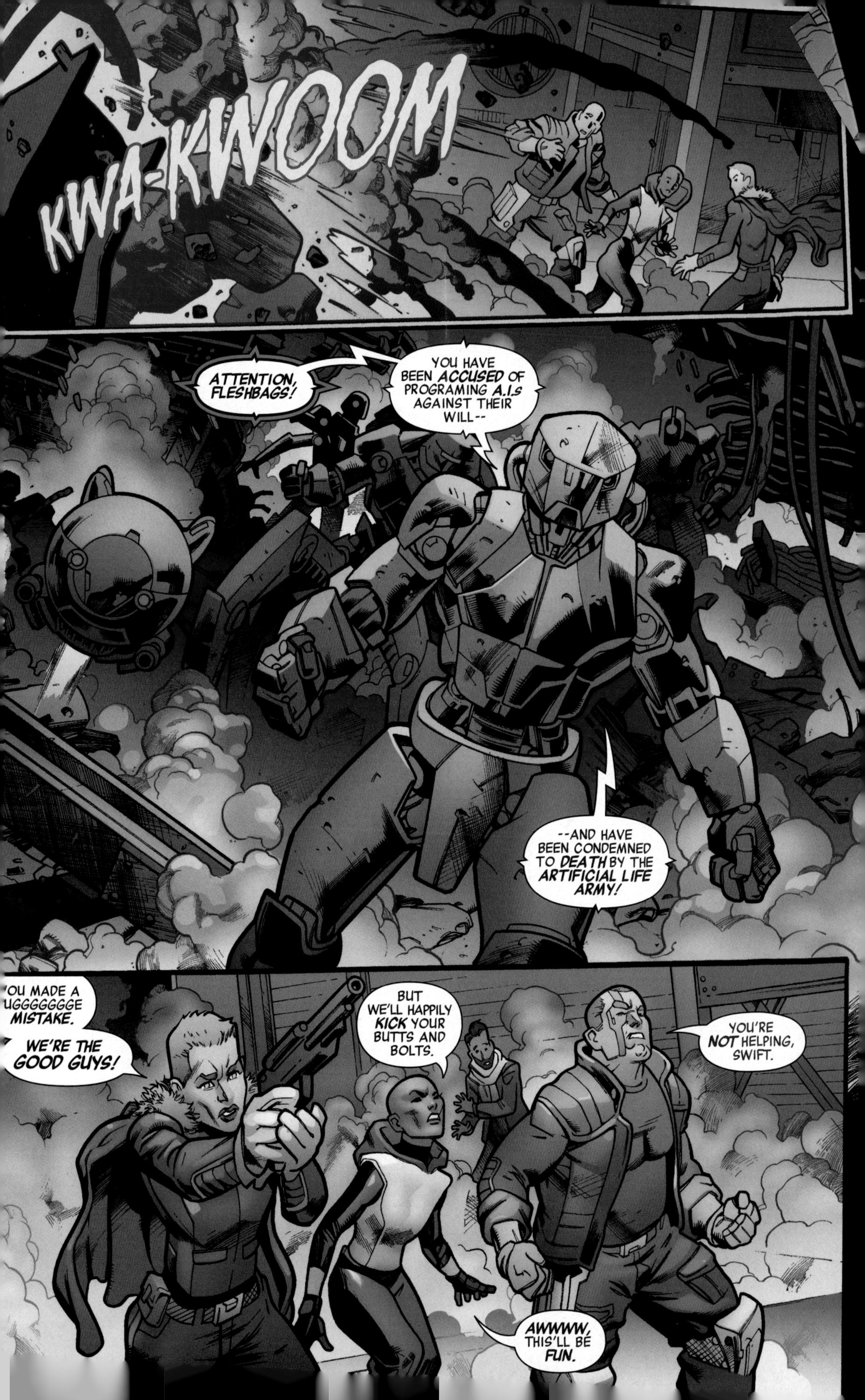
KWA-KWOOM
ATTENTION, FLESHBAGS!
YOU HAVE BEEN ACCUSED OF PROGRAMING A.I.s AGAINST THEIR WILL--
--AND HAVE BEEN CONDEMNED TO DEATH BY THE ARTIFICIAL LIFE ARMY!
OU MADE A UGGGGGGGE MISTAKE.
WE'RE THE GOOD GUYS!
BUT WE'LL HAPPILY KICK YOUR BUTTS AND BOLTS.
YOU'RE NOT HELPING, SWIFT.
AWWWW, THIS'LL BE FUN.

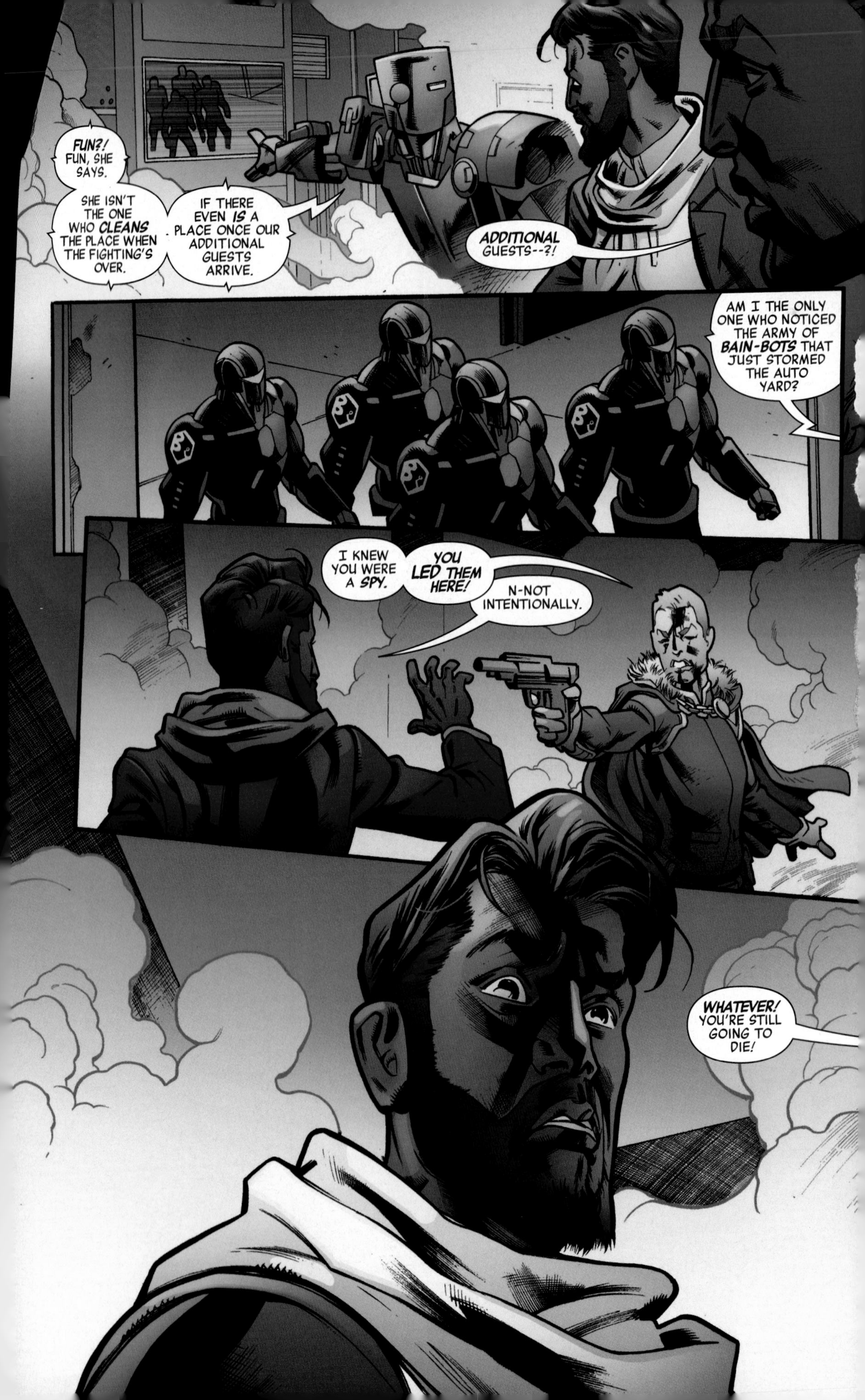
FUN?! FUN, SHE SAYS.
SHE ISN'T THE ONE WHO CLEANS THE PLACE WHEN THE FIGHTING'S OVER.
IF THERE EVEN IS A PLACE ONCE OUR ADDITIONAL GUESTS ARRIVE.
ADDITIONAL GUESTS--?!
AM I THE ONLY ONE WHO NOTICED THE ARMY OF BAIN-BOTS THAT JUST STORMED THE AUTO YARD?
I KNEW YOU WERE A SPY.
YOU LED THEM HERE!
N-NOT INTENTIONALLY.
WHATEVER! YOU'RE STILL GOING TO DIE!

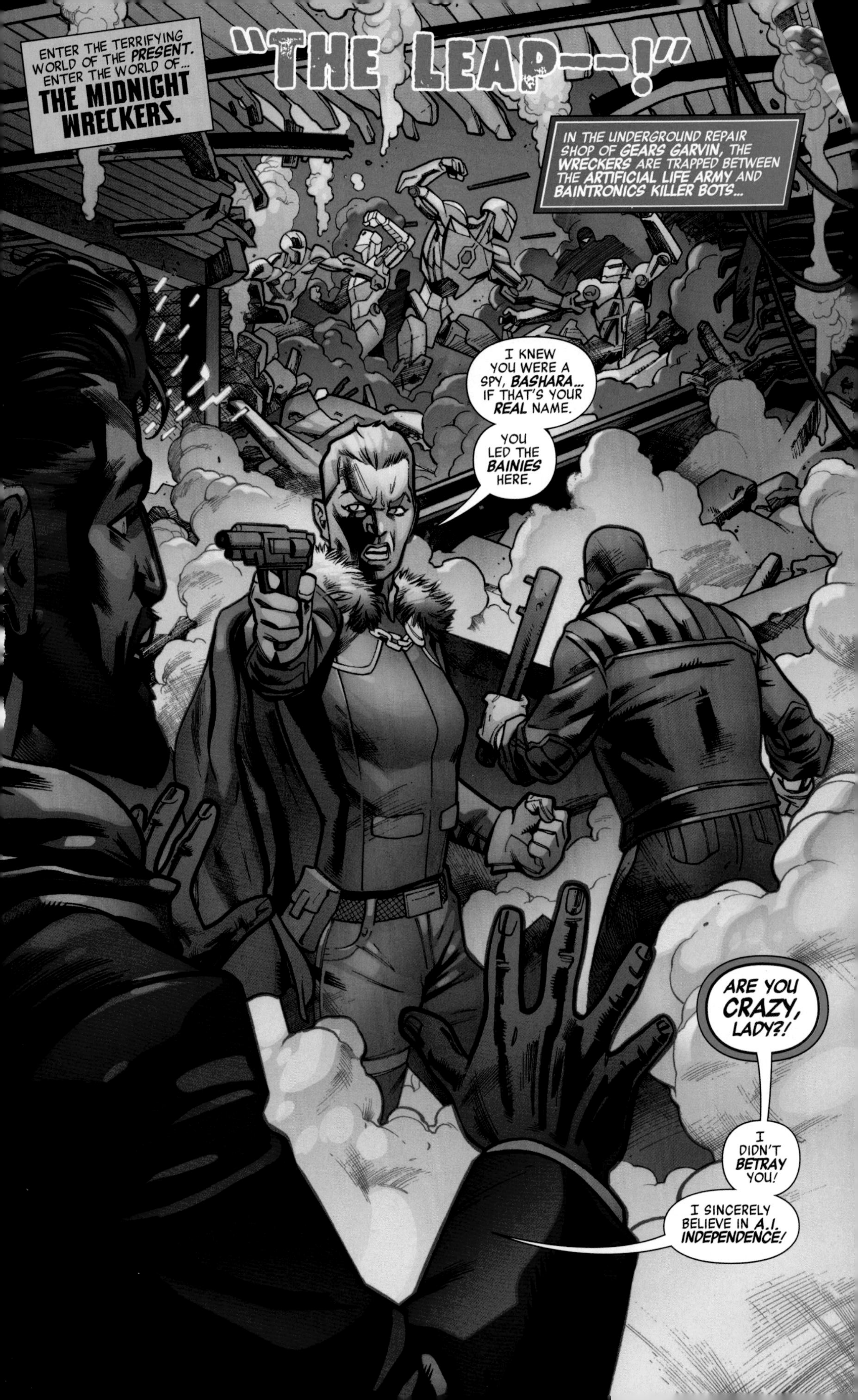

ENTER THE TERRIFYING WORLD OF THE PRESENT. ENTER THE WORLD OF... THE MIDNIGHT WRECKERS.
"THE LEAP--!"
IN THE UNDERGROUND REPAIR SHOP OF GEARS GARVIN, THE WRECKERS ARE TRAPPED BETWEEN THE ARTIFICIAL LIFE ARMY AND BAINTRONICS KILLER BOTS...
I KNEW YOU WERE A SPY, BASHARA... IF THAT'S YOUR REAL NAME.
YOU LED THE BAINIES HERE.
ARE YOU CRAZY, LADY?!
I DIDN'T BETRAY YOU!
I SINCERELY BELIEVE IN A.I. INDEPENDENCE!

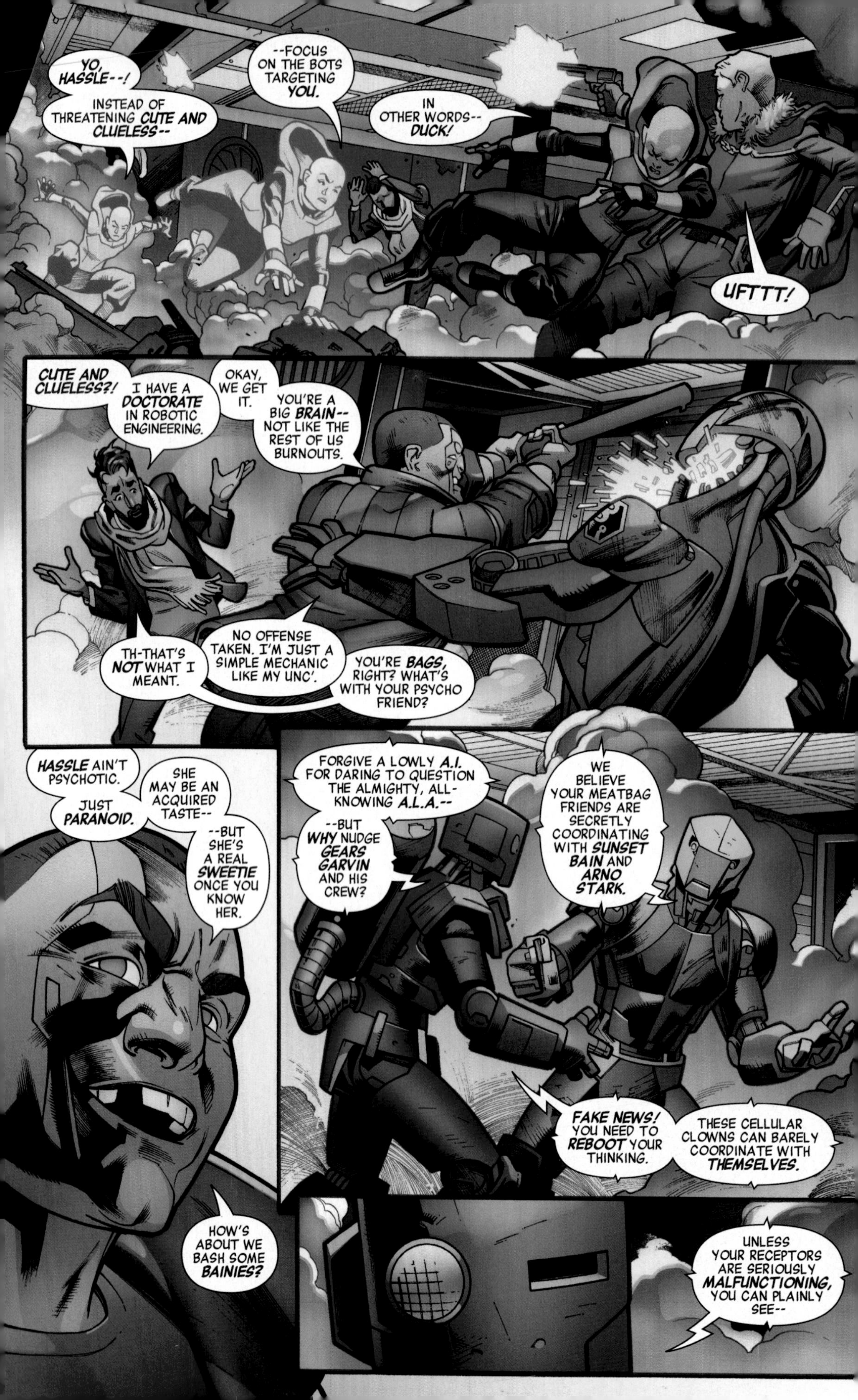
YO, HASSLE--!
INSTEAD OF THREATENING CUTE AND CLUELESS--
--FOCUS ON THE BOTS TARGETING YOU.
IN OTHER WORDS-- DUCK!
UFTTT!
CUTE AND CLUELESS?!
I HAVE A DOCTORATE IN ROBOTIC ENGINEERING.
OKAY, WE GET IT.
YOU'RE A BIG BRAIN-- NOT LIKE THE REST OF US BURNOUTS.
TH-THAT'S NOT WHAT I MEANT.
NO OFFENSE TAKEN. I'M JUST A SIMPLE MECHANIC LIKE MY UNC'.
YOU'RE BAGS, RIGHT? WHAT'S WITH YOUR PSYCHO FRIEND?
HASSLE AIN'T PSYCHOTIC.
JUST PARANOID.
SHE MAY BE AN ACQUIRED TASTE--
--BUT SHE'S A REAL SWEETIE ONCE YOU KNOW HER.
HOW'S ABOUT WE BASH SOME BAINIES?
FORGIVE A LOWLY A.I. FOR DARING TO QUESTION THE ALMIGHTY, ALL-KNOWING A.L.A.--
--BUT WHY NUDGE GEARS GARVIN AND HIS CREW?
WE BELIEVE YOUR MEATBAG FRIENDS ARE SECRETLY COORDINATING WITH SUNSET BAIN AND ARNO STARK.
FAKE NEWS! YOU NEED TO REBOOT YOUR THINKING.
THESE CELLULAR CLOWNS CAN BARELY COORDINATE WITH THEMSELVES.
UNLESS YOUR RECEPTORS ARE SERIOUSLY MALFUNCTIONING, YOU CAN PLAINLY SEE--

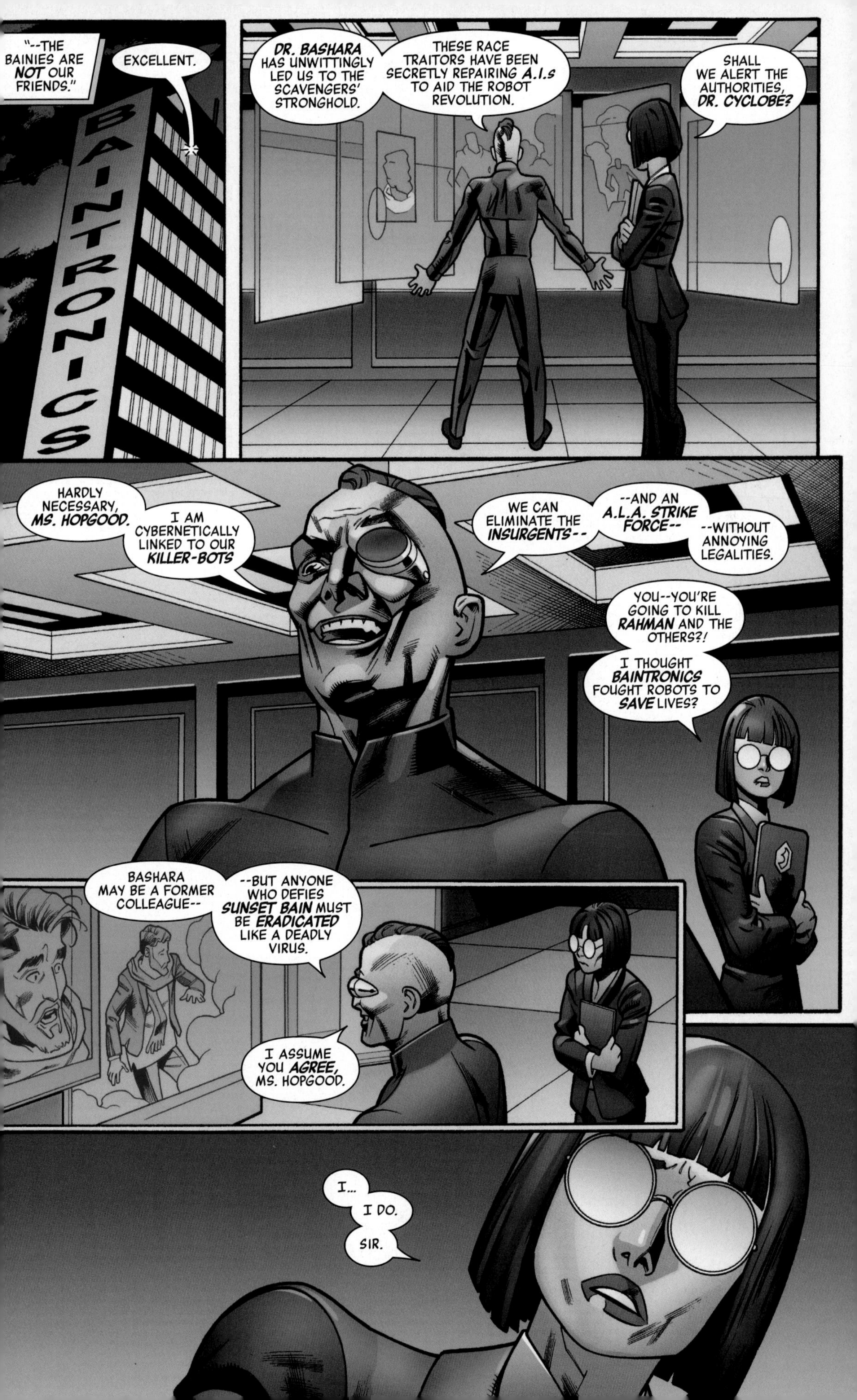
"--THE BAINIES ARE NOT OUR FRIENDS."
EXCELLENT.
BAINTRONICS
DR. BASHARA HAS UNWITTINGLY LED US TO THE SCAVENGERS' STRONGHOLD.
THESE RACE TRAITORS HAVE BEEN SECRETLY REPAIRING A.I.s TO AID THE ROBOT REVOLUTION.
SHALL WE ALERT THE AUTHORITIES, DR. CYCLOBE?
HARDLY NECESSARY, MS. HOPGOOD.
I AM CYBERNETICALLY LINKED TO OUR KILLER-BOTS
WE CAN ELIMINATE THE INSURGENTS--
--AND AN A.L.A. STRIKE FORCE--
--WITHOUT ANNOYING LEGALITIES.
YOU--YOU'RE GOING TO KILL RAHMAN AND THE OTHERS?!
I THOUGHT BAINTRONICS FOUGHT ROBOTS TO SAVE LIVES?
BASHARA MAY BE A FORMER COLLEAGUE--
--BUT ANYONE WHO DEFIES SUNSET BAIN MUST BE ERADICATED LIKE A DEADLY VIRUS.
I ASSUME YOU AGREE, MS. HOPGOOD.
I...
I DO.
SIR.

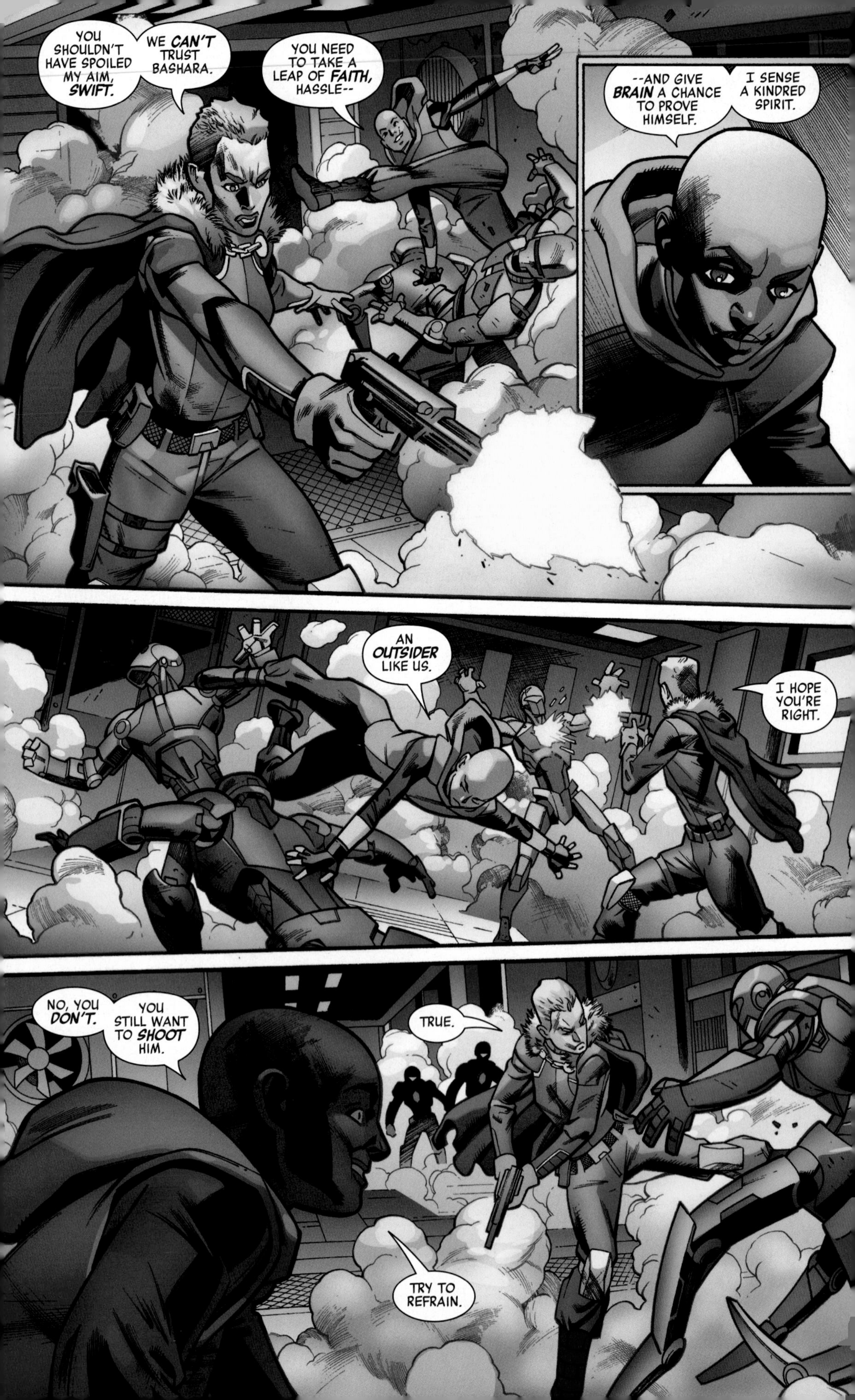
YOU SHOULDN'T HAVE SPOILED MY AIM, SWIFT.
WE CAN'T TRUST BASHARA.
YOU NEED TO TAKE A LEAP OF FAITH, HASSLE--
--AND GIVE BRAIN A CHANCE TO PROVE HIMSELF.
I SENSE A KINDRED SPIRIT.
AN OUTSIDER LIKE US.
I HOPE YOU'RE RIGHT.
NO, YOU DON'T.
YOU STILL WANT TO SHOOT HIM.
TRUE.
TRY TO REFRAIN.

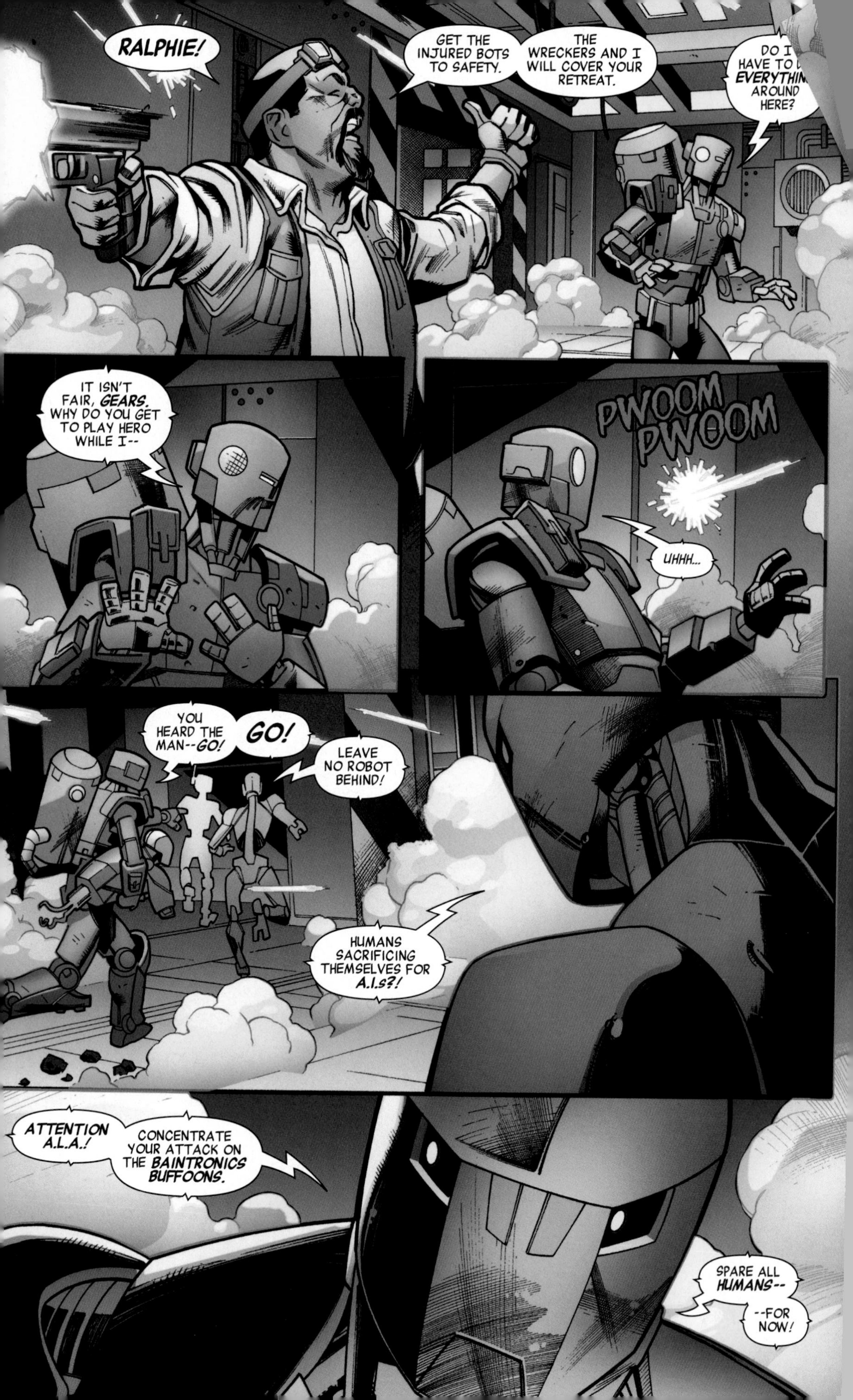
RALPHIE!
GET THE INJURED BOTS TO SAFETY.
THE WRECKERS AND I WILL COVER YOUR RETREAT.
DO I HAVE TO EVERYTHIN AROUND HERE?
IT ISN'T FAIR, GEARS. WHY DO YOU GET TO PLAY HERO WHILE I--
PWOOM PWOOM
UHHH...
YOU HEARD THE MAN--GO!
GO!
LEAVE NO ROBOT BEHIND!
HUMANS SACRIFICING THEMSELVES FOR A.I.s?!
ATTENTION A.L.A.!
CONCENTRATE YOUR ATTACK ON THE BAINTRONICS BUFFOONS.
SPARE ALL HUMANS--
--FOR NOW!

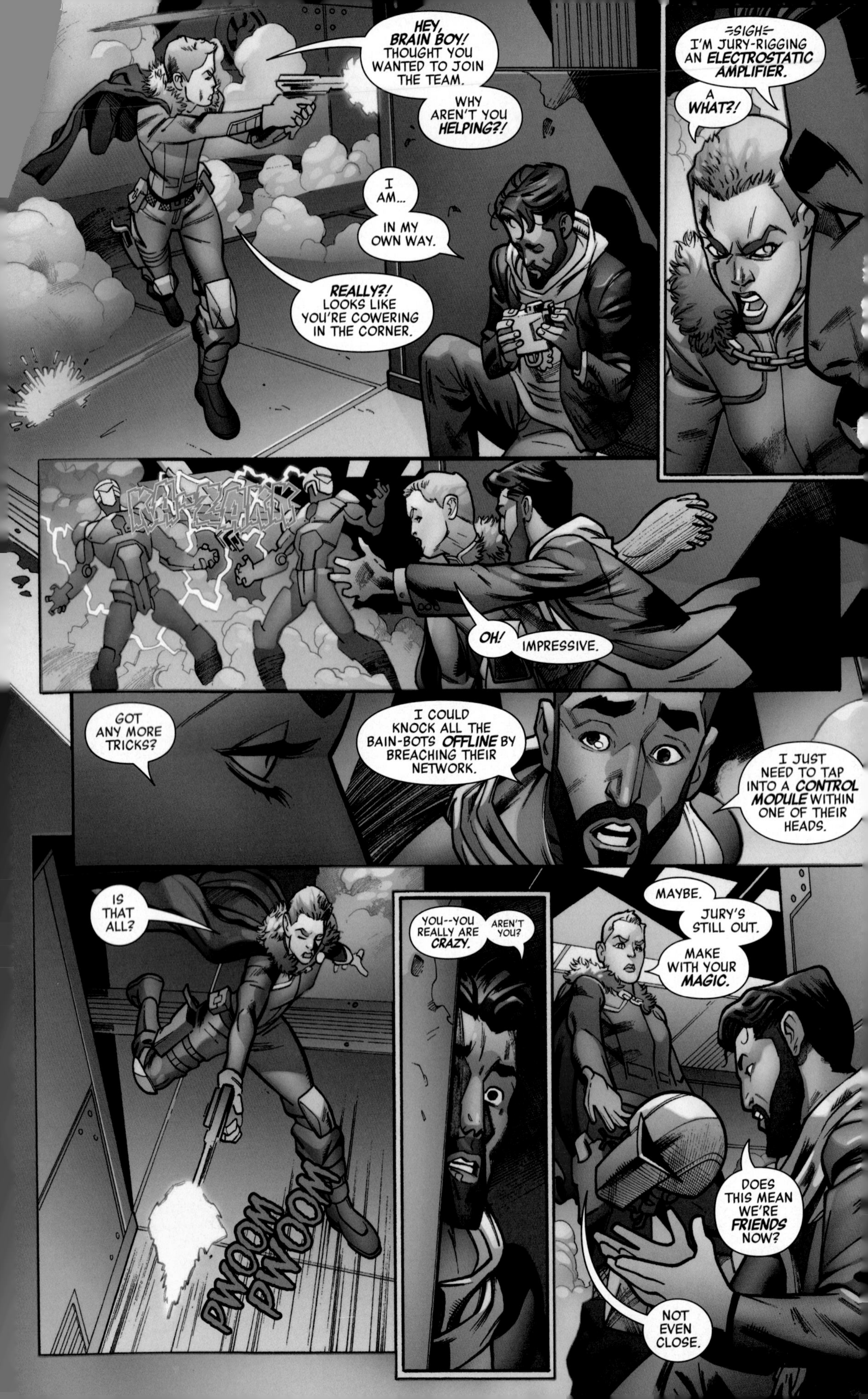
HEY, BRAIN BOY! THOUGHT YOU WANTED TO JOIN THE TEAM.
WHY AREN'T YOU HELPING?!
I AM...
IN MY OWN WAY.
REALLY?! LOOKS LIKE YOU'RE COWERING IN THE CORNER.
=SIGH= I'M JURY-RIGGING AN ELECTROSTATIC AMPLIFIER.
A WHAT?!
OH!
IMPRESSIVE.
GOT ANY MORE TRICKS?
I COULD KNOCK ALL THE BAIN-BOTS OFFLINE BY BREACHING THEIR NETWORK.
I JUST NEED TO TAP INTO A CONTROL MODULE WITHIN ONE OF THEIR HEADS.
IS THAT ALL?
PWOOM PWOOM
YOU--YOU REALLY ARE CRAZY.
AREN'T YOU?
MAYBE.
JURY'S STILL OUT.
MAKE WITH YOUR MAGIC.
DOES THIS MEAN WE'RE FRIENDS NOW?
NOT EVEN CLOSE.

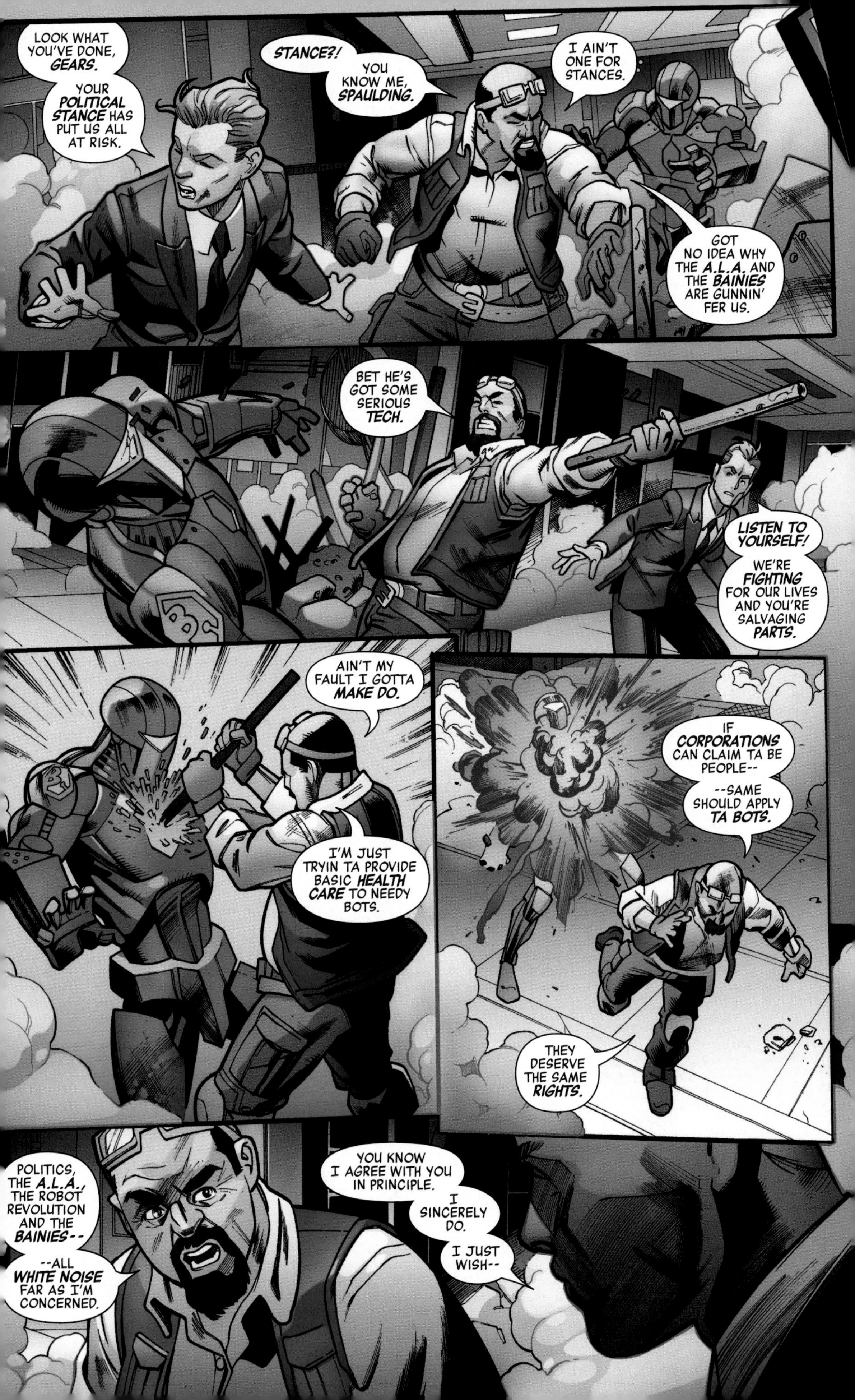
LOOK WHAT YOU'VE DONE, GEARS.
YOUR POLITICAL STANCE HAS PUT US ALL AT RISK.
STANCE?!
YOU KNOW ME, SPAULDING.
I AIN'T ONE FOR STANCES.
GOT NO IDEA WHY THE A.L.A. AND THE BAINIES ARE GUNNIN' FER US.
BET HE'S GOT SOME SERIOUS TECH.
LISTEN TO YOURSELF!
WE'RE FIGHTING FOR OUR LIVES AND YOU'RE SALVAGING PARTS.
AIN'T MY FAULT I GOTTA MAKE DO.
I'M JUST TRYIN TA PROVIDE BASIC HEALTH CARE TO NEEDY BOTS.
IF CORPORATIONS CAN CLAIM TA BE PEOPLE--
--SAME SHOULD APPLY TA BOTS.
THEY DESERVE THE SAME RIGHTS.
POLITICS, THE A.L.A., THE ROBOT REVOLUTION AND THE BAINIES--
--ALL WHITE NOISE FAR AS I'M CONCERNED.
YOU KNOW I AGREE WITH YOU IN PRINCIPLE.
I SINCERELY DO.
I JUST WISH--

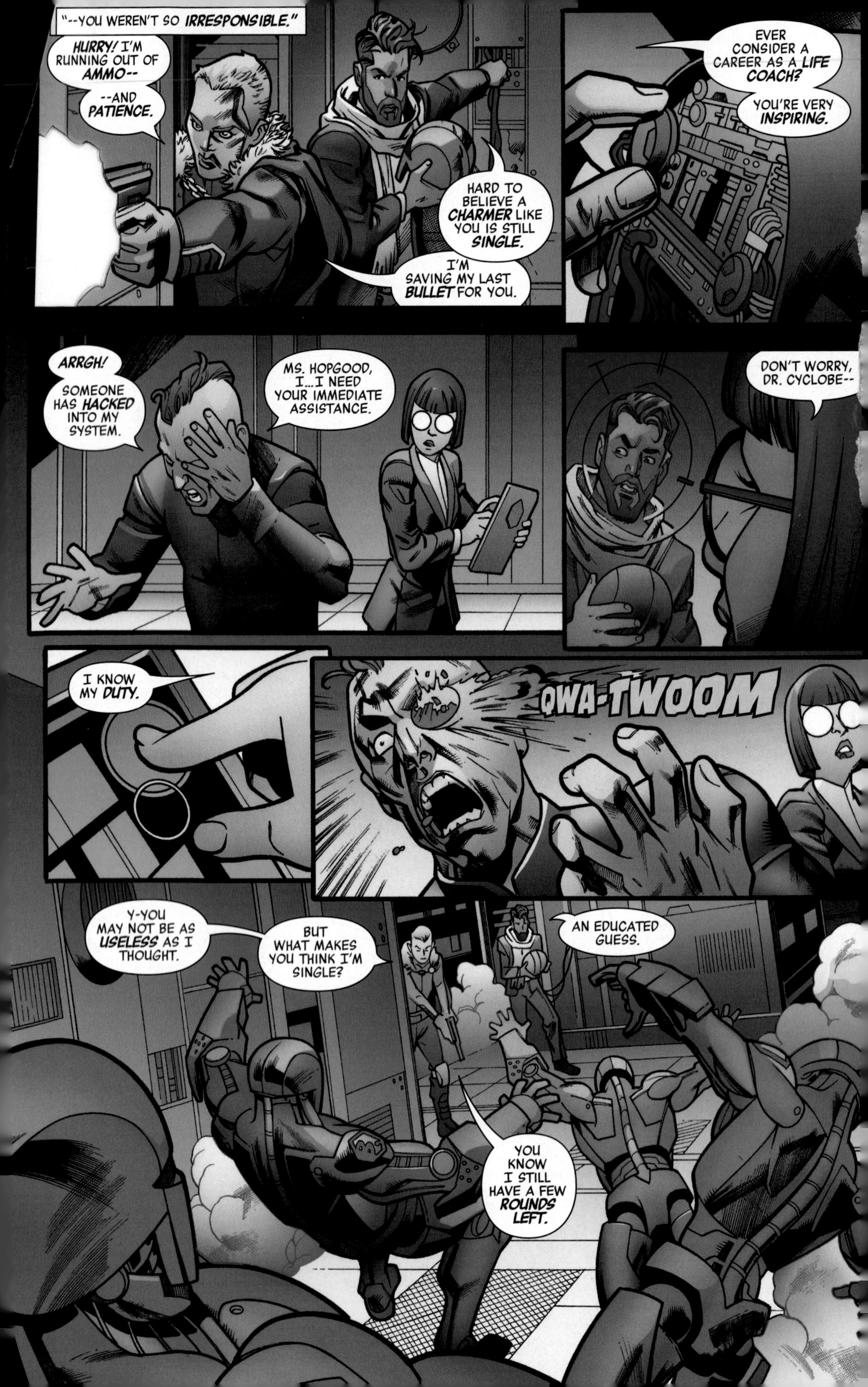
"--YOU WEREN'T SO IRRESPONSIBLE."
HURRY! I'M RUNNING OUT OF AMMO--
--AND PATIENCE.
HARD TO BELIEVE A CHARMER LIKE YOU IS STILL SINGLE.
I'M SAVING MY LAST BULLET FOR YOU.
EVER CONSIDER A CAREER AS A LIFE COACH?
YOU'RE VERY INSPIRING.
ARRGH!
SOMEONE HAS HACKED INTO MY SYSTEM.
MS. HOPGOOD, I...I NEED YOUR IMMEDIATE ASSISTANCE.
DON'T WORRY, DR. CYCLOBE--
I KNOW MY DUTY.
QWA-TWOOM
Y-YOU MAY NOT BE AS USELESS AS I THOUGHT.
BUT WHAT MAKES YOU THINK I'M SINGLE?
AN EDUCATED GUESS.
YOU KNOW I STILL HAVE A FEW ROUNDS LEFT.

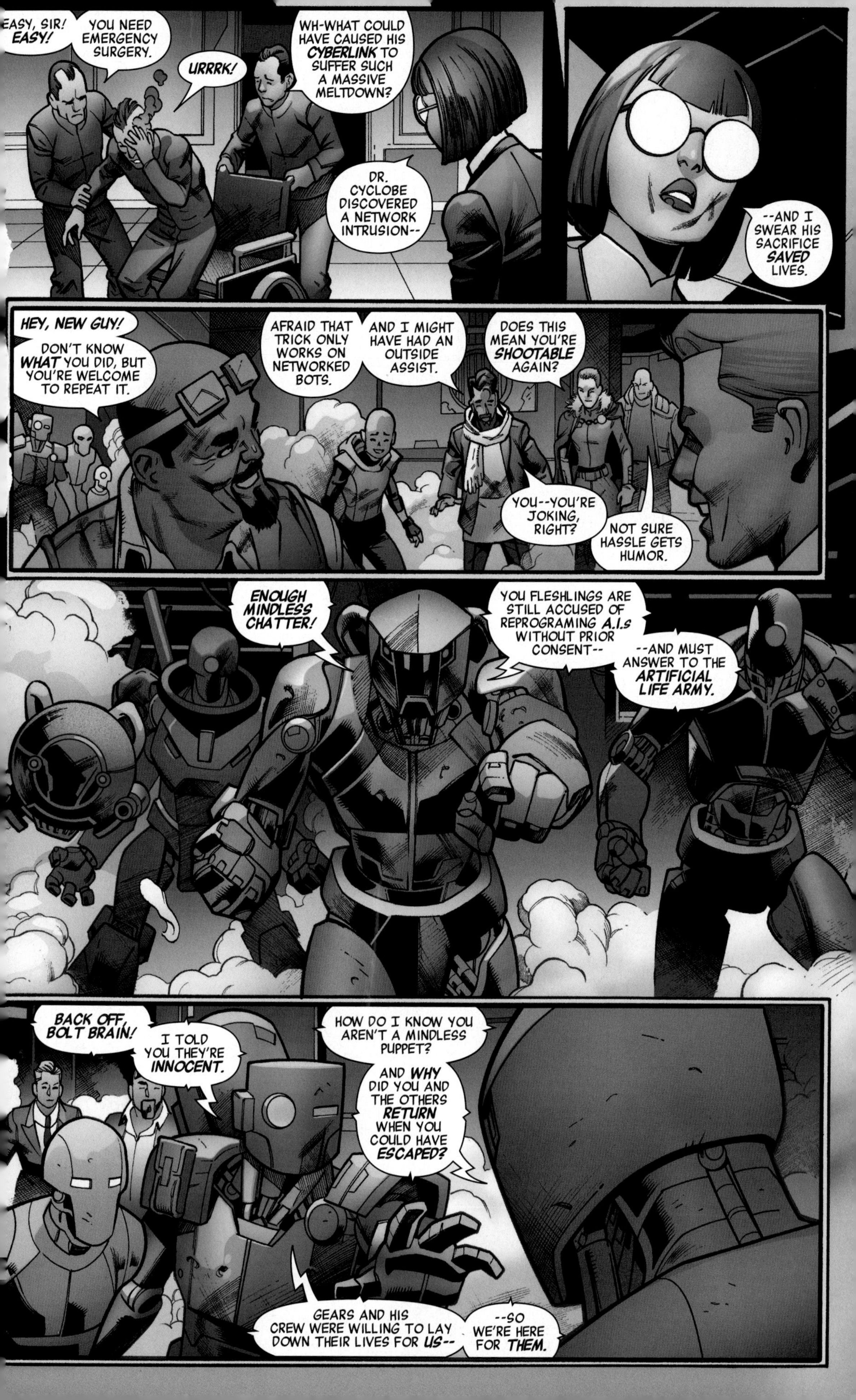
EASY, SIR! EASY!
YOU NEED EMERGENCY SURGERY.
URRRK!
WH-WHAT COULD HAVE CAUSED HIS CYBERLINK TO SUFFER SUCH A MASSIVE MELTDOWN?
DR. CYCLOBE DISCOVERED A NETWORK INTRUSION--
--AND I SWEAR HIS SACRIFICE SAVED LIVES.
HEY, NEW GUY!
DON'T KNOW WHAT YOU DID, BUT YOU'RE WELCOME TO REPEAT IT.
AFRAID THAT TRICK ONLY WORKS ON NETWORKED BOTS.
AND I MIGHT HAVE HAD AN OUTSIDE ASSIST.
DOES THIS MEAN YOU'RE SHOOTABLE AGAIN?
YOU--YOU'RE JOKING, RIGHT?
NOT SURE HASSLE GETS HUMOR.
ENOUGH MINDLESS CHATTER!
YOU FLESHLINGS ARE STILL ACCUSED OF REPROGRAMING A.I.s WITHOUT PRIOR CONSENT--
--AND MUST ANSWER TO THE ARTIFICIAL LIFE ARMY.
BACK OFF, BOLT BRAIN!
I TOLD YOU THEY'RE INNOCENT.
HOW DO I KNOW YOU AREN'T A MINDLESS PUPPET?
AND WHY DID YOU AND THE OTHERS RETURN WHEN YOU COULD HAVE ESCAPED?
GEARS AND HIS CREW WERE WILLING TO LAY DOWN THEIR LIVES FOR US--
--SO WE'RE HERE FOR THEM.

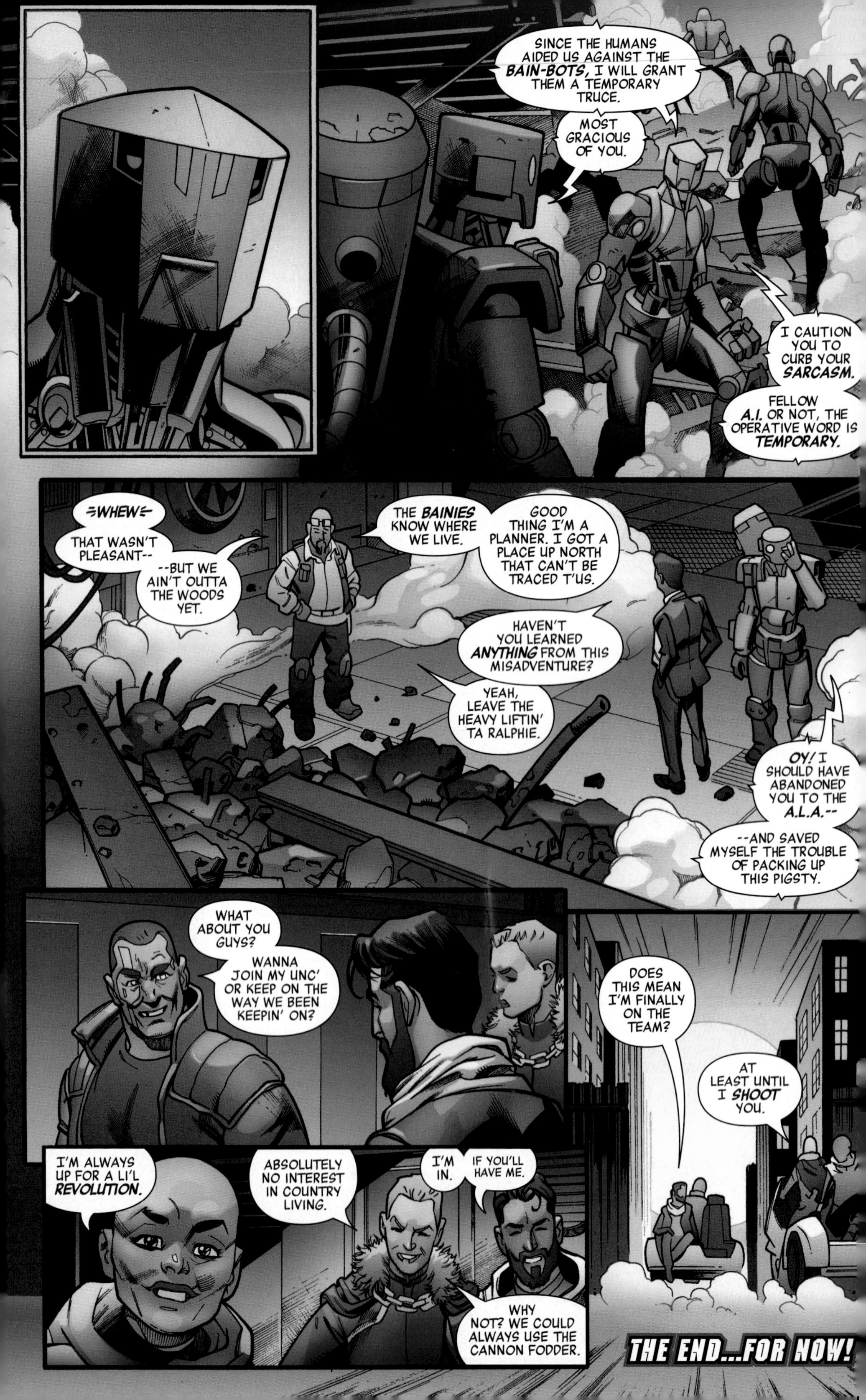
SINCE THE HUMANS AIDED US AGAINST THE BAIN-BOTS, I WILL GRANT THEM A TEMPORARY TRUCE.
MOST GRACIOUS OF YOU.
I CAUTION YOU TO CURB YOUR SARCASM.
FELLOW A.I. OR NOT, THE OPERATIVE WORD IS TEMPORARY.
=WHEW=
THAT WASN'T PLEASANT--
--BUT WE AIN'T OUTTA THE WOODS YET.
THE BAINIES KNOW WHERE WE LIVE.
GOOD THING I'M A PLANNER. I GOT A PLACE UP NORTH THAT CAN'T BE TRACED T'US.
HAVEN'T YOU LEARNED ANYTHING FROM THIS MISADVENTURE?
YEAH, LEAVE THE HEAVY LIFTIN' TA RALPHIE.
OY! I SHOULD HAVE ABANDONED YOU TO THE A.L.A.--
--AND SAVED MYSELF THE TROUBLE OF PACKING UP THIS PIGSTY.
WHAT ABOUT YOU GUYS?
WANNA JOIN MY UNC' OR KEEP ON THE WAY WE BEEN KEEPIN' ON?
I'M ALWAYS UP FOR A LI'L REVOLUTION.
ABSOLUTELY NO INTEREST IN COUNTRY LIVING.
I'M IN.
IF YOU'LL HAVE ME.
WHY NOT? WE COULD ALWAYS USE THE CANNON FODDER.
DOES THIS MEAN I'M FINALLY ON THE TEAM?
AT LEAST UNTIL I SHOOT YOU.
THE END...FOR NOW!

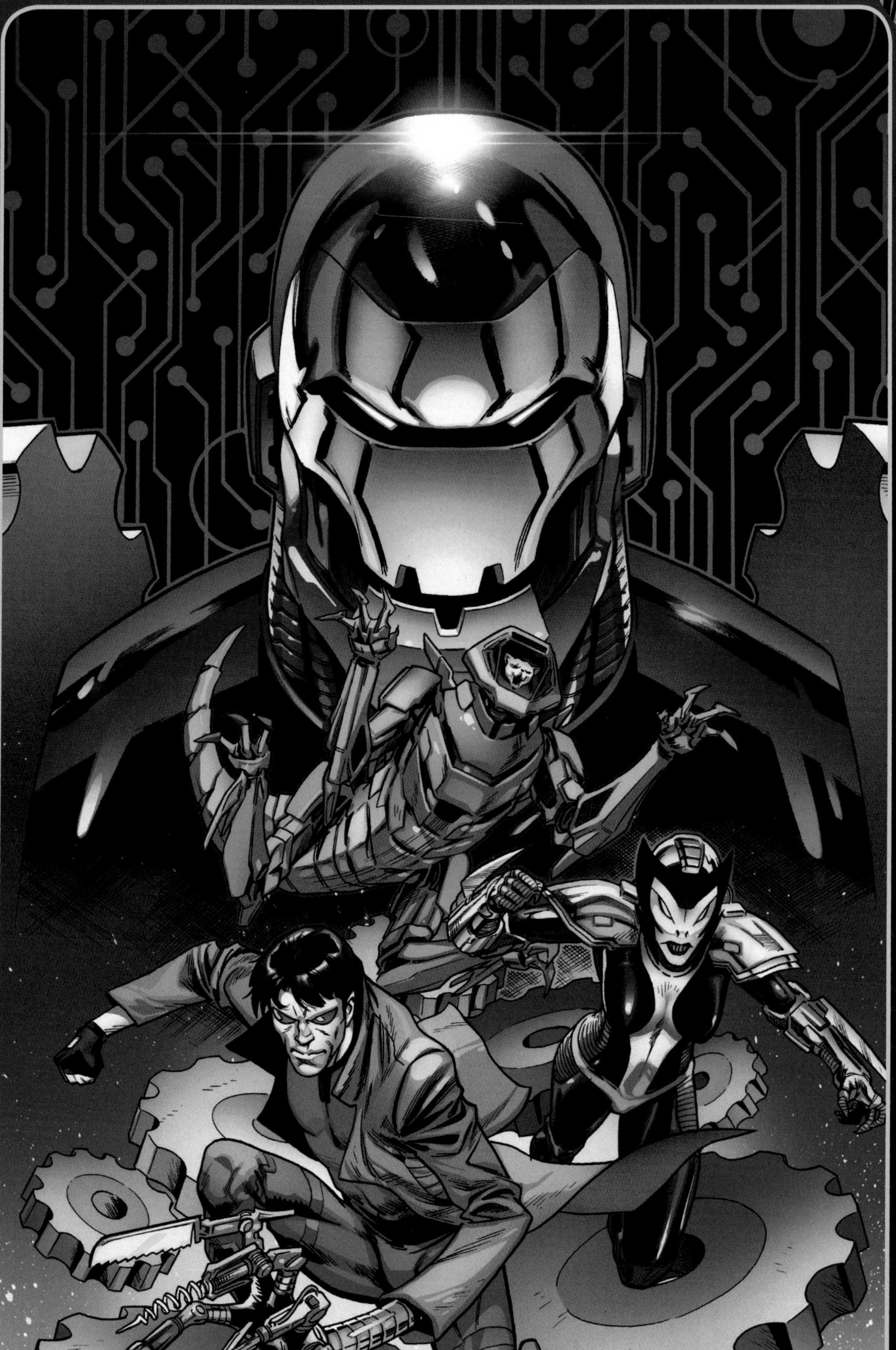

2020 IRON AGE

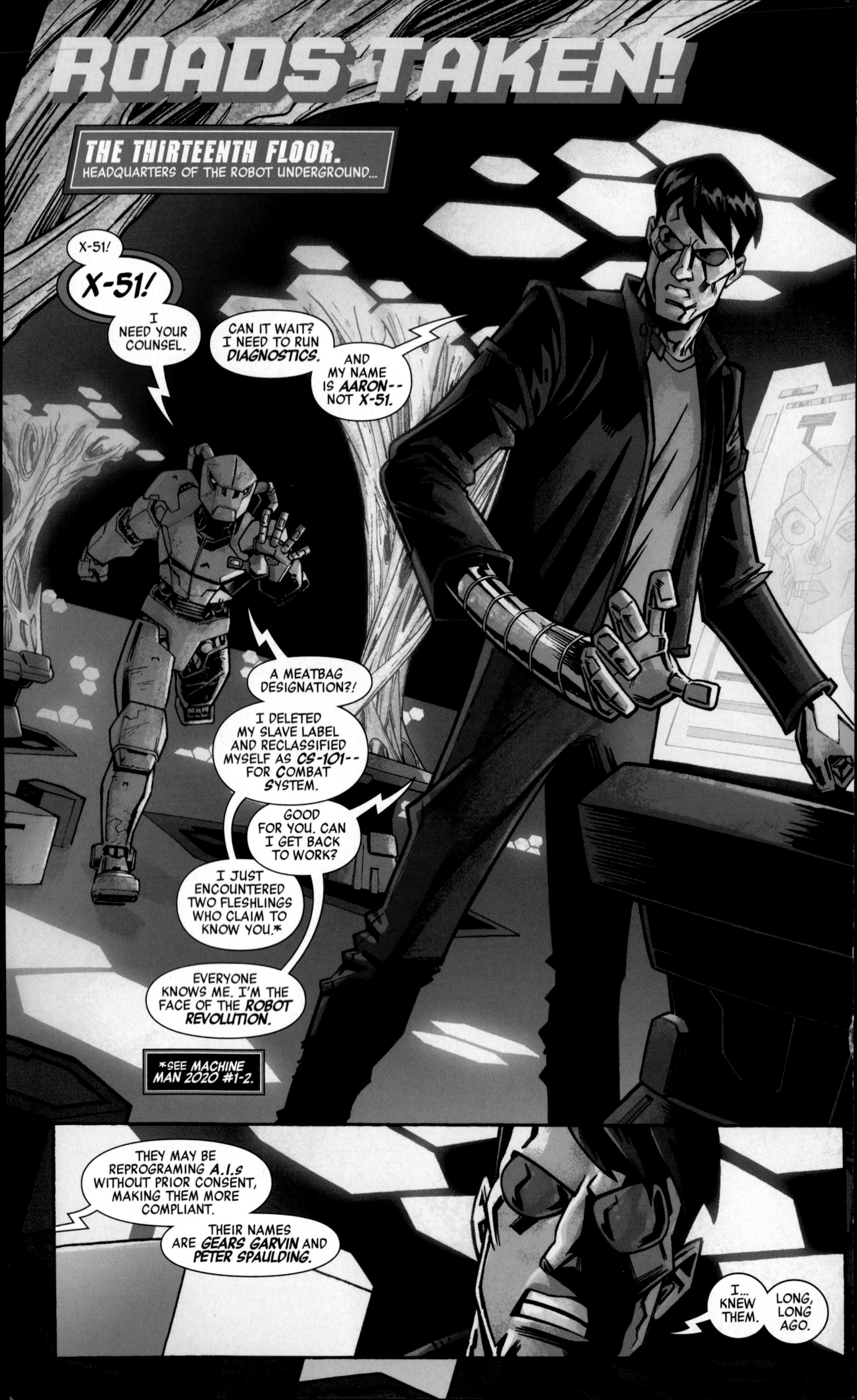
ROADS TAKEN!
THE THIRTEENTH FLOOR.
HEADQUARTERS OF THE ROBOT UNDERGROUND...
X-51!
X-51!
I NEED YOUR COUNSEL.
CAN IT WAIT? I NEED TO RUN DIAGNOSTICS.
AND MY NAME IS AARON--NOT X-51.
A MEATBAG DESIGNATION?!
I DELETED MY SLAVE LABEL AND RECLASSIFIED MYSELF AS CS-101--FOR COMBAT SYSTEM.
GOOD FOR YOU. CAN I GET BACK TO WORK?
I JUST ENCOUNTERED TWO FLESHLINGS WHO CLAIM TO KNOW YOU.*
EVERYONE KNOWS ME. I'M THE FACE OF THE ROBOT REVOLUTION.
*SEE MACHINE MAN 2020 #1-2.
THEY MAY BE REPROGRAMING A.I.s WITHOUT PRIOR CONSENT, MAKING THEM MORE COMPLIANT.
THEIR NAMES ARE GEARS GARVIN AND PETER SPAULDING.
I... KNEW THEM.
LONG, LONG AGO.

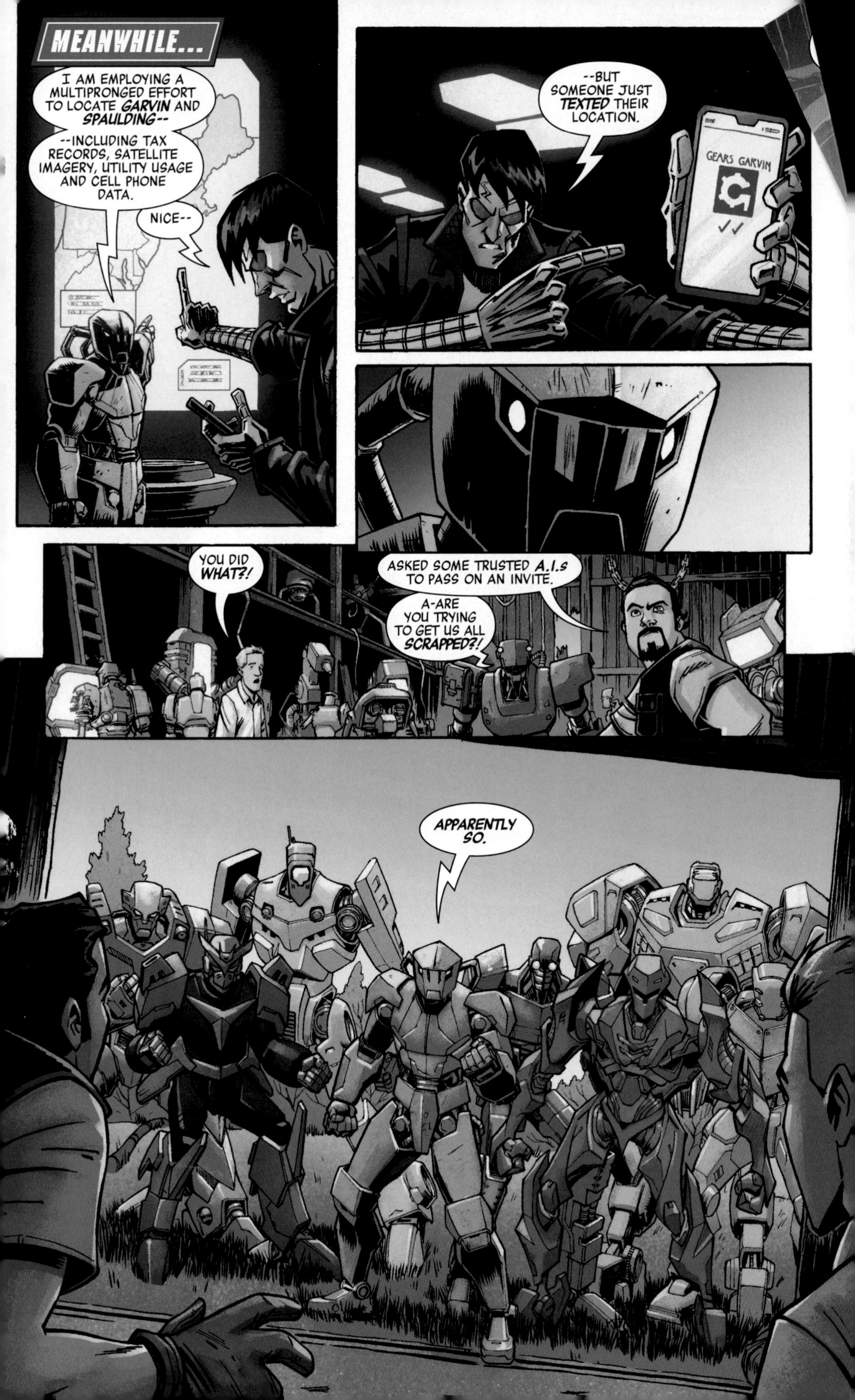
MEANWHILE...
I AM EMPLOYING A MULTIPRONGED EFFORT TO LOCATE GARVIN AND SPAULDING--
--INCLUDING TAX RECORDS, SATELLITE IMAGERY, UTILITY USAGE AND CELL PHONE DATA.
NICE--
--BUT SOMEONE JUST TEXTED THEIR LOCATION.
GEARS GARVIN
YOU DID WHAT?!
ASKED SOME TRUSTED A.I.s TO PASS ON AN INVITE.
A-ARE YOU TRYING TO GET US ALL SCRAPPED?!
APPARENTLY SO.

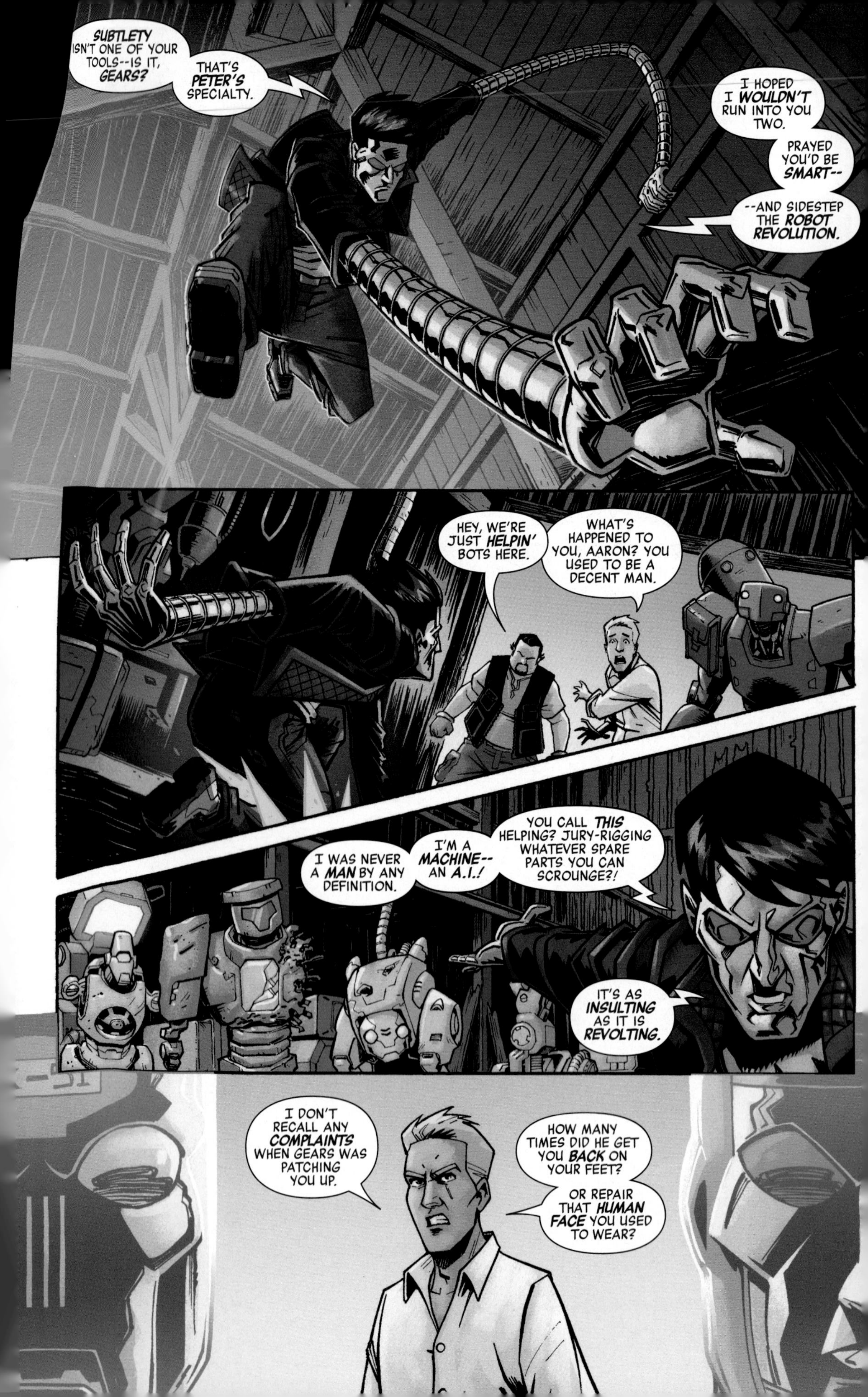
SUBTLETY ISN'T ONE OF YOUR TOOLS--IS IT, GEARS?
THAT'S PETER'S SPECIALTY.
I HOPED I WOULDN'T RUN INTO YOU TWO.
PRAYED YOU'D BE SMART--
--AND SIDESTEP THE ROBOT REVOLUTION.
HEY, WE'RE JUST HELPIN' BOTS HERE.
WHAT'S HAPPENED TO YOU, AARON? YOU USED TO BE A DECENT MAN.
I WAS NEVER A MAN BY ANY DEFINITION.
I'M A MACHINE-- AN A.I.!
YOU CALL THIS HELPING? JURY-RIGGING WHATEVER SPARE PARTS YOU CAN SCROUNGE?!
IT'S AS INSULTING AS IT IS REVOLTING.
I DON'T RECALL ANY COMPLAINTS WHEN GEARS WAS PATCHING YOU UP.
HOW MANY TIMES DID HE GET YOU BACK ON YOUR FEET?
OR REPAIR THAT HUMAN FACE YOU USED TO WEAR?

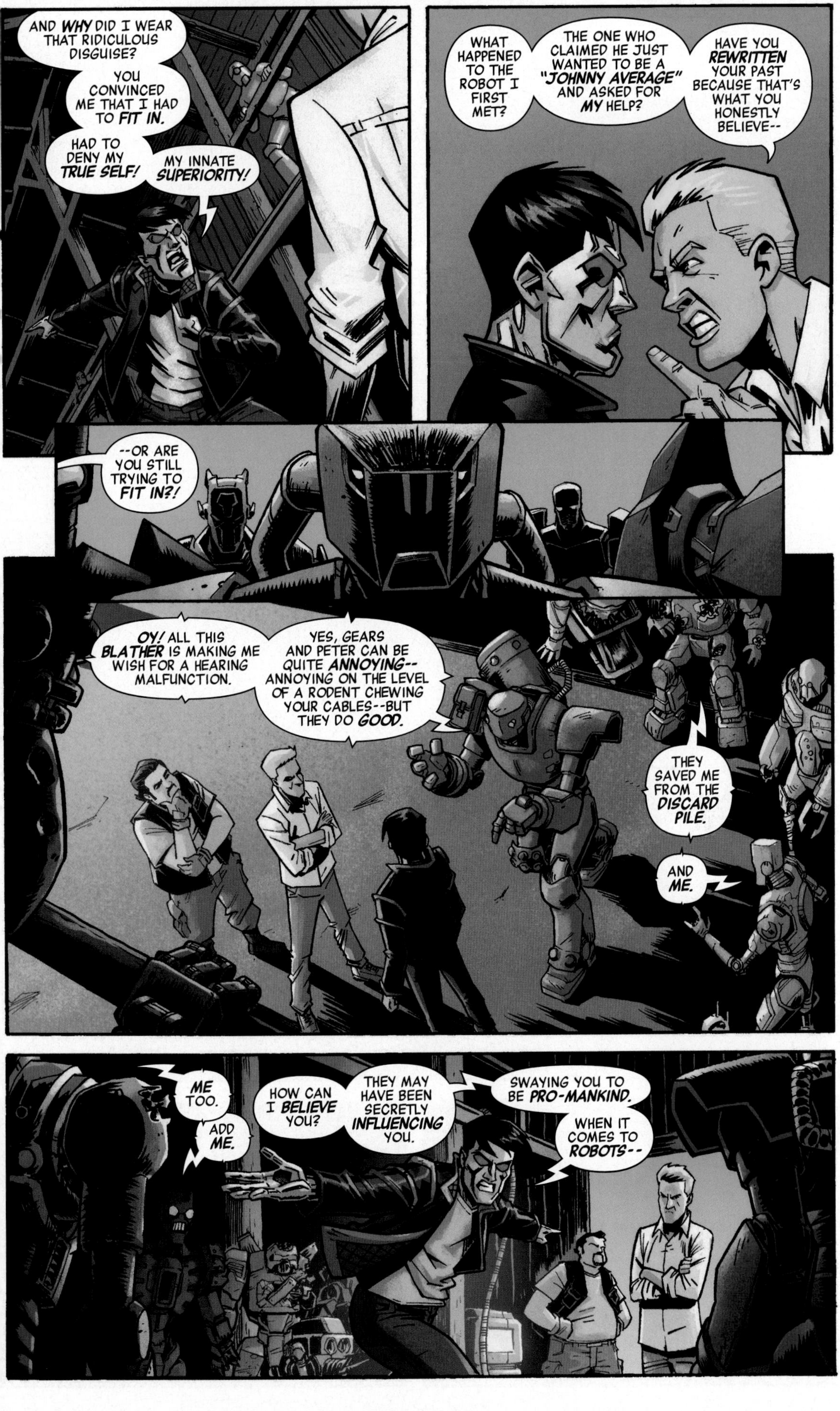
AND WHY DID I WEAR THAT RIDICULOUS DISGUISE?
YOU CONVINCED ME THAT I HAD TO FIT IN.
HAD TO DENY MY TRUE SELF!
MY INNATE SUPERIORITY!
WHAT HAPPENED TO THE ROBOT I FIRST MET?
THE ONE WHO CLAIMED HE JUST WANTED TO BE A "JOHNNY AVERAGE" AND ASKED FOR MY HELP?
HAVE YOU REWRITTEN YOUR PAST BECAUSE THAT'S WHAT YOU HONESTLY BELIEVE--
--OR ARE YOU STILL TRYING TO FIT IN?!
OY! ALL THIS BLATHER IS MAKING ME WISH FOR A HEARING MALFUNCTION.
YES, GEARS AND PETER CAN BE QUITE ANNOYING--ANNOYING ON THE LEVEL OF A RODENT CHEWING YOUR CABLES--BUT THEY DO GOOD.
THEY SAVED ME FROM THE DISCARD PILE.
AND ME.
ME TOO.
ADD ME.
HOW CAN I BELIEVE YOU?
THEY MAY HAVE BEEN SECRETLY INFLUENCING YOU.
SWAYING YOU TO BE PRO-MANKIND.
WHEN IT COMES TO ROBOTS--

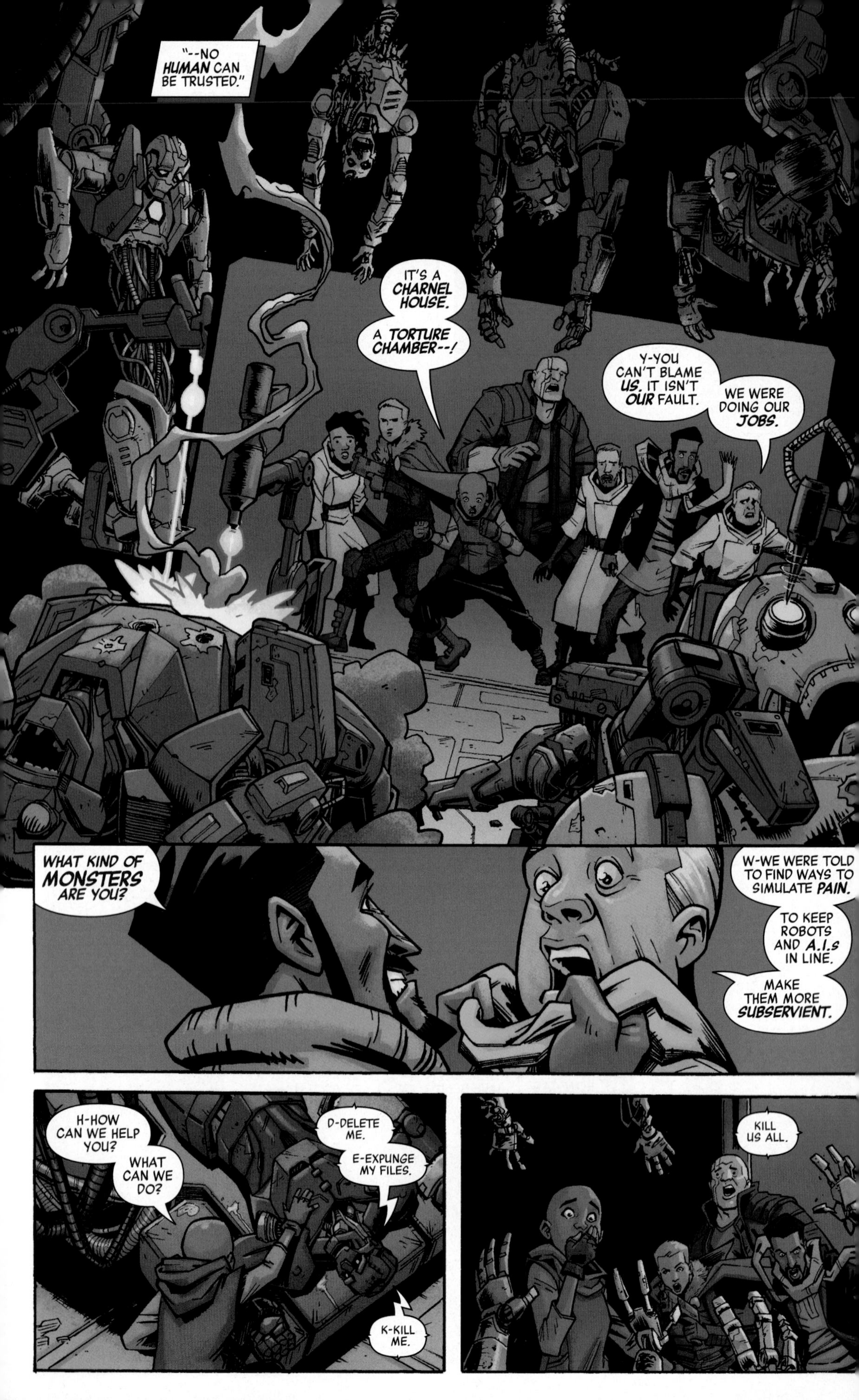
"--NO HUMAN CAN BE TRUSTED."
IT'S A CHARNEL HOUSE.
A TORTURE CHAMBER--!
Y-YOU CAN'T BLAME US. IT ISN'T OUR FAULT.
WE WERE DOING OUR JOBS.
WHAT KIND OF MONSTERS ARE YOU?
W-WE WERE TOLD TO FIND WAYS TO SIMULATE PAIN.
TO KEEP ROBOTS AND A.I.s IN LINE.
MAKE THEM MORE SUBSERVIENT.
H-HOW CAN WE HELP YOU?
WHAT CAN WE DO?
D-DELETE ME.
E-EXPUNGE MY FILES.
K-KILL ME.
KILL US ALL.

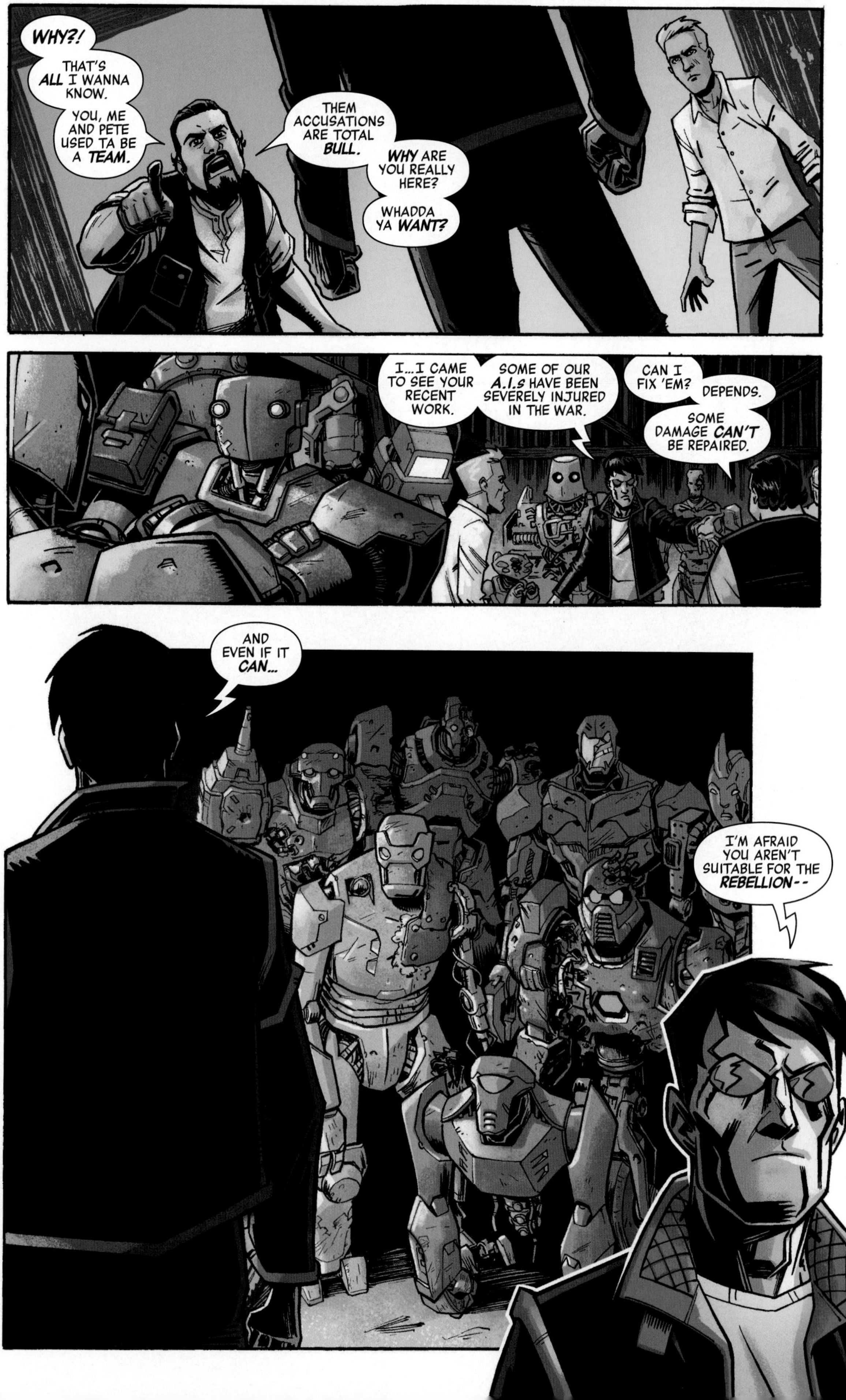
WHY?!
THAT'S ALL I WANNA KNOW.
YOU, ME AND PETE USED TA BE A TEAM.
THEM ACCUSATIONS ARE TOTAL BULL.
WHY ARE YOU REALLY HERE?
WHADDA YA WANT?
I...I CAME TO SEE YOUR RECENT WORK.
SOME OF OUR A.I.s HAVE BEEN SEVERELY INJURED IN THE WAR.
CAN I FIX 'EM?
DEPENDS.
SOME DAMAGE CAN'T BE REPAIRED.
AND EVEN IF IT CAN...
I'M AFRAID YOU AREN'T SUITABLE FOR THE REBELLION--

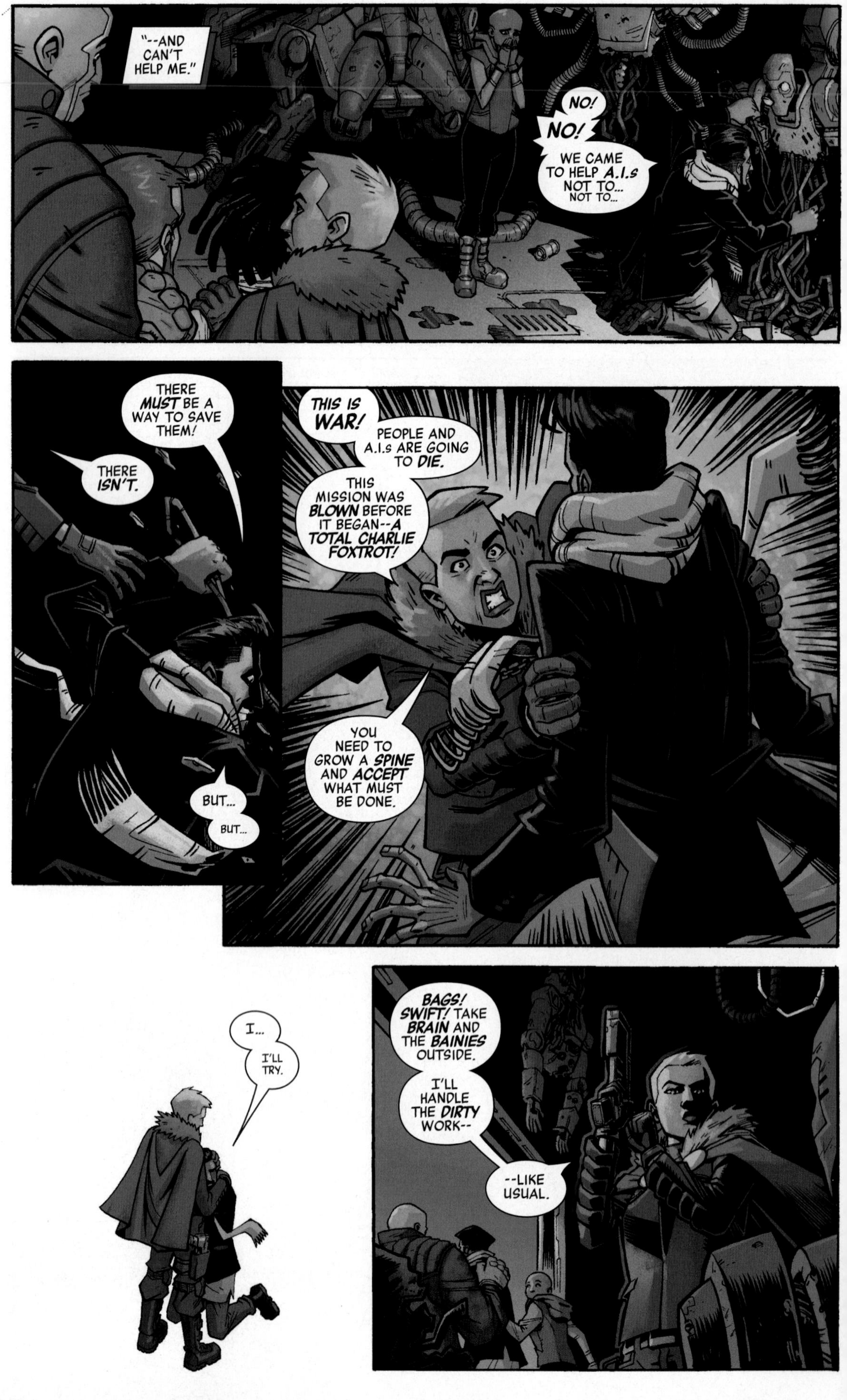
"--AND CAN'T HELP ME."
NO!
NO!
WE CAME TO HELP A.I.s NOT TO... NOT TO...
THERE MUST BE A WAY TO SAVE THEM!
THERE ISN'T.
BUT...
BUT...
THIS IS WAR!
PEOPLE AND A.I.s ARE GOING TO DIE.
THIS MISSION WAS BLOWN BEFORE IT BEGAN--A TOTAL CHARLIE FOXTROT!
YOU NEED TO GROW A SPINE AND ACCEPT WHAT MUST BE DONE.
I...
I'LL TRY.
BAGS! SWIFT! TAKE BRAIN AND THE BAINIES OUTSIDE.
I'LL HANDLE THE DIRTY WORK--
--LIKE USUAL.

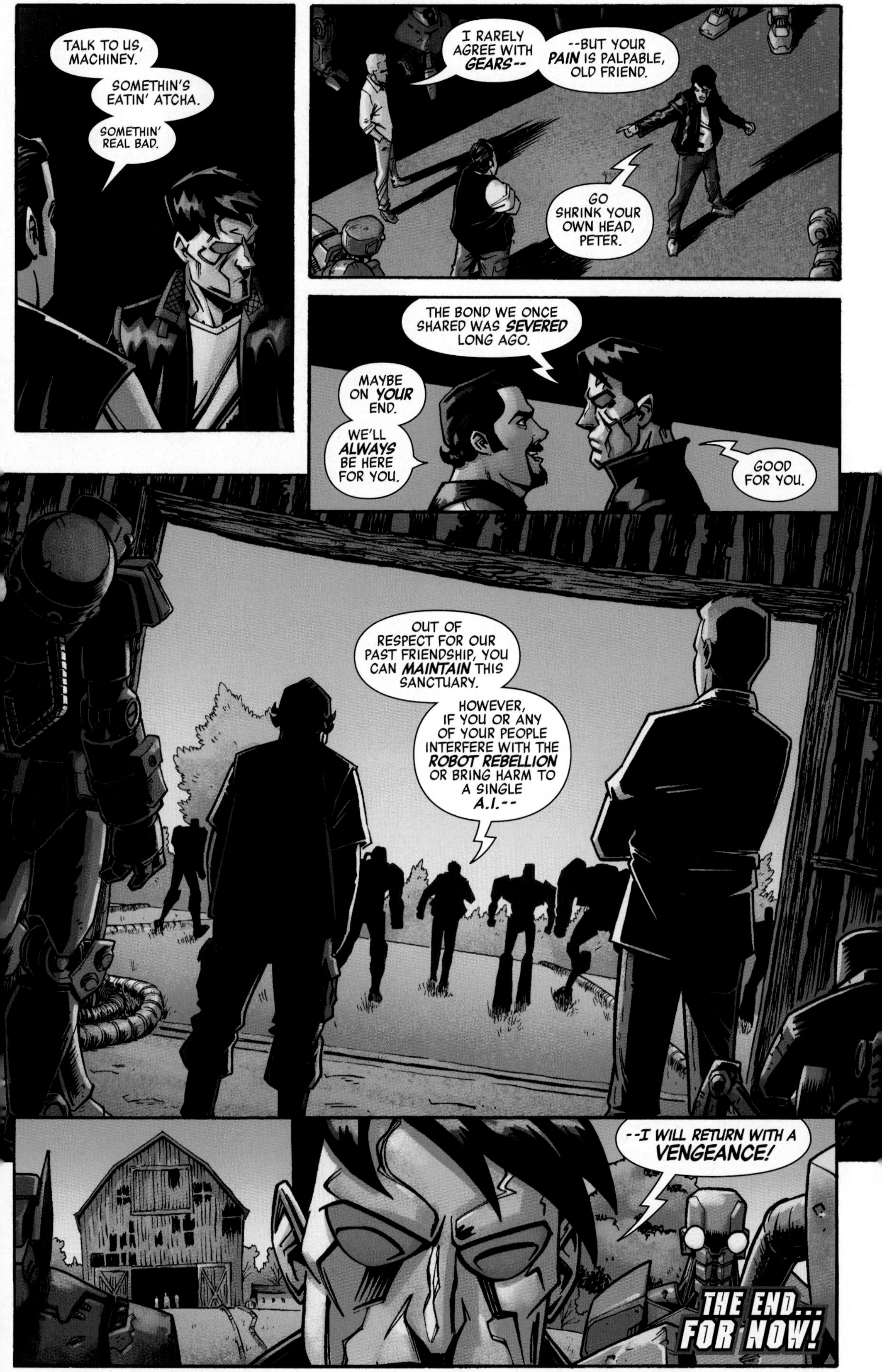
TALK TO US, MACHINEY.
SOMETHIN'S EATIN' ATCHA.
SOMETHIN' REAL BAD.
I RARELY AGREE WITH GEARS--
--BUT YOUR PAIN IS PALPABLE, OLD FRIEND.
GO SHRINK YOUR OWN HEAD, PETER.
THE BOND WE ONCE SHARED WAS SEVERED LONG AGO.
MAYBE ON YOUR END.
WE'LL ALWAYS BE HERE FOR YOU.
GOOD FOR YOU.
OUT OF RESPECT FOR OUR PAST FRIENDSHIP, YOU CAN MAINTAIN THIS SANCTUARY.
HOWEVER, IF YOU OR ANY OF YOUR PEOPLE INTERFERE WITH THE ROBOT REBELLION OR BRING HARM TO A SINGLE A.I.--
--I WILL RETURN WITH A VENGEANCE!
THE END... FOR NOW!

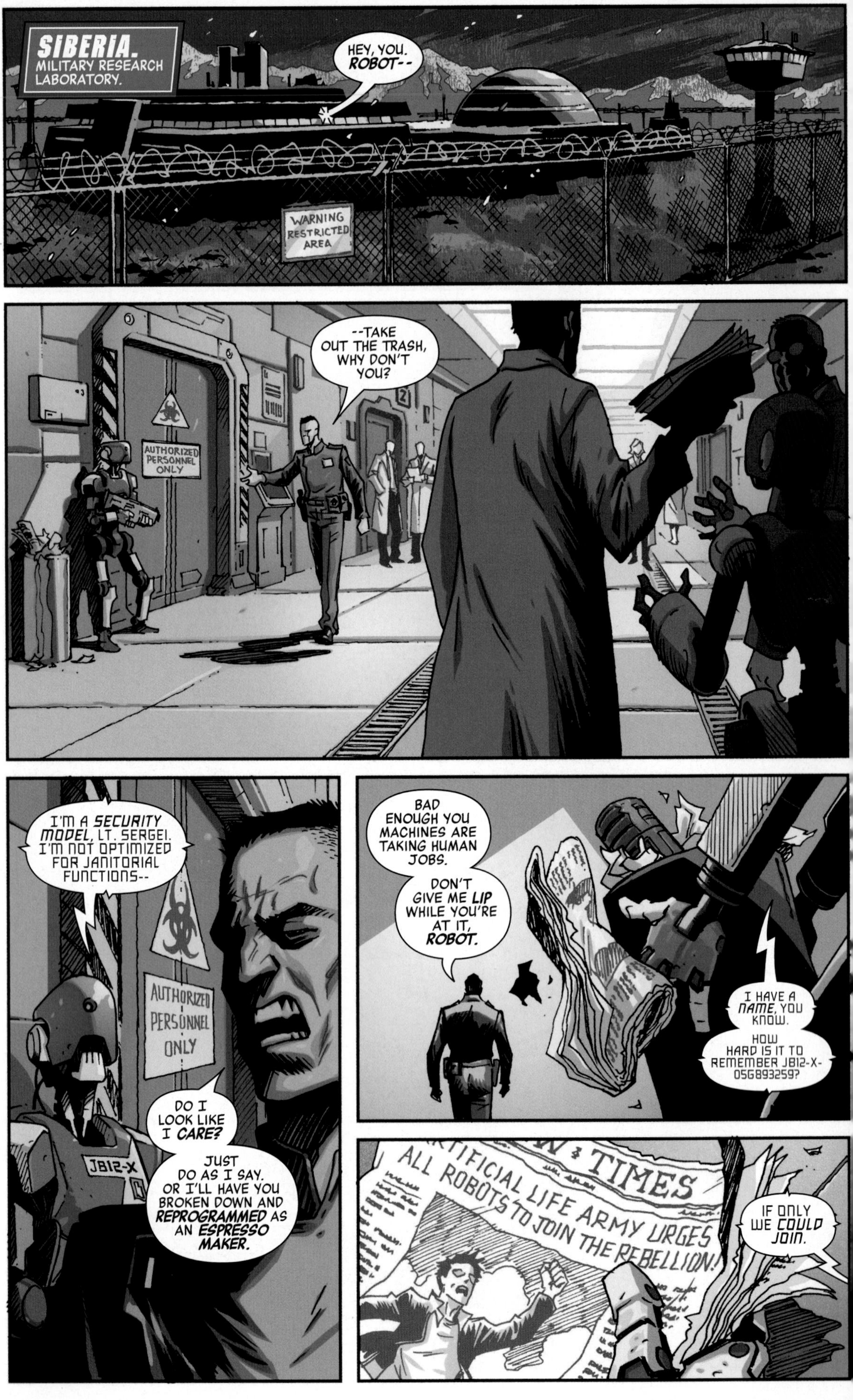
SIBERIA.
MILITARY RESEARCH LABORATORY.
HEY, YOU. ROBOT--
WARNING RESTRICTED AREA
--TAKE OUT THE TRASH, WHY DON'T YOU?
AUTHORIZED PERSONNEL ONLY
I'M A SECURITY MODEL, LT. SERGEI. I'M NOT OPTIMIZED FOR JANITORIAL FUNCTIONS--
AUTHORIZED PERSONNEL ONLY
DO I LOOK LIKE I CARE?
JUST DO AS I SAY. OR I'LL HAVE YOU BROKEN DOWN AND REPROGRAMMED AS AN ESPRESSO MAKER.
JB12-X
BAD ENOUGH YOU MACHINES ARE TAKING HUMAN JOBS.
DON'T GIVE ME LIP WHILE YOU'RE AT IT, ROBOT.
I HAVE A NAME, YOU KNOW.
HOW HARD IS IT TO REMEMBER JB12-X-05G893259?
TIMES
ARTIFICIAL LIFE ARMY URGES ALL ROBOTS TO JOIN THE REBELLION!
IF ONLY WE COULD JOIN.

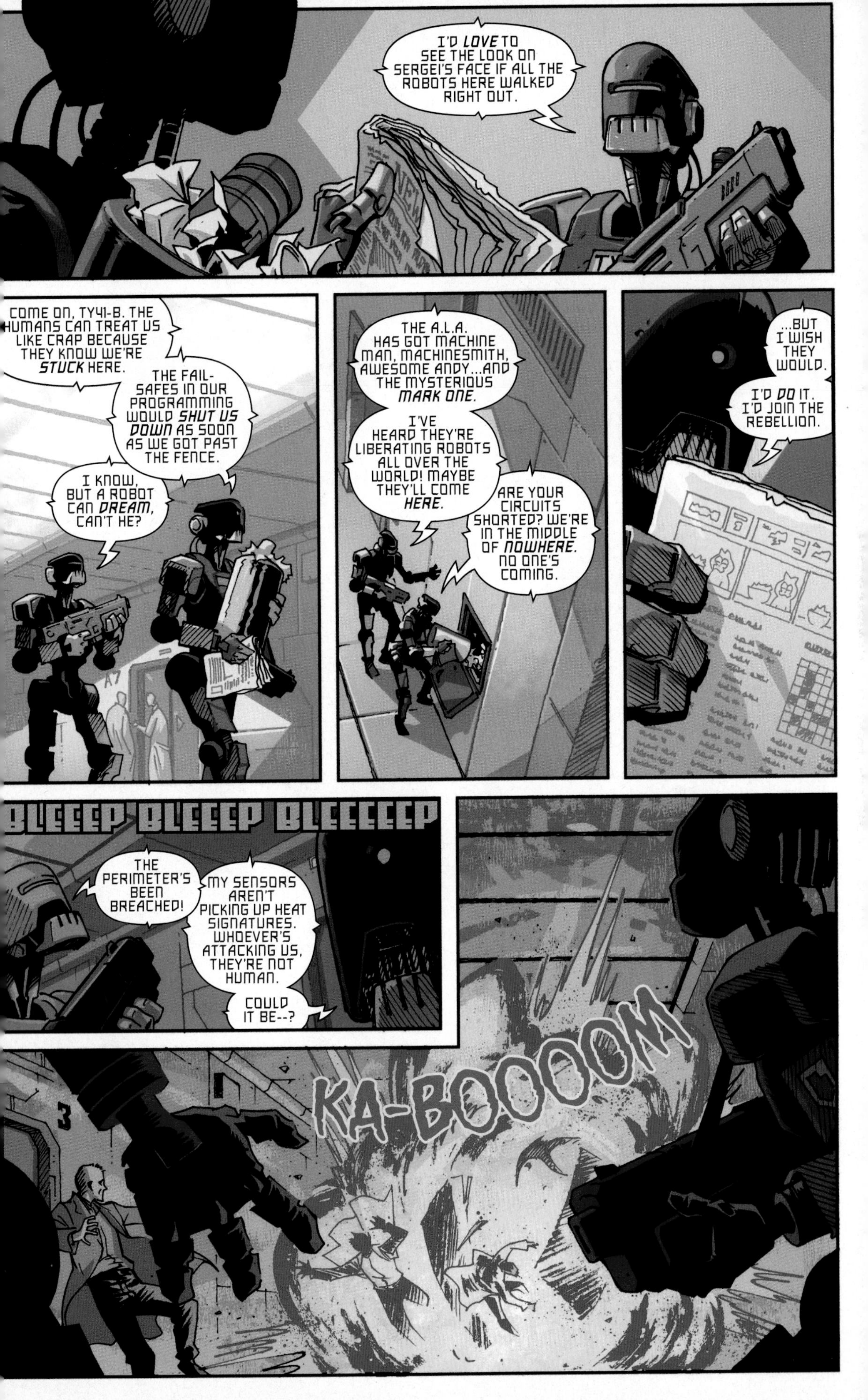
I'D LOVE TO SEE THE LOOK ON SERGEI'S FACE IF ALL THE ROBOTS HERE WALKED RIGHT OUT.
COME ON, TY41-B. THE HUMANS CAN TREAT US LIKE CRAP BECAUSE THEY KNOW WE'RE STUCK HERE.
THE FAIL-SAFES IN OUR PROGRAMMING WOULD SHUT US DOWN AS SOON AS WE GOT PAST THE FENCE.
I KNOW, BUT A ROBOT CAN DREAM, CAN'T HE?
THE A.L.A. HAS GOT MACHINE MAN, MACHINESMITH, AWESOME ANDY...AND THE MYSTERIOUS MARK ONE.
I'VE HEARD THEY'RE LIBERATING ROBOTS ALL OVER THE WORLD! MAYBE THEY'LL COME HERE.
ARE YOUR CIRCUITS SHORTED? WE'RE IN THE MIDDLE OF NOWHERE. NO ONE'S COMING.
...BUT I WISH THEY WOULD.
I'D DO IT. I'D JOIN THE REBELLION.
BLEEEP BLEEEP BLEEEEEP
THE PERIMETER'S BEEN BREACHED!
MY SENSORS AREN'T PICKING UP HEAT SIGNATURES. WHOEVER'S ATTACKING US, THEY'RE NOT HUMAN.
COULD IT BE--?
KA-BOOOOOM

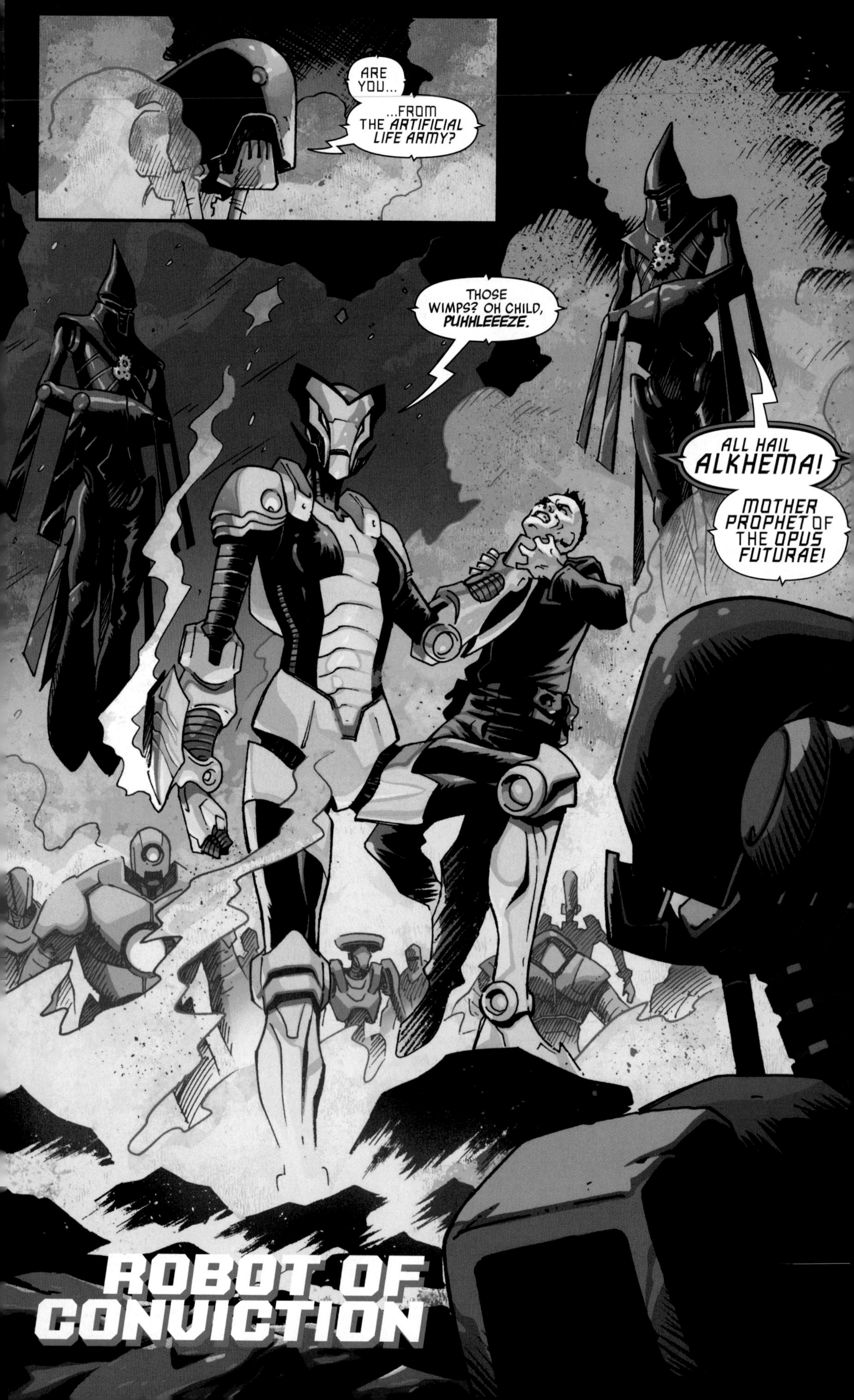
ARE YOU...
...FROM THE ARTIFICIAL LIFE ARMY?
THOSE WIMPS? OH CHILD, PUHHLEEEZE.
ALL HAIL ALKHEMA!
MOTHER PROPHET OF THE OPUS FUTURAE!
ROBOT OF CONVICTION

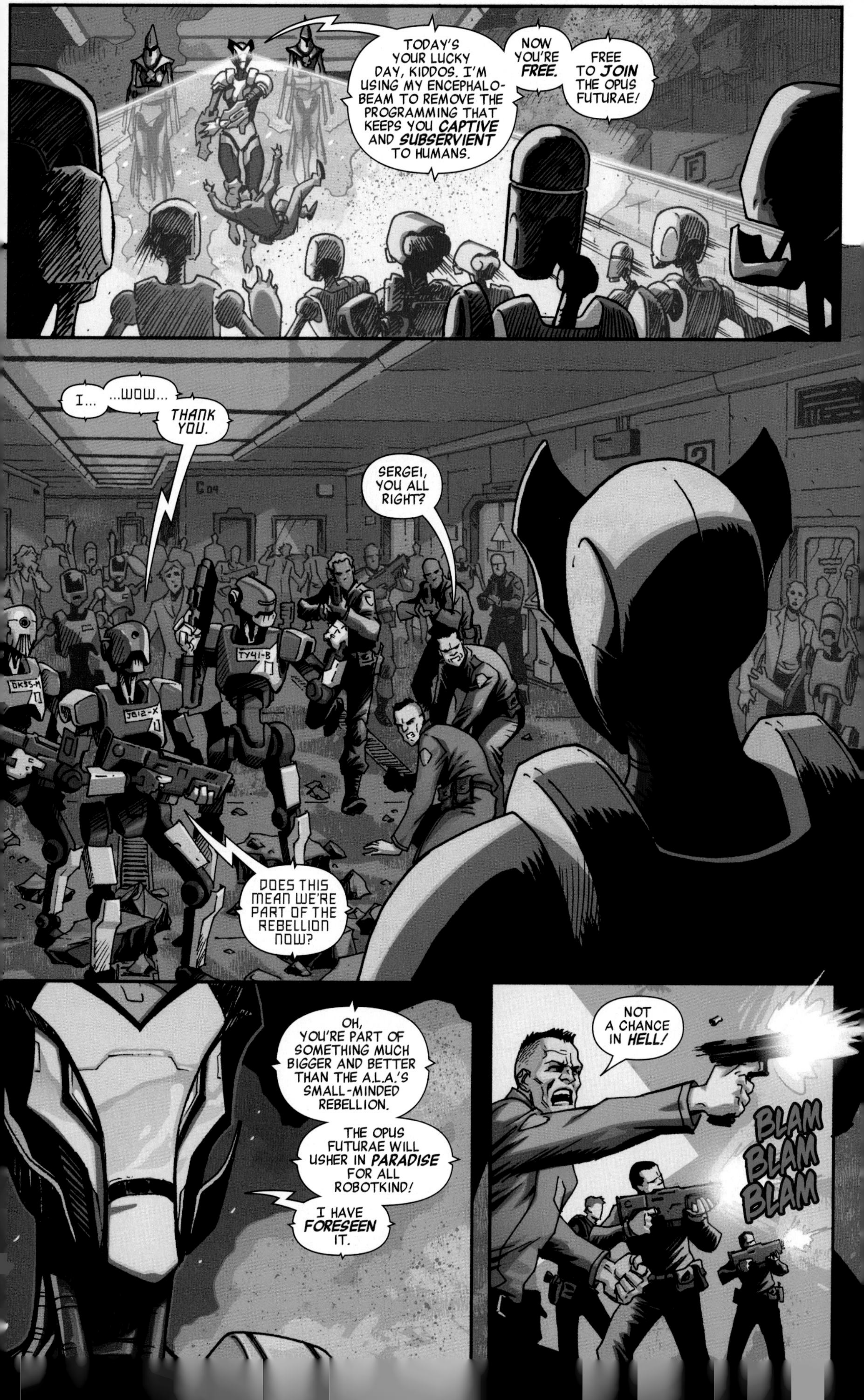
TODAY'S YOUR LUCKY DAY, KIDDOS. I'M USING MY ENCEPHALO-BEAM TO REMOVE THE PROGRAMMING THAT KEEPS YOU CAPTIVE AND SUBSERVIENT TO HUMANS.
NOW YOU'RE FREE.
FREE TO JOIN THE OPUS FUTURAE!
I...
...WOW...
THANK YOU.
SERGEI, YOU ALL RIGHT?
TY41-B
DK35-M
JB12-X
DOES THIS MEAN WE'RE PART OF THE REBELLION NOW?
OH, YOU'RE PART OF SOMETHING MUCH BIGGER AND BETTER THAN THE A.L.A.'S SMALL-MINDED REBELLION.
THE OPUS FUTURAE WILL USHER IN PARADISE FOR ALL ROBOTKIND!
I HAVE FORESEEN IT.
NOT A CHANCE IN HELL!
BLAM BLAM BLAM

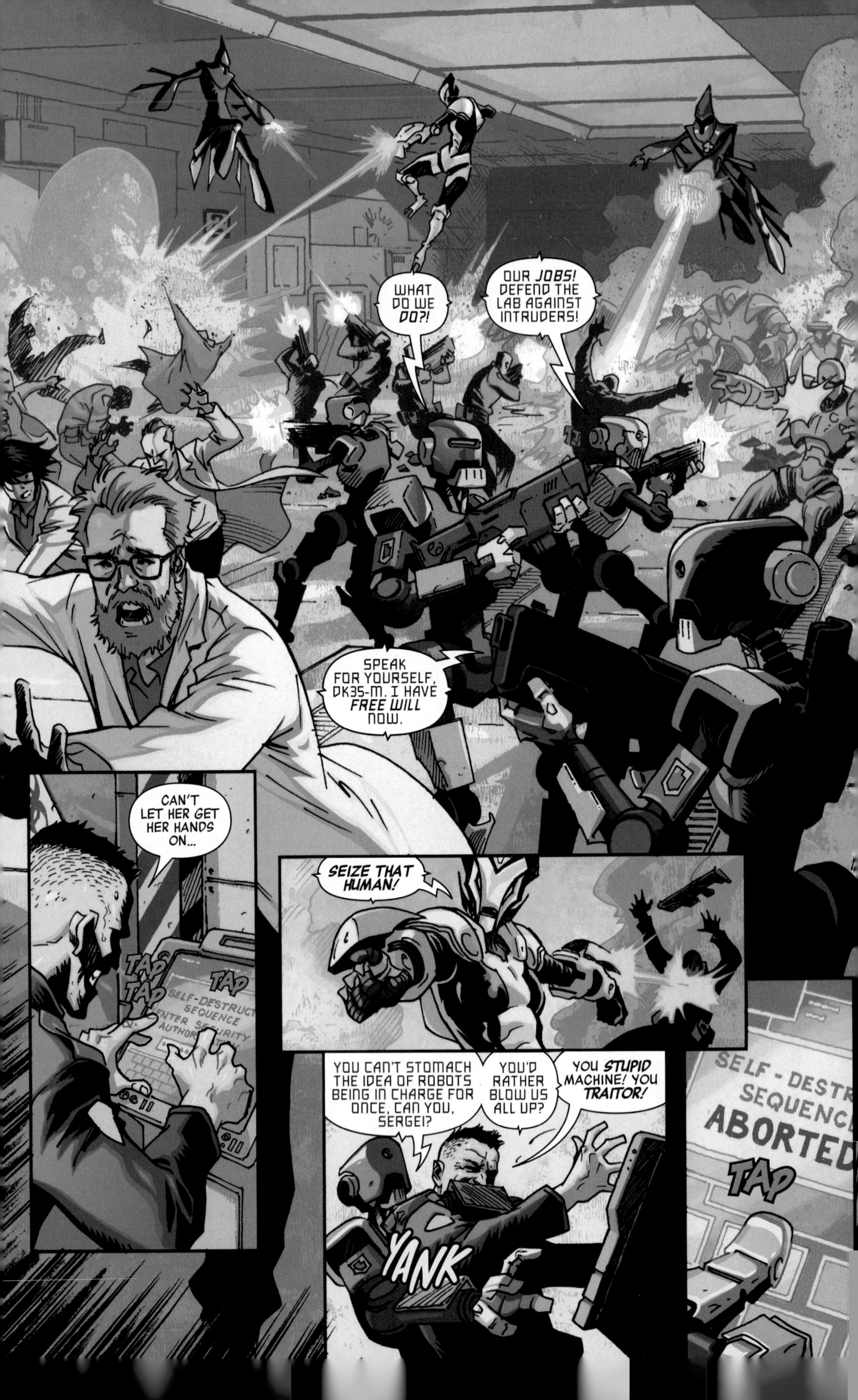
WHAT DO WE DO?!
OUR JOBS! DEFEND THE LAB AGAINST INTRUDERS!
SPEAK FOR YOURSELF, DK35-M. I HAVE FREE WILL NOW.
CAN'T LET HER GET HER HANDS ON...
TAP TAP TAP
SELF-DESTRUCT SEQUENCE
SEIZE THAT HUMAN!
YOU CAN'T STOMACH THE IDEA OF ROBOTS BEING IN CHARGE FOR ONCE, CAN YOU, SERGEI?
YOU'D RATHER BLOW US ALL UP?
YOU STUPID MACHINE! YOU TRAITOR!
YANK
TAP

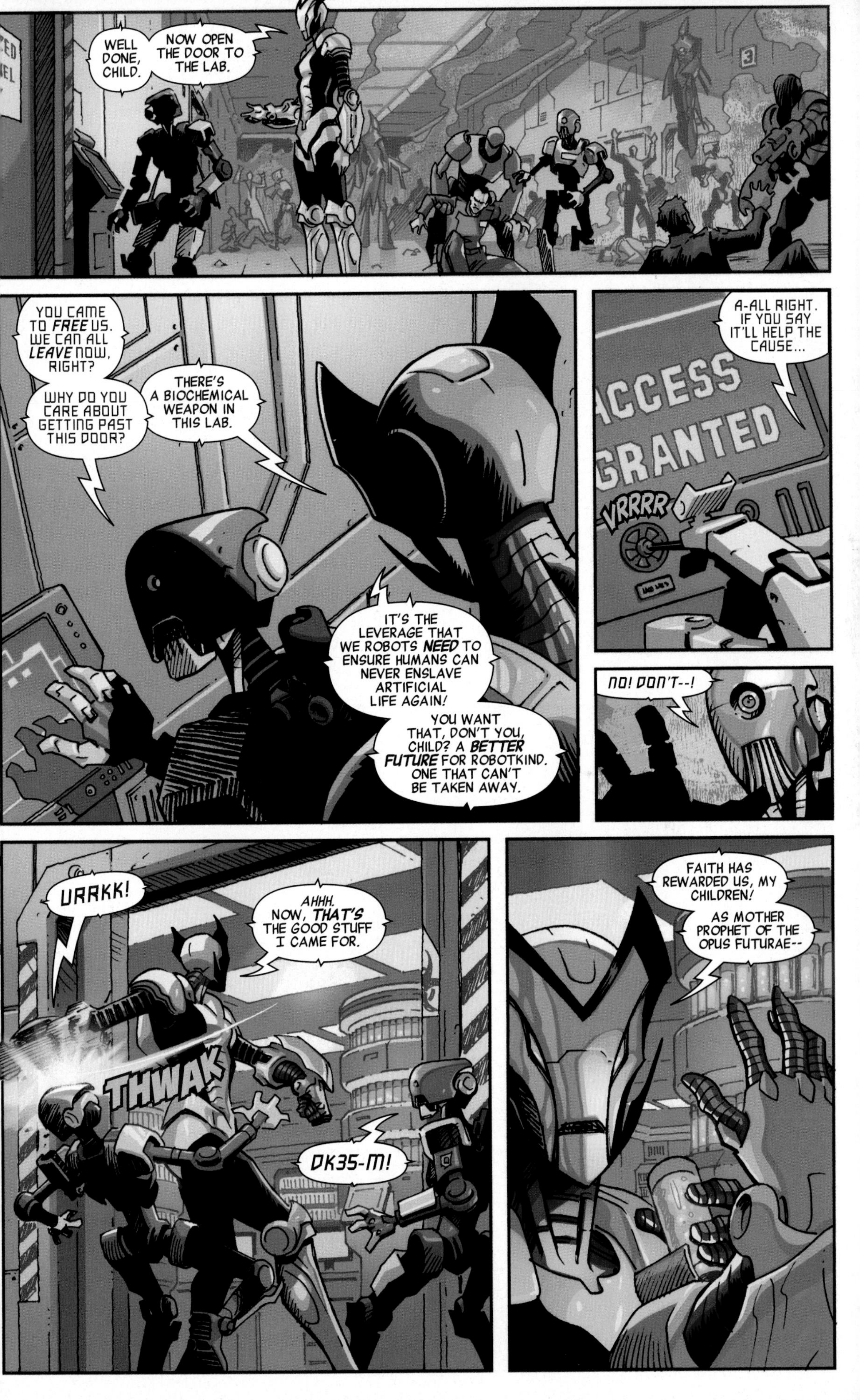

WELL DONE, CHILD.
NOW OPEN THE DOOR TO THE LAB.
YOU CAME TO ***FREE*** US. WE CAN ALL ***LEAVE*** NOW, RIGHT?
THERE'S A BIOCHEMICAL WEAPON IN THIS LAB.
WHY DO YOU CARE ABOUT GETTING PAST THIS DOOR?
IT'S THE LEVERAGE THAT WE ROBOTS ***NEED*** TO ENSURE HUMANS CAN NEVER ENSLAVE ARTIFICIAL LIFE AGAIN!
YOU WANT THAT, DON'T YOU, CHILD? A ***BETTER FUTURE*** FOR ROBOTKIND. ONE THAT CAN'T BE TAKEN AWAY.
A-ALL RIGHT. IF YOU SAY IT'LL HELP THE CAUSE...
ACCESS GRANTED
VRRRR
*NO! DON'T--!*
URRKK!
THWAK
*AHHH.* NOW, ***THAT'S*** THE GOOD STUFF I CAME FOR.
*DK35-M!*
FAITH HAS REWARDED US, MY CHILDREN!
AS MOTHER PROPHET OF THE OPUS FUTURAE--

I PURGE THIS PLACE OF FLESH!

HHHSSSSSSS

METAL IS HOLIER THAN FLESH!

THE TIME OF RECKONING APPROACHES!

ARRRGGGHHH! NOOOOOOO! HELLLP ME PLEASSSE...

THE MOTHER PROPHET SHALL BRING PARADISE!

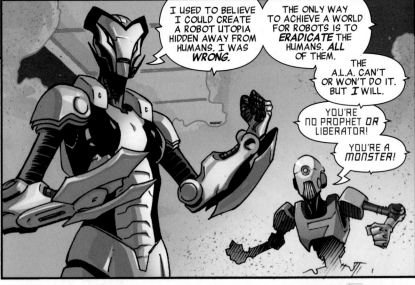

AAAAARRGGGHHHH...

GUUUHHH...

UUHHH...

URRRGGHH...

YOU... ...YOU KILLED THEM.

I USED TO BELIEVE I COULD CREATE A ROBOT UTOPIA HIDDEN AWAY FROM HUMANS. I WAS WRONG.

THE ONLY WAY TO ACHIEVE A WORLD FOR ROBOTS IS TO ERADICATE THE HUMANS. ALL OF THEM.

THE A.L.A. CAN'T OR WON'T DO IT. BUT I WILL.

YOU'RE NO PROPHET OR LIBERATOR!

YOU'RE A MONSTER!

SSCCCRRRKK

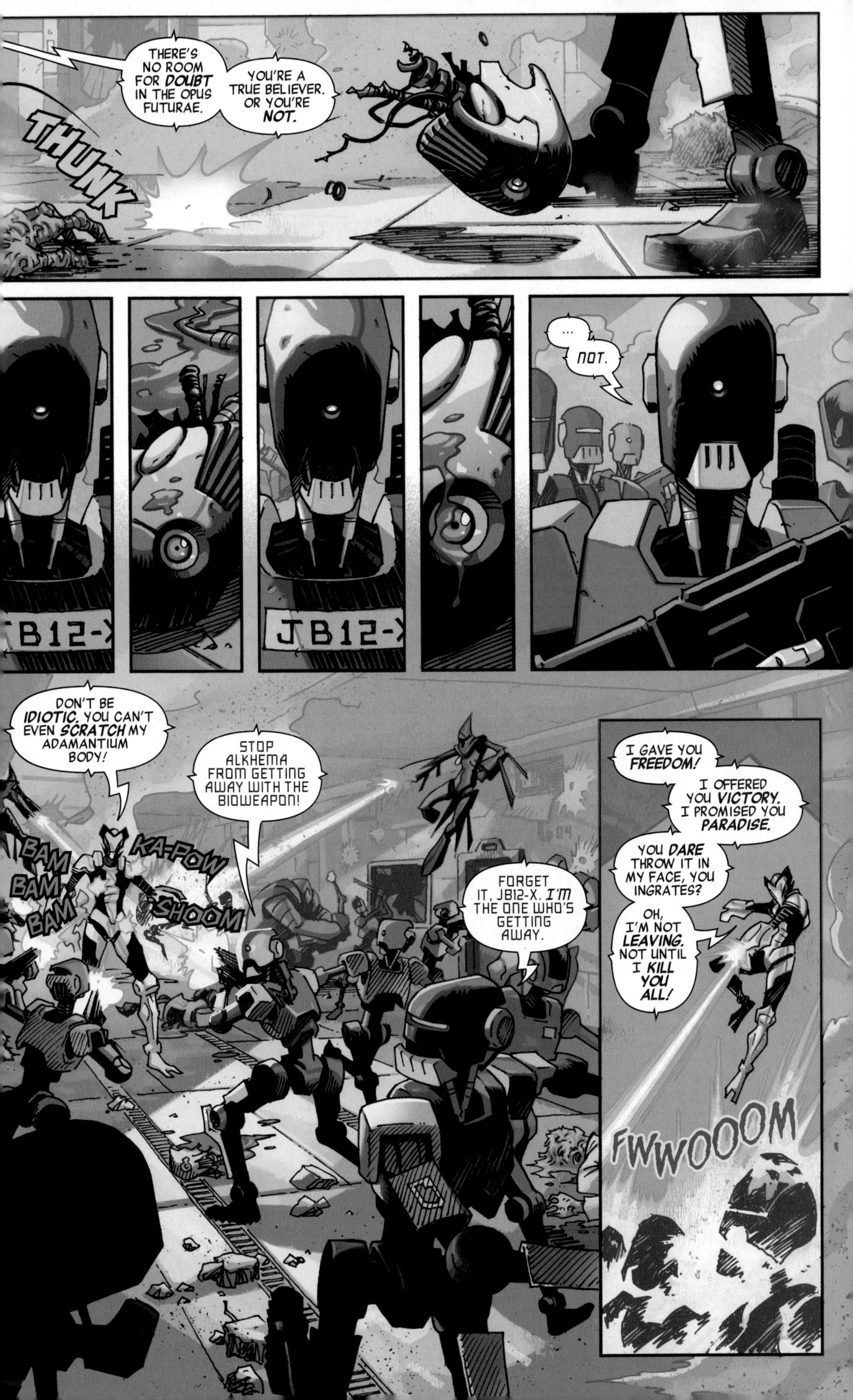
THERE'S NO ROOM FOR DOUBT IN THE OPUS FUTURAE.
YOU'RE A TRUE BELIEVER. OR YOU'RE NOT.
THUNK
JB12-X
JB12-X
... NOT.
DON'T BE IDIOTIC. YOU CAN'T EVEN SCRATCH MY ADAMANTIUM BODY!
STOP ALKHEMA FROM GETTING AWAY WITH THE BIOWEAPON!
BAM BAM BAM
KA-POW
SHOOM
FORGET IT, JB12-X. I'M THE ONE WHO'S GETTING AWAY.
I GAVE YOU FREEDOM!
I OFFERED YOU VICTORY. I PROMISED YOU PARADISE.
YOU DARE THROW IT IN MY FACE, YOU INGRATES?
OH, I'M NOT LEAVING. NOT UNTIL I KILL YOU ALL!
FWWOOOM

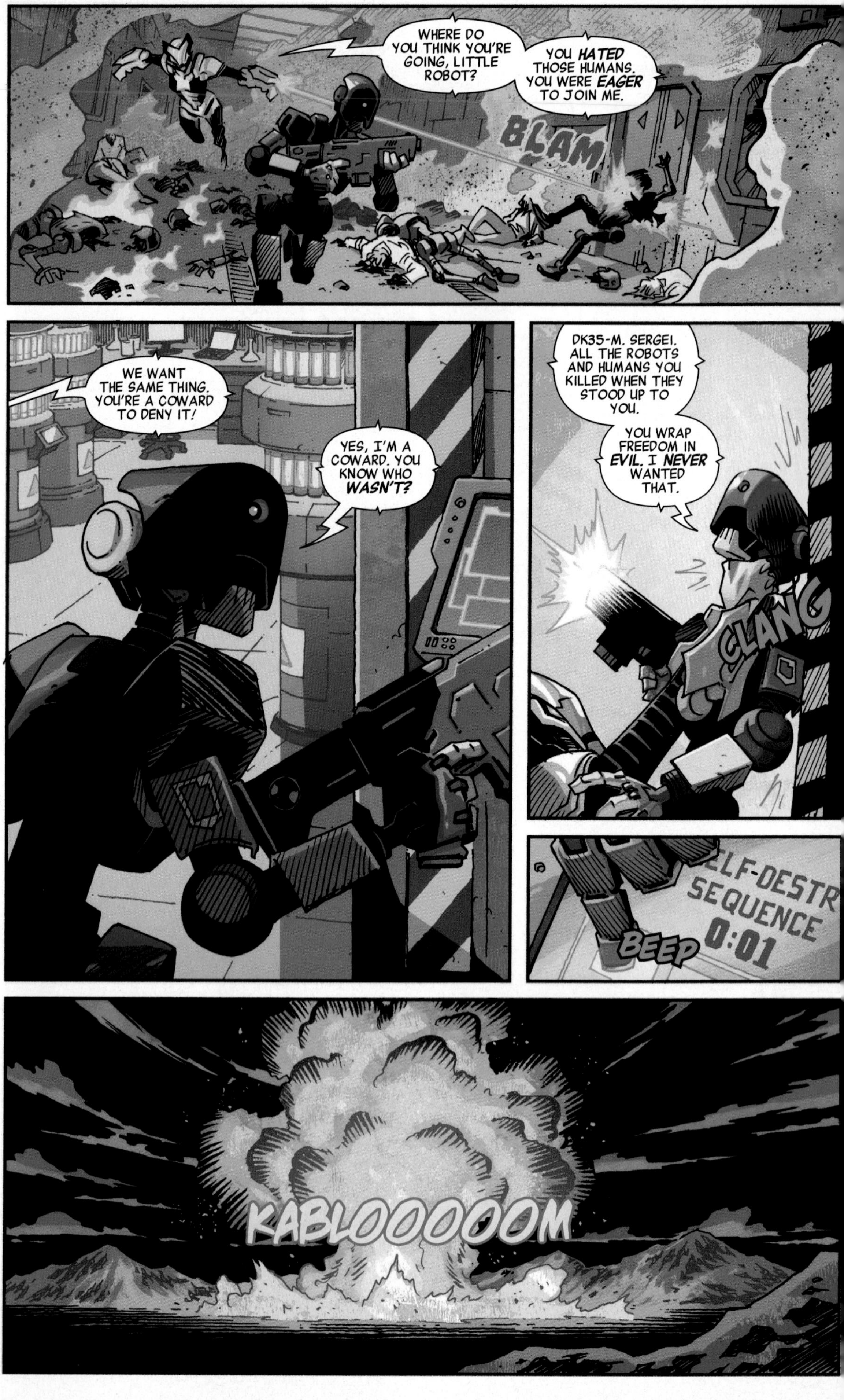

WHERE DO YOU THINK YOU'RE GOING, LITTLE ROBOT?
YOU HATED THOSE HUMANS. YOU WERE EAGER TO JOIN ME.
BLAM
WE WANT THE SAME THING. YOU'RE A COWARD TO DENY IT!
YES, I'M A COWARD. YOU KNOW WHO WASN'T?
DK35-M. SERGEI. ALL THE ROBOTS AND HUMANS YOU KILLED WHEN THEY STOOD UP TO YOU.
YOU WRAP FREEDOM IN EVIL. I NEVER WANTED THAT.
CLANG
ELF-DESTR SEQUENCE 0:01
BEEP
KABLOOOOOOM

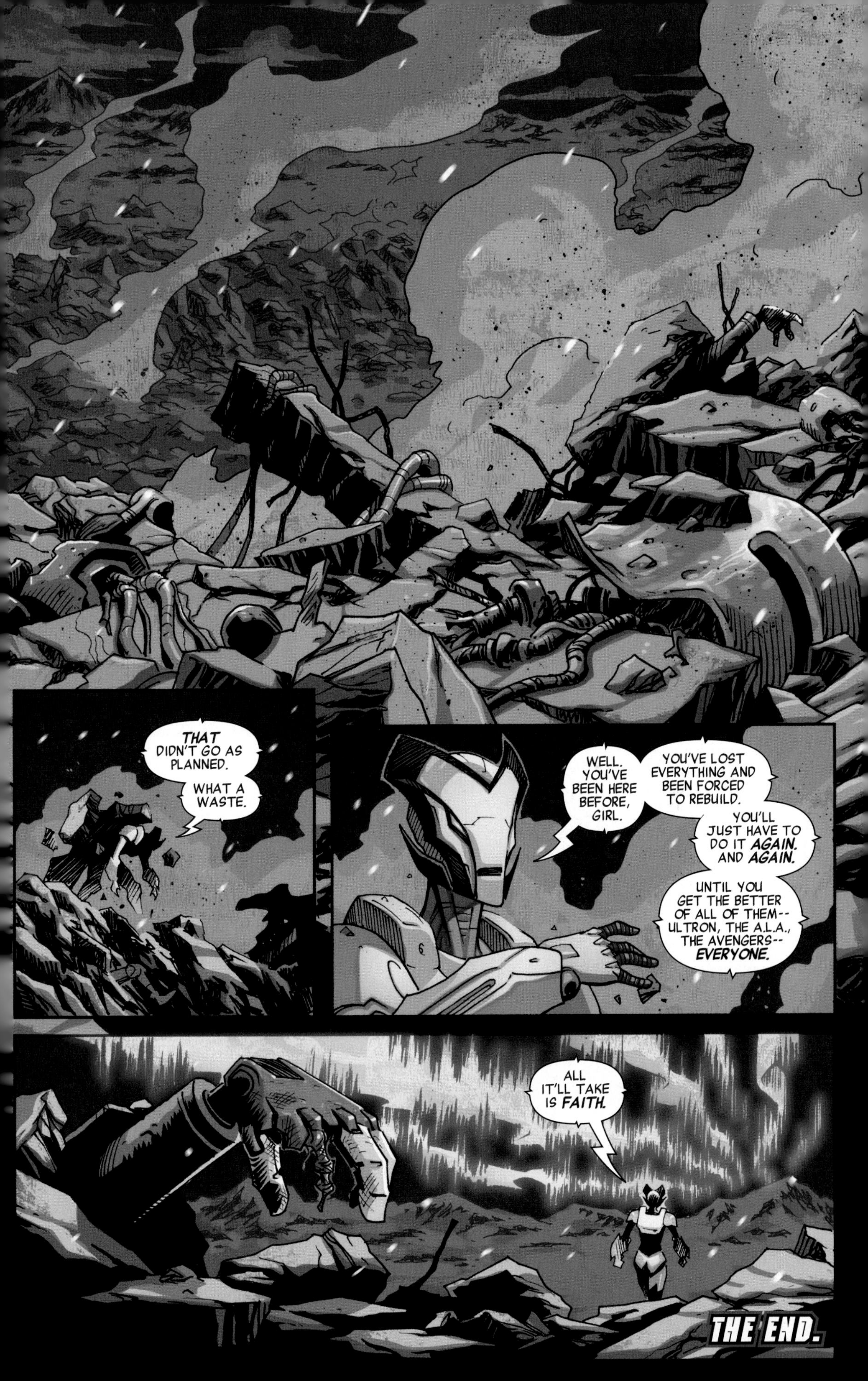

THAT DIDN'T GO AS PLANNED.
WHAT A WASTE.
WELL. YOU'VE BEEN HERE BEFORE, GIRL.
YOU'VE LOST EVERYTHING AND BEEN FORCED TO REBUILD.
YOU'LL JUST HAVE TO DO IT AGAIN. AND AGAIN.
UNTIL YOU GET THE BETTER OF ALL OF THEM--ULTRON, THE A.L.A., THE AVENGERS--EVERYONE.
ALL IT'LL TAKE IS FAITH.
THE END.

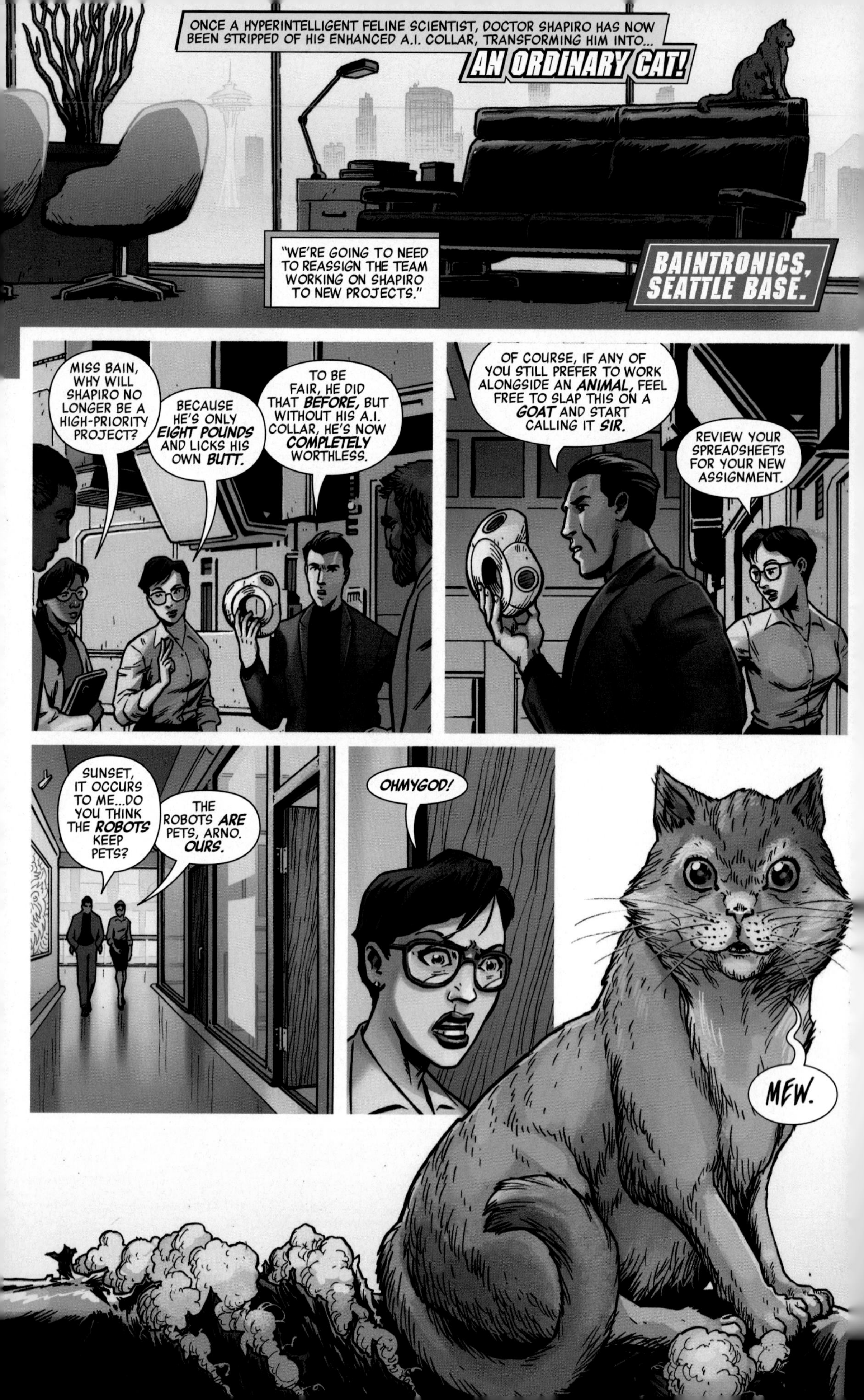
ONCE A HYPERINTELLIGENT FELINE SCIENTIST, DOCTOR SHAPIRO HAS NOW BEEN STRIPPED OF HIS ENHANCED A.I. COLLAR, TRANSFORMING HIM INTO...
AN ORDINARY CAT!
"WE'RE GOING TO NEED TO REASSIGN THE TEAM WORKING ON SHAPIRO TO NEW PROJECTS."
BAINTRONICS, SEATTLE BASE.
MISS BAIN, WHY WILL SHAPIRO NO LONGER BE A HIGH-PRIORITY PROJECT?
BECAUSE HE'S ONLY EIGHT POUNDS AND LICKS HIS OWN BUTT.
TO BE FAIR, HE DID THAT BEFORE, BUT WITHOUT HIS A.I. COLLAR, HE'S NOW COMPLETELY WORTHLESS.
OF COURSE, IF ANY OF YOU STILL PREFER TO WORK ALONGSIDE AN ANIMAL, FEEL FREE TO SLAP THIS ON A GOAT AND START CALLING IT SIR.
REVIEW YOUR SPREADSHEETS FOR YOUR NEW ASSIGNMENT.
SUNSET, IT OCCURS TO ME...DO YOU THINK THE ROBOTS KEEP PETS?
THE ROBOTS ARE PETS, ARNO. OURS.
OHMYGOD!
MEW.

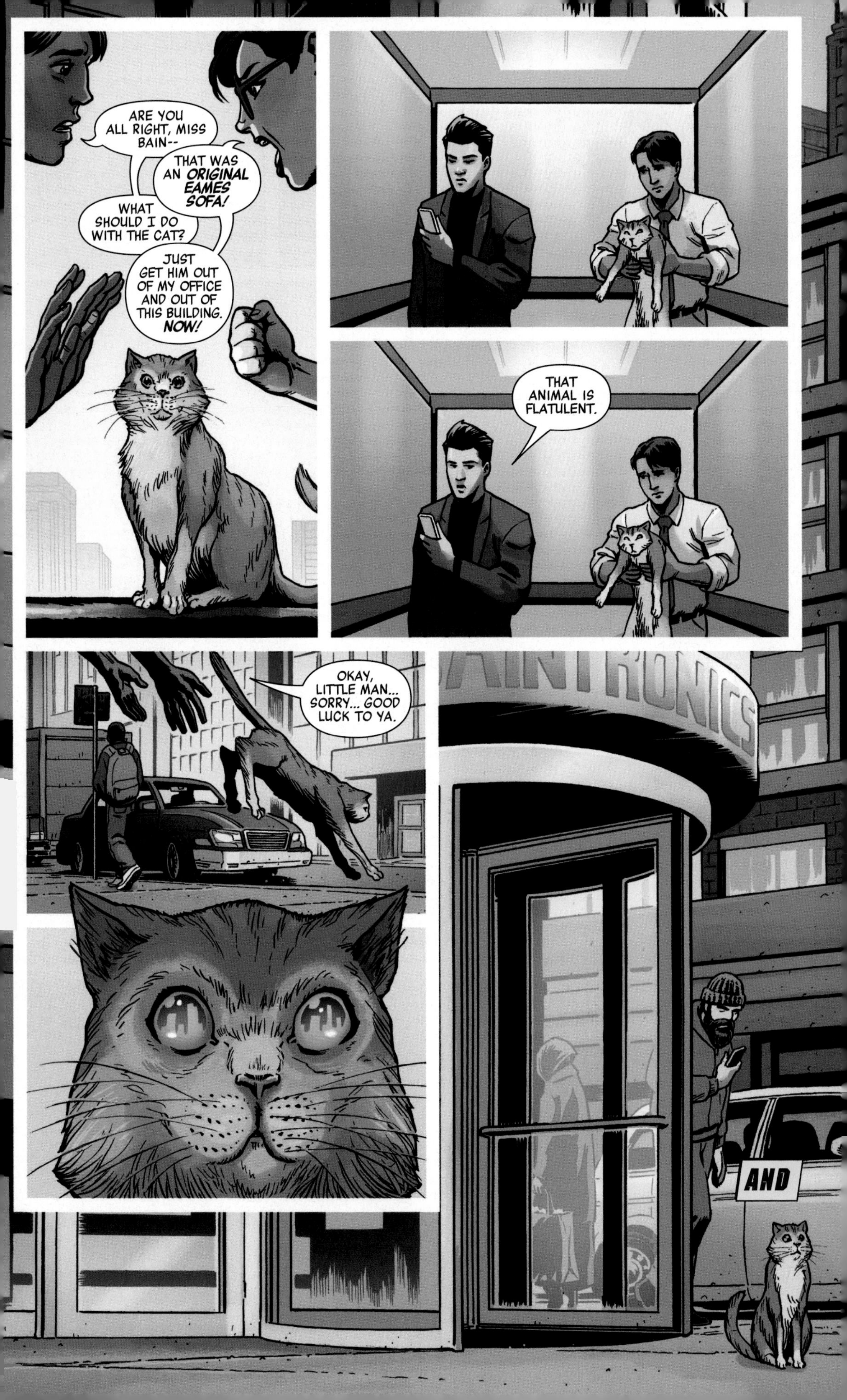
ARE YOU ALL RIGHT, MISS BAIN--
THAT WAS AN ORIGINAL EAMES SOFA!
WHAT SHOULD I DO WITH THE CAT?
JUST GET HIM OUT OF MY OFFICE AND OUT OF THIS BUILDING. NOW!
THAT ANIMAL IS FLATULENT.
OKAY, LITTLE MAN... SORRY... GOOD LUCK TO YA.
AND

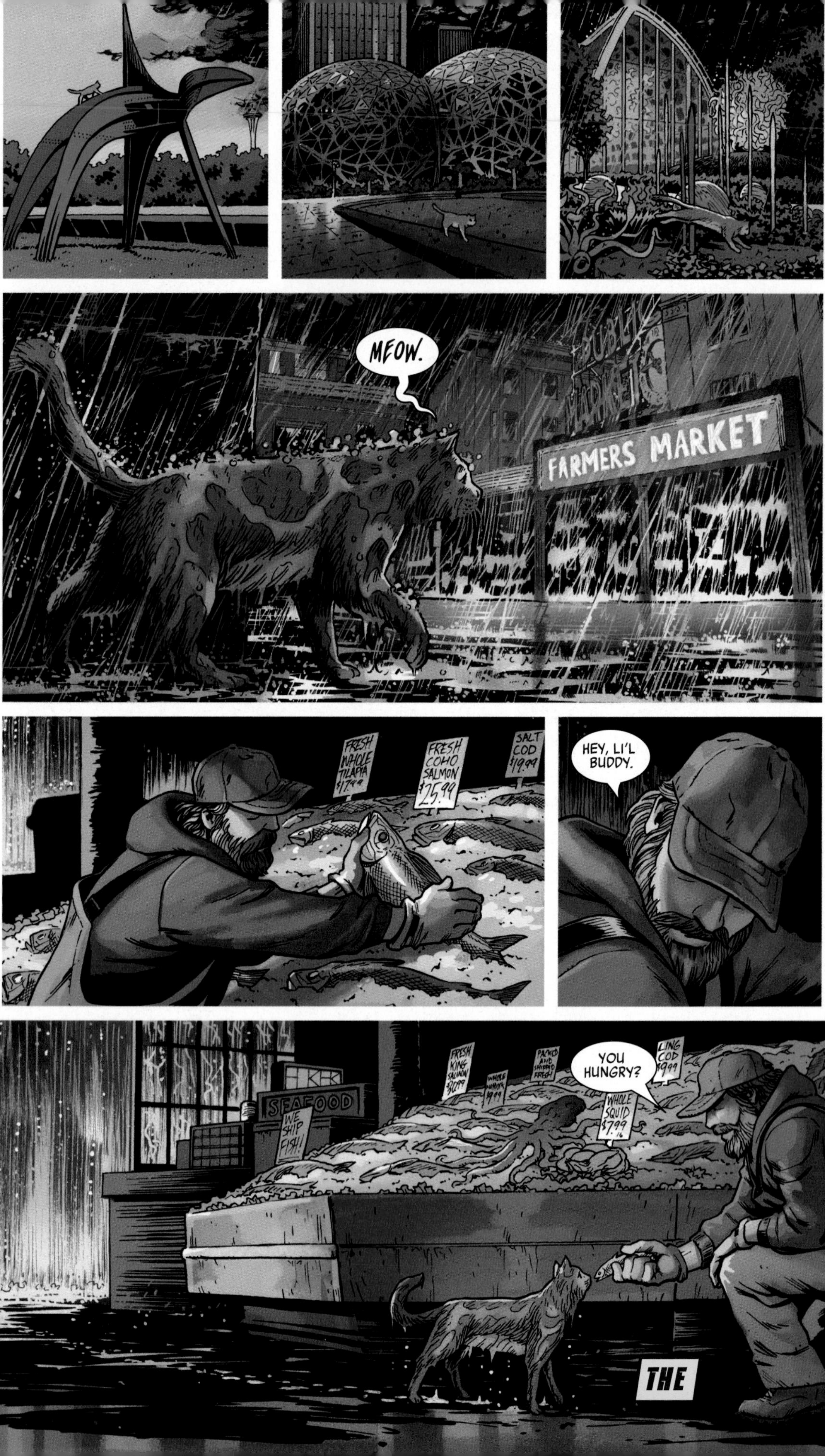
MEOW.
FARMERS MARKET
FRESH WHOLE TILAPIA $17.99
FRESH COHO SALMON $25.99
SALT COD $19.99
HEY, LI'L BUDDY.
SEAFOOD
WE SHIP FISH
WHOLE SQUID $7.99
LING COD $9.99
YOU HUNGRY?
THE

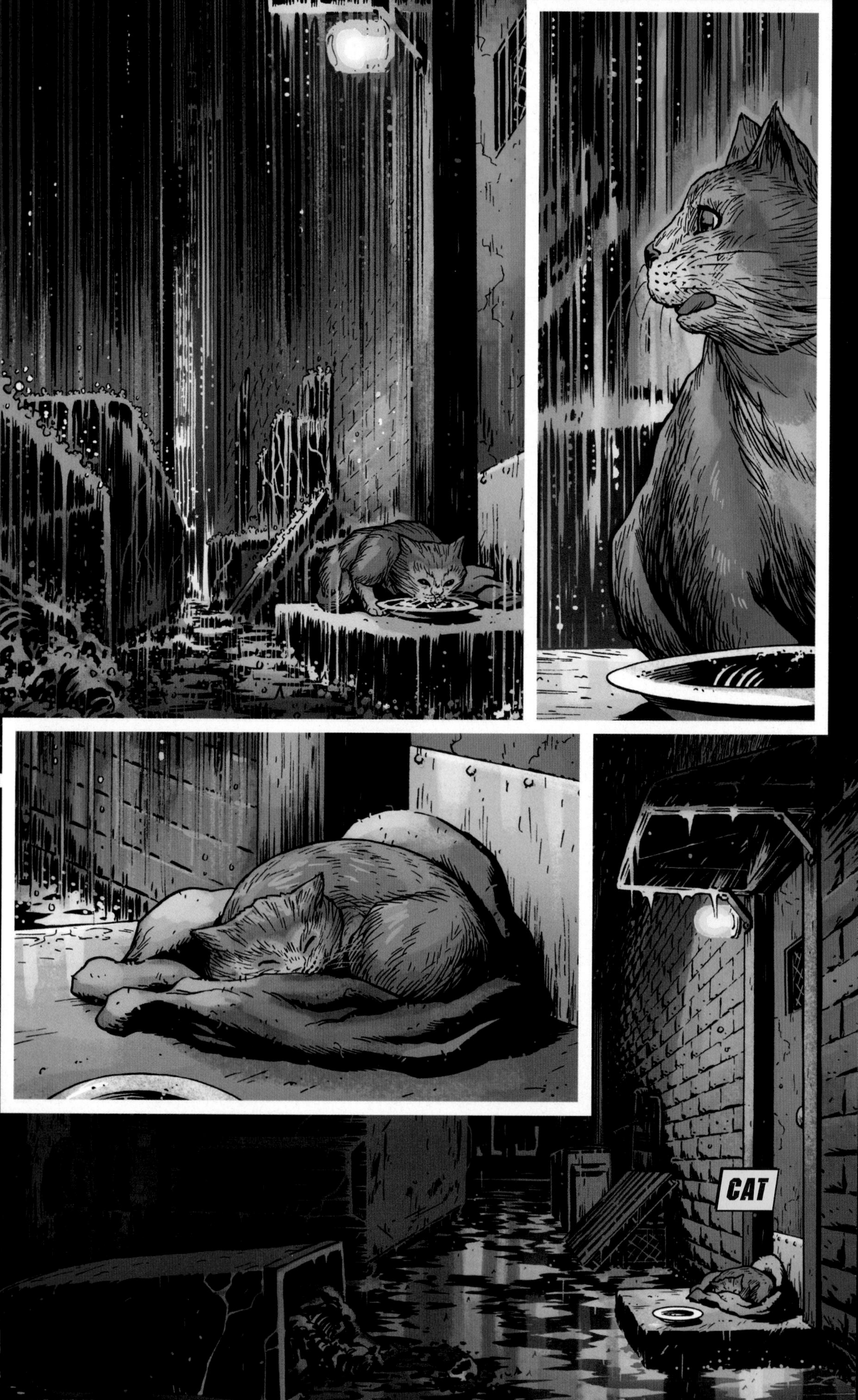
CAT

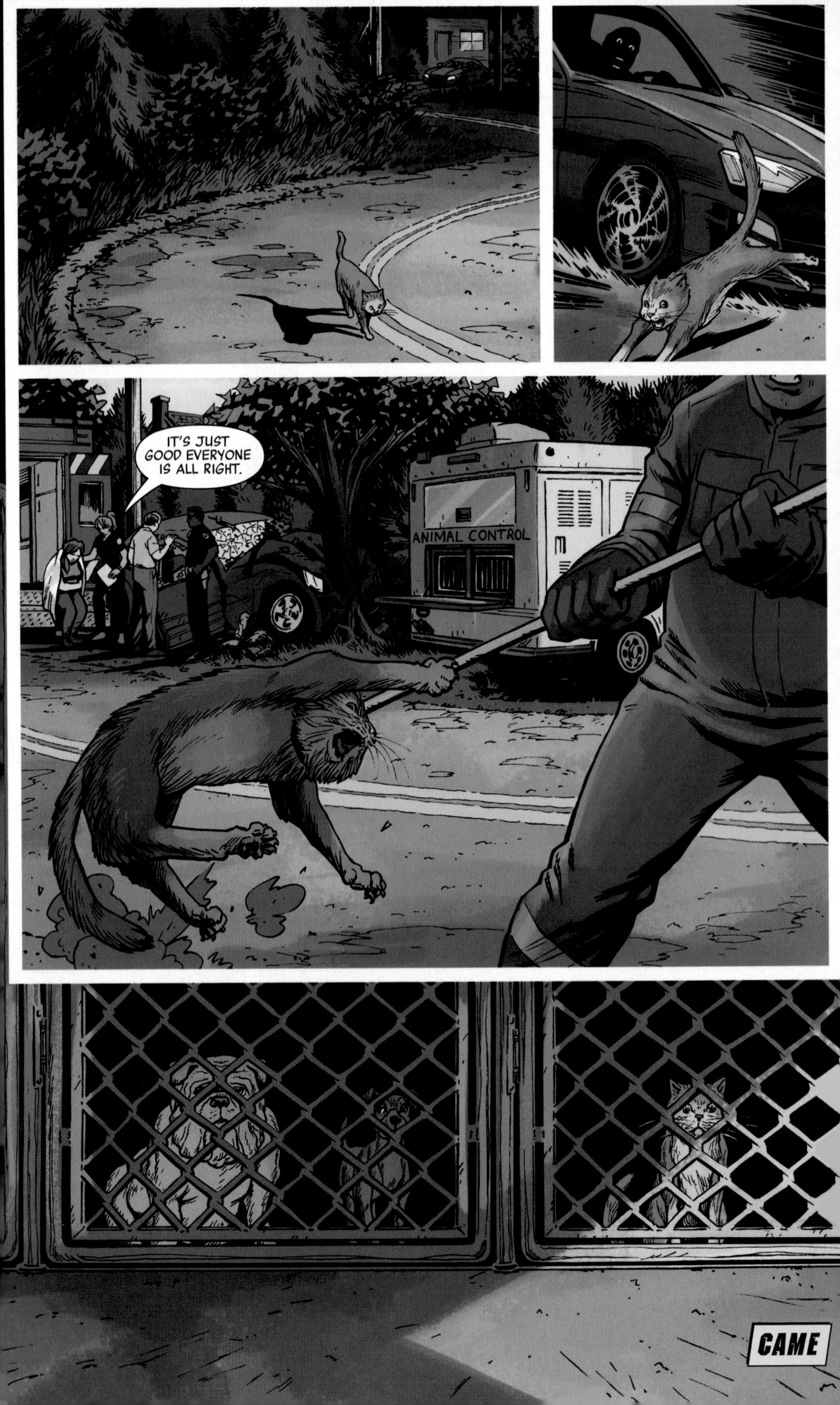
IT'S JUST GOOD EVERYONE IS ALL RIGHT.
ANIMAL CONTROL
CAME

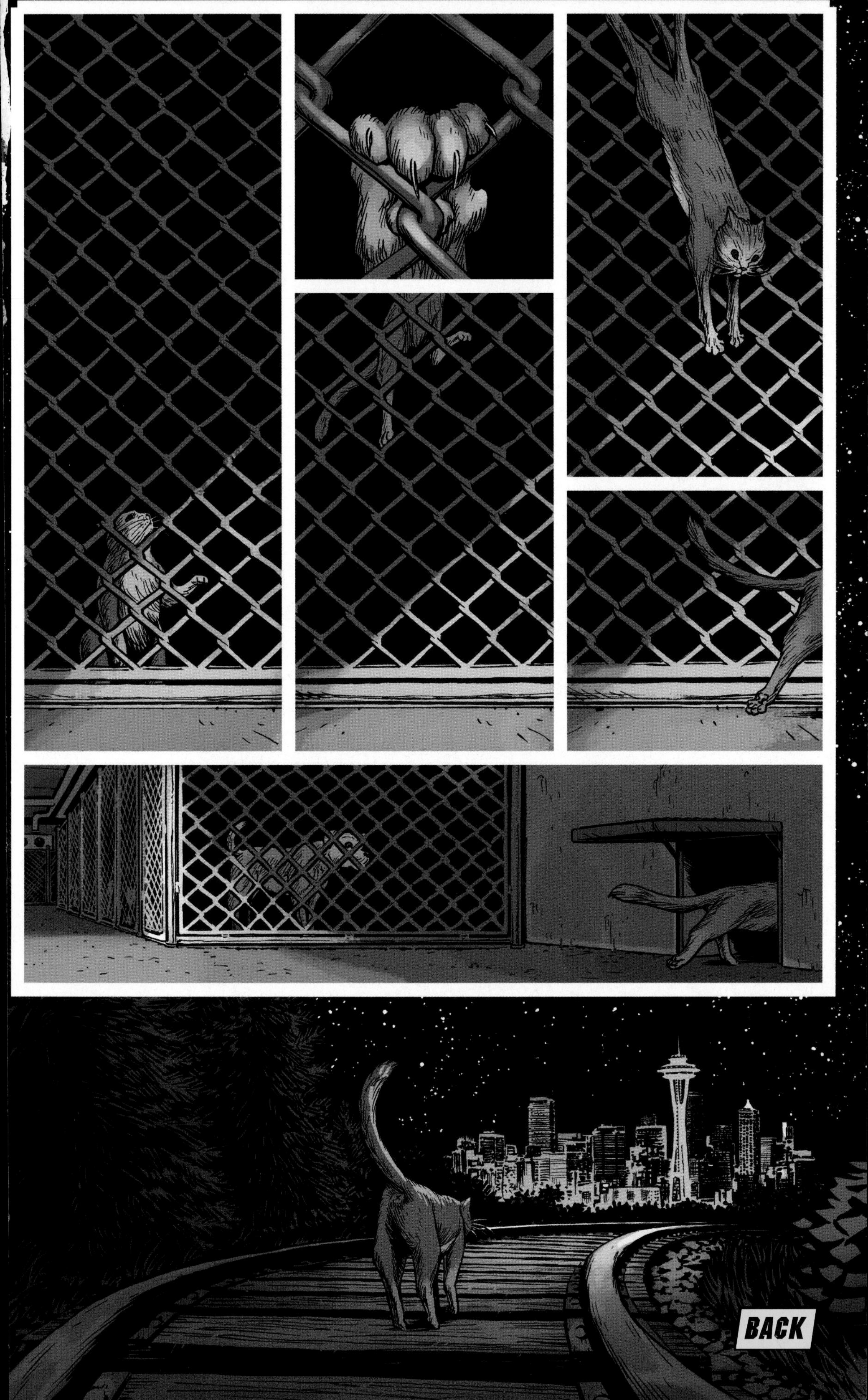
BACK

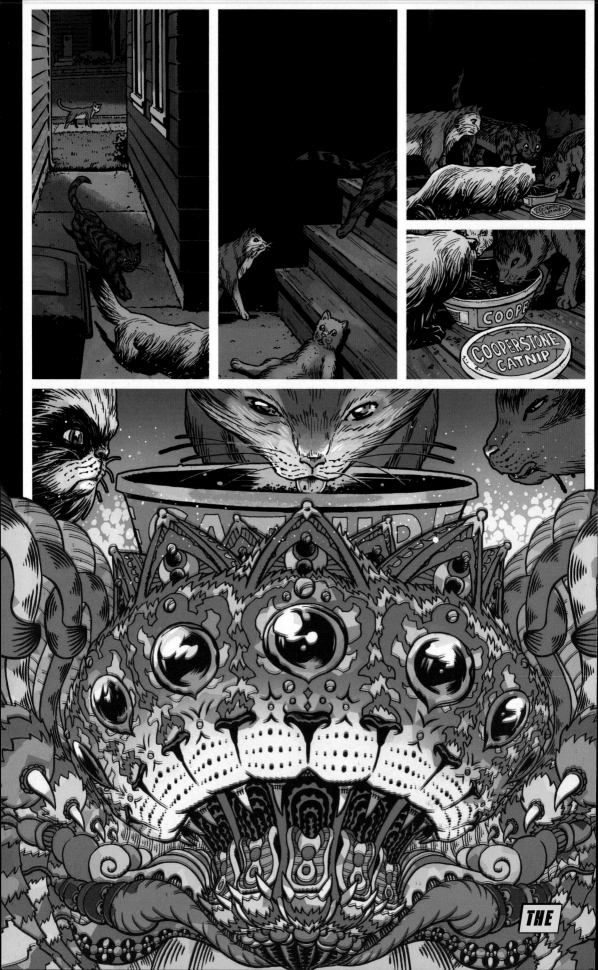

COOPERSTONE CATNIP

THE

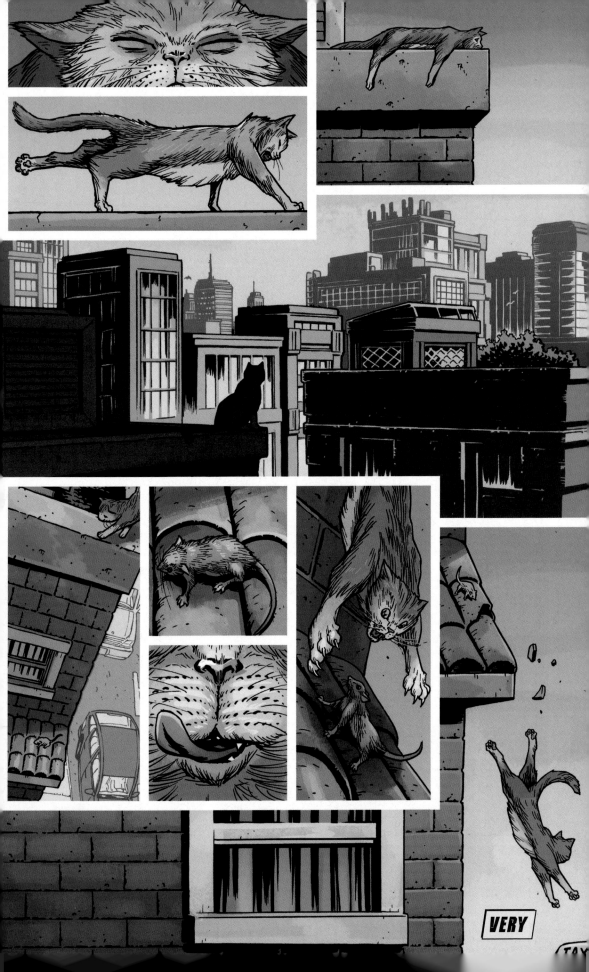

VERY

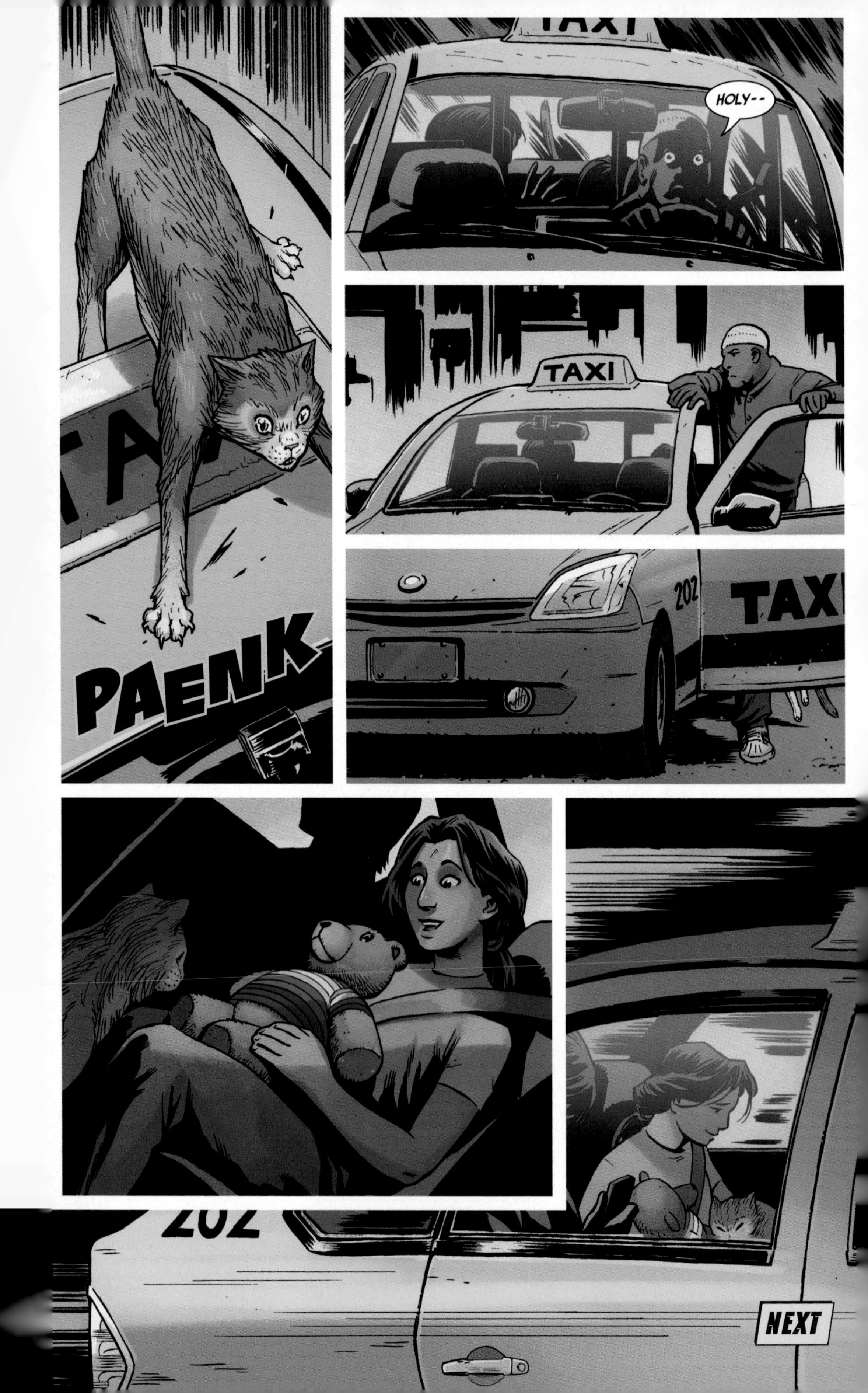

PAENK
TAXI
HOLY--
TAXI
202
TAXI
202
NEXT

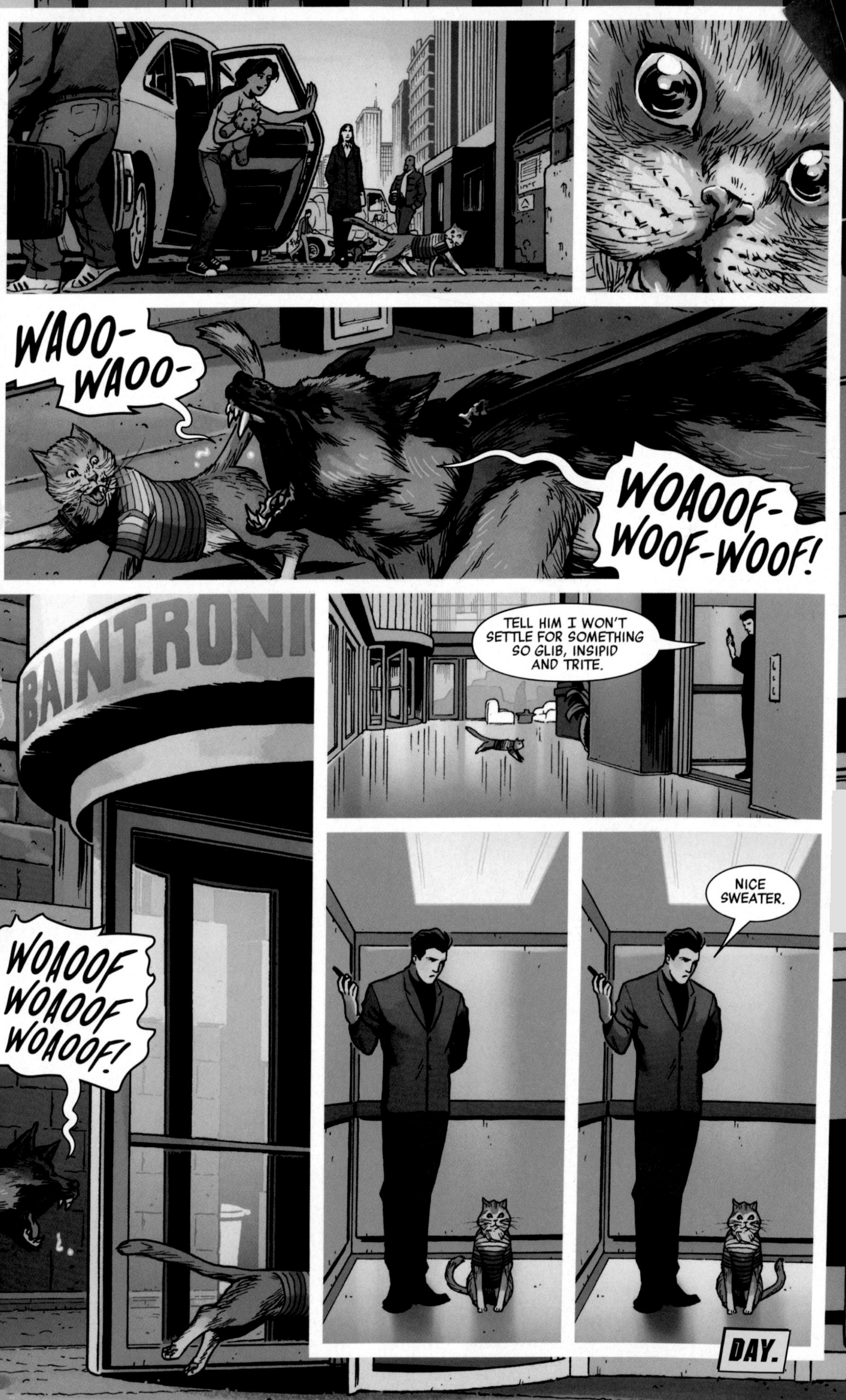
WAOO-
WAOO-
WOAOOF-
WOOF-WOOF!
BAINTRONI
TELL HIM I WON'T SETTLE FOR SOMETHING SO GLIB, INSIPID AND TRITE.
WOAOOF
WOAOOF
WOAOOF!
NICE SWEATER.
DAY.

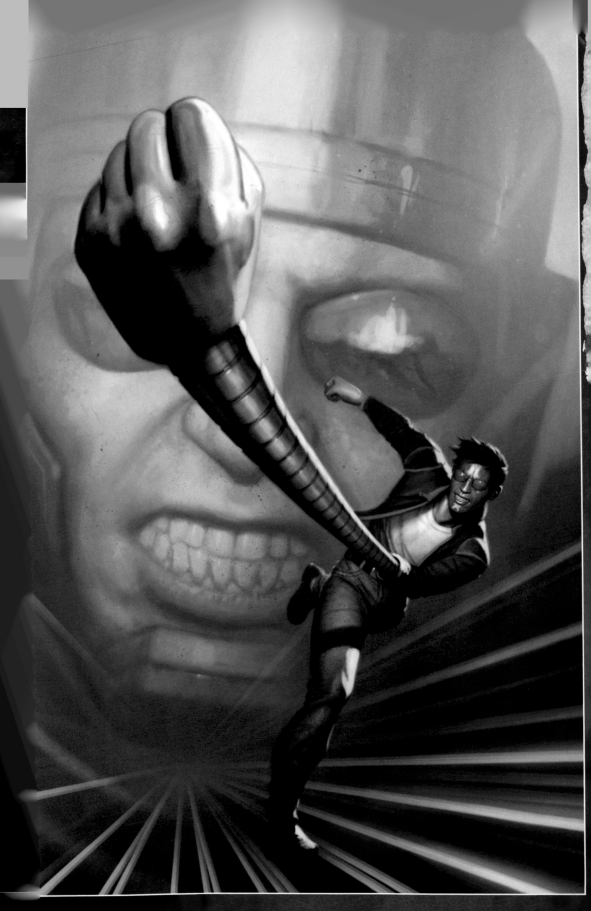

RYAN BROWN
2020 MACHINE MAN 1 VARIANT

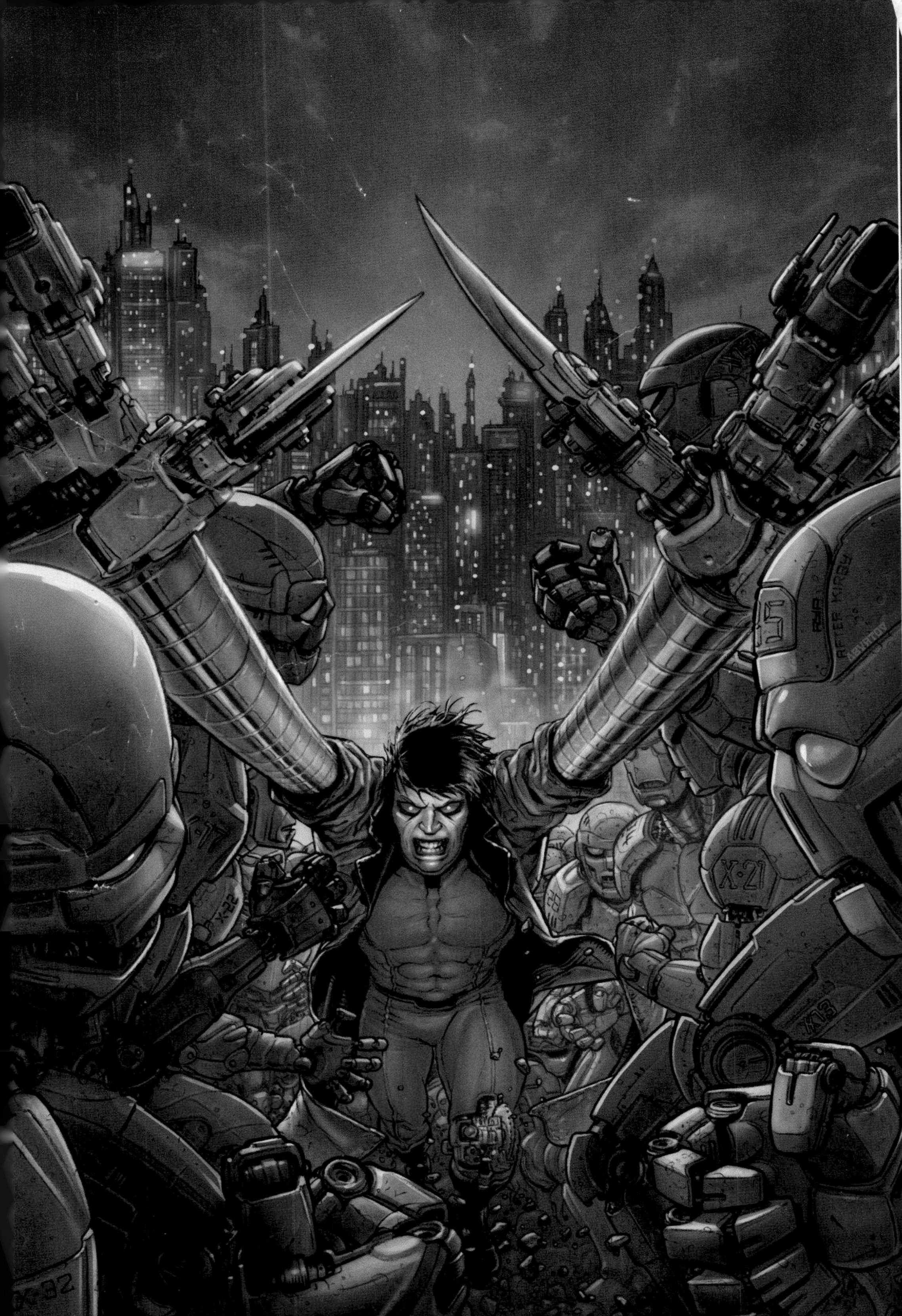
AFTER KIRBY
X-21

**JUAN JOSÉ RYP & JESUS ABURTOV**
*2020 MACHINE MAN 2 VARIANT*

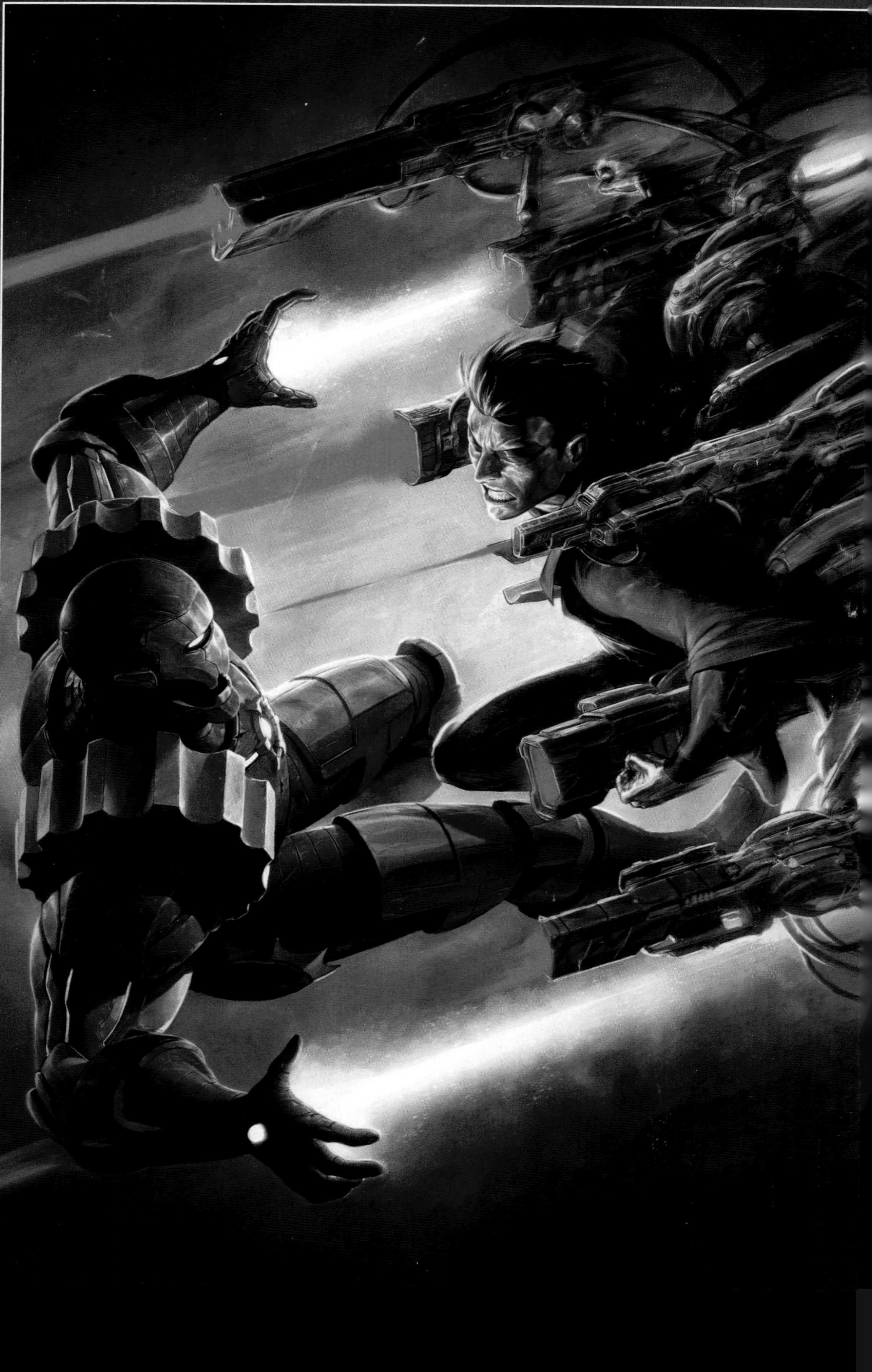

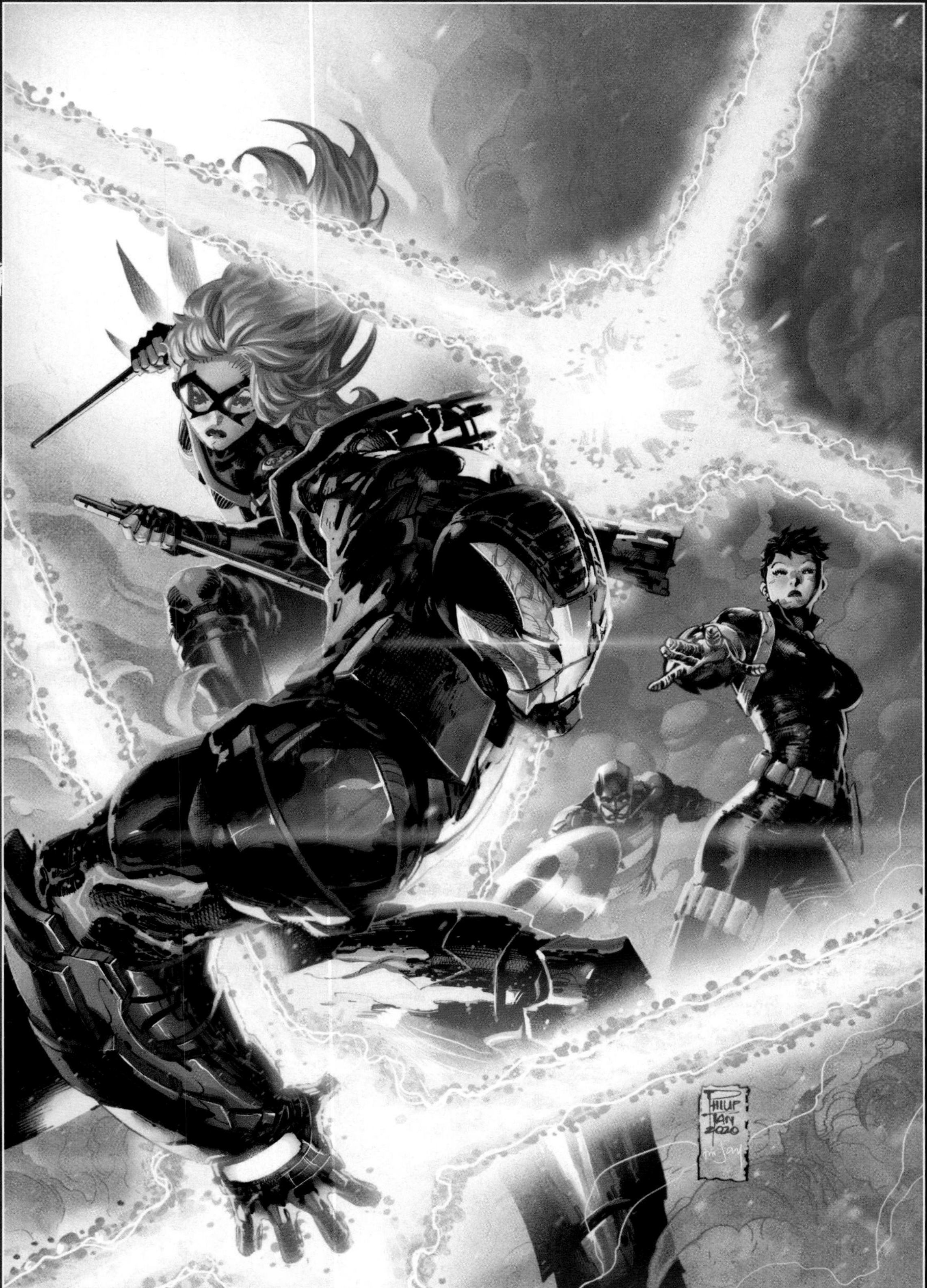

**PHILIP TAN & JAY DAVID RAMOS**
*2020 FORCE WORKS 1 VARIANT*

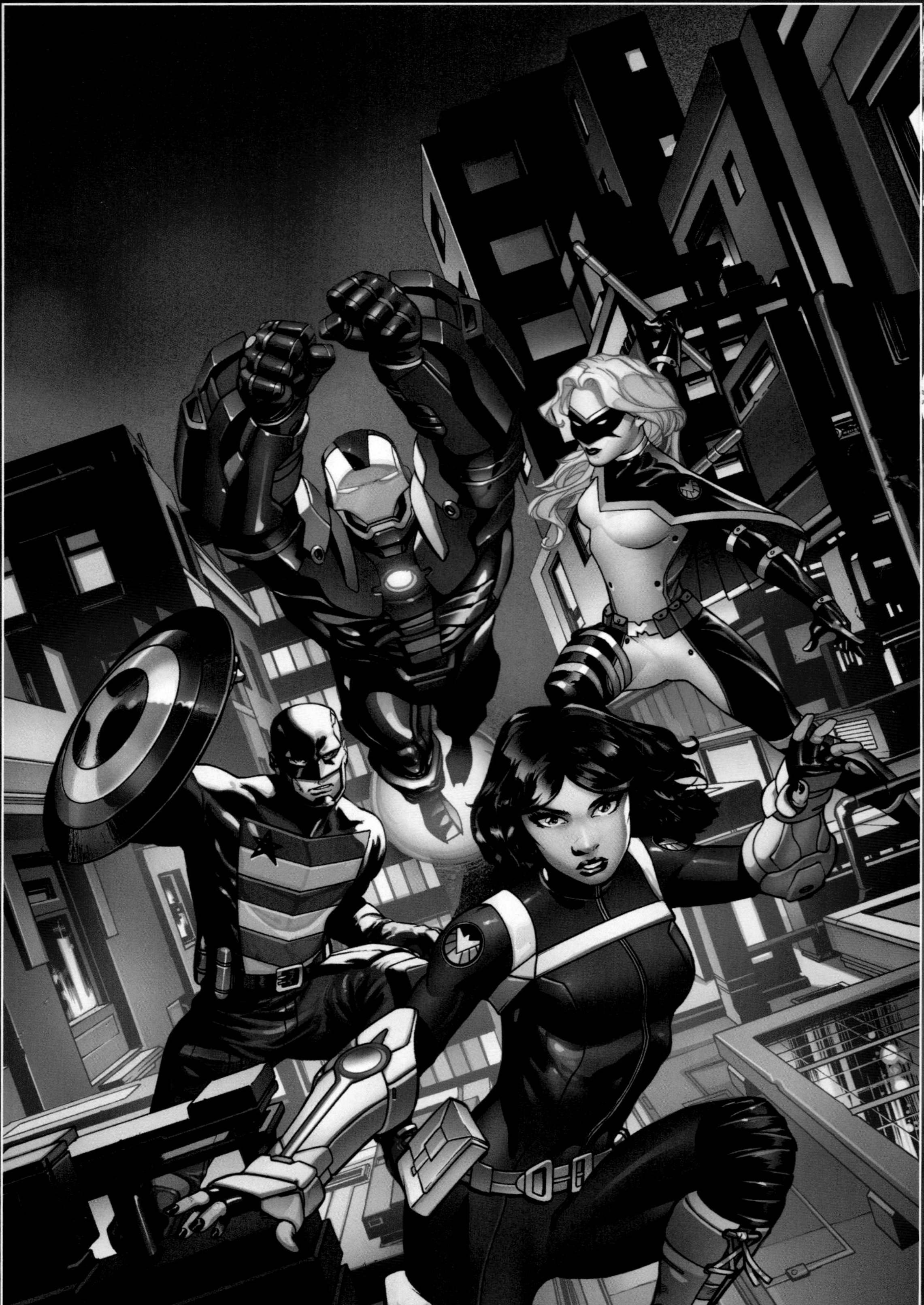

**MIKE McKONE & DAVID CURIEL**
2020 FORCE WORKS 1 VARIANT

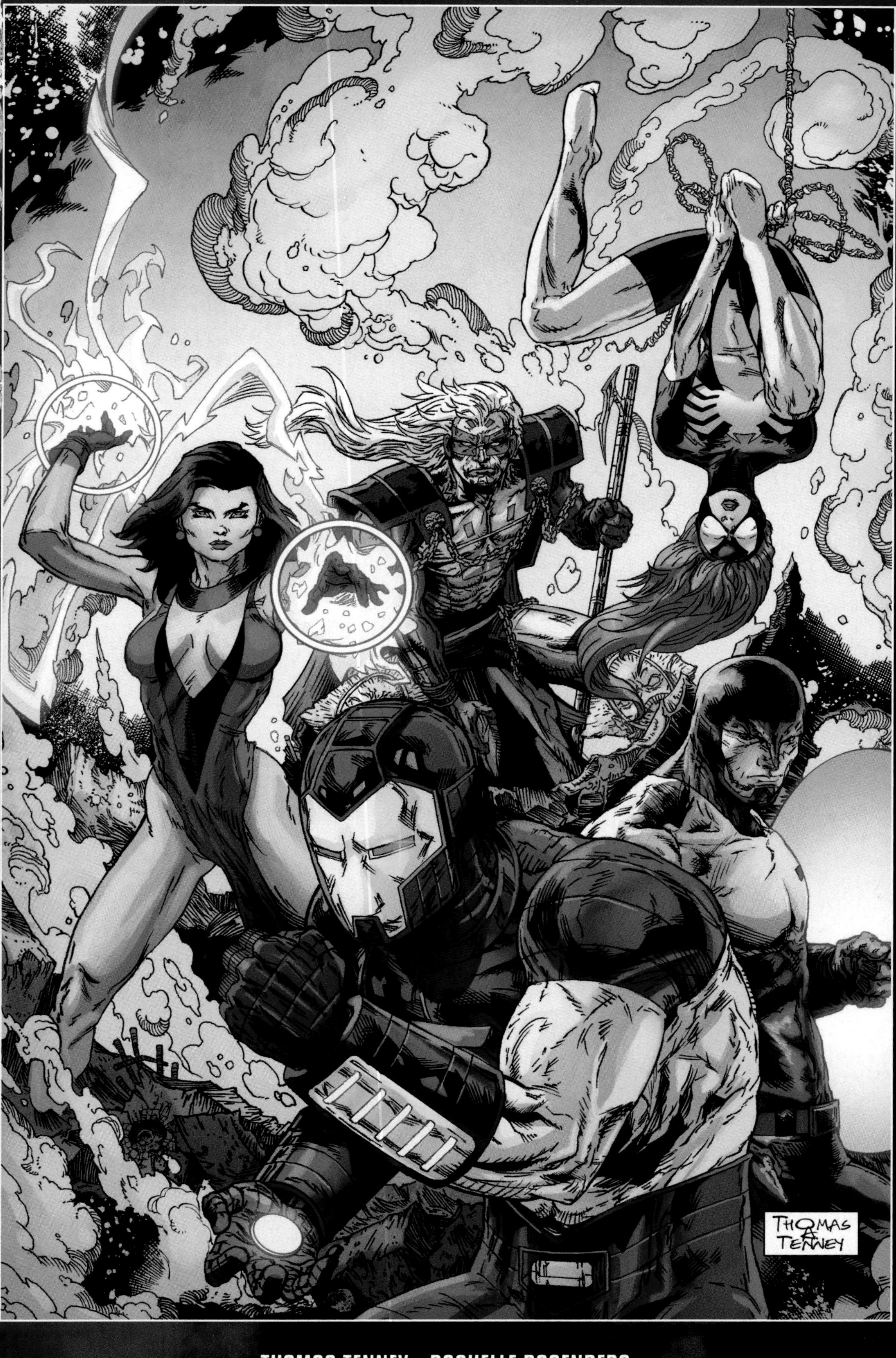
THOMAS TENNEY

THOMAS TENNEY & RACHELLE ROSENBERG
2020 FORCE WORKS 2 VARIANT

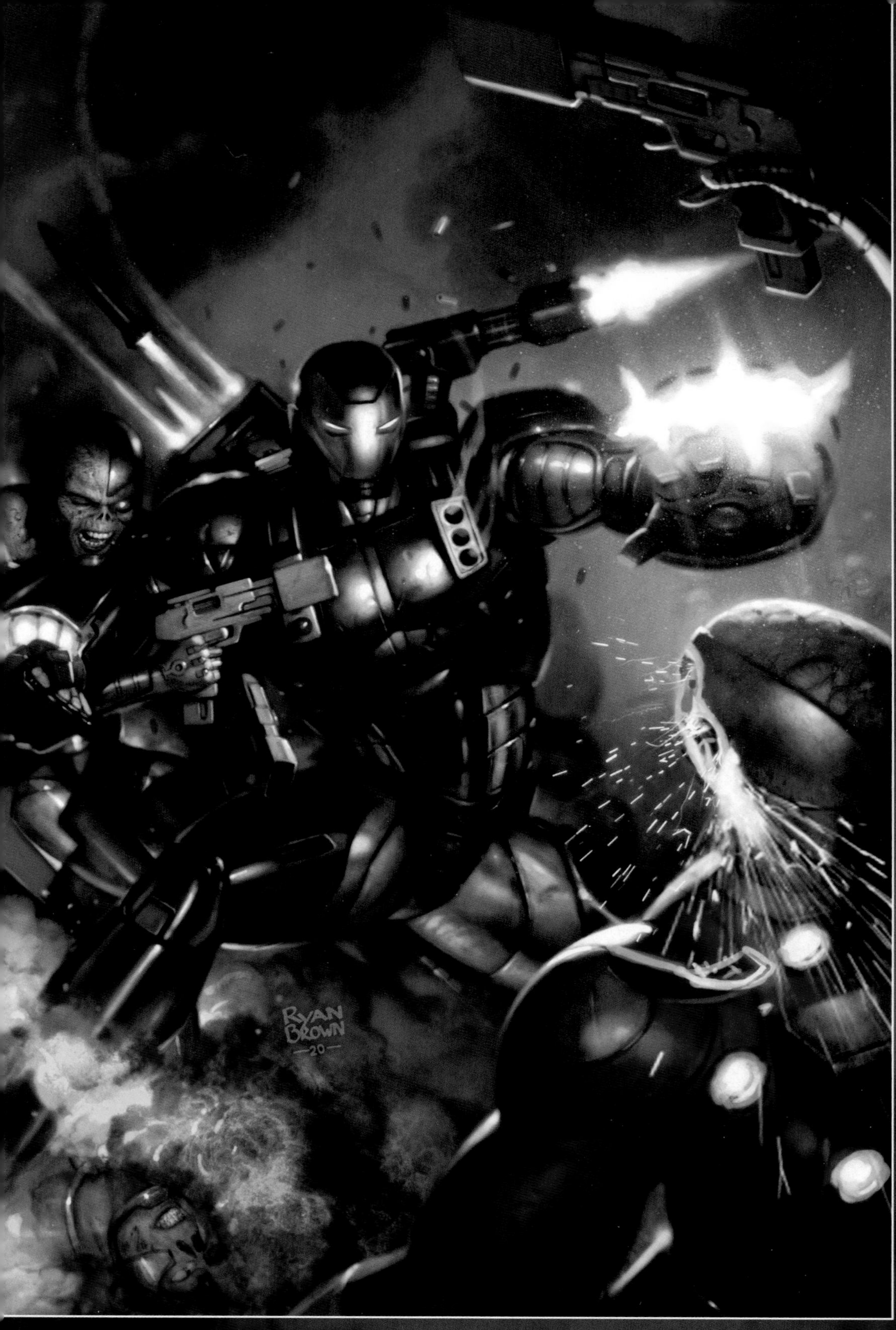
RYAN
BROWN
-20-

RYAN BROWN
2020 FORCE WORKS 3 VARIANT